CHILD ABUSE

Contents

Preface

The children in our society are among the deprived and neglected. Barring a fistful number of fortunate ones, the majority of them begins with suffering and roll into the practical life in the same vein. For any nation, children reflect its health. They are in fact a strength in reserve for the country. If they are healthy, active, educated, informed, disciplined, then, in their hands, the future of a nation is well secured.

It is an acknowledged fact that child servitude is a harsh reality, fostered by socio-economic and historical compulsions. It is believed that poverty, unemployment, population growth and illiteracy are the main reasons for the malady and that their redress is a pre-requisite for eliminating child servitude. It should be noted that the growth rate of the population is much higher among those communities, in which unemployment is rampant.

If child labour is not controlled, impoverished parents would continue to succumb to the 'necessity' of enlarging the number of earning members in the family. Similarly, there exists a correlation between illiteracy and child servitude. In the areas, where there are more job opportunities for children, the dropout rate in schools is extremely high. Now, the situation is; if we do not liberate millions of children from their jobs today, we shall be responsible for keeping them illiterate for their entire lives.

Notably, the Minimum Age Convention, 1973 is a landmark achievement in the struggle against child abuse. A large number of both industrialised and developing countries have already adopted child labour legislation, which as a whole, is progressive and reasonably close to international standards.

As per census, nearly 40 per cent of our population consists of children below the age of fourteen. The Constitution of India, as expounded by the Supreme Court, makes free and compulsory education up to that age, a fundamental right. However, large masses of children in that age group, not only have no such blessing but, on the contrary, are condemned to back-breaking labour under harrowing conditions. Ironically it is lack of political commitment and not economic constraints that devastated the country with the curse of illiteracy. In fact, total prohibition of child labour and the provision of free, compulsory and universal primary education should invariably go hand in hand.

Child labour cannot be totally eliminated without providing and sustaining avenues to free, compulsory and universal primary education. But, these may not be meaningful, while children continue to be at the work place, whether hazardous or not. Ironically, the fact remains that we have failed to reach the goal and should honestly and candidly acknowledge this.

This study is an attempt to construct a comprehensive picture, relating to the problems of child labour. The undersigned does not claim to provide ready made answers to all the questions, pertaining to child abuse. However, she has not delved into child slavery, sale of children, street children etc., as it requires a separate book. Hopefully, this modest work would be taken by readers as acceptable and helpful, in some way.

New Delhi

Arunima Baruah

INTRODUCTION

A few people may know that the Convention on the Rights of the Child recognizes the exceptional vulnerability of children and proclaims that childhood is entitled to special care and assistance. It obligates the state to respect and ensure that children get a fair and equitable deal in society. It emphasized the importance of the family and the need to create an environment that is conducive to the healthy growth and development of children. It advocates public action by all individuals and agencies—governmental and non-governmental, local, regional, national, and international—to promote the rights of the child.

The convention in a sense, is a means of empowering children and creating in which all children are able to live securely and realize their full potential in life. It highlights four basic rights— the right to survival, the right to protection, the right to development, The right to participation.

The National Policy for Children, 1974 affirmed the Constitutional provisions— "it shall be the policy of the state to provide adequate services to children both before and after birth and through the period of growth to ensure their full physical, mental and social development"

With such excellent intentions and policies children should have had a better deal but unfortunately this is not so. Article 39 of the Directive Principles of State Policy states "that the health and strength of workers, men and women, and the tender age of children are not abused and the citizens are not forced by economic necessity to enter vocations unsuited to their age or strength", "that children are given opportunities and facilities to develop in a healthy manner and in conditions of freedom and dignity and that childhood and youth are protected against exploitation and against moral and meterial abandonment". Similarly, Article 24 stipulates that "no child below the age of fourteen years shall be employed to work in any factory or mine or engaged in any other hazardous employment".

These conventions, Constitutional provisions are for the empowerment and protection of all children. But in a society that is divided on the basis of caste, class, religion and sex, and where poor, marginalised parents and guardians are also discriminated against with the majority, powerful on top of the social ladder taking away most of the benefits, children on the lowest rung of the ladder face four times more discrimination and exploitation. It is these children we need to focus upon. These are the children of the weaker sections, especially the scheduled castes and scheduled tribes, who are almost 35 per cent of the total child population of India and among them the girl children.

Children of the Marginalized Sections

While all children need their rights to be recognised and ensured—their right to survival, good health and adequate standard of living.

(a) their right to development, education, leisure, recreation and proper and balanced development.

(b) their right to participation, freedom of expression and thought, access to information.

(c) their right to protection from exploitation, abuse, inhuman and degrading treatment, special protection in times of emergency and armed conflict, children of the marginalised sections need protection from all kinds of exploitation and violence prevalent in society. It is these children who are bonded in various jobs, domestic workers, street children, child prostitutes, beggars, rag pickers and the desrted. Of them the girl child is further exploited because of her sex.

How do we protect these children? Laws are there but social awareness about the plight of these children is missing and also ignored. These are the same children who are denied all other facilities with regard to health, education freedom to choose and participate, and abused by the existing socio-cultural structure of society.

According to the Convention on the Rights of a Child "...a child means every human being below the age of eighteen years unless, under the law applicable to the child, majority is attained earlier". (Article 1)

The legal conception of a child varies depending upon the purpose: whether it is for imposing legal disabilities (e.g., in the juvenile justice systems), for affording protection (e.g., in the political rights sphere), for spelling out duties and obligations (e.g., in juvenile justice systems), for affording protection (e.g., from exploitative or hazardous employment), or for establishing eligibility to receive benefits or special services (e.g., health, education and maintenance benefits). Underlying these alternative definitions are also very different conceptions of the child. These include viewing children as a burden which invoke rights to maintenance and support; regarding children as undergoing temporary disabilities making for rights to special treatment and discrimination; treating children as specially vulnerable for ensuring rights of protection; and recognizing children as resources for the country's development giving rise to rights of nurturing and advancement. Under different economic and socio-cultural circumstances, the child has also been regarded as a commodity, as an insurance, as a source of labour, and as a social burden.

In India too, the definition of a child varies with the purpose. The Census of India treats persons below the age of fourteen as "children". While making use of standard demographic data, social scientists include females in the age group of 15-19 years under the category of the "girl child". According to the Constitution, no child below the age of fourteen years shall be employed to work in any factory or mine or engaged in any other hazardous employment (Article 23). The legal definition of a "child" depends very much upon the specific legislation.

The ways to protect these children must be:

(i) Recognition of the fact that the socio-cultural structure has marginalised them, we need to promote attitudinal changes among people so that unconstitutional cultural traditional factors are challenged and unaccepted and not practised. (ii) Poverty and ignorance need to be combated through policies that specifically address these issues. (iii)Restructuring of development policies so that rural areas are economically developed and poverty alleviation programmes become possible. (iv) Free compulsory primary education with necessary infrastructure—buildings, study material, uniforms and food be immediately implemented through legal measures. (v) Child Marriage Restraint Act be changed to Child Marriage Abolition Act and measures for the punishment for those who violate the law be made more stringent. (vi) Registration of all marriages to prevent child marriage and false marriages which are one of the means of recruitment into prostitution. (vii) Immediate action be made possible in cases of child abuse, assault, rape of children, especially of the marginalised. The law and order machinery be especially trained and advised to take up their cases. A special cell to handle cases of child abuse to be set up at police stations. (viii) What we demand is—complete control of trafficking of children and young women into prostitution; and rehabilitation to those children in prostitution and children of prostitutes, and women, young and old, who can be weaned out of this system. (ix) Change in existing legislation providing for new laws is a must, along with coordination among all existing laws J.J. Act, IPTA, Police Act, Cr. P.C. and IPC is necessary, especially in their applications. (x) Setting up of more educational boarding schools, vocational training centres, where they can be accommodated along with others so that they are not isolated as criminals carrying a stigma. (xi) Activate anganwadi workers, gram panchayat and other rural and grassroots functionaries like school teachers, medical workers, police, etc. to take up their job seriously and thus protect the children from harm. (xii)Networking of NGOs and relationship with all law and order agencies for suitable joint action. (xiii) Participation of society in the form of watchdog committees in rural and urban areas to identify people, areas, and families that indulge in the business of forcing children into labour and prostitution, and break the existing laws. Take immediate action with law enforcement agencies against them. (xiv) Other facilities for health, nutrition, counselling be provided. (xv) Role of the media be more sensitive and responsive. Need for general awareness and sensitization programmes for media professionals so that they can evolve healthy media campaigns to sensitize the public.

There is a need for concerted effort to develop a new set of social norms and cultural practices which will enable equitable distribution of wealth, rural regeneration, eradication of poverty, removal of illiteracy, sex and caste bias and promotion of legal reform and law enforcement. Only then can all children be protected and developed as responsible citizens.

PART - I

THE CHILD

ONE

WHO IS A CHILD?

Interestingly, the Census of India defines persons below the age of fourteen as children. Law in India illustrates a 'child' as follows:

1. *Criminal Law Indian Penal Code:* Nothing is an offence which is done by a child under the age of seven years. The age of criminal responsibility is raised to 12 years if the child is found to have not attained the ability to understand the nature and consequences of his/her act.

    Attainment of sixteen years of age for a girl is necessary for giving sexual consent, which is not less than fifteen years in case she is married.
2. *Juvenile Law: Juvenile Justice Act, 1960:* A juvenile is a child who has not completed the age of 16 years in case of a boy, or the age of 18 years in the case of girls. A delinquent juvenile cannot be sentenced to imprisonment. If a juvenile who has attained the age of 14 years commits an offence of a serious nature and is found not to be in his interest or in the interest of other juveniles to send him to a special home then the juvenile court may order the delinquent juvenile to be kept in safe custody in such place and manner as it thinks fit. Detention in police stations or jails is specifically prohibited under the Act.
3. *Family Law: Child Marriage Restraint Act, 1926:* Child means a person who, if a male, has not completed 21 years of age and, if a female, has not completed 18 years of age.
4. *Labour Law-Apprentices Act, 1961:* A person is qualified to be engaged as an apprentice only if he is not less than fourteen years of age and satisfies such standards of education and physical fitness as may be prescribed.
5. *Factories Act, 1948:* A child below 14 years of age is not allowed to work in any factory. An adolescent between 15 and 18 years can be employed in a factory only if he obtains a certificate of fitness from an authorised medical doctor. A child

between 14 and 18 years of age cannot be employed for more than four and a half hours.

6. *Mines Amendment Act:* No person below eighteen years of age shall be allowed to work in any mine or part thereof.
7. *The Child Labour (Prohibition and Regulation) Act, 1966:* Child means a person who has not completed his fourteenth year of age,
8. *Army Headquarters Regulations.*
   (a) The age of recruitment in the Army is from 16 to 25 years. Persons who are recruited at the age of 16 years undergo Basic Military Training for up to two-and-a-half years from the date of enrolment and are then inducted into regular service.
9. *Indian Contract Act, 1870:* A person below the age of 18 years has no capacity to contract.
10. *Provision of Free and Compulsory Education:* Article 45 of the Constitution states that the State shall endeavour to provide within a period of ten years from the commencement of this Constitution, for free and compulsory education for all children till they complete the age of fourteen years.

The word "child" has been used in various legislations as a term denoting relationship, as a term indicating capacity; and as a term of special protection. Underlying these alternative specifications are very different concepts about the child. These include viewing children as a burden which invokes rights to maintenance and support; regarding children as undergoing temporary disabilities making for rights to special treatment and special discrimination, treating children as specially vulnerable for ensuring rights of protection; and recognising children as resources for the country's development necessitating their nurturing and advancement.

The question of review of definition of the "child", in the light of Article 1 of the Convention on Rights of the Child has been referred to the Law Commission of India to be considered by the Commission while undertaking a comprehensive review of the Code of Criminal Procedure and the Indian Penal Code. The Law Commission has already reviewed the Code of Criminal Procedure and is likely to undertake a comprehensive review of the Indian Penal Code and the Indian Evidence Act shortly.

Legal enactments invoke differential age-specifics creating a dilemma whether the same human being is or is not a child and, depends upon the law which is being invoked in a given case. Given the fact that the deprived child's birth is either inadequately/incorrectly recorded, the reliability and impact of the laws thus cannot be fully regulated in terms of age. The laws which relate to transgression by the child, are under the general rubric of juvenile, which distinguishes treatment vis-a-vis the adult, for offences like begging/stealing/drug taking/peddling or crime. Free legal aid is available, under the public utility litigation provisions. But the disparity between the age-identified child and the laws applicable in terms of maturity levels and the child's ability to articulate needs, requires congruent thinking in policy, law statements and their enactments.

The acceptance of the definition of the child as given by the UN Convention on the rights of the child is likely to have implications on programme planning and budgetary provisions. The Government of India is, therefore, reviewing the legislation and is considering, adopting the definition of the child as stated in Article 1 of the Convention, wherever it is feasible and applicable, so that the rights of children are protected in the society under all circumstances.

Children in India

The Indian population is relatively young with nearly 37 per cent of it below the age of fifteen, i.e. two out of every five persons are below 15 years. The total child population of India in the 0-14 age group is 297 m. out of a total population of 846 m. according to 1991 census. Of this 203 m. are in the age group of 5—14, the school-going age. Of this, 112m. are reported to have been enrolled in the formal school system, about 7 m. are in the NFE, and about 100 m. are out of school or 'nowhere children'.

Notwithstanding considerable investment and political will and commitment, and sincere efforts to bring down the rate of growth of the population and also the absolute number of people, India's population is growing at a much faster rate than that of the rest of the world. Every year some 13 to 14 m. infants which is equivalent of the population of a very large country like Australia, are being added to the Indian population without any assurance of availability of hygiene, sanitation, immunization, literacy, and education.

An estimated 77 per cent of India's children live in rural areas. According to one projection, about 99.4 m. children, or nearly two-fifths of the total Indian child population, live in conditions that are dangerous to life. Of them 48.5 m. or nearly half are under six-years old. Today about 21m. babies are born annually. Of them about 8 m. die, leaving about 13m. children.

There have undoubtedly been rapid strides in the reduction of the infant mortality rate (IMR) which is a key indicator of social wel-fare in a given population. The IMR, which used to be approximately 110 in 1000 live births, has now fallen to 76. Even that is quite high and continues to be one of the major areas of concern. Of the seventy-six children who die out of 1000 live births, 40 per cent are those under 5 years of age and about 50 per cent are less than a year old. In the lowest age group of 0—12 months, 50 per cent of the deaths are due to dysentry, diarrhoea, respiratory diseases, and gastro-intestinal disorders.

Life expectancy at birth has increased from 23.63 for male and 23.96 for females in 1901 to 61.5 and 62.1 respectively in 1996. This could be straightaway attributed to an extensive network of ove 2000 Community Health Centres, 22,000 Primary Health Centres an 131,000 village level sub-centres.

Today there is a growing awareness of the value of invest-ment in early childhood care and development (ECCD). The impor-tance of trying to 'prevent' or 'manage' the problems of children wh are the future adults has been clearly recognized.

The introduction of Integrated Child Development Service (ICDS) Project in 1975 marked the beginning of a multi-sectoral ap-proach combining health, nutrition, and early childhood education. Th universal immunization programme, oral rehydration therapy, and series of indirect nutrition support programmes such as those relatin to poverty alleviation, public distribution of food, health, family we-fare, adult and non-formal education which were simultaneousl launched along with ICDS in 1975 were major path-breaking exer-cises. It was in many ways a model of integration.

Despite all these positive initiatives and significant achieve-ments there are wide gaps between the expected and actual outcom and these gaps that exist in areas of major concern very adversely afre the development and growth of children. The ICDS has been in opera-tion for over 20 years and has undoubtedly focused on micro-nutrient particularly vitamin A and iron in areas covered by the programm but substantial part of the country is not covered by the scheme (tl ICDS serves 4200 of 5575 Community Development Blocks). Ev with the package of services for health, nutrition, and pre-primary education under the ICDS, malnourishment has not been fully overcome because of a variety of factors. Supplementary nutrition serves as an inadequate 'main meal' for poor children. About 7 per cent of the rural households and 3 per cent of the urban ones still do not have access to two square meals a day. This is a reflection of the acute poverty of some households. Lack of stability and durability of employment, non-payment of minimum wages (not to speak of a fair or living wage), the continually spiralling prices of essential commodities, the progressive decline in the purchasing power of the rupee, and an effete and inefficient public distribution system are largely responsible for this deplorable state of affairs. Cultural practices such as faulty cooking methods, inadequate and improper feeding of infants, neglect of pregnant women in a male dominated and discriminatory society awash with fads and taboos leading to malnourish-ment and resultant undernourishment and death of infants are important contributory factors to malnutrition. Poor sanitation and the indifferent quality of water that causes a high incidence of infection and diarrhoea are other major contributory factors. While claims are made that severe malnutrition fell to less than 9 per cent for India as a whole in 1990, there remain areas in Bihar where severe malnutrition is around 25 per cent. The chronic malnutrition among preschool children remains disturbing.

It is estimated that about 2.5 m. children in India are threatened by blindness in early childhood. Over a million children suffer from severe vitamin A deficiency, as a result of which 12,000 to 14,000 children in the 3-6 age group go blind every year. The peak incidence of such blindness is in the age group 1 to 5 years, and three-fourths of the children in this age group have body weights that are 75 per cent below the standard weight of well-nourished children and only 3 per cent can be considered to have normal body weights. Anaemia in young children is associated with impaired cognitive performance, psychomotor developments and scholastic achievement.

It is estimated that 30 per cent of all school-going children suffer from one form of ailment or another. Of the various types that are reported to health centres, 56 per cent purportedly relate to intestinal infections, respiratory complaints, and nutritional disorders.

Education

Education figures in the concurrent list of distribution of powers. This was made possible by the 42nd amendment to the Constitution (1976) with a view to providing a national direction for orderly and coordinated development of education at all levels throughout the country and is a continuation of the thrust provided by the framers of the Constitution (Art. 30, 45, 350 A).

Few claim that the policy of the national government has not been positive and supportive of the proper evolution and growth of education both prior to and after Independence. Providing free, compulsory, universal primary education or basic education has been an article of faith and commitment of the government of both pre-independent and independent India. The educational infrastructure at all levels has grown enormously over the past five decades since Independence. There has been substantial growth in investment inasmuch as expenditure on education as a percentage of National Income increased from 1.2 per cent in 1950-1 to 3.9 per cent in 1986-7, and it is now proposed to be raised to 6 per cent. There has been a phenomenal growth of recognized educational institutions at all levels, i.e. primary, upper primary, secondary, higher secondary, intermediate, undergraduate and post-graduate. The number of teachers and teachers' training institutions has also kept pace with the growth in the number of teaching institutions. There is perceptible improvement in access to educational opportunity reflected by the increase in the percentage of enrolment of both boys and girls, as also in absolute numbers. The net impact of all this has been an overall improvement in the rate of literacy (both male and female as also the national average).

The challenges to the educational system have been many. An expanded educational infrastructure by itself has not ensured equity in access to education. The urban-rural and male-female divide, and economic and regional disparities have taken a heavy toll on the ideal of providing equitable access to education to all. Despite the phenomenal increase in the number of educational institutions and improvement in enrolment, over a 100 m. children are out of school of whom 60 per cent are girls. While the present enrolment is 148 m., we have to ensure the enrolment of an additional 32.9 m. children by 2001 which by any reckoning is a task of gigantic proportions. The impact of high enrolment is neutralized by low retention. Though the drop-out rates are declining they continue to be very high at all stages and in particular for girls (the average rate being 36.3 per cent at the primary and 52.7 per cent at the upper primary level). Although there was an appreciable increase of 16.67 per cent in the rate of literacy in the 1991 census over that of 1951, we have in terms of absolute numbers over

200 m. illiterates which is the single largest illiterate population in the world. The differences in the rate of literacy are also equally pronounced, as the following percentages show:

		Percentage
Regional	Kerala	89.0
	Rajasthan	20.0
Social	SC	37.4
	ST	29.0
Gender	Male	64.0
	Female	39.0
	General	52.1

These gaps are further accentuated by vast differentials between the achievement of boys and girls, between members of the Scheduled castes and tribes and others, and between levels of proficiency in arithmetic, the mother tongue, the physical and social sciences.

An ongoing status appraisal report on 'Primary Education in India' prepared by a core group on Citizen's Initiative on Primary Education comprising Professor C. J. Daswani, Sanjay Ghose, social activist and J. Acharya has highlighted the following problems, constraints, and challenges in achieving the goal of universal primary education:

- The share of plan allocations to education declined from 7.8 per cent in the First Five Year Plan to 2.7 per cent in the Sixth Plan.
- Even when the share has increased in the recent past, it continues to be considerably lower than it used to be in the first plan.
- Nearly 98 per cent of the total expenditure is recurring, and of this nearly 96 per cent is spent on salaries. Teachers' salaries alone accounts for 94 per cent of the recurring expenditure, meaning thereby that very little is spent on the maintenance of the existing facilities.
- Local community level initiatives to improve the functioning of schools are lacking.
- The unaided private sector continues to expand and thrive despite the fact that successive educational policies have favoured a common school pattern in India.

- Efficiency, accountability, and responsiveness of the educational system are elusive.
- Of every 100 girls enrolled in Class I, there are only 40 who continue up to Class V, only 18 up to Class VIII, only 9 up to Class IX, and only one up to Class XII.
- A vast majority of children in the 6-14 year age group work not in the organized sector but in the unorganized and informal sector, often helping their parents in different vocations.
- The bulk of the out-of-school children can be deemed to be working children as their parents do not permit them to attend school.
- The problem of educating the vast mass of 100 m. plus working children cannot be solved in one stroke through a single model of alternative schooling.
- We need to experiment with a variety of alternatives to formal school education, to make these alternatives known to the children and their parents, and implement these with their full knowledge and approval. Till then they will continue to remain 'out-of-school' children and 'nowhere' children.
- The problem is further compounded by 2.6 m. disabled or severely handicapped children in the 4—15 age group.
- There are around 1.7 m. children who are mentally handicapped and suffer from severe learning disabilities.
- One of the major tasks ahead is to address the issue of inter-regional, inter-group and gender disparities, in educational development.
- In many instances and locales especially in remote and inaccessible rural areas and in the case of certain targeted groups, the school may not perhaps be the most appropriate institutional arrangement with which to spread the message of primary education.
- Irrespective of the curriculum, students are not learning all that they are expected to at the primary level. This has more to do with curriculum transaction than curriculum design.
- The future of primary education depends on the success achieved in catalyzing local social pressures to improve the system.
- Nehruvian socialism envisaged the paramount role of the state in ensuring social justice with economic growth. In the actual

process of implementation, the compulsions of economic growth have overtaken the rationale for social justice. Educational strategies and programmes were evolved more on the basis of cost considerations than on those of the genuine needs and requirements of education.

- Compulsory education of every child below 14 years was, therefore, never seriously implemented because considerations of cost supervened over the desirability of the objective.
- Resources were spread too thinly, making the investments unproductive and ineffective. Schools were set up without adequate buildings, with very little or no teaching materials, and without an adequate number of qualified teachers. It was almost as if providing a school in name was more important than in creating conditions for its effective functioning.
- The national policy, system, and programme of education were designed to provide access to education of comparable quality to all students irrespective of caste, religion, location or sex. What in practice happened however, was a trend towards uniformity in school education which is neither possible nor desirable. The national curricular framework has led to greater uniformity than diversity suited to the changing social and cultural milieu of the state.
- Uniformity in structure as well as in content at the national level, sacrificing there by principles of local relevance and pluralism, essential in a pluralistic society, has been an unfortunate corollary of the national policy of education.
- The role of local bodies became a casualty in the raging debate between centralization versus decentralization.
- Together with English there are fifty-one languages that are currently used as the medium of instruction at the primary level, yet there are millions of children whose early education is in a language other than their mother tongue.
- As in every other aspect of educational planning the issue of the medium of instruction at the primary level is perceived only from the urban point of view. The mother tongue being the most effective medium of instruction, at the primary school level, all children must be taught through it. Besides, the mother tongue is also one of the most effective means of socialization.

- A teacher is not merely a tool or agency for the implementation of models and directions of the state. S/he is an independent being, endowed with a capacity for original thought, creativity, and academic action, and should not be reduced to the position of a mere appendage to the system.
- To empower teachers a participative, communicative, and effective model of teachers' training needs to be introduced. Teachers' training unfortunately remains a poorly rated academic activity, and has remained largely untouched by academic grounding in modern child-centred pedagogy.
- An evaluation of the content, process, and impact of learning is extremely important. The present system of evaluation gives greater legitimacy to external examination while paying lip service to continuous and comprehensive self-evaluation.

TWO

WHAT IS CHILD LABOUR ?

The world over, the number of working children is increasing from year to year. Some reasons are economic situation of their family, lack of employment opportunities for the adult member, and the preference of the employers to hire children to save on production costs. The child loses all the pleasures of life and potentials of growth and development.

There is worldwide awareness and laws have been enacted to prohibit children from being employed. Illegal recruitment of children still continues. There is also a great scope for exploitation and abuse of child. The social workers and activists from the trade unions are finding it difficult to help the child because of the existing legislations and other social factors. Such workers do not get proper empirically verified research data on the nature, causes and conditions of child labour, on one side, and feelings and aspirations of the children on the other.

A survey of the urban working children was conducted in 1984-85 by the Institute for Cultural Research and Action, Bangalore. This became the basis for drafting Child Labour Bill, 1985. Besides, the study also helped working children to acquire skills, knowledge and training so as to become productive workers. The findings of this survey along with a blueprint for elimination of child labour in the long run are presented. Problem of child labour at the macro-level with reference to India, methodology of the study giving context to the survey, profiles of child workers and their families, employment and working conditions, wages and income, educational and career interests of the working children, the urban working children and the concerns for the working children are presented.

As children always participated in economic activities, their workplace was an extension of home and children were not given hazardous tasks. However, with the advent of industrialisation, labour now became a marketable commodity.

If a family cannot afford to feed its children, that is not a problem relating to labour, but it may lead to a child being sent out, or even sold, to supplement the family income. Or it may be a cause of a child not being provided with education. That may not necessarily be rectified even if the child is not at work, but it is less likely to be rectified if the child is working every waking hour. If a child is being abused or ill-treated, it does not follow that the offender is the employer, but much of the abuse and ill-treatment of which we know is by employers.

In 1919, at its first session, the International Labour Organisation (ILO) adopted the Minimum Age Convention, providing that in industry there should be no employment of those under the age of 14. But industry, of course, touched only the fringes of the problem. There has been a subsequent total of 14 HD conventions on the subject of child labour.

The Minimum Age Convention of 1973 extended the prohibition to all child labour. It provided that no child should be in full-time employment under the age within that system of completing compulsory schooling, and in no case under the age of 15. Between 13 and 15, a child might be employed on light work, provided that it was not such as to prejudice his or her attendance at school or training. And the Convention provides that, up to the age of 18, no one is to be employed in work likely to jeopardise his or her health, safety or morals.

In 1981, the UN estimated that 145 million children in the world under the age of 14 were in employment, mostly full-time. The ILO estimates that the highest rates of child labour are in Africa. But the degree of suffering among employed children is probably greater in Asia.

The Bonded Labour Liberation Front of India, in 1989, convened the South-East Asia Seminar on Child Servitude. It was attended by 60 delegates from five countries in the region. Governments were not represented, but there was an ILO delegate, and a number of Human Rights workers, academics and judges. They were able to collate a great deal of evidence. What was unique is that they brought along a number of children to give their own evidence. That was no easy task. There was an element of risk both for workers and for children.

The reasons which lead to child employment vary substantially with local conditions and local cultures. Where a family simply cannot afford to keep a child at home, so he or she is put out to earn. It may be at a wage, or the father may be employed, and simply take along his family to help, in order to maximise his earnings. The earnings are then paid to the father. The employer may then have no record of an individual child, a situation which has advantages in the unlikely event of an inspector asking questions. But even if no records exist, a child who tries to escape may discover that is the employer's business. The child may live at home, or in accommodation provided by the employer.

There are children whose families cannot afford to keep them at home, so realise whatever financial value they may have on the market. The parents may be told that the child can be adopted, where it can have a better life. Daughters may be married off as children. A bride price is paid, and the child then enters the household of the new family to do whatever work, in whatever conditions, they decide.

In many regions of Asia, poor people earn just enough to keep themselves and their families. There is nothing over to put by for emergencies. But occasions arise when a substantial sum is needed. Social conventions may require that when a child is married, the family provides a wedding feast. They may need to provide a dowry for a daughter. Even if the family is part of a community which has no status in the eyes of the more privileged majority, they need to hold up their heads within their own community. But the need to borrow money does not always arise from maintaining status.

Often, there is simply not enough money or produce to keep the family through the monsoon season. Either way, a father may have to go to the local landowner, or to someone with resources and ask for a loan. And the condition may be that he must work for the creditor until the loan is repaid. Then the problems begin. The debtor has to accept whatever wage is on offer. He cannot now work his own piece of ground so effectively, and a substantial part of his remuneration is deducted to repay the debt. But the interest rate may be very high, so that frequently he is working simply to pay off the interest, leaving the debt undiminished. Often, indeed, the debt continues to increase. The debtor is probably illiterate and in any event is not given an account book, so he has to rely on what the creditor tells him. He may then have to borrow further and one of the children will be given in bond for the debt.

The child, after all, is the parent's property, and the transaction is like pawning a chattel. The child works without any wages and must continue to work for the creditor until the debt is paid. But frequently, it is never paid. An unscrupulous creditor will make deductions for food or for shelter, whatever food or shelter may have been provided, or for damage or breakages, and the debt continues to grow. The debt does not cease with the death of the father, so the child may be in bondage for the remainder of its life. And if a debtor dies, leaving a debt, the debt devolves on the children, so that many children are born into bondage, a bondage which they never escape from birth until death. There are families who have been in slavery for generations because of a debt incurred by a remote ancestor.

In most Asian countries debt bondage is no longer lawful. In India, in particular, a series of statutes forbids it, but the victims do not know about them. In many areas, officials are not sympathetic with the debtors. There are those who devote themselves to enforcing the law or improving conditions, and a number of organisations now follow in the footsteps of the Bonded Labour Liberation Front, but for all we know to the contrary, there are families falling into debt-bondage as quickly as others are being released.

A survey of some of the industries where bonded labour applies are described below. Most Indian handmade carpets are produced in the Mirzapur carpet industry. The industry employs some hundred thousand children, many of whom serve as bonded labourers or are simply kidnapped.

The Bonded Labour Liberation Front of India discovered in 1984 that 32 children aged 6 to 14, were employed by the same loom-owner. They were brought before the Supreme Court and the judge was horrified on hearing the evidence. He ordered their release and exercising a power which is available to the Supreme Court in India, he appointed a commissioner to make a study. The case was taken up by the media and debated in the Human Rights Commission. Many more children were released, but there is still far to go. If children are not available as bonded labourers, they are frequently replaced by simply kidnapping others.

The government quickly realised that there was little purpose in ordering the release of children unless they had somewhere to go, some way of earning a living, and some training. Money was set aside for this purpose, but little seems to have reached those for whom it was intended. In one instance, an eight-year-old boy was given his release certificate, plus a total of Rs. 650. His employer simply seized Rs. 500. And when his parents came to collect him, the employer demanded Rs. 1,300 which he said he had spent on the boy's training. The parents could not pay and did not know where to go for advice. The owner simply sold the boy to someone else. Enforcement is so relaxed that some loom-owners are alleged to have claimed that a child is working in unlawful debt bondage when it is not, because in that way they get their hands on some of the rehabilitation money.

There is now in India a carpet manufacturing industry a Child Labour Group, which arranges for their processes to be inspected and a certificate issued that carpets are produced in accordance with good practice. Many of the larger exporters are joining. Arrangements are under way for some European importers to look for those certificates before purchasing.

In India another industry which employs a substantial number of children under the bonded labour system is stone quarrying, particularly in the outskirts of Delhi. In November 1988, the Bonded Labour Liberation Front learned of 48 people, including 15 children, working as bonded labourers, all in one village. They secured their release. Their health had suffered from the dust, but it was said that the worst effects were psychological. Most of them were totally apathetic about their condition. All resistance had been drained from them.

The brick kiln industry in Pakistan absorbs many bonded labourers. It has been estimated that some two million families in Pakistan are still subject to bonded labour. In 1992, the Government of Pakistan legislated against bonded labour. But the problem, as in India, remains one of enforcement. As long ago as 1988, on a complaint sponsored by the Bonded Labour Liberation Front of Pakistan, the Supreme Court held that the practice in the brick kiln industry was unconstitutional and ordered the release of the victim.

Outside South-East Asia, evidence is constantly emerging of children employed in horrifying conditions. In the United Arab Emirates and in Dubai, camel racing is a popular sport. Jockeys need to be small and light. Until recently, there was a flourishing trade in children from the Indian subcontinent, taken as bonded labcurers, kidnapped, or simply enticed by prospects of earnings. A child thrown off and dragged along by a charging camel can be seriously injured. And there was little information on what happened to children when they grew too big to be jockeys. Things have improved since a programme on the BBC World Service, made as a result of efforts by Anti-Slavery International, was shown. There is now more effective legislation to protect children. The maximum weight imposed by the sport has been replaced by legislation requiring a minimum weight, to ensure sufficient strength for safety.

The economy of Dominican Republic depends largely on sugarcane. Work in the plantations with large knives used to cut cane, is harsh, unpleasant and dangerous. It is not easy to find a willing labour force. Workers are imported from neighbouring Haiti. They are recruited with stories which paint a very false picture, but once there they are trapped. Often they are held there against their will, by armed guards. Americas watch were recently able to inspect some of the working conditions and were horrified at what they saw. Frequently, there is no sanitary accommodation, and dysentery and similar diseases are rampant. The victims receive little sympathy from the local Dominican population, who dismiss people from Haiti as inferior.

Since they are not citizens of Dominica, they have virtually no legal rights. Many of the workers are children, who either come with their parents, or who have been kidnapped or recruited with stories of high earnings. Their plight has been brought to the notice of the world by some church workers, particularly Fr. Edwin Paraison, an episcopal priest, himself from Haiti. Although in great danger himself, it is said that he has helped large numbers of children to escape.

Some Asian cities, such as Bangkok, provide facilities for paedophiles. Regularly, children arrive in large numbers at the main railway station, where they have been brought by kidnappers or, more usually, they have simply come to the city to find a living, waiting at the station are people known as fishermen, who take control of them and sell them on to employers looking for cheap labour. The attractive ones are sold to brothels, to satisfy the needs of paedophiles, and there they remain as slaves, often until they die of disease, or simply of exhaustion. Some years ago, a group was formed in Thailand to campaign against those practices. They formed End Child Prostitution in Asian Tourism (ECPAT). They addressed themselves to tour operators, to airlines and to governments, hoping to persuade governments to take extraterritorial jurisdiction to try offences by European tourists in Asia.

Some Western governments are now passing 'Longreach Laws', taking jurisdiction to prosecute their citizens for offences of this kind committed abroad. Sweden has its own police agents in Bangkok and Manila. The Australian government instructs its diplomats to watch visiting Australians whom they have reason to suspect.

Another group of children who need to be consider are those who are either orphaned, turned out by their families to fend for themselves, or who have run away from the conditions which we have just been contemplating and who are now living on the streets. For companionship and support they have to look to other children, and they live in gangs, making a living in whatever way presents itself, begging, guiding tourists, or doing odd jobs. Many make a living by looking through the city's garbage, collecting paper, bottles, rags and bones. There are retailers who take what they find and pay them something, however small. Frequently, they have arrangements delineating their territory, so they have to be up before the city is stirring to ensure that no one poaches on their territory. Many suffer accidents from sharp glass or tins, or bites from rabid dogs.

In major cities in Europe and in America, street children are organised in gangs by criminals, who send them out to pick pockets, burgle houses and generally organise them. Many of them from poverty-stricken families in Eastern Europe, particularly the gypsy population of the Balkans, are taken to other countries for this purpose. In some areas of South America, street children are going into business on their own, for example, distributing drugs. There may be a gang with its own territory, and sometimes there are territorial wars between rival gangs, as in Chicago in the 1930s. But the gangs are gangs of children, and there are cases of children being murdered by other children.

Children on the streets are sometimes seen as a nuisance, or worse. Their escapades evoke anger and sometimes they develop a running feud with the police. Usually, the police limit their reaction within acceptable bounds, but there is at least one example in Brazil where the police reaction went over the top.

There is nothing new in campaigners seeking to draw attention to the suffering of children from poor backgrounds. At the end of the First World War, in Europe, devastated by war, children were the first victims. The movement 'Save the Children', organised relief and campaign for more structured protection. In 1923, 'Save the Children' drafted the Declaration of Geneva. The five principles set out by the Declaration are the following:

i) The child must be have the means requisite for its normal development, both material and spiritually,
ii) The child that is hungry must be fed, the child that is sick must be nursed, the child that is backward must be helped, the delinquent child must be reclaimed and the orphan and the waif must be sheltered and succoured.
iii) The child must be the first to receive relief in times of distress.
iv) The child must be put in a position to earn a livelihood and must be protected against any form of exploitation.
v) The child must be brought up in the consciousness that its talents must be devoted to service of its fellowmen.

In 1956, the UN adopted the Supplementary Convention on the Abolition of Slavery, providing, *inter alia,* that states should abolish the practice of the delivering a child by its parents to another person with a view to the exploitation of his labour.

In 1959, the UN adopted a further declaration on the rights of the child. It set out ten principles. For the first time, it addressed the question of discrimination and specifically provided that every child should enjoy all the rights set out in the declaration, without discrimination on grounds of race, colour, sex or creed. It provided that every child should be given facilities to develop physically, mentally morally, spiritually and socially, and that the best interests of the child should he paramount. This introduced an important principle, which has subsequently been developed. The Declaration proceeded to set out particular rights, such as a health care education, protection from cruelty, recreation and appropriate treatment for the handicapped.

In the 1970s, there was a discussion about a possible Convention which could identify with the obligations of governments which would have the force of law and which at least might make provision for monitoring the efforts which governments were making to implement it. The year 1979 was declared by the United Nations to be the International Year of the Child. In the course of the year the Polish Government proposed that they should begin work on a Convention. The UN Human Rights Commission established a working group to draft a Convention. They set themselves the objective of having the Convention approved by the General Assembly within ten years. If that appears a somewhat relaxed view of urgency, it must be seen in the context of the way in which the UN works.

National delegations have to obtain instructions from their governments, and within governments, each department insists on its input. Each government has a different idea of the priorities. Some will be anxious to include a particular provision which others will find embarrassing, because of some domestic problem. There will be horse trading, adjournments for consultation, debates and further private discussion.

In 1989, the General Assembly adopted unanimously the new Convention consisting of 54 articles. A child is defined as a human being below the age 18. Four principles are worth singling out.

Firstly, the rights set out in the Convention are to apply without discrimination of any kind, in respect of race, sex, religion, ethnic or social origins, disability or other status. Thus the Convention takes it other areas of work which have been carried out on human rights.

Secondly, the obligation is upon states to ensure that the rights are implemented. And the obligation applies to ever child within the jurisdiction and thus not only to the state's own citizens.

Thirdly, the primary consideration should be in it has the best interests of the child. And to ensure that the child's best interests are not simply as interpreted by a provision that due weight should be given to the views of the child, of course in accordance with the age and maturity of the child. Indeed, it is specifically provided that the child should have the right freely to express its views.

The fourth provision has proved not wholly uncontroversial. First, it emphasises the distinction between the interests of the child and that of the parents. Secondly, children have a right not simply to be protected but to be heard. This may impose some burden on our patience and our common sense. There were suggestions that the Convention should be called 'A Convention for the Protection of Children'.

To speak of the rights of a child appears to entail that the child should be able to initiate some process for their enforcement. We protect ancient buildings, but we do not speak of their having rights. There are then a series of articles setting out substantive rights.

There are articles on basic needs, food, health care, education, recreation and play. There are articles relating to protection, from child labour, drug abuse, sexual exploitation, trafficking and abduction. There are articles on civil rights, freedom of expression, freedom of thought, conscience and religion, protection of privacy, access to appropriate information and protection of justice and dignity within the penal system. There are three articles on what may be called enforcement.

Article 43 establishes a Committee on the Rights of the Child, consisting of ten experts, elected by the states parties. States undertake to submit to the Committee reports on the measures taken to give effect to the rights in the Convention. The first report is to be within two years of the date when the state ratifies, and thereafter every five years.

Article 49 provides that the Convention should enter into force when there have been twenty ratifications or accessions. This was achieved in September 1990. In the same month, presidents and prime ministers from 70 countries gathered at the World Summit for Children in New York, and agreed on a Plan of Action for Children, endorsed by 159 states. The intention was to undertake progressive implementation of the rights in the Convention. It declared that children should have the first call on resources. And it set out targets for the year 2000, particularly relating to the elimination of certain diseases. It requires each state to prepare a National Plan of Action, including target dates and anticipated resource requirements.

As early as 1988, United Nations International Child's Emergency Fund (UNICEF) established the Children's Centre in Florence to advise on child rights, and to encourage initiatives by publication of information and thinkpieces. At the Human Rights Summit in Vienna in June 1993, children were high on the agenda. Stephen Lewis, the Special Representative of UNICEF's Executive Director, spoke of children as the cutting edge of human rights. We can narrow the disparities between the privileged and the underprivileged, he explained, by what he called a jump start early in people's lives. So the problems of children in Mirzapur, in Rio de Janeiro, and in Dominica are very much a topic of discussion among diplomats and politicians and lawyers.

But human rights stand or fall not in conference rooms, but in streets and cellars. We cannot eliminate the problems instantly like switching off a light. People have to work at it. None the less, it concentrates the minds of governments to know that the world is asking questions. Even the most indifferent of governments likes to be loved in international circles. What is important is that the questions should keep coming.

Initiatives and impetus for human rights have always come principally from the NGOs. That is not to say that governments are always hostile to Human Rights, or even totally, indifferent. Within governments there are those who care about human rights, either generally or in specific areas. But the whole scheme of International human rights enforcement is to place on governments the responsibility for ensuring that the standards are met in their respective countries, a consequence of the fact that the UN is orientated towards nation-states, and very much subject to the assertion of national sovereignty.

National governments would prefer enforcing human rights themselves to having others asking questions within their boundaries. So it is not surprising that governments are less than enthusiastic to make a rod for their own backs. It was principally NGOs who made the running in relation to children's rights before, during and after the Convention process. And implementation will depend largely on the pressure which they can maintain.

There is an NGO Group on the Rights of the Child, to help maintain the impetus. It is based in Geneva, at the premises of Care of

Children International. It works closely with NGOs like Anti-Slavery International, maintaining pressure at the UN Sub-commission on minorities and similar international bodies. Anti-Slavery International presents an award each year to someone whose contribution to the fight against slavery should be recognised. The first award was to Swami Agnivesh, of the Bonded Labour Liberation Front of India. The second was to Fr Ricardo Rezende, a Catholic priest in Brazil, for his work among rurai communities.

After the Second World War, the lives of children in industrialised countries improved substantially. Between 1950 and 1990, European countries achieved the fastest reduction in infant mortality ever recorded. But in the last 15 years there has been a growing number of problems relating to children. In Europe, a high proportion of children live in families with low incomes, but the figures must be adjusted to take account of redistributive taxation and social security policies. In Germany, 2.8 per cent of children can be said to be living in poverty, in France 4.6 per cent, in the UK 7.4 per cent, and in the US 20 per cent.

There are further problems with families who must rely increasingly on the incomes of both parents, with consequently less time to spend caring for children, playing with them or teaching them. And this appears to be particularly true in the US and the UK. They are living with what Dr. Sylvia Ann Hewlett in her study *Child Neglect in Rich Nations* published by UNICEF, calls the cult of the workaholic. There is a disturbing body of research revealing what is possibly obvious that the more time children are left on their own, the more likely they are to develop behavioural problems, such as drug abuse.

In UK, children in employment are protected by a formidable body of legal provisions, so many that Caroline Moorhead, who wrote a booklet on the subject for Anti-Slavery International, described them as a patchwork of laws, some new, some still drawing heavily on provisions passed in the last century. They prescribe the times at which children may work, the number of hours, what work they may do, and in what conditions. The bad news is that they are rarely enforced. Caroline Moorhead found in 1985 that remuneration depended largely on wages, inspectors of whom there were 119 for the whole of Great Britain.

In the whole of England and Wales there were 3,000 educational welfare officers, one per 970 children. Safety was the concern of the Factories Inspectorate, and there were 500 inspectors for the whole of the UK. We know how many industrial accidents relating to children are reported, and the number is quite small, but the low pay unit found that in their sample. 31.6 per cent of the boys and 29 per cent of the girls had received some injury while working.

The Gulbenkian Foundation established the Children's Rights Development Unit in March 1992 to initiate a national agenda for monitoring and implementing the Convention, article by article, and promoting awareness of its provisions. Gulbenkian have also published a proposal by Martin Rosenbaum and Peter Newell for the appointment of a Children's Rights Commissioner along the lines of the Health Service Ombudsman and the Local Government Ombudsman.

The UK duly ratified the Convention on 16 December 1991, subject to six reservations or declarations.

i) It interprets the Convention as applicable only following a live birth, so that it leaves open questions about abortion.
ii) There is some limitation on the construction of the word 'parents' to conform with UK law.
iii) The government will be bound by the provisions only so far as they are not in conflict with existing provisions on the right to remain in the UK.
iv) A child is not to be construed for all employment purposes as a person under 18. British law recognises young people as a separate category with different rights and obligations.
v) While the Convention requires that young offenders should not be detained with adults, the UK provides that they shall be subject to facilities being available, and to cases where it may be thought beneficial to detain them with adults.
vi) The right to legal representation set out in the Convention is not to apply to children's hearings in Scotland.

The Children's Committee's first report fell due in December of 1993. The Committee has expressed the hope that reports shall include consultation with NGOs. The UK government distributed the draft report to some NGOs out of several hundred interested in the subject, and distributed it on 15 December, with a requirement to send comments by the end of December. Not only were organisations given a mere fortnight in which to distribute the report to their members, read it, discuss it and react, but they were required to do so over Christmas.

Background

The issue of child labour has acquired a great deal of prominence since April 1994 when, in the wake of the conclusion of the last Uruguay round of negotiations, an agreement was signed at Mar-rakesh, to which India was a signatory. It had earlier attracted attention and concern, after July 1991, when India's economic reforms were launched at the national level, ushering in a new era of liberalization and privatization, in an attempt to integrate the national economy with the global economy. It is not as if the issue of child labour had not surfaced even earlier. It was very much a part of the social and national consciousness, but the issue acquired a new meaning and significance in the context of contemporary competitiveness where labour cost is one of the important contributory factors and child labour has certain connotations, mostly negative, in the context of labour cost and international trade. Apart from the ILO, which took a lead in this area since its inception, the issue of child labour is, very validly, being raised today in many international fora. International agencies and the UN system as a whole have pledged their support to eliminate child labour by signing a joint declaration at New Delhi in August 1998. Numerous declarations are being made and documents published, but as an issue, child labour is far more complex and multifaceted than is apparent in them. It is necessary to view the various implications of the issue in a holistic perspective encompassing the history, economics, and sociology of child labour, the constitutional and legal framework, policy postulates obtaining at the national and international level, and the adoption of possible strategies towards the total elimination of child labour.

A child is born. 'It is a soul with a being, a nature and capacity of its own, who must be helped to find them, to grow into their maturity, into a fullness of physical and vital energy and the utmost breadth, depth and height of its emotional, intellectual and spiritual being.' This is how Justice P. N. Bhagawati described the birth of a child, and the excitement and joy associated with that birth, in a judgement on international adoption of children in 1985. This perception is writ large in our ancient thought and culture. Tagore, in *Sadhana* (1979) said that 'Civilization must be judged and prized not by the amount of power it has developed but by how much it has evolved and given expression to by its laws and institutions, the love of humanity.' And this noble thought echoes in the Introduction to the *Progress of Nations,* an annual publication of UNICEF, for 1997:

The day will come when nations will be judged not by their military or economic strength, nor by the splendour of their capital cities and public buildings but by the well being of their people; by the levels of health, nutrition and education; by the opportunities to earn a fair reward for their labour; by their ability to participate in the decisions that affect their lives; by the respect that is shown for their civil and political liberties; by the provision that is made for those who are vulnerable and disadvantaged and by the protection that is afforded to the growing minds and bodies of their children.

The birth of a child is a moment of great rejoicing for parents; a joy that is unfortunately shortlived. The child is subjected to a process of sex-based discrimination that acts as a process of ruthless exploitation. Deploring this phenomenon, the Supreme Court of India, in *Bandhua Mukti Morcha,* etc. v. *Union of India and Others,* while disposing of the writ petition (C) No. 12125 of 1984 (under Art. 32 of the Constitution of India) observed:

A child of today cannot develop to fee a responsible and productive member of tomorrow's society unless an environment which is conducive to his social and physical health is assured to him. Every nation, developed or developing, links its future with the status of the child. Childhood holds the potential and also sets the limit to the future development of the society. Children are the greatest gift to humanity. The parents themselves live for them. They embody the joy of life and in their innocence relieve the fatigue and drudgery in their struggle of daily life. Parents regain peace and happiness in the company of children. Children signify eternal optimism in the human being and always provide the potential for human development. Neglecting children means loss to the society as a whole. If children are deprived of their childhood—socially, economically, physically and mentally—the nation gets deprived of potential human resources for social progress, economic empowerment and peace and order, social stability and good citizenry.

Every form of work, whether hazardous or not, entails some degree of stress. Hazardous work cripples the health, psyche, and personality of a child, while non-hazardous work connotes other forms of deprivation, such as denial of access to education and denial of the pleasurable activities associated with childhood. The fact remains, in any event, that there has to be a minimum age for entry into the workforce, whether it is for wages, or for a living, or otherwise. That age should be determined in physical, emotional, and psychological terms. Only when a person has the physical strength, the mental and emotional maturity to think and to act rationally and scientifically, that s/he can cope with the stress that is imposed by the work in which s/he is engaged.

This was the basis on which minimum age of entry into employment, Convention No. 138, was designed and adopted at the International Labour Conference in June 1973. The Convention clearly spelt out that no child below a particular age, say fifteen, was to work, but was instead required to attend school and receive an education. The age of entry to work would vary from country to country, state to state, and region to region. This was because geographical, topographical, climatological, and demographic conditions vary widely, and these have an impact on the growth and evolution of children. These variations notwithstanding, it is necessary to adopt a minimum age for entry to employment and work in order to protect those below this age from the adverse consequences of so doing.

This was evidently the rationale that weighed in the minds of the founding fathers of the Constitution when they prohibited the employment of children in factories, mines, and every hazardous workplace. The spirit of the ILO Convention was also clearly and unambiguously enshrined in Art. 45 of the Constitution which mandates that the state shall endeavour to provide free and compulsory education for all children until they complete the age of fourteen.

There is a dichotomy between the provisions of Art. 24 and Art. 45 and, though unintentional, it is necessary that this dichotomy be stated clearly and unambiguously. If the employment of children is prohibited in hazardous operations, does this imply that children are permitted to work in non-hazardous operations? If that is so, how does one reconcile, on the one hand, the fundamental right to receive free primary education at a particular age and, on the other the possibility of working at that age. If children between 6 and 14 years of age are expected to go to school, how can they, at the same time be permitted to work, even if the nature of their work is non-hazardous? Does it mean that education with work and earning with learning can be combined under non-hazardous conditions of work?

This is precisely what the Supreme Court has stated in its judgement in civil writ application No. 465 dated 10 December 1996. According to this judgement, paragraph No. 31(10), children should be permitted to work for 4— 6 hours a day in non-hazardous employment while receiving education for two hours a day. The Supreme Court judgement, however, rests on the existing law itself, which is a by-product of Art. 24 of the Constitution. The Child Labour (Prohibition and Regulation) Act, 1986 which repealed the Employment of Children Act, 1940, permits children to work in industries other than those specified in Part (A) and (B) of the Act.

Combining education with work and earning with learning, is in my opinion a myth. Let us see why this combination is neither possible nor desirable.

Who are the children in India that are subjected to work? They are children from the families of agricultural labourers, sharecroppers, families of rural artisans, fishermen and women, those of inter-state migrant workmen, *beedi* workers, weavers, leather workers, salt workers, building and construction workers, brick-kiln and stone-quarry workers, and those of collectors of minor forest produce in tribal areas.

They are by-products of the families of the rural poor, many of whom have been victims of social discrimination and economic deprivation for generations. They are subjected to hard manual labour for long hours at a very early age. Such work often tends to be arduous drudgery, resulting in continuous fatigue, which is further compounded by acute malnutrition. In the process of exposure to seemingly innocuous work, children contract infections and become victims of occupational diseases. To illustrate: the working conditions of child garbage- and ragpickers increase the risk of disease and disability through exposure to lead and mercury, buckling of the back because they have to lift heavy sacks of rags, and the presence of parasites. Even children in agricultural work are exposed to and adversely affected by toxic chemicals, accidents from sharpened tools, and motorized equipment such as tractors. In the tripartite sectoral committee meeting on working conditions of agricultural workers held at Geneva from 23 to 27 September 1996 it transpired that 15,000 children working in agriculture in Costa Rica later became impotent as a consequence of their exposure to toxic chemicals.

It is true that learning productive work could be exciting and enjoyable for persons at the proper age if the work environment were safe, clean, and congenial, and if all the requisite safety equipment were provided. ILO Convention No. 138 prescribes fifteen as the minimum age of entry to employment, as it is at this stage that one is physically and mentally equipped to cope with the stress and strain work imposes. This is the minimum age at which one is aware of the nature of work, the impact of work on the psyche and personality, and of devices to protect oneself from the risks and hazards it entails.

The distinction between 'hazardous' and 'non-hazardous' work is in this sense more artificial than real; it is a distinction of degree and not of kind, and, therefore, needs to be discounted. What appears on the surface to be non-hazardous and innocuous may not in reality be so.

The next point that militates against the combination of education with work is the quality of education that can be provided within two hours. Education is meant for productive efficiency and the empowerment of the individual. Some empowerment is possible if there is a judicious and balanced combination of proficiency in the mother tongue, proficiency in arithmetic, and proficiency in physical and social sciences as well as general and social awareness. The acquisition of minimum levels of learning and proficiency in these depends upon a host of factors such as:

- prevalence of a literate environment where literacy and education are valued and prized by the society as a whole;
- a warm and convivial environment in the school;
- committed teachers willing to live in the local habitat, who open the school in time, are humane and sensitive in their approach to students, are good communicators, and act more as promoters, facilitators, and catalysts than as controllers or regulators, will promote and encourage self-evaluation as an important tool of learning, and the like;
- effective teachers' training that is participative and communicative and acts as a tool of empowerment of the teacher;
- Curriculum, course content and textual materials that are need-based and relevant, designed in a participative workshop, and their suitability certified before adoption.

Regretfully this is not the reality today. The educational system at all levels, in particular at the primary, upper primary, and elementary level, is fragmented, and largely non-functional. We have about six lakh villages and about 5.81 lakh schools. In other words, we do not have a school for every village. Some schools are beyond a radius of two kilometre making it virtually impossible for mothers to send their children (particularly girl children) to school. We do not have a minimum of two teachers in every school, and wherever they exist, the second teacher is not necessarily a woman—largely on account of the low rate of female literacy, and hence the non-availability of qualified and trained women teachers. The teachers do not live in the village and often tend to run the school more by proxy. Teachers' absenteeism in the northern states (particularly in Bihar, MP, UP, and Rajasthan) is very high. Teachers' motivation and commitment to use education as a tool for integrated and holistic development of children as extremely low. This is partly because of their socio-economic background, partly on account of faulty teacher training, and their interest being focused solely on the perquisites of office, but largely on account of an environment characterized by a lack of probity, and transparency. While the curriculum and course content are largely irrelevant and the motivation of parents and children is at an all time low, the overall educational environment is dull, demotivating, and suffocating.

The major flaw in the present system of education is that it stifles reativity and originality. Professor Yash Pal, who was Chairman of the National Advisory Committee on Education appointed to look into the issue of the load of school satchels, and submitted his well-known report 'Learning without Burden', is of the view that the resent system of education does not emphasize real learning but only memorization for successful performance in exams. There is no proper learning environment in the class conducive to encourage students to inquisitive about the world around them, and motivate them to discover things for themselves. After nearly four decades since the constitutional directive was made, we are today caught in a web: unable to decide whether the earlier emphasis on expansion of the stem should be replaced by qualitative development.

Definitions and Concepts

There are widely varying perceptions about the definition and concept of child labour. Related to this there are three clearly divided schools of thought. The views of these are summed up below.

The first school of thought treats education as the fundamental human right of every child in 5-14 age group and holds that any child in this age group who is out of school should be treated as a working child. According to 1991 census we have a total child population of 297 m. in the 0-14 age group. Of this, children in school-going age i.e 5-14, constitute 203 m. Every year 21 m. children are born, 8 m. die, and 13m. survive. Multiplied at this rate, 78 m. children would have been added to 297 m. children between 1991-7 totalling 375 m. Similarly, judging by the rate of enrolment, the rate of retention and drop-out, and rate of participation of children in the school system (both formal and non-formal) the number of children of school-going age (5-

14 years) would by now have grown to at least 220 m. Of this, 112 m. go to formal school, about 7 m. to non-formal school, and the rest, i.e 100 m. plus are children who do not attend school. According to the first school of thought, it is the responsibility of the state to create the infrastructure for facilitating free, compulsory, and universal access to both primary and elementary education. They believe that there can be no excuse for over 100 m. children in the 5-14 age group being outside the school system, whether formal and non-formal. They are firmly of the view that access to educational opportunity for all children in the 5-14 age group is barest minimum obligation of the state and that the state cannot absolve itself from the obligation either on the ground of poverty and other economic compulsions or due to lack of infrastructure, logistical support, and resources. They are also firmly of the view that it is child labour that induces poverty rather than poverty that induces child labour. According to them, a child below 15 years is not physically and emotionally mature and fit to enter the world of work. If children in the 5-14 age group are being forced to work rather than being sent to school on account of social, economic, and cultural compulsions, such a process is bound to result in retardation and impoverishment of their evolution and growth, and this to such a degree that when they cross the threshold of childhood they will be too bereft of physical strength and energy to be productive and responsive adult members of society.

According to them again, all children of school-going age who are out of school should be presumed to be doing some form of work or the other. It is immaterial whether or not the job is hazardous, as the concept of childhood does not fit into the world of work. They are therefore, of the opinion that the distinction between hazardous and non-hazardous is at best artificial, and we cannot put up with a situation in which millions of children are out of school spending their days at home or doing some work at home without wages or outside home for wages.

According to the second school of thought the magnitude of the problem is so enormous that the state will find it extremely difficult to create the environment and provide the infrastructure, logistical support, and resources to send the additional 100 m. plus children to school, whether formal or non-formal. The total resources that would be required to ensure free, compulsory primary education would be of the order of Rs 40,000 cr. or 12 bn US dollars annually and the availability of resources of such a magnitude is a mirage. This school of thought, therefore, advocates a gradual, sequential, and selective approach to the entire issue of out of school children vis-a-vis working children. Its votaries hold that we should first concentrate on those employed in hazardous occupations/processes, release and rehabilitate them through education, nutrition, and skills training, and subsequently those children working in non-hazardous occupations/ industries/ processes. According to them, elimination of child labour should be viewed as a long-term goal to be achieved progressively rather than at a stroke. They also believe that total elimination of child labour by law is not possible and, therefore, advocate a dual approach of prohibition and regulation, which is in sharp contrast with the viewpoint of first school of thought advocating total prohibition.

There is a third school of thought that believes that both civil society and the state as the agent of the society has abjectly failed in, (a) making education a fundamental human right, (b) creating the appropriate infrastructure and environment, and providing incentives to ensure access to educational opportunities to all, and (c) creating a positive and conducive school environment that will enable universal retention and participation of children who have enrolled themselves in school and also make it possible for them to achieve at least the minimum levels of learning. They, therefore, advocate a point of view that militates against that of both the other schools of thought, in holding that it should be left to the children themselves to decide whether or not they want to go to school. If they want free universal elementary education, the necessary infrastructure, logistical support, and environment for this should be created by the state on behalf of civil society. If, however, the children find that the educational system is dull, demotivating, and irrelevant, and would prefer to work, the state on behalf of the civil society should create opportunities for forms of work that is in consonance with their physical and mental capacities.

Each of the three schools of thought has its merits and demerits. I shall pointless not enter into a debate on the superiority of one over another, or which should take precedence. The fact, however, remains that every child is also a human being and human beings are the finest products of creation. Childhood is a stage in the evolution and growth in human life: its most tender, formative, and impressionable. While, undoubtedly, access to health, hygiene, sanitation and nutrition for every child in the 0—6 age group is extremely important to ensure sustained physical growth, access to primary and elementary education at the age of 5 plus is almost an equally important social need. It is true that most children receive some form of early childhood education either through the Anganwadi centres of the Integrated Child Development Services (ICDS) or through simple interaction with their parents, but these at best may be viewed as an important stage in preparing them for entry into the world of primary and elementary education. To the extent the family is literate and numerate, this literate environment will enrich the quality of preparation and facilitate access to educational opportunity. Regretfully, however, over 100 m. households are non-literate and non-numerate, and are, therefore, not able to provide a literate environment for the child that is conducive to his/her learning. It is, therefore, evident that there is great force in the point of view of the first school of thought, i.e. that (a) education is a fundamental human right; (b) the state as the agent of civil society must create the infrastructure, provide the logistical support and environment for access to free, compulsory, primary education; (c) the state must also simultaneously create the opportunities and provide the facilities for participation, universal retention, and achievement of the minimum levels of learning. Once this is accepted as the irreducible minimum goal of every decent and civilized society it will be impossible for the state to shirk or sidetrack this important responsibility. Intensive efforts must, therefore, be made to awaken the consciousness of all sections of the society, namely, opinion moulders, policy-makers, and programme im-plementors, to this and thus create conditions that are conducive to the mobilization and motivation of parents, and the universal realization of the importance of education for every child in the 5-14 age group regardless of background or sex.

There is nothing new in this, in as much as a number of international instruments have imposed a legal obligation on all their member countries to provide the much needed access to educational opportunity to every child together with other forms of protection. These are:

- UN Convention on the Rights of the Child (1989)
- International Covenant on Economic, Social and Cultural Rights (1966)
- The International Covenant on Civil and Political Rights (1966)
- Supplementary Convention on the Abolition of Slavery, the Slave Trade, and Institutions and Practices Similar to Slavery (1957)
- Convention for the Suppression of the Traffic in Persons and of the Exploitation of the Prostitution of Others (1949)

These covenants have been supplemented and their guiding

spirit of dignity and respect for children's rights has been reinforced by numerous declarations adopted in international conferences such as:

- 1990 World Summit for children and the world declaration on the survival, protection and development of children
- 1990 World Conference on Education for All
- 1995 Conference of Labour Ministers of non-aligned countries and the declaration that was adopted at the close of the conference
- The Stockholm Congress on commercial sexual exploitation of children held in August 1996
- The third SAARC Ministerial Conference on the children of South Asia in August 1996 and the Declaration for eliminating bonded child labour by the year 2000 with total elimination of child labour in the region by 2010
- The declaration adopted at the close of the two day International Conference held at Amsterdam in February 1997 (25-26 February 1997)
- The declaration and the action programme adopted at the close of the four day International Conference held at Oslo between 27 and 30 October 1997.

THREE

CHILD LABOUR IN INDIA

Throughout the history child labour has always existed but it was only in the nineteenth century in industrialized countries that it came to be seen as a social problem. Industrialization led to a growing separation between home and the place of work. Production that had formerly been carried out within the family was now done in workshops and factories. In the early workshops, it was still possible to maintain family and group ties. Children accompanied their parents to the workshop or factory where they acted as helpers. In the absence of technical education centres, this was a useful way of teaching the children a trade.

The women and children employed in these early workshops were always paid lower wages than men, so when mechanization reduced the number of operations requiring a lot of muscle power they became an attractive source of labour.

The twentieth century is sometimes referred to as the **Century of the Child**. For the first time in history, the rights of the child were put on the international agenda. As far back as 1919 the International Labour Organisation (ILO) drew up a convention aimed at restricting child labour in industry by setting minimum age (ILO Convention 5). It was followed by various other conventions on the minimum employment age for different sectors, including shipping, agriculture and non-industrial occupations. In 1973, the ILO drew up a universal convention on the minimum employment age, applicable to virtually all sectors (ILO Convention 138). India has ratified this convention.

India has the largest number of working children in the world. The government itself acknowledges that at least 17.5 million children are working. An Indian research institute often cited by the ILO—the Operations Research Group, Baroda—estimates the number of working children at 44 million.

It is impossible to collect correct figure of the children employed in mines, factories, fireworks, brickfield, poultry, bidi-factory, building-construction, hotels and sweet-meat shops or as domestic servants or in polishing works and many other less hazardous works like agro or non-agro industries. In 1987, laws were made to ban child-labours in non-agro industries. In 1987, laws were made to ban child-labours in hazardous works. Still out of 3 child labourers of the world, two live in India and the larger number of them are engaged in non-organised sectors, agro-industries and private industries based on low capital where the industrial environment is prone to cancer of liver, nerve and eye. According to survey of WHO, one third of the children of the world suffer from the diseases caused due to poisonous effect of pesticides in our country.

The ICFTU's regional organisation in Asia—APRO—puts the figure of working children at 50 million. One private institution in India, however—the Centre for Concern for Working Children—which has carried out an inquiry into the number of children not attending schools, estimates the number of working children in India at 100 million.

In the absence of agreed criteria and reliable data, several agencies have computed the figure on the basis of people below the poverty line and children not enrolled in schools. For example, the Balai Data Bank, Manila considers that the number of children is likely to be over 100 million. The Campaign against Child Labour (CACL), an umbrella organisation covering about 1000 NGO,s (Non-Governmental Organisations), estimates that "there are 70-80 million child labourers, based on the number of non-school going children and families living in destitution".

According to the 1991 census, there are about 11.20 million full-time and 10.70 million part-time child labourers in India. This excludes the unorganised sector and the self-employed children in which there are about another 20 to 25 million children. About a quarter of the working children in the metropolitan area suffer from over work, inadequate pay and physical abuse. They soon fall victim to the street culture of drug abuse, smoking, gambling, drinking, vagrancy, stealing and prostitution. Most of these remain untouched by social welfare programmes.

According to the Asian Labour Monitor, every third household in India has a working child. Further, according to the same journal, the extent of child labour can be gauged by the fact that in the age group of 5-15, every fourth child is employed, 20 per cent of all children in the age group of 10-14 years are employed in one form or the other, and over 20 per cent of the Gross National Product (GNP) of India is contributed by child labourers.

According to a study conducted by the All India Guild of Law Graduates, 6.7 per cent of the workforce consists of children, below

Public Co-operation and Child Development revealed that 24.7 per cent child labourers surveyed in Bombay, started work between the ages of six and nine, 48.4 per cent, between ten and twelve and 26.9 per cent, between the ages of thirteen and fifteen.

Children Working in Different Areas of Employment

Sl. *No.*	Nature of Activity	1971 Census *No. of Child workers in age groups 0-14 years. (in thousands)*	1971 Census Percentage	1981 Census *No. of Child workers in age groups 0-14 years. (in thousands)*	1981 Census *Percentage*
1.	Cultivators	3,870	36.05	4,013	35.95
2.	Agricultural labourers	4,586	42.72	4,774	42.76
3.	Livestock, forestry, fishing, hunting plantations etc.	885	8.25	704	6.30
4.	Minning and quarring	24	0.22	27	0.23
	processing servicing repairs, etc.	653	6.08	965	8.63
	(a) Housing industry	338	3.15	425	3.79
	(b) Others	315	2.93	540	4.84
6.	Construction	59	0.55	79	0.72
7.	Transport, storage and communication	42	0.39	34	0.29
8.	Trade and commerce	211	1.97	246	2.20
	Total	10,739	100.00	111,68	100.00

From the above table, we find that about 85 per cent of working children are to be found in the agricultural sector and that the overwhelming chunk in any sector are from the scheduled castes and tribes.

Agricultural Sector : Child labour has always been common in sector, especially in small family farms. Generally speaking, Indian rural families have a strong sense of community and it is taken for granted that every member will contribute to family resources. It is rural families have a strong sense of community and it is taken for granted that every member will contribute to family resources. It is impressed upon children from a very early age that they must show their solidarity by contributing to the family income. Many children, therefore, consider it quite normal that they should start working from a very early age and this situation is reinforced if the schools are a long way from where the children live or if the parents do not have the money to send their children to school. Moreover, while in many farming castes and communities-education is no guarantee for a better future, the contribution in work and income made by children is often essential to the survival in impoverished rural families.

Traditional rural customs often persist after the family has migrated to urban area. All too many parents take off their children from school at an early age and send them out to earn their living as domestic servants, street traders or factory workers.

Service Sector : Due to migration from the countryside to the city, increasing unemployment and a lack of social security, a growing section of the population in India is obliged to generate its own employment in the **"informal"** sector.

Our children are often found working in small factories, motor garages, food stalls, doing shoeshining, as domestic helps, rag pickers and even as beggars. No education policy could make the parents interested to send their children to schools as earning by them is more lucrative for a poor family than education. The wages paid to children are normally lower than the prevalent rate while the exploitation is abnormally high to turn them into bonded labourers or child prostitutes. Sex tourism is another factor that is contributing to increasing child prostitution in India too.

In the match and firework factories at Sivakasi (Tamil Nadu), 40,000 children (out of a total workforce of 70,000) are employed. In other industries as well, such as bidi-manufacturing, diamond-polishing, handicrafts, agriculture, rag-picking and the hotel industry, children form a major portion of the total labour employed.

The Gurupadaswamy Committee Report in 1979 identified sectors of the economy where there were substantial numbers of working children, namely, bidi-factories, glass factories, the carpet industry, the handloom industry, in jari making and embroidery, in polishing precious stones, in match and fireworks, foundries and repair shops, in hospitals, restaurants, canteens, tea stalls, shops and establishments, service stations, construction sites, as rag pickers and as casual labourers. The prevalent gender bias of the society is naturally reflected in this world too. In the field of child labour, girls have outnumbered the boys and consequently, in illiteracy, their number is double to that of the boys.

The girls are engaged in work at an earlier age and deprived of literacy. They are thrust into unpaid or unproductive activities from their very tender age and made easy prey to physical violence and sexual abuse, in addition. As these child labourers come mostly from the poor families, the combined effect of impoverishment, lack of access to education and health, physical labour and their social condition bring them to accept poverty and violence in their later lives.

It is traditional for very young girls from poor families to be sent to work in the homes of wealthier families in return for boarding and lodging. Many impoverished parents prefer their daughters to work in some other family's household rather than in a workshop, factory or as a street vendor, because they imagine that it is safer for them. Maidservants work long hours, have little or no leisure and receive little or no pay. There is virtually no official inspection of the conditions under which these domestic slaves work.

The number of children—especially girls—working as domestic servants has risen over the past few decades. As more and more girls from the lower middle classes go out to work, the demand for cheap domestic labour keeps rising. In metropolitan cities like Delhi and Mumbai, for example, this has led to the emergence of a new category of middlemen who ruthlessly recruit children for domestic work. In addition to this, all too many child refugees end up in host families where they are treated as domestic slaves.

Other types of service where child labour is on the increase occur in the informal tourist and entertainment industry, for instance, in restaurants, guest houses and brothels. Poverty, war and violence expose children to new dangers and new forms of exploitations.

Industry and Mining : Only a small percentage of child labour is accounted for by large, export-oriented enterprises in mining and industry. This is related to the fact that these enterprises are subject to more government control and that trade union influence is often greater there. Child labour mostly occurs in unorganized and small sectors such as in the match and carpet industries in India.

There are few statistics on child labour among children under the age of ten. In the first instance, this is because work by very young children is rarely recognized as such or because it is simply overlooked by census-takers. Such young "domestic helpers" are either recorded as adoptees or uncounted because they are unpaid. A second reason for the inadequate registration has to do with the fact that labour by very young children is illegal in all countries and as such is hushed up or deliberately concealed.

Most of the children work in the so-called informal economy—both in the cities and in the countryside—where protective labour laws and regulations regarding working hours, pay, social security and working conditions are generally absent. Children usually work in situations where it is difficult, if not impossible, to offer them any protection, such as, on the streets, in unregistered enterprises, workplaces, small factories, guest houses, cafes, restaurants, eating-houses, shops, family businesses, clothing workshops, buildings sites, small private mines and in remote farming areas.

It is estimated that only a small percentage of working children—roughly five per cent work directly in export-oriented industries. Examples can be found in the production of clothing, carpets and shoes, in the diamond industry, the food processing industry, in tanneries and furniture makers. On the other hand, the practice of contracting work out via middlemen makes it difficult to estimate how many children are indirectly involved in production for the world market.

In India and many other developing countries, poverty has risen sharply in recent decades as a result of the Structural Adjustment Prgrammes (SAPs) imposed by the International Monetary Fund (IMF) and the World Bank. These have led to privatization, a decrease in government expenditure on social services (including education and health), a deterioration in social security, promotion of export-oriented production, deregulation and flexibilization of industrial relations, and a dilution of trade union rights. The percentage of Indian Union Government's expenditures (1919-97) allocated only one per cent on health, two per cent on education and thirteen per cent on defence.

United Nations International Children's Emergency Fund [now United Nations Children's Fund] (UNICEF) warned as early as 1984 that SAPs were having a devastating effect on poor families in general, and on the welfare of children, in particular. Experts in various countries have shown that the increase in child labour is one of the direct consequences of economic crisis and structural adjustment. Much of the social costs of SAPs is passed on to women in poor families, a process that is sometimes described as the "faminization of poverty". The sectors hardest hit by privatization and government cut-backs are also those sectors which employ a lot of women, such as, education and health care, child care, telephone and postal services. For most of the women, there is no alternative employment available except in the informal sector which is where many laid-off women workers end up.

Growing unemployment and rising prices lead to a reduction in spending power and an increase in women's workload. Families affected by unemployment generally have no financial reserves to fall back on. Impoverished families who can no longer afford the rising cost of education and child care find themselves obliged either to keep their children home or to send them out to earn some money so as to at least keep the family unit afloat. Poverty and despair lead to an increase in violence within the family. When their own income proves inadequate men tend to force women and children out to work. The number of deserted women with children is on the increase, partly owing to the growing number of migrating men going in search of work, elsewhere. In 30 per cent of the families, according to the United Nations, women have to bear the burden of looking after their families alone. The majority of such families are among the poorest in the world. Women caught in these situations tend to be physically and mentally exhausted and in the absence of alternative resources they often have no choice but to let the children work for the sake of their families as a whole. Children from poor families run a high risk of ending up as street children. Child workers in Calcutta do a variety of jobs ranging from self-employment to employment in the service sector.

Dicussions with NGOs reveal that children who are just 4 to 5 years old do manual labour several hours each day in Calcutta. The kids break apart batteries with rocks and hammers, separating the acid and lead for re-sale, often poisoning themselves in the process. There are other child workers who make flip-flop sandals with scissors, sometimes as long as their arms, or work in light bulb factories where they breathe in fine glass dust particles that can scar their lungs. Many do not appear in the records and become invisible in statistics. A large number of girl children are surrogate mothers to their siblings while also helping their mothers in domestic or piece rate work.

There are others, who look after cars, shine shoes, sell newspapers, etc., and the average earning of a child labour in Calcutta is less than US $3 in a month. Sometimes, they stay out on the streets and meet up with youth gangs or groups of children who live on the streets. The worse the child's home situation, the greater the chance that it will join these street children instead of returning home. Such children all too often end up in the criminal circuit.

The unloading of the social costs of the SAPs onto families is referred to in a UNICEF study as "invisible adjustment". This invisible exploitation of individuals affects not only the socio-economic rights of the women, but also the living conditions and future prospects of their children, a process that is further reinforced by the inequality between men and women.

While on the one hand the supply of child workers is rising as a result of poverty, on the other hand, changes in the production process are leading to an increased demand for child labour. The growth in subcontracting, flexibilization and deregulation, the emergence of free zones and the informalization of labour appear to have made child labour more attractive and easier for employers.

Many sectors are increasingly contracting out parts of the production process. This saves larger companies high labour costs and enables them to make use of the cheapest employees, which include children. The client firm and the actual workers are often separated by a long chain of middlemen and subcontractors. Multinationals contract local firms in India to fill orders. These local firms compete fiercely with one another to land the limited number of multinational orders; they look for the cheapest labour and where possible they use child labour in their own factories or contract out work to informal workshops or the home workers, who in turn enlist children in order to boost the family income.

It is often difficult to discover who is really employing the children working in grimy workshops or at home, pressured to work for eight to eleven hours a day to reach the production norm and often paid a pittance for their efforts. In a number of industries, such as shoe and cloth manufacturing, a few specific parts of the end product are made by children. These are then exported to the big factories for further processing by adult employees before finally exported to Europe and the United States.

Most of the children work for over 12 hours a day under inhuman conditions, on starvation wages. Child labour is cheap and unorganised. Since child workers have no legal status, even unions are also helpless. They suffer from severe mental and physical retardation. In case of accidents, employers easily get away by paying a pittance by way of compensation.

In almost all cases, there is extreme exploitation of working children. There are laws to protect them, but no proper enforcement agency. Punitive measures are laughably flimsy. In 1986, the Supreme

Court released 800 children from Palamau in Bihar, from where they were taken as slaves to work in the carpet weaving industry in the Mirzapur belt. They had been branded, tortured and made to work 20 hours a day. The local magistrate reportedly fined the exploiting employers a mere Rs. 40 a head.

It is irony of the fact that Article 24 of the Indian Constitution reads—

"No child below the age of 14 years shall be employed to work in any factory or mine or engaged in any other hazardous employment."

India has stood for constitutional, statutory and developmental measures that are required to eliminate child labour. India has ratified six ILO Conventions relating to the child labour and three of them as early as in the first quarter of the twentieth century. Following the directions of the Constitution, the child labour (Prohibition and Regulation) Act-1986 was formulated to encounter the magnitudious problem of increasing child labour. This act bans employment of children below the age of fourteen in certain fields such as port, railways, transport, fireworks, etc., and in other cases if a child is engaged, cannot be made to work for more than six hours a day. The violator of this act shall be punishable with imprisonment for a term of three months to one year or with fine which may extend from Rs. 10,000 to Rs. 20,000 or with both. But the pathetic side of this act is that it nowhere decleares child labour illegal and the provisions for monitoring over the proper implementation of the act is very poor. Result is the frequent violation of childhood prerogatives.

It has been pointed out time and again that there is no need for child labour in a country where there is large scale adult unemployment. In many cases, industries employ children as cheap labourers while their parents sit idle because from the employer's point of view, little children spell big profits. Children are more amenable to discipline and can be ruthlessly bullied by adult supervisors without fear of protest; they cost less, are more active, agile and quick; further, since in certain industrial sectors child labour is illegal, no laws apply; and finally, most children work in the unorganised sector in any case and hence find it doubly difficult to organise and fight for their rights.

The UN Convention on the Rights of the Child is the most frequently ratified international human rights treaty. It was passed by the General Assembly of the United Nations on 20 November 1989 and by October 1993, it had been ratified by 152 countries including India. This universal acceptance makes the conventions an important instrument in improving the situation of children and adolescents.

The central message of the UN Convention is that children may demand their own rights. It thereby gives expression to a new perception of childhood, one that has been almost universally accepted during the course of the twentieth century—the Century of the Child. Children are no longer seen as a "possession" which parents, educators and other adults can dispose of at their own discretion, but as having their own individual and socio-economic rights to life, to their own name and nationality, to well-being, love and care, as well as a right to free expression, a right to freedom of association and assembly, a right to free expression, a right to freedom of association and assembly, a right to access to information, a right to the best possible health and health care, a right to free and compulsory primary schooling, and a right to harmonious development, recreation, art and culture. These are just some of the rights that are dealt with in the UN Convention.

Article 45 of the Indian Constitution says that:

"The State shall endeavour to provide, within a period of ten years from the commencement of this Constitution, for free and compulsory education for all children until they complete the age of fourteen years".

The absence of adequate, competent and afforable educational facilities is often a major contribution factor to the existence of child labour. In India, the simple fact is that children who are not at school are mostly at workplace.

The largest number of illiterate live in our country. Academic atmosphere, infrastructure, the teacher and the taught and the teaching-system are entirely pathetic. There is no teacher in 2624 primary schools, there is only one teacher in each of 1,48,033. There are only two teachers in each of 28.5 per cent, there is no building for 7 per cent schools. The schools are run under open sky. Twenty per cent schools are run in thatched huts or in tents. There are 6 lakhs primary schools and number of students is 110 million. The number of drop-outs is thirty-six per cent before they are promoted to class V and fifty-two per cent students leave school before they are promoted to class VII. Six and a half crore children are out of the periphery of academic institution and out of three such children, two are females. The spectacle is more pitiful than of Pakistan and Sri Lanka. Notwithstanding, the allocation of money in national budget for education is gradually decreasing: 1990-91—4 per cent, 1992-93—3.6 per cent 1993-94—3.5 per cent.

According to the State of World's Children 1999 Report, in India, over eighty per cent of children in urban areas are enrolled in school, but in rural areas, the rate is about sixty per cent. But there is great variation between the states. Though Kerala is not a rich state of India, nine out of ten primary school age children go to school, while in Bihar only half do.

Nearly fifty-three per cent population of India lives in severe poverty, earning less than one dollar a day. Child labour is a persistent problem, a cause and consequence of low enrolment and high drop out rates. Students-teacher ratio is very high (greater than 60 to 1 in India), particularly in the primary schools. There are many single teacher primary schools, in which at least four different classes of students from standard I to standard IV are to be taken at the same time by one teacher.

According to Mabhub-ul-Haq, the noted economist, "Education is the true essence of human development. Without education, development can be neither broad-based nor sustained". But the educational situation is so much worse in India that the percentage of primary school entrants reaching grade V (1990-95) is 62 per cent and secondary school enrolment ratio is as follows:

Sl.No.	*Particulars*	*Year*	*Male*	*Female*
1.	Secondary School Enrolment Ratio (Gross)	1990-96	59	38
2.	Adult Literacy Rate	1995	66	38

However, educational participation statistics are sometimes an accurate guide to the extent of child labour. Child workers, such as many child newpaper sellers, tea stall workers, particularly in the cities, often do manage to attend school. Indeed, they sometimes work in order to be able to pay for their education. Often, children work eight or more hours a day in addition to the hours they spend at school, a practice that ends in mental and/or physical exhaustion.

A major factor influencing the extent of child labour is the introduction of compulsory education: without it, government will find it difficult to enforce child labour legislation. According to the American Professor Myron Werner, no country has succeeded in putting an end to child labour without first introducing and enforcing compulsory education. It is very important that the upper age limit for compulsory education should correspond to the minimum age limit for employment.

The extent of child labour is partly influenced by the way in which the Indian society reacts to the problem. In India, marked indifference or lack of conviction stands in the way of tackling the problem effectively. Therefore, the Government confines itself to enacting legislation without providing the instruments for enforcing the laws nor are trade unions always as interested in the problem as they might be, because their members often work for large companies where child labour is less prevalent. Even parents from backward communities display indifference to the importance of education, as educational opportunities were denied to all the backward communities in India for thousands of years, preferring to let their children work rather than "waste their time at school". The media pay little attention to the problem because where child labour is regarded as demand actions are mostly coming from some committed individuals and NGOs.

The importance of political will can be illustrated by the example of Kerala. The government there decided to give priority to education. By spending more than double, the national average in education, Kerala has succeeded in providing virtually all children with primary education and almost 90 per cent with secondary schooling. The upshot is that only about three per cent of children in Kerala work while in other Indian states the figure can be as much as ten times higher.

In order to tackle the child labour problem, the following recommendations have been passed by the State Education Ministers Committee: • Fundamental duty of all parents is to ensure that their children upto fourteen years of age attend school. Punishment for "defaulting" parents. • Establishment of primary schools within a distance of one to one and half km from rural habitations. • Set up upper primary schools within a distance of three km from a village with a population of 500 people. • "Deserving private schools should be given adequate opportunity" to help them operate in remote and inaccessible areas.

The government considers Child Labour a "necessary evil" and the Child Labour Act, 1986 does not completely ban, but only seeks to "protect" working children. But the question remains—if earlier laws could not protect children from exploitation, what is the guarantee that new ones will. And where is the will or the machinery to enforce such laws.

The argument given in favour of not banning child labour is that such a ban would affect industries employing child labour. The authorities talk in terms of profits, and foreign exchange earned by industries (carpet, gun polishing) employing child labour. No wonder, there is reluctance to face the issue head on. But no one cares about the effect of such exploitative and dangerous working conditions on the children.

So, the 1986 Act was drafted with the view that child labour cannot be banned. Social activists immediately attacked it as regressive. The Act covered only ten per cent of the total working children.

Those working in an unorganised sector are not protected. The Ministry of Labour did not find it necessary to include the glass industry among the list of occupations hazardous to children even though there is enough evidence to prove that glass works are dangerous for children (high temperature, burn injuries, toxic fumes). The slate pencil industry, where workers succumb to silicosis and other respiratory ailments before they even reach middle age was excluded from the purview of the Bill. However, after prolonged movements, these industries are now included in the list of hazardous industries, prohibiting children's employment.

Considering the magnitude of the problem of working children, the Government of India has formulated the National Policy on Child Labour in 1987 and has committed to undertake the following measures for the welfare of the children: (a)Comprehensive health programme for all children. (b) Programme to provide nutrition services for removing deficiencies in the diet of the children. (c) Free and compulsory education for all children upto the age of 14. (d) Physical education, games, sports and other types of recreational as well as cultural and scientific activities in schools, community centres and such other institutions. (e) Special assistance to children belonging to weaker sections of the society. (f) Special attention to children who have become delinquent or have been forced to take to begging or are otherwise, in distress. Facilities for education, training and rehabilitation shall be provided so that such children are helped to become useful citizens. (g) Protection of the children against cruelty, neglect and exploitation. (h) No child under the age of 14 years shall be permitted to be engaged in any hazardous occupation or be made to undertake heavy work. (i)Facilities for special treatment, education, rehabilitation and care of children who are physically handicapped. (j)Priority to children in relief operations in times of distress or natural calamities.

The celebrated Child Labour (Prohibition and Regulation) Act, which was passed on December 23, 1986 is today years old. Even a cursory assessment presents a dismal picture. The Central Advisory Board on Child Labour set up a Task Force under senior advocate L.M. Sanghvi to implement the Act. The report of the Task Force submitted in December 1989 highlighted that the Act had lowered the age for a child's entry into certain types of employment and had prohibited night employment of children below the age of 17 years as had the earlier Employment of Children Act, 1938. Most important, the report pointed out that children working in the agricultural sector and in homes and home-based industries were left outside the purview of the Act. The list of "hazardous" industries was badly defined and that the only yardstick of harm used was physical harm, claimed the report.

CACL reports that between 1986 and 1993, there were only 3488 prosecutions under the Act with 1426 convictions all over the country. Not one employer has been put behind bars in the entire history.

Apart from requiring enforcement of legal provisions to protect the interest of children, the National Policy envisages focussing on general development programmes for the benefit of child labour and project-based plan of action in areas of high concentration of child labourers. Under the project action plan of the policy, National Child Labour Programme (NCLP) have been undertaken in different areas to rehabilitate child labour.

A major activity undertaken under the NCLP is the establishment of special schools to provide non-formal education, vocational training, supplementary nutrition etc. to children withdrawn from employment. At present, it has 2528 schools in 76 districts and covers about 1.5 million children only. On August 15, 1994, the-then Prime Minister P.V. Narsimha Rao had proclaimed with much fanfare that child labour would be eliminated from hazardous industries by the year 2000.

Subsequently, a sum of Rs. 850 crore was announced for the purpose; a National Authority for the Elimination of Child Labour was set up to provide educational and nutritional support to children withdrawn from hazardous industries. They were to be given vocational training to enable them to become productive adults. However, for the year 1995-96 a meagerly sum of 34.4 crore was spent covering 140 districts and 12 States; this was spent on awareness generation, surveys and direct action programmes.

India has also been participating in the International Programme for Elimination of Child Labour (IPEC) launched by International Labour Organisation (ILO) since 1991. However, according to Government reports, the total number of children covered by all these projects is about two lakh (0.2 million) only. Now the question arises, when do we reach the target of rehabilitating all the working children of India?

The grey areas of enforcement of the child labour laws as well as the slow progress in the implementation of special welfare measures for working children are a clear indication of the lack of concern at the official level for the plight of these children. Even the money spent so far has not resulted in any substantial change in the condition of the children who are "covered" by these welfare projects.

For example, most of the special schools set up for the working children are inefficiently run, and studies have demostrated that non-formal education for working children has very little impact in the rehabilitation process, unless an integrated approach is undertaken in this regard.

The Chairperson of the government-appointed Commission on Labour Standards and International Trade, Subramaniam Swamy, asserted in September 1995 that child labour was growing at the rate of four per cent per annum as opposed to the population growth rate of two per cent per annum. "He also put forward a forceful plea for a National Labour Standards Act, superseding all existing disparate laws, in this context, to arrest, reverse and eliminate its growth." (*The Pioneer*, September 2, 1996)

Further, the Commission estimated that to meet the avowed target of eliminating child labour from hazardous industries by 2010 would cost a whopping Rs. 15,000 crore. If a "shorter target" was to be met i.e. by the year 2004 then the bill would climb to Rs. 45,000 crore. The figures have been arrived at by taking into account factors like payment of salaries of child labourers to their families and the cost of educating them, claims Swamy. Now for the punch line: "India seeks international cost-sharing through a Global Social Facility and Fund located in the ILO and UNESCO." Bending words and shopping for finance are the trademarks of our politicians as is the setting-up of committees and commissions a substitute for action.

The Supreme Court judgement in M.C. Mehta v/s State of Tamil Nadu [1996 SCC 756] delivered on December, 10, 1996 brought the issue of child labour under the spotlight for a few weeks. Hailed as a major victory for the cause of child labourers, the judgement directs the setting-up of a fund called "the Child Rehabilitation-cum-Welfare Fund" to which offending employers of child labour in hazardous industries are to contribute Rs. 20,000 and the appropriate state government is to contribute Rs. 5000 per child; the child's family is to be paid a monthly amount from the interest accruing on the corpus of Rs. 25,000. The Court also directed the State governments to complete surveys and report to the court within a period of six months. The judgement adheres to the distinction between hazardous and non-hazardous work that is the bane of the Child Labour (Prohibition and Regulation) Act, 1986 and does not address the issue of agricultural child workers at all.

On December 10, 1996 a three-judge Bench of the Supreme Court comprising Justice Kuldip Sing, Justice B.L. Hansaria and Justice S.B. Majumdar delivered a judgement in writ petition No. 465 of 1986 M.C. Mehta v/s State of Tamil Nadu [(1996 6 SCC 756] which falls in the category of the much-worked phrase, "landmark" or "path-breaking" where child labour has been recognised as a "national problem."

Despite several constitutional provisions, both Fundamental Rights and Directive Principles of State Policy, several National Policies and Plans of Action and ratification of the Convention of the Rights of the Child in 1992, children are being forced to work in sub-human conditions and at wages well below par.

Poverty is no excuse for denying a child the basic rights to survival, protection, development and participation. In fact, the Supreme Court judges have rightly pointed out that poverty as such has not stood in the way of other developing countries such as Zambia, Ghana, Ivory Coast, Libya and Zimbabwe from taking care of child labourers.

The Court has also asked the state to ensure that an adult member of the working child's family gets a job in place of the child. In case this was impossible, Rs. 5,000 be contributed to the rehabilitation fund for each child. In view of the magnitude of the task, a separate cell in the Labour Department of the appropriate government would also be created. Nine major industries have also been identified as hazardous. Some of these are match-making at Sivakasi, diamond polishing at Surat, Ferozabad's glass industry, previous stone polishing industry at Jaipur, brassware industry at Muradabad, handmade carpet at Mirzapur, lock-making industry at Aligarh, slate industry at Markapur, slate industry at Mandsaur etc.

The issue of child labour is a very sensitive one and apt to provoke an emotional response. The question is not so much whether child labour is permissible or not. Child labour is almost universally rejected and regarded as reprehensible, as is witnessed by the widespread ratification of the UN Convention on the Rights of the Child.

A purposeful and coherent national policy is of overriding importance in the fight against child labour. In the last instance, it is up to the government and people of India to give priority to the abolition of child labour. If we lack the necessary political will, all action from outside is doomed to fail. Nevertheless, that political will can be stimulated by the international community, both by govenment and by the trade union movements and NGOs, who have assembled in this august gathering.

Effective legislation: Improved legislation on the minimum age for employment and for monitoring its observation is an essential requirement for combating child labour.

Creative and effective education: Another important factor in a coherent approach to child labour is creative and effective education. Education is the most important instrument in preventing children from entering the job market at an early age. Millions of children never even complete primary education. In India, the dropout rates are extremely high. Compulsory education is, therefore, of vital importance. There should be however, one provision: primary education and school meals must be free, otherwise, children from poor families will simply be kept at home.

Improved status of Women: A third element concerns improving the socio-economic status of women from poor families. The campaign to abolish child labour cannot be separated from women's struggle for recognition, decision of paid and unpaid work, and from structural measures to combat poverty and violence.

Research has shown that the social welfare of children is closely related to the status of women. Throughout the world, it is women who spend most time looking after and raising children. Women who have an income of their own give priority to expenditure that contributes to the welfare of the children. Not that this should be allowed to release men from their obligations as fathers. Men and women must be made aware of their responsibility for future generations. Special attention must be given to reinforching the status of women from poor families via trade union organisation, education, vocational training, the promotion of equal opportunities for employment and income and the creation of facilities that make it possible to combine paid work with family responsibilities, for an increasing number of women in India and all the developing countries, good quality child care is vitally important for both their own position and that of the child.

Consciousness-raising campaign: The fourth element consists of consciousness-raising campaigns. Because child labour is regarded as a "fact of life" in India, increasing public awareness is of vital importance. The media are a particulary important target in this context but also employers, employees, parents and the children themselves.

Replacing children with adults: Very often, children have to work while their parents or older relations remain unemployed. The latter would often be only too happy to take the place of a child if only the employer would agree. An anti-child labour campaign by the LAMP of West Bengal has achieved some positive results with this approach. Some firms have replaced children with adults from the same family so that the family is ensured of a steady income. LAMP believes that special government incentives and trade Union Campaigns should be used to persuade employers to co-operate in such a programme to replace child workers with adults from the same family.

Promoting the interests of child workers: It is important to establish and support local programmes concerned with improving the lot of child workers. Sometimes, these programmes are initiated by the children themselves, sometimes by other organisations.

Abolition of work under extreme conditions and by young children: Finally, strict measures are needed to ban all child labour that is in any way—physically, mentally or morally—hazardous for the child.

It goes without saying that the trade union movement has an important role to play in combating child labour. After all, trade unions represent worker's interests and that includes the interests of child workers. Despite this, the trade union movement has been less directly involved with specific anti-child labour actions than might be expected. One major reason for this is that trade union representation in India is strongest in the larger enterprises where, partly as a result of the union presence, there is relatively little child labour. Most child labour occurs in the informal sector, agriculture and at the family level where the trade union movement has less influence. The result has been fewer specific activities and more attention to general measures against child labour.

In coming years, trade unions in India and all other developing countries should concentrate on sectors with a low rate of organisation where extreme forms of child labour occur. Collaboration should be ought with NGOs, women's organisations, etc., already active in this rea.

From our experiences,[9] what is urgently needed is a commitment) protect all young children and provide compulsory schooling for very child under the age of 14. Tackling adult unemployment is also n urgent necessity. It is also obvious that poverty, unemployment, onded labour, rural indebtedness and women's low status are directly nked to the exploitation of child labour. These larger issues have to e dealt with on a priority basis in order to restore happy childhood to l children including working children of India.

References

The Census of India, 1971, Office of the Registrar General and Census Commissioner, Govt. of India, New Delhi.

The Census of India, 1981, Office of the Registrar General and Census Commissioner, Govt. of India, New Delhi.

State of World's Children 1999 Report, UNICEF.

Chiled Labour, published by Legal Education and AID Society, Madras, 1991.

Eliminating Child Labour—Stichting FNV, Amsterdam, The Netherlands.

The Lawyers Collective—Vol. 12, No. 4, April, 1997.

National Policy on Child Labour, 1987, Govt. of India.

Constitution of India, Govt. of India Publication.

The Pioneer, September 2, 1996.

FOUR

DEPRIVATION AND SURVIVAL

In the vast sea of humanity, children are the most vulnerable section living on the edge of mercy of others, nearly as animals. "Children are all around us. They represent about a quarter of the world's population. They are not equipped to defend themselves. They depend on what is given to them. They are victims of circumstances. They bring us joy, they bring us tears, they are our reason to hope. They are your children, they are my children, they are children of the world", said Eddie Adams.

The philosophy behind the UN Convention on the Right of the Child is that children, too, are equals but they are not alike. This calls for extension of special support to childhood in the best interests of the child. Article 3.1 thus enjoins all responsibility in the following words:

"In all actions concerning children, whether undertaken by public or private social welfare institutions, courts of law, administrative authorities or legislative bodies, the best interest of the child shall be a primary consideration."

India's (now) outdated National Children Policy (1979) declared that " The Nation's Children are supremely important asset. Their nurture and solicitude are our responsibility. Children's programme should find a prominent part in our national plans for the development of human resources, so that our children grow up to become robust citizens, physically fit, mentally alert and morally healthy, endowed with the skills and motivations needed by the society. Equal opportunity for development to all children during the period of growth should be our aim, for this would serve our larger purpose of reducing and ensuring social justice."

Now, how we have treated our "supremely important asset" in all these years. Even at the micro level, children's interests and rights are no longer identical with those of their parents. In Indian context, the twin blades of poverty and greed play a rather antipathetic role in many such relationships. Yet the general defence of paternalism by the Master of the Rolls in Re S (1993) is understandable where he claimed, "... a child is, after all, a child":

" The reason why the law is particularly solicititous in protecting the interests of children is because they are liable to be vulnerable and impressionable, lacking the maturity to weigh the longer term against the shorter, lacking the insight to know how they will react and the imagination to know how others will react in certain situations, lacking the experience to measure the probable against the possible".

Indian Constitution provides for the foundational framework of the care and protection of the Child in Articles like 24, 39 (e) and (f). In backing up these constitutional provisions, general legal framework has not been evolved although piecemeal legislations like Factories Act and Child Labour Prohibition and Regulation Act take a little care of the field. According to Art. 24 'No child below the age of fourteen years shall be employed to work in any factory or mine or engaged in any other hazardous employment'. This solemn declaration, is hardly respected and regularly violated. Nearly 11 million children are forcibly employed in hazardous sectors like fireworks and bangle making industry. In Sivakasi alone which has some 200 units producing 90 per cent of the country's fireworks employ 1,25,000 children in the age group of 10-14 years by perpetuation of the system of contracting and sub-contracting. In the process, children are exploited "and sacrificed as flies in the fine plays of the adult from the blast to the bursting. Nearly one and a half lakh children inhale substantial quantity of gunpowder in their workplace, making them unsuitable for jobs in later day life as they suffer from respiratory diseases, says CRY report (Asian Age dt. 5.11.99). Then finally, who are the majority of victims of fireworks at funsport? Diwali — a festival of light meant darkness for life to many child victims who were treated among 220 burn patients admitted within a span of 3 hours in Ram Manohar Lohia Hospital Delhi recently. This number has remained almost the same for last six years. Delhi High Court in its Order dated 5.10.99 instructed the Government Hospitals to make special arrangements with additional manpower, dressing material, linen and medicines for treatment of burn patients being a repeat of the Order on yearly succession (vide Order dt. 9.10.98). According to a study made by a Bio-medical Engineer of IIT, Delhi, 77 per cent of the burns caused by fireworks otherwise considered safe by the people are due to e.g. *Anars*—flowers pots *chakris*—rotating wheels—again mostly used by the children.

Article 39(e) speaks in terms of health and strength of the workers and seeks to raise a protective shield against abuse and exploitation of the tender age of children. This age is a formative stage best protected by parental care and schooling and insulation from the uncaring labour market of domestic seritude and wayside cantons of canteen. Obviously, Art.39 (f) sounds hollow and rhetoric although its lofty spirit is undisputably a piece of the moon everybody aims at. The demand "that children are given opportunities and facilities to develop in a health manner and in conditions of freedom and dignity and that childhood and youth are protected against exploitation and against moral and material abandonment" has to be looked into with a free mind and fresh outlook. Childhood belongs to the child. Let us return it back to him. "Mankind owes to the child the best it has to give" (UNDRC):

Deprivation of Childhood Health

Deprivation, in this context, include a wide range of material and non-material entitlements or benefits and more than just monetary wealth. Natural disasters and calamities apart, parental and societal deprivation of the children are rampant throughout the world. Orphanage total or partial, either in a loss of father or mother, early separation from them in-house or outward, absence of company for long hours or even neglect at home are not quite uncommon. Since the development of an individual is affected not only by his geographical and physical environment but also by psychological and social factors, our concern should be to see how best to avoid or minimise the extent of deprivation of early childhood of the children. Parents' care is the best insurance against a variety of deprivations due to bio-medical reasons. The degree and quality of attention, affection, association and appropriation are impartible by outside agencies and cannot therefore, be imparted. What is needed most is to understand and accept that the mother is central figure and force to reckon within any scheme of orderly planning of parenthood. A child is born from the mother's womb. What goes on before the birth of the child determines the health of the child to be. Drinking, smoking, drugs with their side-effects tell tons on the congenital defects and disability of the children. If that be the case, thalasmia is preventable by blood tests before marriage whereas medical check-up is yet to form part of the legal framework for instituting marriage. Nutrition is a major determinant of child's health in his life-long episode beginning from the foetal growth in mother's womb. American Journal of Clinical Nutrition reporting results of research by a team of scientists of the University of Amsterdam on women reveals that mothers conceived during the period of famine of 1944-45 after Nazi occupation gave birth to children among whom the female group developed obesity in their fifties relatively higher than the general group—an inheritance from the mothers of malnutrition. Obesity, surely then is not merely a by-product of living style of the rich due to environmental and societal contribution. Nutrition Foundation of India in its study 'Prevalence of Obesity in Urban Delhi' identified obesity as fast emerging health hazards of the rich but the poor mothers of the slums will have their own contribution to the problem in generational legacy through the process of inheritance. (HT dt. 13.11.99). The problem of Acute Limphoblastic Leukaemia (ALL) of children is a disturbing feature of the child health scenario globally.

Results of research published in 'the Lancet' claims that Cancer Research Institute, London has found first direct evidence that child leukaemia is not inherited but is caused by a gene defect (mutated or altered) which takes place during the development of blood cells in foetus which again is affected by environmental conditions such as pollution. So, if the children are to be saved from this fatal diseases, remedial measures must address to the source of attack. Children are also to be protected against inheritance of HIV virus which is playing havoc to a large number of innocent children. According to UNAIDS' estimate, about 1000 infants are infected with HIV virus each day although pre-natal HIV is preventable currently by ZDV drug treatment.

School at early age and early school hour

On the one hand, children are booked for admission to school at a very early age sometime below or around the age of 2 years on the other, large number of grown-up children are not sent to school. This Indian experience of thoughtless handling makes the children victims for life. Paediatricians now warn that it is injurious for the children's long-term interest to force the learning process too early, that too, with overload of books physically and the pressure of homework mentally. The fear of getting up early in unearthly hour leads to constant anxiety. Exposing the child to bitter dawn cold results in upper respiratory tract infections. Irregular food habits cause listlessness, low stamina and poor concentration. The daily trauma can seriously harm the health of the child in the form of blood sugar, anaemia, stress and bowel disorder. The general pattern of ill-treatment met by children at the hands of their parents is indicated by the following rituals:

Dragging the child out of bed while it is pitch dark.

Literally force-feeding him or her, often without success.

Waiting at the bus stop in the cold and darkness, or dangerously driving through fog.

Making the child wear shorts even in the depths of winter as some schools insist children below a certain age cannot wear long pants.

Have the child return with bronchitis because he or she has attended morning assembly or been made to stand in the 'late line' out in the cold and fog.

It is surprising to gauge the extent of tolerance stretching to the extreme, probably unique to India. In England schools are gifting alarm clocks to young children to remove their anxiety as a measure of incentive to come to school punctually. Yet, more than 100,000 children run away from home in Britain each year, according to the Children's Society Survey. These run-aways did not fit the stereotype image of being from poor, inner city homes. The problem was spread almost evenly across society, children having been forced to leave in many cases. Emotional conflicts, neglect, apathy and indifference are the root causes for isolation of the children in the lonely island in the uncaring crowd of the family.

Here again, blaming the parents is not absolving. It has been observed that the kind of support networks available to mothers working or not, are crucially important for social and cognitive development of the child- (Jaykody, Chatter and Taylor, 1993). All it means, conditions at home must be right for the children. Children want to live with nature and be natural, to be aware of the seasons, to smell trees, grass and flowers, and to hear and see birds. Freedom with check can only assure their well-being. "In the little world in which children have their existence, whosoever brings them up, there is nothing so finely perceived and so finally felt as injustice" finely cut by Charles Dickens.

The Issue of Survival

The principle most directly related to children's economic and social rights is formulated in the right-to-life Article. The Article in the UN Convention goes further than just granting children the right not to be killed. It definitely includes the right to survival and development with dignity. So Art. 6.2 says:

"State shall ensure to the maximum extent possible the survival and development of the child".

The extensive meaning conferred to the word 'survival' points to the need of preventive action such as immunisation. While immunisation is good and necessary, the overburden of vaccination has been ignored totally and their side-effects side-lined from the point of view of long-term safety.

Girl Child

According to 'Save the Children' Report* published recently even in Australia, 3733 children with a sizeable percentage belonging to the age-group below 10 years are selling the body merely to survive. Of the total number of rapes in U.S. about 30 per cent of the victims are below 16 years—747 (5.4 per cent) are reported to be below 10 years and 3320 (24.1 per cent) belong to 10-16 years age group.** Whereas throughout the world, girl child rarely finds the right kind of assurance with regard to a safe dwelling abode, sanitary and wholesome provisions of privacy. The mother-child life cycle starting with the girl child is a disturbing lot of an affair. The goals of the UN Convention have been earmarked as survival, development, protection. It gets first shock at prenatal stage of the USG Table. Only the lucky ones are allowed to see the light of the day. There is none to speak on behalf of the unborn child —the child *en ventre sa mere*. The neglect starts with the growing girl child, the mother-to-be in the form of deprivation of the correct level of nutrition at post-natal stage. As a result, out of 200 million children under five from the developing countries, 36 per cent have been found to be under weight (1989-90 ACC/SCN 1992). In India, the launching of the ICDS (1975) programme made no difference to the situation qualitatively. The programme expanded from its original objectives, failed to take care of the girl children on the street. A modest step in the right direction has been the effort of IPER schools. In Calcutta, the Child in Need Institute runs home shelter of the street girl children—a limited scale of laudable venture.

Specific needs of the Street Child

Privacy and Toilet, Residing place, Night Shelter, Clothing, Protection against sexual harassment, Educational Facilities and Access to sporting activities.We talk a lot about right to privacy. The question of survival of the street children especially of the girl children is the prime consideration. Of course, the NGOs like Sulabh International can extend the convenience of toilet and bathing facility to the girl children on the street to bring a shade of sanity and improvement to the situation further. More shelters need be constructed and it can serve multiple objectives in view of the devastating cyclonic disasters recently experienced in Orissa which brought miseries to 15 lakh children.

Poor children's clothing should be part of the kit given free of cost and their timely supply is equally important as delay in procurement of warm clothing this year is going to affect large number of poor students of the capital city itself.

Mobile school scheme for street children can be initiated. The main handicap is posed by the economic value of the time investment in education by this unfortunate lot of street children working as ragpickers. Alternative jobs or allowances as incentive to registration for schooling is now less attractive as the opportunity cost for them is too high. Thus, an NGO's plan to introduce this measure remained still-born, after all the need of the moment is immediate and children are unwilling to accept Rs. 1000 as monthly dole against their current earning level of around Rs. 3000 in Calcutta in this regard, Delhi High Court judgement upholding the banning order on recycling of plastic material is a correct one as it kills two birds with one stone.

Sexual harassment to street children should be made a separate category. They are the most unprotected species as far as rape victims are concerned. In the U.S. nearly 30 per cent rape victims are children below 16 years. If they are on the street, the probability of harassment is even greater everywhere.

Conclusion

A heartening note to be taken into account is that of the 183 ILO conventions nineteen relate to child labour of which seven have been satisfied by India as against only three by Germany and only one by the U.S.A. But there is a difference at the ground level situation. In the U.S. several legislations are in the pipeline notably, Child Labour Deterrence Act which seeks to prohibit use of products made by child labour. The Child Labour Free Consumer Information Act (s.554) imposing labelling standard (Rugmark as a monitoring body and symbol) is going to be enforced and effective as the certification procedure stipulated is quite rigorous. These legislative measures are of relevance and significantly important to our Indian exporters.

Thus, a strategy to free the market from child labour and their rehabilitation in a concerted fashion with a collaborative and cooperative approach from the industry and the government will have to be devised in larger national interest. One positive step taken by the Government at the behest of the Human Rights Commission in the form of amendment of the Civil Service Rule prohibiting employment of children below certain age as domestic hands is a charitable gesture setting the mode in top gear for a welcome change, can bring salutary effects in course of time. We should now think about forming an independent Children Rights Commission to take care of the entire gamut of children's issues cropping up in the new millennium.

References

1. Nagar, Divya, Deprived Children (1992), Printwell, Jaipur.
2. MacPherson, Stewart. Five Hundred Million Children (1987), Wheatsheaf Book, Sussex.
3. Devasia Leelamma, Girl Child in India (1991), Ashish Publishing House, New Delhi.
4. De Souza, Alfred. Children in India (1979), Mandhar, New Delhi.
5. Franklin, Bob. The Handbook of Children Rights (1995), Routledge, London.
6. S. Nayana Tara. Integrated Child Development Services (1988), Ashish Publishing House, New Delhi.
7. Kewalramani, G.S. Child Abuse (1992), Rawat Publications, New Delhi.
8. Chopra, Kamala. Reinforcement Among Infants (1983), National Psychological Corporation, Agra.
9. Ginzberg, Eli. The Nation's Children (1960), Columbia University Press, New York.

* Asian Age, dt. 11.11.99
* Shelter: Vol.2, No. 1, Jan, 1999
* Shelter: Vol. No. 1, Jan, 99.

PART - II

THE VICTIMS

FIVE

VICTIMS OF CRIME

I

The contemporary victimological vision is expanding its horizons to visualise the trials and tribulations of a wide variety of those victims of crime about whom the justice-oriented policy perspectives with regard to their plight and problems are far from being clear. The indifference of traditional victimological vision to unravel the ground realities of children's abuse and exploitations is one such area where empirical insight is both partial and perfunctory. To make up for this deficiency of our current knowledge on the subject, victimologists are trying hard to build a substantial database largely on the non-criminological forms of child abuse and exploitation—globally, nationally, regionally and locally.

Having resolved to look at the problems and predicaments of child victims of crime, the victimologists everywhere are trying to understand and analyse the situation under which criminal victimization of children occurs. In fact, the subject of juvenile victimization has not yet been extensively discussed and debated in India.

II

The victimization of children is by no means a new phenomenon. In fact, history is replete with examples of various forms of child abuse and exploitation. What is new is the recognition of the problem. The growing societal concern about the problem, the forms it has taken—and the cruel realities that these forms often reflect—are due to a number of developments, prominent among them being (i) the recognition of the rights of child and the ratification of these rights by large number of nations and, (ii) the world declaration on the survival, protection and development of children. In conformity with these developments, governments across the globe are now feeling sufficiently concerned with the preservation, protection and promotion of children's rights and to the prevention, control and eradication of all forms and practices derogatory to children's rights and injurious to their safety, health and well-being. In consonance with the concerns voiced both globally and nationally, everywhere the governments have now come up with policy statements, legal instruments, programme formalization and the implementation of the State's agenda for the care, protection, treatment, training and development of the children. The commitment that has arisen out of the concern for some of the atrocious and unthinkable forms of juvenile victimization offers hope for a better deal to children who are helpless victims of adult abuse and exploitation, and in some extreme cases, of barbaric brutalization.

The issue here is not the presence or absence of the beautifully-worded policy statements and rhetoric on the rights of the child. The issue indeed is how far the policy and programme related rhetoric have travelled to the realm of a progressive and positive empirical reality for children in general and victimised children in particular. When we look at the children's condition in the developing countries, we come across a depressing reality—a situation that makes us hang our heads in shame. Millions of children in many of the developing countries of Asia, Africa and Latin America are dumb sufferers of mass poverty, wide-spread malnutrition, hunger, hopelessness, illiteracy, ignorance, dearth, desertion, destitution, disability, disease and death. We know the harsh reality and the misfortune of millions of children woefully into conditions of life from where there is no escape, except for a degrading, disgraceful and dehumanised existence.

Children's situation in India is no better and we cannot afford to be complacent about it. Anyone who is familiar or concerned about the disadvantaged children, or children in especially difficult circumstances, knows that there are problems galore. The brazen and bizarre incidents of children's abuse and exploitation occur with frightening regularity compelling us to think of our hypocrisy about the nation's commitment to those constitutional commandments which obligate the state to do so many good things for children. The horrifying realities of child abuse and exploitation give a lie to a defining sentence in the National Policy for Children: "Children are supremely important assets and their nurture and solicitude is the nation's primary responsibility".

The magnitude of the problem of child abuse and exploitation is so gigantic, the causes so complex and confounding, the resources so limited, the indifference and unconcern so wide-spread and the states' unwillingness to act in a determined manner so obvious, that there is an all-round disappointment and despondency. Majority of us are becoming cynical because most of our past and present policy statements do not invite credibility any more. The huge expenditures on several programmes and activities of child development have not brought us any closer to solutions. It is no wonder then that we have a huge problem of child abuse and exploitation on hand.

This work intends to delimit the outreach of the discussion to the problem of "Criminal victimization of children", namely, the analysis, examination and articulation of the problems, policies, programmes and the current perspectives on combating the menace of criminal victimization of the juvenile, in other words, the unravelling of issues and perspectives on child victims of crime.

The victimologists (included criminologists) may not be in a position to competently analyse or examine some of obvious, yet very important non-criminological manifestations of the problem of child abuse and exploitation. The reference is to the problem of child labour, or to the problems of street children, handicapped children, destitute children, neglected children and other varieties of children vulnerable to non-criminal victimization. Let us, therefore, avoid any detailed discussion on non-criminal aspects of juvenile victimization, and better concentrate on criminal victimization of children, which, in itself, is a big subject for deliberations. Let us also avoid getting bogged down to problems and issues concerning children's well-being and move on the specific varieties of criminal victimization of children.

III

The fact that children in all societies and at all times have been loved and loathed, healed and hurt, protected and punished, endeared and endangered, shows that benevolence for and violence against children runs parallel throughout history. Crimes against children continue to be committed everywhere, perhaps in the same manner as before. The criminal victimization of children in its subtle and bizarre forms continues to be the burden of societal benevolence towards children. The victimization of children through various forms of violence—physical and emotional, social and economic—has been the persistent and pervasive problem of the past and continues to be the problem of the present. It is a different matter though that most of the societies (including Indian society) have long ignored violence against children as a tolerable aberration of certain families troubled by the traumas of domestic disorganisation.

Domestic violence against children has, therefore, not been recognised as a problem of any serious concern. It continues to be perceived as a private family matter not fit to be discussed with any outsider. Talking about it is incongruent without idealised notions of paternal care of children. Subjecting children to harsh disciplinary measures is still the parents' privilege and supposedly the surest way of teaching a child the early lessons of discipline and obedience. The issue of cruelty does not figure prominently in the large portion of parental violence directed against their own children. But herein arise certain questions; whether domestic violence is a private issue, or a matter of public concern; should parental violence against their own children be regarded as 'disciplining' or be treated as a form of child victimization? Or, where and under what circumstances parental violence ceases to be beneficial or benevolent and assumes that character of victimization? These questions, in Indian context, defy easy explanations and continue to be problematic. It is for reasons of cultural conditioning that one tends to ignore child-centred domestic violence and refuse to threat it as a problem.

Another issue for consideration is: whether child-centred domestic violence has reached such serious proportions that treating it as a social problem has become necessary? There are no straight answers to this question, atleast for now. Many of us will not feel comfortable to follow the western (basically American) line of thinking where children have been privileged to approach police against parental mistreatment, cruel or unusual treatment or punishment.

Against this backdrop, we often come across an empirical reality which makes sordid revelations about the cruelties (read crimes) being inflicted on children in certain families. The bizarre incidents of family-centred juvenile victimization make us confused about how to help such victims of domestic violence. These incidents also make us overwhelmed by the seeming impossibility of intervening into the situation and rendering some help or succour to the child. Our feelings towards the plight of such children are often passionate and intense, involving national concern, quite often outrage, but that is where our concern ends and helplessness takes over.

Since an overwhelming number of such incidents go unreported and never enter the official police records, we are in no position to gauge the actual extent or the magnitude of the problem. We do not know the names or the numbers of such children or the whereabouts of their victimisers (parents and employers). The cases that come to the knowledge of official agencies—hospitals, nursing homes, police stations, etc., just reveal the tip of the iceberg. Given the kind of social milieu we live in, the extent of domestic victimization of children is impossible to be disciplined. As yet, we don't have reliable data to tell us as to where such families are and where are such agents of juvenile victimization? Whatever rudimentary awareness we have about such children and their victimizers, we do not know how to deal with them. This is in reality the dilemma of the situation.

The problem of latent criminal victimization of children is perhaps as much disconcerting as is the problem of child victims of crimes reported in the *Crime in India* figures. It is therefore, imperative that we should also understand the nature of hidden criminal victimization of children, since that alone would help us devise some practical measures for preventive, combative or corrective strategies without fuller understanding of the dark figures of domestic crimes against children would only turn out to be a futile academic exercise.

IV

The offences committed against children, or the crimes in which children are the victims, are called 'crimes against children'. The Indian Penal Code and various protective and preventive "Special and Local Laws" specifically mention the offences wherein children are known to be the victims. The cases in which the children are victimized and abused are categorized under two broad heads: (i) crimes committed against children which are punishable under Indian Penal Code; and (ii) crimes committed against children which are punishable under special and local laws.

The crimes which are punishable under the Indian Penal Code include: (a) foeticide (crime against unborn child) Sections 315 and 316 IPC; (b) infanticide (crime against newly born child) Section 315 IPC; (c) exposure and abandonment (crime against children by parents or others to expose or leave them with the intention of abandonment) Section 317 IPC; (d) Kidnapping and abduction for exporting, Section 360 IPC; Kidnapping for ransom Section 363 read with Section 384 IPC; for camel racing, Section 363 IPC; for begging Section 363-A IPC; to compel for marriage Section 366 IPC; and for slavery Section 367 IPC; (e) procurement of minor girls (for inducement to force or seduce to illicit intercourse) Section 366-A IPC; (f) selling of girls for prostitution, Section 372 IPC; (g) buying of girls for prostitution, Section 373 IPC; (h) rape and unnatural offences.

Crimes against children which are punishable under special and local laws fall under the ambit of: (a) Immoral Traffic Prevention Act 1956; (b) Child Marriage Restraint Act 1979; (c) Child Labour

(Prohibition and Regulation) Act 1986; and (d) Juvenile Justice Act 1986.

While the available official statistics on crimes against children (as annually reported in *Crime in India* do not indicate the actual extent of the criminal victimization of children owing to large number of cases remaining unreported or unregistered. These statistics, however, provide us with a peep into the nature of crimes which come to the knowledge of the police.

A report of (1997) *Crime in India* tells us that amongst the 10 types of crime against children, child rape tops the list followed in descending order by kidnapping and abduction; procuration of minor girls, selling of girls for prostitution; buying of girls for prostitution; abetment of suicide; exposure and abandonment, infanticide; foeticide and marriage of minor children.

Child rape (up to 16 years) has shown noticeable size in its reported incidence from 1993 to 1997, and percentage variation has been 8.1 per cent over 1993 figure. Almost similar increase was noticed in other crime heads. A further probe into the rising incidence of child rape revealed that: (i) of all the victims in rape cases during 1997, children alone accounted for 28.8 per cent; (ii) the cases of rape of children below the age of 10 years were on a rise every year in the country except in 1996 since 1993; (iii) for the first time in the last 5 years, the year 1997 witnessed a sharp rise of 26.6 per cent, a rise of 4.0 per cent in victims in the age group of 10-16 years; (iv) the child rape victims below 10 years reported steep increase in 1997 over 1996.

Having shown a continuous rise in the reported cases of crime against children, the *Crime in India* report called for a "humane approach" to issues relating to child victims of crime. This is a very relevant observation coming from a Home Ministry outfit, namely, the National Crime Records Bureau. Before we come to question of approaches and strategies, let us understand the multifaceted character of criminal victimization of children.

V

For purposes of clarity, patterns of juvenile victimization must be preceded by some kind of an operational definition of 'victimization'. Keeping in mind the fact that non-criminal victimization (victimization arising out of exploitation and abuse which is illegally forbidden, though considered bad, evilsome and problematic) is not the central issue, we can have this tentative definition: "Criminal Victimization" is the process and outcome of condition/circumstances emerging out of crimes/

criminal acts committed against a child that cause him/her the physical, mental, sexual, social and economic hardship, hurt, humiliation, inconvenience, discomfort or annoyance. Subject to acceptance of this definition, I may like to add that criminal victimization of children includes cruelty, injury, pain, suffering, shame, humiliation, rejection and other kinds of social denigration. On the basis of these physical, psychological and social ramifications of crimes committed against children, we may construct a tentative topology of their victimization. This topology may comprise the following five broad forms of victimization.

1. **Physical Victimization** includes putting (forcing) children to hard physical labour under hazardous conditions, causing ill-health, physical injury, permanent or temporary disability or, in worst cases, death. Victimization of working and street children undoubtedly fits into this category. The most brutal and inhuman forms of physical victimization is the crime of maiming (kidnapped) children for purposes of begging.

2. **Sexual Victimization** includes exposing or exploiting children for immoral and sexual purposes; forcible child rape; child prostitution; paedophilia, incest involving children. The most reprehensible form of sexual victimization is the problem of child prostitution.

3. **Psychological Victimization** includes different types of emotional deprivation, rejection or treating the child in manners that he or she may feel unwanted.

4. **Social Victimization** includes parental/familial neglect, abandonment or turning the child out of home.

5. **Economic Victimization** includes cornering the earning of the child; denying the child the payment of adequate or prescribed minimum wages; keeping him as bonded labour and taking the economic advantage of the work done by the child.

The forces conspiring to cause the aforesaid forms of victimization depend upon the number of factors which govern the existential conditions/circumstances may also be dependent upon: (i) child's family milieu-disorganisational domestic conditions poverty and penury of parents, and the parents' attitude and behaviour of neglect, ill-treatment, etc. and (ii) external conditions making the child vulnerable to be victimized by persons other than parents/family members. Therefore, the forms that juvenile victimization takes depend on the child's social and economic background; situations of destitution and disability and conditions conducive to the criminal victimization of the child.

The etiology of each of these forms of juvenile victimization needs separate discussion. However, some discussion must take place on the kidnapping of children for criminal purposes and disgraceful sexual exploitation and abuse. Child prostitution is one such form which has already assumed menacing proportions. This problem needs to be discussed with a sense of urgency. A thought may also be spared for assessing the devastating psychological/social impact of victimization on the personality of the children. The western researches on the subject show that most of the victimized children develop such sense of hostility against their victimizers or society in general, which in future years, may well be channelled into violence. These researches also aver that there is a high probability that victimized children may turn out to be tomorrow's victimizers, or perpetrators of crime and violence. We certainly need some empirical data to approve or disapprove of these western assertions.

VI

Having explained the probelmatique of the child victims of crime, and having understood the forms and patterns of juvenile victimization, we finally need to address ourselves to the mechanisms and measures which could prevent victimization of children, and help us devise effective strategies and approaches to combat with the problem. Coming straight to the question of strategy, we should keep in mind that complexity of the problem does not permit any further room for complacency and does not allow us to look for simple quick-fix solutions. Good intentions and bold policy statements have outlined their utility, for, we had enough rhetoric on child welfare, child development and the rights of child. There is a need to develop a long-term view and evolve possible potential solutions as opposed to short-run crisis management, Band-Aid approach—all too common in popular thinking and official responses. We need to devise, develop and operationalise variety of approaches—social, psychological, and legal to prevent juvenile victimization and to protect children from the traumas of their abhorrent abuse and exploitation. Without being more elaborate in describing the three major approaches, let us outline their salient features.

The Social Approach includes launching of public campaigns designed to call nation's attention to the problematique of children's criminal victimization. Organised social movement, involving mass action is the prerequisite for mobilizing the support of the powerful members of society who can exert profound influence and activise the state to take effective action, in respect of preventing child abuse and exploitation and promoting children's care, protection, treatment, education, training and rehabilitation. Providing assistance of an advocate (legal counsel) to the victim is one of the most important requirements, and, as such, services of a lawyer should be considered mandatory, right from the beginning. The Supreme Court of India, in the case of Delhi Domestic Working Women's Forum vs. Union of India and Others (Crl. WP No. 362/93), has laid down the broad parameters in assisting the victims of rape. Some of these parameters are relevant in case of child sexual abuse as well. The Court had laid down that: (a) Legal representation should be provided to the complainants of sexual abuse; (b) competent, sensitive and child-friendly advocates be appointed by the Court to represent the indigent/needy complainants; (c) legal assistance be provided at the police station itself; (d) the police has to inform the victim about his/her right for legal representation, even before any questions are asked; (d) the cases of sexual victimization be tried in an atmosphere where anonymity of the victim could be maintained as far as necessary; and (f) a list of child-friendly and willing lawyers should remain available at the police station.

Law-Enforcement Approach requires the demonstration of greater sensitivity in the handling of the complaints of the child victims of sexual abuse. For example crimes should be examined in seclusion and in a child-friendly domestic environment, which is congenial for the child to be examined. Basic decency and courtesy should be maintained while examining the child victims of crime, especially the victims of sexual abuse. The case should be taken to ensure that the secondary victimization be avoided and human rights of the child victim are not violated.

To ensure a sensitive and humane handling of child victims of crime, low-level police functionaries have to be specially trained in child-friendly methods of policing. The proposed special 'child-friendly' training of police functionaries at the cutting edge level should also include imparting knowledge about the procedural and substantive laws relating to various offences against children, not only in the Indian Penal Code but also under various special and local laws. This is being repeatedly emphasized in view of the fact that on many occasions majority of the lawyer level (Thana level) police functionaries have been found to be blissfully unaware of the large number of laws relating to children. It is also desirable to get prepared a compendium of procedural, substantive, local and special laws and make it available at all police stations.

These approaches, no doubt, hold the promise of providing a better deal to child victims of crime. But given the all-round inertial and indifference, bordering on hopelessness and helplessness, it is unrealistic, however, to believe that the existing preventive, protective, curative and rehabilitative policies and programmes run both by the governmental agencies and large number of non-governmental organisations in the field of child welfare, would produce results better than before.

The police and child serving agencies, valuable as they are, can only treat the symptom and not the roots of the problem. What is needed, therefore, is a more fundamental approach of correcting the societal conditions that make millions of our children vulnerable to abuse and exploitation. This would certainly necessitate catching the culprits and subjecting them to their just deserts.

VII

Let us be little more hopeful and confident that notwithstanding the pessimism over the grim child situation in the country, and the seeming impossibility of combating the problem of juvenile victimization, we must maintain hope that there always exist potentials for easing out the problems of criminal victimization of children. Although we might d esire more pleasant picture of child situation in the country, we cannot avoid encountering many difficult problems. We should not think that being realistic about these problems is any reason for inertia. Quite the contrary, confronting these problems demands creative as well as critical thinking about the possible solutions. The experience of the developed countries (where incidents of juvenile victimization are far too less) indicate that children can be spared the exploitation and abuse if the country is determined to do so, regardless of constraints and difficulties. This is possible only when clear priorities are set, concerted efforts are made, existing programmes are restructured, and other available, but often underutilized resources, are mobilized to energetically tackle the task at hand. Only with persistent efforts at finding pragmatic solutions, we can hope of creating a more just and humane society. Finally and most importantly, an optimistic vision is important, because there is always light at the end of a dark tunnel.

SIX

NEGLECT OF VICTIMS

A victim of crime is a pathetic sight. Not only does he suffer losses, loses dignity, or undergoes deprivation of having a traumatic experience of being a victim of crime when he feels diminished in all respects, he also sees no hope, in near future, of his being fulfilled, satisfied, or compensated. He is heavy with quilt because of the missed opportunity in preventing the crime or protecting himself against it by not following a lonely street or carrying money without adequate precaution or care. He thus suffers guilts, stress, trauma, fear, emotional upset, and psychological distress.

Crime imposes heavy cost upon society in terms of the personal loss (indicated above), the insurance costs, medical expenses, man-days lost, impairment, death, systems costs, etc. It is a drain upon economic resources as the product is usurped by the illegible and unauthorized persons who ought to have contributed to the economy. It is also a strain upon the economy to the extent of costs required to meet the challenge of crime in terms of the infrastructure of the criminal justice system comprising the police, the prosecution, the judiciary, the correctional services, and the prisons. The institutions of the system are expensive and cost the exchequer, ultimately the tax-payer.

So there are two categories of victims of crime. One category pertains to those suffering the direct impact of crime. The other includes the society that bears the cost of the institutions designed to deal with crime in its various phases and processes, even those dealing with crimes that have not happened or been committed; i.e., the preventive action.

Both these categories are pushed to the background in the rush of events when the search for the criminal becomes a predominant management objective for police. Though this is meant to find out the truth of the incident, yet this process is impersonal, unidirectional and related to the victim only to the extent he helps in identification of the culprit or the circumstances under which the crime was committed. Sometimes, this relapse into memory of the unpleasant event creates unpleasantness every time the victim reconstructs the scene for the benefit of the investigating officer.

It is only after the police has succeeded in apprehending the criminal that the response of the court and the efforts of the prosecutors come into play. Since both these institutions have not seen the victim in his raw, original, shattered state, they are remote, methodical, impersonal, and aloof in responses which, at times, appear to be wooden, devoid of any milk of human kindness, or any streak of sympathy.

Whatever be the extent of responses of the system, the moot point is that it is loaded in favour of the criminal. In the process, victimology is a victim of the proverbs which give direction to the functioning of the system. Quotes from the jurisprudence are like proverbs which are not only unhelpful to the victim but also contradictory thus neutralizing the functioning of the system. Proverbs were conceived by the 'wise' to guard against the arbitrariness of the autocrats, and yet-to-be-just regimes. These are short crisp sentences which etch deeply in the psyche of the law enforcement officers, the judiciary, and all others concerned with the system. These are polestars, touchstones, astrolabes, guidelines, and tests of the system.

There is a large category of the safeguards for criminals in the form of proverbs. They are 'he is innocent till proved guilty', 'he is entitled to benefit of doubt', 'bail is his right (bail and not jail)', 'the case has to be proved beyond reasonable doubt', 'let 99 criminals get away but not one innocent person indicated', 'he is entitled to all right under the Constitution', 'since he is a citizen, he is entitled to all the basic needs in the prison, including the legal aid'.

All these principles are couched in the beautiful, jargonized language, very convincing, well reasoned out. Taken one by one, there is a lot of force in these tenets. All by themselves, they stand erect. But they are too solid to meet each other, bend for a compromise and make for a coherent system. They clash. They are uncompromising because their interests come into conflict. If a criminal is innocent till proved guilty, then why is he incarcerated as an 'undertrial' awaiting the finalisation of the case. If 'bail and not jail' is the principle, how is it that so many (perhaps 85 per cent) prisoners are languishing in prisons. And how does one trace out a criminal released on personal bond? Why should 99 criminals be left out? Why should, the criminal who has rights not perform his fundamental duty of eschewing violence or following the law? And then after a prolonged incarceration, he gets benefit of doubt and all traces of criminality are washed from his face.

Victim of crime is a fact; criminal is a conjecture. Not much effort is required to know the plight of the victim. But law has to protect the innocent who can be a victim of a conjecture. Since the criminal is unknown, the law enforcement agency has to be circumspect and ensure against miscarriage of justice upon the innocent. Yet who can deny that there are criminals. After all, crime is a matter of fact; so is a victim. But the criminal either eludes or deludes under the support of the jurisprudential shibboleths. No surprise that many get scot free after a protracted trial which is more gruesome for the victim than a criminal for the former loses and the latter gains.

The processes of the system are a zero sum game. It is here that the distinction between truth and proof is necessary. The truth shall come out and it does. But the proof is elusive because witness may not be available, may become hostile, may not cooperate, may forget the incident thus introducing contradictions and creating a scope for incredibility. So in spite of the fact of crime, the perpetrator escapes from the net. The large scale latitude shown to the lot of the criminal is responsible for a low rate of conviction and search for a parallel system of justice. It is equally a powerful tenet that justice delayed is justice denied. But the distribution of justice does get delayed. Hence the denial, leading to frustration, and then personal initiatives to seek justice as per one's will. This is a symptom of desperation. This has been the cause of Bhagalpur incident and continues to intrigue the police under pressure to 'show results' and resort to short cuts and other unauthorized practices.

It will not be far fetched to suggest that brutalization of force is attributed to delay and then denial of justice. The rise of the parallel system too can be attributed to the vacuum caused by the system's inadequacies and limping progress. At the initial stage when crime is committed or has come to light, the state is all for the victim of crime. The police swoops over the site of crime, speaks to the victim, gets his report and then evidence, is all anxious to 'work out' the case, as the detection of crime is called. And then other institutions are responsible to complete the process. But with the lapse of time, the concern for the victim decreases. The element of time works as a scourge. Time heels the wounds of the victim and the sensitivities of the enforcement agency.

More the time, less the concern; less the time, more the concern. The result is that the victim is not heeded to when he wants to find out the progress of the case. He has no response from the inaccessible court whom he cannot, for fear of contempt, even ask the reason for delay or make a suggestion for an expeditious disposal. The other reason for diminishing interest is the piling up of cases with all agencies. The latest in time pushes the earlier ones backwards. The new gets the priority. The fresh is in limelight. Hence resources have to be expanded upon the most recent. The 'more' engulf the one which may be the concern of the individual but not that of the organization. Third factor that lessens the interest is the element of familiarity. Once the case is familiar to the officials, it loses its sting. The victim then subsequently becomes a burden to be avoided. It mostly happens when the case is not worked out and the victim is compelled to knock at the door of police, even if for the purpose of satisfaction. With time, the victim also gets acclimatized to deprivation, loss, humiliation. Mental adjustment is made, justification provided, and coping strategies devised. Under the incomplete system, the problem is how to create a sense of justice. There are two aspects which must be considered. The CJS is expected to produce justice which means speedy, sure and sufficient disposal of case and penalties where necessary. We must get over the overbearing influence of the proverbs which have succeeded in creating a mindset, and found a theory of justice that satisfies the victim, the criminal, and the social order. This is an intricate task. However incomplete and inadequate, an attempt must be made.

Let us examine the system as dealing with three parties when crime is committed.

If appears that the system has accountability to all three participants. Whereas its role towards the criminal is well defined in the shape of crisp short sentences, its role to the victim and social order is excluded in the scheme of things. The safeguards granted to the criminal are given, cannot be altered because each one is well reasoned and stands on its firm feet. There is thus a need to search roles that appease or satisfy the victim and take care of the public interest and social order. The present system is loaded in favour of the criminal. There is a need to balance and bring about an equalization. How to do this? We may try a few principles.

1. **Rule of the prima facie:** This principle is based on the preponderance of evidence. It is this which puts the criminal in the dock to face a trial. If it is risky to see an innocent being punished, it is equally unjust to let a criminal go by in spite of the preponderance of evidence. And what is the sanctity of the benefit of doubt? Why only in favour of the criminal? Why not to assist the victim? Truth is a fact whereas proof is a construction. If construction fails, the ground must not give way. It is wellknown

that statements US 161 Cr PC are not signed, that witnesses turn hostile, often become forgetful, develop a soft corner for the criminal, enter into compromises, are cajoled, threatened and endangered. In the light of all these possibilities, how is it that the 'principle of innocence' should be so overbearing as to stifle the fact. So the probabilities cannot be set aside and circumstances doubted every time the evidence whittles down under the various pressures to the disadvantage and disappointment of the victim who is left in the lurch by all around him. The prosecution might fail, but the victim loses. The victim is betrayed by the process. The majority works against him as his testimony is said not to be supported by evidence. In spite of the fact, he becomes unreliable. Such is the power of the rule of corroboration. The so-called corroborated are not victims; so they can shift their allegiance, leaving the victim high and dry, not to be counted upon. He appears an unreliable wretch.

2. **Right to be heard:** Every victim of crime has a right to be heard. Often this right is denied to him by means of subterfuges practised by police who are reluctant to register cases not realizing that the process of investigation cannot start unless cognizance of crime is taken. This is, in fact, a fundamental right subsumed under the rubric of 'equality before law and equal protection of laws'.

There shall be no denial of registration with regard to any cognizable crime. Law must take its course, whatever be the compulsions (statistical, resource, work-load) of the police. Similarly, he has a right to be heard by the court which is more indulgent in giving adjournments, generally on the request of defence counsel. Every postponement of the trial is a pain to the victim who gets feeling of being ignored by the system.

3. **Right to know/information:** The victim has every right to know the progress of his case both from police and the court. Though the channel of communication in the court is one-sided, i.e., from the court to the client, with no questions or doubts permitted, yet this does not satisfy the victim who must seek court's indulgence and patronage in being heard and his problem resolved. The plight of the victim and the witnesses in the corridors of courts is well known. The atmosphere is impersonal, remote from compassion,

sympathy, balmy touch. It is formal, standardized, commercial and matter-of-fact, at times verging on the insensitive. It is here that the victim is grilled, harassed, put to inconvenience, not cared for by anyone, and running from pillar to post.

The anxiety of the victim must, therefore, be appeased by the police or court informing him of the progress or reason for delay. He must not be in doubt about the efficacy of the system and must understand its genuine compulsions or else he shall have his own interpretations of the unjustness which he is a prey to. This requires a sensitive approach.

4. **Right to decent treatment:** What is most urgently required is that the system decides the problem expeditiously. It involves three things. One, it must not permit delay being caused; two, it must deliver the result; and three, it must be humane to the victim till the process is complete. This analysis highlights the need to give decent treatment to the victim who undergoes privations till the decision of the case. If the processes cannot be expedited, the least that the system can do is to extend a proper treatment to the victim and not humiliate him by asking him to come again and again or refusing to inform him of the progress or considering him as a burden, an imposition, or denying him the basic facilities of waiting, toilet, clarity of orders, giving him copies, if he so desires, etc.

5. **Minimization of pain, inconvenience, humiliation:** One of the methods of coping with plight of victim is to minimize the inconvenience caused by procedures and processes. This can be done by the sensitization of the agents to the travails of the victims. It involves two things. First, not doing what is not permitted. If a woman or a child under the age of 15 years is not to be called to the police station, this should not be done (Sec. 160 Cr PC). If statement of the complainant is to be taken, it must be done at the earliest so that he gets the feeling that it has been done. Often, the statements u/s 161 Cr PC are written later on, based on the FIR. Statements, should not only be taken at the earliest, but also appear to be recorded by giving this feeling to the victim. If the victim has an appointment to meet the investigation officer, this must be honoured or the victim informed of the change, if it is unavoidable.

This aspect also includes the compensation to victims and all efforts which are necessary to secure it. For instance, a victim of road accident or the survivors must be assisted in getting the insurance on self, insurance as per third party commitment, and other support which the Accident Claims Tribunal can provide. All this requires copies of police reports, documents, certificates and other supporting material which police and others concerned must provide without hassles. In this aspect is also relevant to the issue of Final Report so that the victim can get relief. Even getting the postmortem expedited in unnatural death cases is a great succour to the survivors.

The principle involved is getting the victim what is due to him. If there are various proverbs which come to the assistance of a criminal, there ought to be a few which help the victim. One of these can be 'do not do unto others what you do not like to be done to you.' This is a negative moral ethic propounded by Sandra Pralong, a totally practical rule and in consonance with Popper's principle of 'minimizing avoidable suffering', propounded in his book, *The Open Society and its Enemies.*

6. **Training in sensitivities:** The agencies must be made to realize that the principles are important, practical, desirable, and enforceable. The officials at all levels must be sensitized to the problems of the victim. Policing, which had so far concerned itself with the crimes and criminals, must extend its concerns to the victim. So at every incident, there are two things which it has to do. Firstly, make efforts to catch the criminal. Secondly, to give all possible support to the victim of crime.

This sensitization will come to a sensitive person only and not every one. So while dealing with organization, one must institutionalize inputs and drill in the attitudes to be converted into behaviour.

7. **Monitoring and follow up:** The conversion of attitude to behaviour is possible only when the senior officers ensure that along with efforts to trace the perpetrators of crime, efforts are made to alleviate the condition of the victim. The latter endeavour does not require many resources. It only requires a proper handling. All that ought to be done for the victim must be done because it is in one's control, whereas catching a criminal is a big adventure, a riddle, a charade.

REFERENCES

1. The concept of 'proverbs' was used by Herbert A Simon in Administrative Behaviour; The Free Press; New York, 1976.
2. Sandra Pralong; Is there an ethics of the Open Society in Popper's Open Society after 50 years; ed. Ian Jarvie & Sandra Pralong; Routlege; 1999.

SEVEN

JUDICIAL SCRUTINY FOR PROTECTION

Scriptures may proclaim God manifests in the innocent smile of a child, a philosopher may gaze at the sparkling eyes of a growing child to feel the quintessence of the universe and a poet laureate may announce with divine dolemnity that a child is the father of the nation. But in recent times, there has been unpleasant and unfortunate incidents against the female children, and it becomes a nostalgia, when she succumbs to become a victim of the most inferior bestial propensities of lowly human nature. Mesmerised, she is forced to expose before a perverse impulse of a ravishing man. Unknowingly, she shatters her serene innocence which deprives her from the life time privilege of cherishment of the childhood. She remains to recollect them in memory in poised tranquillity which compels her to embrace despair and forces her to bear the brunt of an incurable stigma.

For the past some time, the subject of sexual abuse against the girl child had received considerable attention due to increase in the number of incidents. At one time, it was felt that law relating to sexual offences did not contain adequate provisions for protection of victims. The victim of sexual abuse who had undergone the trauma have to live with the tragedy. Her nightmarish experience shakes her foundation of living a life worth of any kind. Further, suffer form its effect for a long term and impair her capacity to build relationship or remould their behaviour for a virtuous living and in the process generate endless fear for anything around her. In addition to the trauma of becoming a victim of sexual abuse, the victims have to suffer further agony during the legal proceedings.

The antiquated laws governing the cases of sexual abuse, particularly rape[1] remained unchanged since 1860 for quite some time.[2] The law was amended as a result of sustained campaign against an infamous Supreme Court judgement in the Mathura case.[3] Incidentally in *Mathura,* a sixteen years tribal girl was raped by policemen within a police compound. The trial court held that since the victim eloped with her boy friend and was habituated to sexual intercourse, the charges of rape against the policemen could not be sustained. On appeal, the High Court held differently that mere passive or helpless surrender, induced by threat or fear cannot be equated by desire or will and held the policemen guilty of offence. But the Supreme Court adjudicated that as the victim did not raise any alarm at the time of commission of offence, the allegations of rape were considered to be untrue and accordingly acquitted the policemen.

Such a judgement triggered off a campaign for the changes of the rape law as it became extremely difficult for a rape victim to prove 'beyond all reasonable doubts' that she did not consent for the sexual abuse. The Law Commission accordingly recommended that not only the onus of proof about the allegation should lie on the accused, but also the past sexual history of the victim should be ignored in all such trials. In response to the feelings of public, the government introduced, necessary to the feelings of public, changes in the Indian Penal Code,[4] Criminal Procedure Code,[5] as well as in the Indian Evidence Act.[6] In the Indian Penal Code, new provisions were added which made sexual intercourse by persons in custodial situations, such as policemen, public servants, managers of public hospitals and remand homes, etc., would amount to rape even if it was with the consent of the victim.[7]

Judicial Scrutiny

The Supreme Court held that rape is not only a crime against the victim but it is a crime against the entire society. It destroys the entire psychology of the victim and pushes her into deep emotional crisis. It is her sheer will power which helps her to rehabilitate in spite of the fact that the society looks down upon her in derision and contempt. Therefore in all cases of rape, law should take care about the social aspect of the matter.[8]

In *Delhi Domestic Working Women's Forum v. Union*[9], the Supreme Court recognised the right of the victim for compensation and even to the extent of payment of interim compensation[10] in certain cases.

The Supreme Court held that in cases of sexual abuse, supposed considerations, which have no material effect on the veracity of the prosecution case or where there are discrepancies in the testimony of the prosecution, it should not be ordinarily disallowed by the court unless such discrepancies are fatal in nature or are based on compelling reasons which necessitate looking for corroboration,[11] as corroborative evidence is not an imperative component of judicial credence in every case of rape. It may be stated that corroboration is a condition for judicial reliance on the testimony of the victim and is not requirement of law but a guidance of prudence under a given circumstance.

In *Prem Chand* v. *State of Haryana*[12] the apex court neither characterised the victim as a woman of questionable character nor a person of easy virtue. Thus the character or reputation of the victim has no bearing or relevance in the matter of adjudging the guilt of the accused or imposing the punishment[13].

In *Lankeswar* v. *State of Orissa.*[14] The Orissa High Court held that a woman cannot be treated as an object of pleasure. Therefore no man should entertain the idea that a woman had to depend on man at every stage of life for protection of her dignity and self-respect. Every man conceiving the notion of sexual assault must remember that in the bodily frame of a woman remains the soul of a mother and the essence of purity. Therefore no man has a right to indignify a woman.

Following such an idealism, the Orissa High Court in another case, where a minor girl of eight years old, while grazing bullocks in an open field, having gone to a little distance to bring stray bullocks, was lifted forcibly and raped, held that the accused having offended the dignity of the victim had to undergo punishment.[15]

In another case, it was a sordid tale of extreme brutality and raw unleashed sexuality of a teacher to satisfy his lust upon a thirteen years old girl student who having called her to his room and undressed and raped her.[16] The court following the Supreme Court judgement in *Bharwada v. State of Gujarat,*[17] held that there is no tenebrosity in the position of law that the testimony of a victim of sexual assault should not inspire confidence and found to be unreliable. and accordingly the accused was sentenced.

In *Bansilal v. State of MP*[18] the victim was eight years old and was not only raped at the air strip but also was subjected to unnatural sexual offence by putting the male organ into her mouth and also into her rectum, the court declined to intervene into the punishment inflicted upon the accused.

In *Surendra Kumar Patra v. State of Orissa*[19] the victim was a minor girl of ten years and at the time of occurrence she was watching *Pala* (Night Opera) and was asked by the accused, a known villager, to accompany him to bring *Prasad (Puja offerings),* who on the way took her to a secluded place and raped her. The court while convicting the accused did not pay credence to the medical report.

Significance of Judicial Scrutiny

In Indian setting, refusal to act on the testimony of a victim of sexual abuse, in the absence of corroboration, was considered to be an insult ot the injury already sustained by the victim. There has been a significant judicial observation that the court in India should no more examine the evidence of a girl or woman, subjected to sexual abuse and view the same with the aid of spectacles fitted with lenses tinged with doubt, disbelief or suspicion. In all such cases, the judiciary is of the opinion that the support for the need for corroboration and the relentless or remorseless cross-examinations must be made with a logical mind and not with an opinionated eye. This is for the simple reason that Indian culture is not swept off by westernisation, rather it depended upon its own social values or its own code of living a moral life.

The judiciary also have held that much importance should not be attached to the minor discrepancies for the reason that, by and large, a witness cannot be expected to possess a photographic memory or recall the details of an incidence. Therefore, absence of corroboration notwithstanding the limitations imposed by prudence, the victims evidence is entitled to great weightage in cases of sexual abuse. It was also considered not to put premiums on such defects as they would amount to usurpate upon justice based on defective investigation.

Suggestion and Conclusion

It is suggested that in cases of sexual abuse wherever corroboration is necessary, it should be from an independent source but not necessarily that every part of the evidence of the victim should be confirmed in every details by an independent witness. In most of the cases, such evidence could also be sought from either direct or circumstantial evidence or from both and from the totality of the background of the case. It is also suggested that society should come forward to rescue the victims of sexual abuse. Even law expects them to come forward to help the helpless victim. Although payment of compensation is but poor solace to a victim of sexual abuse, unless people come forward to rescue the victim's human dignity, the victims of sexual abuse will continue to remain under erosion of societal values.

REFERENCES

1. Secs. 375 and 376 IPC.
2. Criminal Law (Amendment) Act, 1983.
3. *Tukaram v. State of Maharashtra,* AIR 1979 SC 185.
4. Changes in Secs. 376, 376A, 376B, 376C and 376D were introduced by Amendment Act, 43 of 1983.
5. Amended Sub-section 372(2) says trial of rape cases could be held in camera, likewise Sub-Section(3) prohibits/regulates publication of names of victims and proceedings; and the consequential Ist Schedule changes. See, Amendment Act 43 of 1983.
6. Section 114A was introduced in the Indian Evidence Act, 1982.
7. A presumption was allowed to the courts as to the absence of consent in certain rape cases under Sec. 376 Sub-Clauses (a), (b), (c), (d), (e), and (g) of IPC.
8. Bodhisattwa Gautam v. Subhra Chakravarti, AIR 1996 SC 922.
9. (1995) 1 SCC 14.
10. Supra fn. 8.
11. State of Punjab v. Gurmit Sing, Air 1996 SC 1393.
12. AIR 1989 SC 937.
13. *State of Haryana v. Prem Chand,* AIR 1991 SC 538.
14. Jail Criminal Appeal No. 332 of 1994 disposed on Dt. 26.11.1996. (Unreported)
15. *Budhia Murmu v. State of Orissa* 1997 (1) OLR 47.
16. *Bhikari Panda v. State of Orissa,* 1997 (1) OLR 338.
17. AIR 1983 SC 753.
18. 1999 (1) Crimes 275.
19. 1997 (II) OLR 49.

EIGHT

CHILD REFUGEES

Introduction

The previous century has produced the largest number of refugees ever in world history. There are in the world today around 15 million people, two-thirds of whom are children, who have fled homes and are now living in exile. Behind this abstract figure lies an immeasurable history of indiscriminate sufferings. The past decade has witnessed a series of civil wars and communal conflicts in which masses of people have been forced to flee for their lives—examples are Burundi, Chechnya, Columbia, Liberia, Rwanda and Sri Lanka.

For many people who are confronted with threats to their lives and liberty, fleeing to another country is the only way in which they can find safety. Sadly, it is becoming increasingly difficult for refugees to find a place of safety beyond the borders of their homeland. Confronted with pressing domestic problems and declining international support, a growing number of countries have closed their borders to the impending large-scale refugee influxes. Moreover, in many parts of the world, people who have taken refuge in another country have been harassed, attacked and even forced to go home against their will.

The use of children as tools of war, where they are manipulated and coerced into being unwitting and unwilling perpetrators of the war's inevitable atrocities and inhumanities, is therefore as pernicious as it is cynical. Mass exodus is too oftern synonymous with a high number of unaccompanied children. Most are not orphans, but have been separated from their parents during conflict or migration. The disintegration of girls particularly, leaves them vulnerable to violence, intimidation and sexual abuse. The children are vulnerable at every stage of their migration—while fleeing a war-zone they risk being raped, physically abused by the soldiers and starved. On arrival at the camps, they risk being sexually exploited by the local security or other refugees. Further, refugees are packed together in refugee camps without hope for their future. Many refugees are worse than the poor of the Third World; aside from lacking proper housing and sufficient food, the refugees, having left their homes, are even more dependent on the outside world. The vast majority of children come from and live in the world's poorest countries and it is their plight that forms the focus of this study.

The United Nations Convention on the Rights of the Child (1989) reaffirms the fundamental place of the family in society, and recognizes that the child should be brought up in the spirit of the ideals in the UN Charter, in particular, peace, dignity, tolerance, freedom and equality. The United Nations High Commissioner for Refugees (UNHCR) was set up to protect refugees. The UNHCR tries to ensure that no refugee is returned involuntarily to country where he or she has reason to fear persecution.

The victimization of refugee children is hardly a recent phenomenon. But as we move into the twenty-first century, knowing the world's desire to protect children, must we accept as inevitable the chronic and escalating pressure of refugee children?

The main aim of this study is to provide a basis for understanding the victimization faced by the refugee children and not to point to the faults or other aspects of refugee relief efforts by the government, international bodies or NGOs.

The Study

The study examines the various socio-psychological aspects of victimization of the child refugees. The sample consists of Sri Lankan children of various age groups who live in the refugee camps in Tamil Nadu. The children (N=31), of both sexes, were chosen using purposive sampling technique from three different camps each consisting of refugees from three different districts of Sri Lanka. The sample chosen were individuals ranging from 10-21 years.

An interview schedule formed the tool of the study to collect relevant data. The data obtained was analyzed and is being discussed below, along with the results. Unstructured interviews were administered on all the children who have been victimized as young children at the time of migration and who were chosen for the study. Further, for a better understanding of the situation of child victimization among refugee children, the heads of the camps from among the refugees, social workers and psychologists from NGOs who work with those children on a voluntary basis, were also interviewed.

A tragic fallout of the ethnic conflict has been the cause of the uprooting of its population with external and internal ramifications. The geographical contiguity and ethnic bonds with Tamil Nadu makes it an attractive asylum at the time of crisis.

It appears from this study that the families lived fairly normal lives, until the situation arrived where they had to leave their houses and flee for two reasons; one is immediate safety to life, and the other is to protect their children from joining the militant groups or the armed forces. In the recent years, more children and youth bear arms in internal armed conflict and violent strifes than ever before. When the conflict drags on for years or even decades, the root causes, such as poverty or repression, are accelerated, galvanizing civilian populations for recruitment into armed groups.

Any conflict has its effect on children. It leaves children and youths orphaned, displaced or responsible as head of households when either one or both the parents are killed or are away at war. Schools, which occupy most of the time in a growing child's life, are either closed for indefinite periods of time, or are destroyed. Their agricultural lands are destroyed. Relatives, neighbours and friends are injured, killed or have fled. Such youths are at risk and become receptive to ideological propaganda. Instances of children and youths having been coerced into joining government and armed forces in Burma (now Myanmar), Ethiopia, Angola, Sudan and Sri Lanka have been well-documented (Child Soldiers: The Role of Children in Armed Conflicts, A Study on Behalf of the Henry Dunant Institute, Geneva, 1994). In this study, a large majority of the sample (81.3 per cent) have not been forced or coerced to join the forces. This is probably because they have not been direct victims (74.2 per cent) the war and have fled before they were attacked.

Therefore, Post Traumatic Stress Disorders (PTSD) symptoms like cognitive symptoms such as confusion in thinking, difficulty in making decisions and disorientation; physical symptoms such as excessive sweating, dizzy spells, increased heart rate, high blood pressure and rapid breathing that may be found in refugees of other countries are unfound in a majority of the children.

It is interesting to note that emotional (anger, shock, grief, etc.) and behavioural symptoms (changes in food habits, withdrawal from others, prolonged silence, etc.) were also non-existent in these children. The grown-up children and youths while relating their experiences revealed that they had to cross dead bodies, some lying just open and mutilated parts of bodies, to get to school. Some of the boys had severe illnesses after seeing mutilated bodies and have not been able to attend school for days. An interesting phenomenon is that, while on their way to school, in groups mostly, when they heard grenades or bombs they laid down flat wherever they were and after the effect just kept moving as if nothing has happened. This shows the effect of their prolonged exposure to war ever since birth.

The families seem to have been financially stabel (87.1 per cent) with own house (45.2 per cent), agricultural land (53.1 per cent) and two-wheeler or cycle. Majority of them (48.4 per cent) have just left the land and fled, while the remaining have either sold their property (22.6 per cent) or left it in someone else's custody (9.4 per cent).

Impact of Victimisation During Migration

The call for migration comes either when their village or colony is going to be attacked by the armed forces or when they are warned to vacate the village by the forces to form a war-base.

Impact of Victimisation After Migration

On reaching the host country, the families are at first kept in a single camp and, thereafter, moved to different camps based on the district to which they belong.

The host government provides cash (depending upon the size of the family) and also basic provisions like rice, kerosene, sugar and pulses. They are permitted to take up employment, a facility incidentally denied to the Chakma refugees. In some instances, the family income is supplemented by funds from relatives abroad. Restriction on their movements have been considerably relaxed in the recent years. They have been included in the category of "weaker sections" and stand eligible for a free supply of clothes and cash and a reservation of seats in schools and professional courses.

To be a refugee is to experience an upheaval. They are torn by the roots from their native soil and often denied the possibility of going back home again. They face new conditions in a new country, and a new environment. Among the Sri Lankan refugees, there are configuration of forces contributing in many cases to family tensions and general estrangement in the parent-child relationship in the pre-adolescent and adolescent periods. As with many other refugee groups, the Sri Lankan refugees have experienced widespread fatigue and depression resulting from relentless economic pressures and cultural alienation. Thus, their abilities to raise their children in a foreign culture are weakened. Often, they lack the energy to discipline their children consistently. Some adults cope with the pressures by abusing alcohol and drugs or by gambling, both of which contribute further to family instability. Half (51.5 per cent) of the children interviewed felt a behavioural change in their parents after migration.

Effects on Children

Many of the families are experiencing crisis in their relationships with their children. These tensions often erupt into child's behaviour, which tends to be destructive to both the children and the families. Such problems include running away, not attending school, engaging in sexual activity, drug and alcohol abuse, child marriage starting in early adolescence and initiating gangs within the camp. A main factor which alienates the parent from the child while he grows, especially when the child is born and brought up in the host country, is that the parent tries to bring up the child in their culture while the child adapts to the host culture. The parents refuse to accept the values of the prevailing culture. Moreover, the parents and the older generation in the camp socially isolate themselves and their children from the outside world (outside the camp).

Adolescent marriage is a serious problem in these camps. The reasons are threefold. One is the close proximity of the houses, which are at times, just partitioned by sheet. Each house measures just around 100 square feet. Second is that, as revealed by the children, the one room accommodation forces all of them to sleep together, this brings about a curiosity in the minds of the children as to watch sexual activities between the parents and some of them have revealed that they keep awake till the wee hours of the morning awaiting such activities. This in turn builds in them the urge to indulge in sexual activities. Third, these children are alienated from the outside world. They live inside the camp, which is composed only of Sri Lankans. In many camps where the child marriage problem persists, the schools are inside the camp, run by Sri Lankans. The NGOs, which render help to these camps, are also run by Sri Lankans. The medical officers, social workers and psychologists are all Sri Lankans.

Most of the families have children between 2 to 4 (56.3 per cent) and 31.2 per cent have children above five and the remaining to a maximum of nine children. Certainly, a catastrophe in the making, with the government providing money and necessities based on the size of the family and increasing the number of camps.

The children, nearly fifty per cent of them, especially the younger children, want to start life afresh. They do feel low at times (48.4 per cent) and generally suicidal tendencies are high. The boys abuse alcohol but not drugs, and do not engage in criminal behaviour. They are treated well in schools of the host country and do not suffer from any problems of discrimination due to their nationality.

A little more than 50 per cent of them like the kind of life they lead in the camps while the other half resent this kind of life and wish to go back to their country some day. Majority of the boys wish to join the armed forces and the girls wish to become doctors. The children who are older and have seen the war and its atrocities are the ones who wish to go back to their country and fight the forces. They miss their friends (92.8 per cent) and school (36.5 per cent). Those who were young when they left their country wish to stay back in this country. A major reason why they do not like life at the camp is not due to restrictions (64.3 per cent) but due to the lack of amenities in the camp (50 per cent) like clean lavatories, clean surroundings, etc. Those who like the camp attribute the feeling mainly to mental (59 per cent) and physical security (65 per cent) that is being away from the war environment.

A majority of them children attend school and very few of them (22.6 per cent) go to work; all of them are boys. The kind of work in which they engage are stone cutting, tailoring and as wage labourers. They do not face any victimization at work in terms of wages, working hours, or discrimination.

Common refugee problems like lack of basic necessities including medical needs is absent in the Sri Lankan refugee camps. The victimization on the whole is centred on the psychological well-being of the child in various ways. The effect of the migration on the parents and their problems in raising their children is unique to these refugees.

This study has broadened our own understanding of the condition of child refugees in the camps. The psychological victimization they face has confirmed the complexity of issues at the level of policies, programmes and repatriation.

This 'war on children' is a 20th century invention. It is said that only five per cent of the casualties in the First World War were civilians. By the Second World War, the proportion has risen to fifty per cent. The civilian share was about eighty per cent most of them women and children (James P. Grant, UNICEF, 1992).

Recommendations

Priority in the list of recommendations would be the need for further research. The psycho-socio impacts of the war and the unique problems faced inside the camp due to camp conditions and the parent society needs to be identified and appropriate steps should be taken to practice innovative and responsive programmes. The children are receptive and look forward to counselling on education, information on education, are interested in computer courses and are also interested in meditation and yoga.

A refugee, therefore, is any person who is unable to return to his or her own country because of persecution on account of race, religion, nationality, membership in particular social group or political opinion. The line of difference between immigrants and refugees lies in the fact that most immigrants leave their country voluntarily while the refugees have been forced to flee their country of origin and have been accepted to live in another country.

The needs of refugees vary depending on who and where they are. In many cases, refugees need immediate assistance in the form of food, water, shelter or medical care. But the most fundamental need of a refugee is to be granted asylum. Article 14 of the Universal Declaration of Human Rights states, "everyone has the right to seek and enjoy in other countries asylum from persecution".

India is a home to thousands of refugees. Giving asylum has been an age-old tradition for which the Rajput kings sometimes paid with their lives and kingdoms. The independence saw millions of Indians become refugees overnight in what was until then their own homes—over fifteen million people crossed the newly-formed borders. In the 1960s over 100,000 Tibetans sought asylum in India. They still live here, mostly in settlements and enjoying almost the same facilities as Indian citizens.

The refugee population of India comprises people mainly from the countries of Tibet, Sri Lanka, Bangladesh and Afghanistan. As of 1997, there were nearly 2,60,000 refugees living in India and the refugee population has remained more or less stable in the last decade of the previous century. In the recent past, 12000 refugees fled to India from Sri Lanka. There are at present 65000 refugees from Sri Lanka in 133 camps in Tamil Nadu, in addition to an unspecified number who live outside the camp.

An information worth mentioning here is that India is not a party to the United Nations Refugee Convention and Protocol, and like the rest of Asia, has no domestic refugee laws. Refugees are treated like other aliens under the Foreigners Act and the Passport Act and are subject to domestic laws governing the entry and stay of foreigners.

Refugee problems are handled on the basis of administrative policies which, though ad hoc in nature, are broadly in line with international refugee law principles. Aid to refugees is generally regarded as humanitarian work. As it has been expressed, "Refugee constitutes one of the powerful labels currently in the repertoire of humanitarian concern". Most of the people can look at their own governments to guarantee and protect their basic rights and security. But in the case of refugees, the country of origin has proved itself unable or unwilling to protect those rights. Deprived of the protection by their country, detached form their families and communities or origin, refugees form a group vulnerable to violence, abuse and victimization of basic human rights.

Infants and children are often the earliest and most frequent victims of violence, disease and malnutrition, which accompany population displacement. A host of studies in war zones around the world, including Jaffna, testify to traumatisation and other extreme adverse effects on children resulting from the ravages of war.

Simple Characteristics

The sample consisted of thirty children with an almost equal number of male (46.9 per cent) and female (53.1 per cent) respondents. All the children were educated or undergoing schooling. Except for one, all are born Sri Lankan citizens. Majority (90.6 per cent) of them have migrated to India before 1994. While in Sri Lanka their parents have either been farmers (31.3 per cent), fishermen (21.9 per cent), tailors (31.3 per cent) or businessmen and their economic conditions while in Sri Lanka was on the whole stable for a large majority (84.4 per cent) of the sample.

Overall Discussion

Victimization in the life of a refugee starts even before he is labelled a refugee. Children are victimized at all levels of their lives, plunging into a future of total darkness.

The trauma undergone by the Sri Lankan children has been assessed here in different stages namely, before migration (while in their homes in Sri Lanka), during migration (the process of shifting to the host country) and after migration (in the camps at the host country).

Impact of Victimisation Before Migration

Although the problems of refugees have become more distinct in the recent times, it cannot be understood without a historical perspective.

A small country with a population of only 18 million, Sri Lanka is one of the largest principal sources of refugees and displaced persons. The origin of flow of refugees can generally be seen in the light of fundamental historical and social processes. The formation of a nation state has been an important process in the case of the Sri Lankan refugees.

Traumatic Experiences and Psychosocial Outcomes

While in Sri Lanka, during the war, the children have been victimized in several ways. They have starved without food (74.2 per cent) and have been shelterless for days (84.4 per cent), unable to go out to the market place (51.6 per cent) or to entertainment or cultural activities (29 per cent) or visit the temple (58.1 per cent) and most of all not being able to attend school (74.2 per cent). Worst, though only a negligible percentage, is that 12.9 per cent of the sample have been sexually abused by the soldiers, that is sexual abuse other than rape, and an equally small percentage (6.5 per cent) have been exposed to sexual abuse. Out of the total sixteen girls who formed part of the sample, there was one rape victim.

Two children were exposed to rape of one of their family members by the soldiers and three children have lost a sibling during the war. About 15.6 per cent of the children have been physically injured during the war. There was a case of an adolescent boy who had lost his leg as a result of the war.

As regards PTSD, interestingly, majority of the children (83.9 per cent) recollect not having experienced any confusion in thinking. This is perhaps true because, firstly they were too young at the time of travel and second reason is one that can be peculiar to Sri Lankan refugees. War has been an everyday happening for all of them as many have been born and brought up in a war-torn situation. Since their birth, they have bitter experiences of witnessing the flee of their friends, relatives and other people most frequently and suddenly. Becuse of such experiences, these children do not understand the context in which their friends and relatives were forced to leave their motherland and the consequences which they are going to face. Hence these children had more excitement than apprehension on leaving their own country.

The homes are vacated overnight and the families flee their houses leaving behind most of their movable and all their immovable properties. In a few families (9.4 per cent), the parents are unable to go with the children for various reasons like lack of finance, etc., have sent only the children either with relatives or neighbour.

There was a case of a family who had lost their parents in the war and the neighbours when fleeing had brought these children with them to Tamil Nadu.

Migration is an expensive matter for these families. Especially when they are large families, as most of them are, migration financially drains them—expenses include charges for packing and transporting their luggage and for their own transportation by boat (93.8 per cent) to the host country. It is during these times that almost all of them have starved for three to four days and wąlked miles to reach the place of embarkation. The children have trekked behind their parents, carrying loads on their backs facing the sun and rain.

Many of the children have expressed that though they were initially excited about going to a foreign country, while crossing the sea they panicked and some of them have also witnessed boats being capsized and many of them being drowned. These scenes come often to their minds leading to depression and isolation. As to PTSD, some of them have expressed having felt certain physical symptoms whole on migration like excessive sweating, increased heart beat, etc. This could also be due to anxiety of travelling abroad and the mode of travelling, which is by boat in the middle of the night.

Nearly all of those who feel this change agreed that their parents did spend time with them and they care for them. They agree that they provide them with all basic necessities.

The change in their behaviour is attributed to alcohol usage in nearly three-fourths of the parents, sixty per cent of these parents also encourage and force their children to abuse alcohol. However, engaging in criminal behaviour by the parents is negligible. They do not physically abuse the children or force them to overwork or prevent them from attending school. A common problem felt by nearly fifty per cent of the children was that their parents were overprotection about them.

Most commonly the family members fall sick, after the tedious travel and the environmental conditions that are prevalent in the camp. This puts a financial pressure on them forcing them to borrow money from money lenders, who exploit the refugees. The interest mounts and in return the money lender offers a job for the mother, where she ente0rtains and provides sex to her clients. As days go by the mother is replaced with the well-grown daughter and the cycle continues. The mothers are offered work abroad as housekeepers. They send their earnings to their children in the camp.

The children feel that their parents refuse to start life afresh (56.3 per cent). A majority of them (68.8 per cent) feel that their parents are depressed most of the time, are under economic pressure (59.5 per cent) and suffer from cultural alienation (75 per cent).

Contributing to this significant malaise in the Sri Lankan community is the trauma of the early nineties during which period most of the parent generation suffered terribly. Almost all of them have experienced the destruction of family members. They still bear the burden of the previous life of terror, starvation and relentless stress.

Socialization, as in any other child, is therefore lacking. They do not have relatives or friends to visit. Therefore, the kind of affection and love a normal child of that age gets out of socialization with the family, relatives, the peer group and the school is lacking for the refugee children. Further to this is the fact that they have a lot of spare time. Therefore, boys in their adolescence and girls just around their teens look to each other for love, affection and sex. Another important point that brings them on the same ground as other children of their age is the mass media. Television is the most common and most accessible form of entertainment to these children. They normally watch two to three movies per day on their own video decks or on common decks. This further instills feelings like love and sex in them.

When the parents oppose to a marriage between them, the children usually resort to attempting suicide either by burning themselves or jumping into a well. Getting married when young is a fad among these children. This brings them a lot of attention from other camp members and friends who look upon them as role models, thus increasing the chain. Another interesting factor is that, these children belong to broken home families. They are either single parent families or one where the parents, most often the mother,is working in a foreign land. The children get married with or without their family's consent The girls stop their schooling from the time of marriage and start having children at a tender age of 13-15 years. A factor worth contemplating about is that, these children who get married do not believe in birth control. Their ultimate motive is to produce as many children as possible and rebuild their lost empire in Sri Lanka.

Surprisingly, a majority of the children (83.9 per cent) do not need any financial help at present. An equal percentage of them feel that educational facilities should be improved. Majority of them (71 per cent) are satisfied with the kind of medical facilities offered but feel the condition of housing and sanitation should be improved (71 per cent).

The statistical records show that a great number of refugees have indeed received help from domestic and international organization. It is considered that the cooperation on behalf of refugees has saved many millions of human lives, and that it provides a rare example of cooperation among governments for the purpose of giving direct assistance to individuals. Even though organizations on behalf of refugees do not bring peace and security to the world; it is emphasized that they do at least give protection and relief to a number of human beings.

Conclusion

The word 'refugee' tends to evoke images of a sprawling camp, housing large numbers of distressed and impoverished people who had to escape from their own country at short notice and with nothing but the clothes on their back. This perception is very true.

It is here that the refugee families of Sri Lanka wait for the day when it is safe enough for them to go back to their homes and resume a normal way of life.

The Sri Lankan refugee children, in all probabilities, do not seem to suffer the kind of victimization child refugees from Bosnia of the Soviet Union do. They have their own unique stand, based on historical and cultural aspects and the duration of the wars.

Although it is impossible to reach out to the thousands of Sri Lankan children who participate and will be participating in the armed conflicts, we can divert the energies of the young in these camps to go back, not as grown-up citizens to die at war but as useful citizens to develop their nation.

What we, here, can probably do is to understand them not as a threat to us but as threatened victims themselves. Public opinion can go a long way towards encouraging governments to adopt policies that could be helpful to them.

There are particularly vulnerable individuals in each refugee situation and for the Sri Lankans it is their young citizens. Special attention is being given by local and international bodies in various ways but what they need is not just an asylum or facilities for their physical survival. They need to be understood as a "unique community with unique needs"—this in turn will safeguard the welfare of the host country too.

Sample Characteristics

Variable	Categories	Freq.	Percentage
Sex	Male	15	46.9
	Female	16	53.1
	TOTAL	31	100.0
Educational Qualification	Below 5th Std.	4	12.9
	5th-10th Std.	17	54.8
	Above 10th Std.	10	32.3
	TOTAL	31	100.0
Year of Migration	Before 1994	29	90.6
	1994-1999	2	9.4
	TOTAL	31	100.0
Employment Status of Parents in Sri Lanka	Fishermen	7	22.6
	Agriculturists	10	32.3
	Tailors	1	3.2
	Businessmen	7	22.6
	Others	6	19.1
	TOTAL	31	100.0
Employment Status of Parents in Tamil Nadu	Tailors	3	9.7
	Wage labourers	9	29.0
	Businessmen	2	7.5
	Unemployed	8	25.8
	Others	9	29.0
	TOTAL	31	100.0

VICTIMIZATION OF CHILD REFUGEES

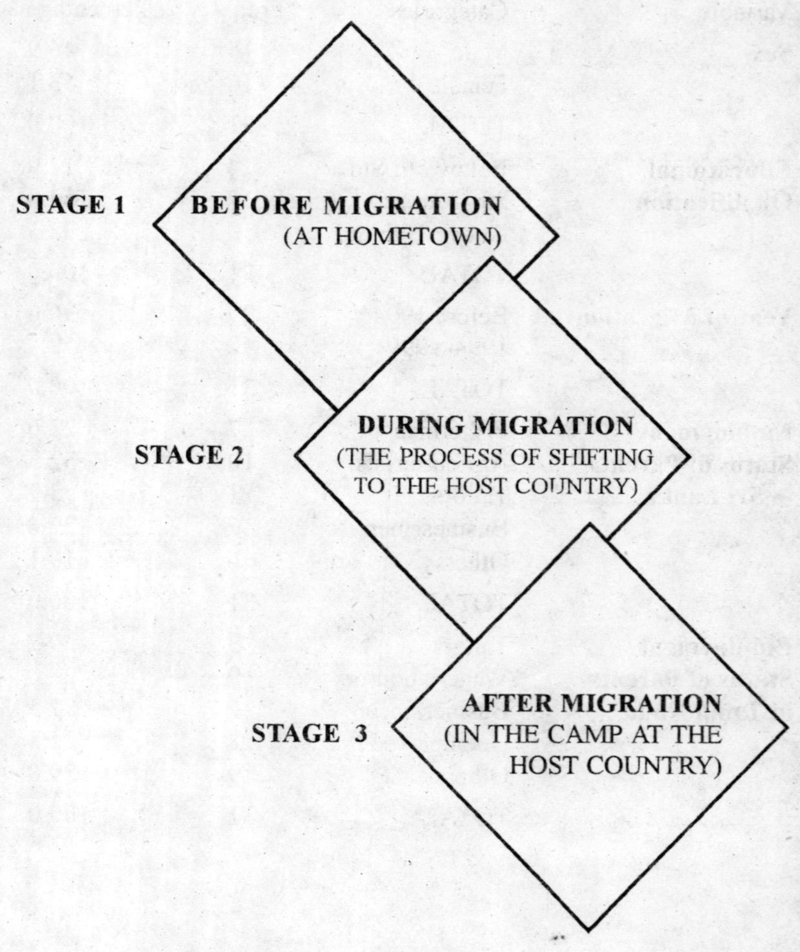

STAGE 1

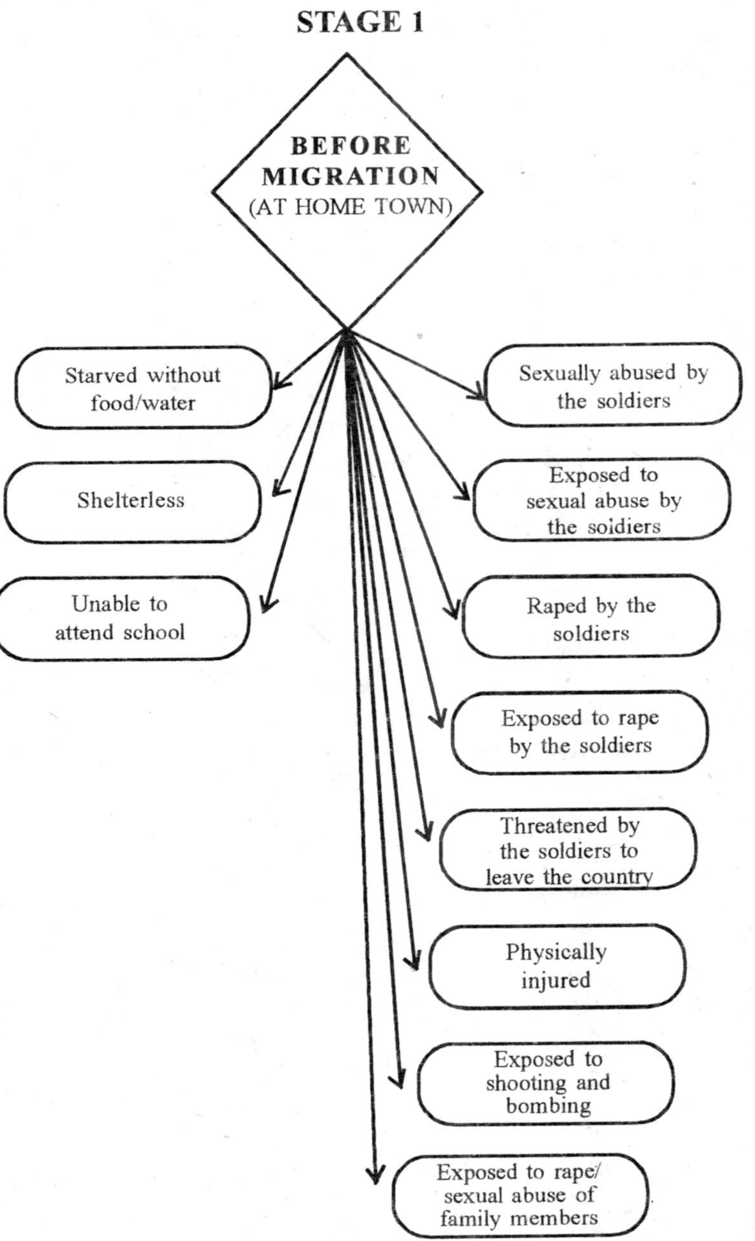
BEFORE
MIGRATION
(AT HOME TOWN)
Starved without food/water
Shelterless
Unable to attend school
Sexually abused by the soldiers
Exposed to sexual abuse by the soldiers
Raped by the soldiers
Exposed to rape by the soldiers
Threatened by the soldiers to leave the country
Physically injured
Exposed to shooting and bombing
Exposed to rape/ sexual abuse of family members

STAGE 2

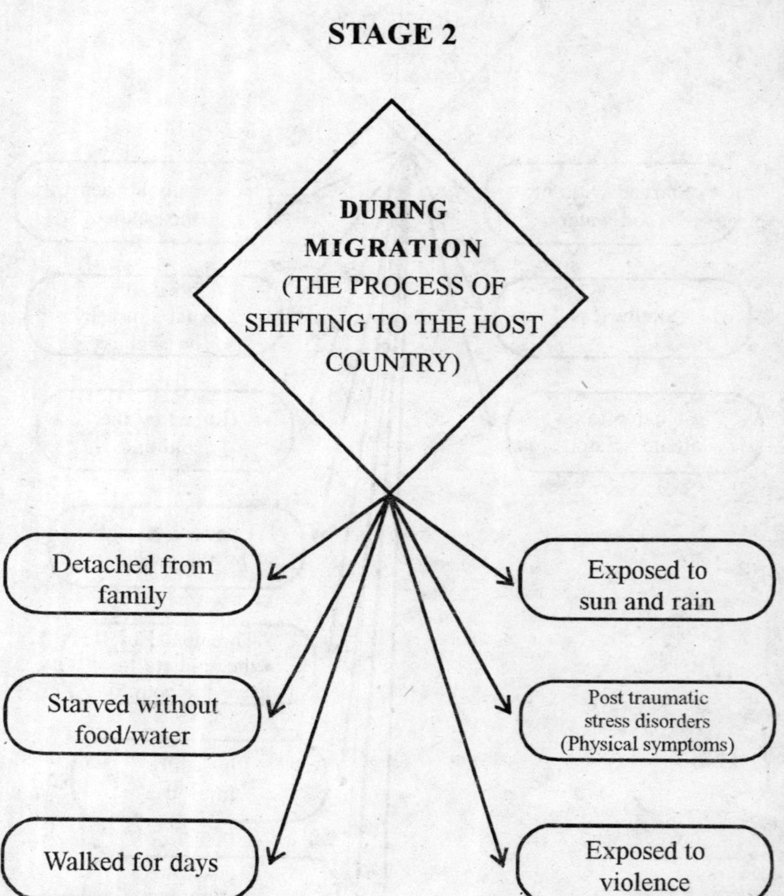
DURING
MIGRATION
(THE PROCESS OF
SHIFTING TO THE HOST
COUNTRY)
Detached from
family
Starved without
food/water
Walked for days
Exposed to
sun and rain
Post traumatic
stress disorders
(Physical symptoms)
Exposed to
violence

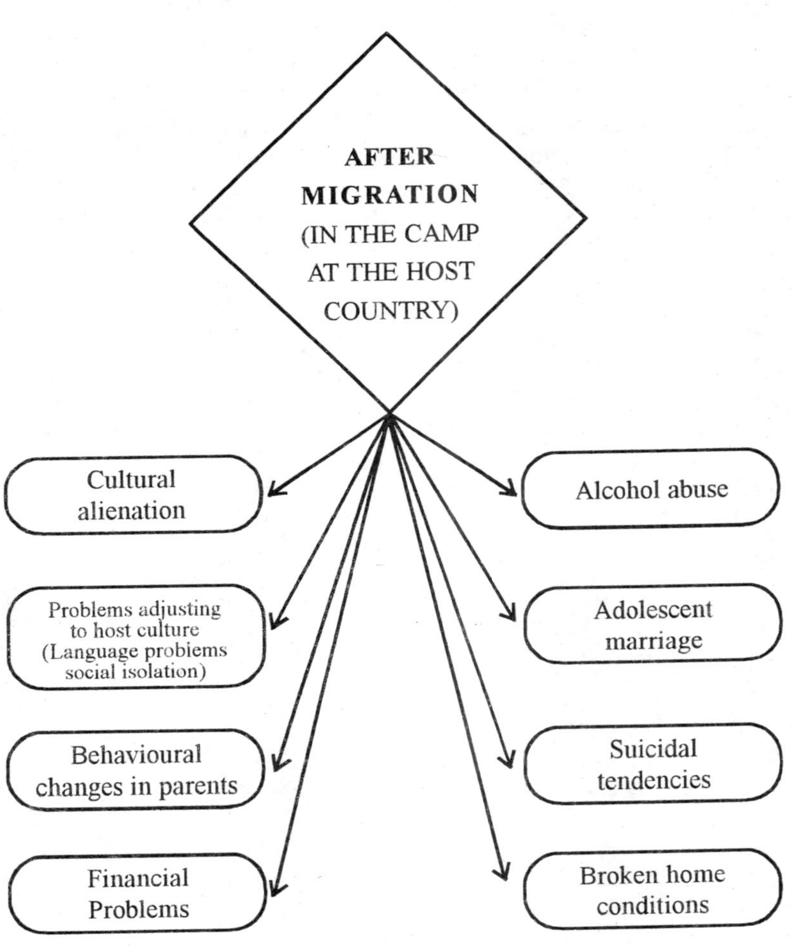
STAGE 3
AFTER MIGRATION (IN THE CAMP AT THE HOST COUNTRY)
Cultural alienation
Problems adjusting to host culture (Language problems social isolation)
Behavioural changes in parents
Financial Problems
Alcohol abuse
Adolescent marriage
Suicidal tendencies
Broken home conditions

References

1. Gill, Guy Goodwin and Cohn Ilene, 1994, Child Soldiers—The Role of Children in Armed Conflicts, A Study on behalf of the Henry Dunant Institute, Geneva, Clarendon Press, Oxford.
2. Salomon, Kim, 1991 Refugees in the Cold War, Lund University Press, Sweden.
3. United Nations High Commissioner for Refugees (UNHCR), June 1996, Human Rights and Refugee Protection, PartII, Specific Issues.
4. United Nations High Commissioner for Refugees (1997-98), The State of the World's Refugees: A Humanitarian Agenda, Oxford University Press.

NINE

ISSUES OF ALCOHOLIC PARENTS

Despite newer knowledge about child development, we seem to have made little progress in applying our minds to the task of understanding the victimization of children affected by their parents' behavioural problems due to alcohol abuse.

Since World War II, social scientists have been conceptualising child development based on the nature of the parent-child relationship. This relationship often called 'bonding' is a vital aspect in child development, one that develops subsequent relationships with family members and ultimately the world at large. Since the child, after birth, is dependent on the parents for a long period of time there evolves a biological repertoire of behaviours, to 'connect' physically, emotionally and psychologically with parents. The connection is not only oral, it is tactile, olfactory, visual and auditory as well (Bowlby, 1958). A child is stimulated by, shaped by, and focused on the parent from the first moments of life. Most of the parents care for their children adequately enough so that children survive. When either one or both the parents become an alcoholic stupor, for various reasons, there occurs a failure or aberration in the normal parent-child bond and the consequent development of psychological, emotional and behavioural problems in the child. Alcoholism is a 'family disease', which affects not only the user but also every member of his or her family. Alcoholics do not drink or recover in isolation. When one person in a family develops alcoholism, the others react to it often with confusion, fear, despair and blame. Alcohol disrupts the consistency and predictability, which should be present in every family. The children, especially, are 'trapped' and left emotionally and situationally helpless. This study attempts to understand and evaluate the intensity and effect of those problems in a growing child.

The Webster's New Dictionary, defines alcoholism as "the habitual excessive drinking of alcoholic liquor, or a resulting diseased condition".

Children of alcoholics face special problems as a result of living in a home disrupted by alcohol problems. No statistical estmiations are available on children of alcoholic parents in India. In the U.S., it is estimated that seven million children out of the total twenty-eight million under the age of eighteen years, live in households with at least one alcoholic parent (Prevention Resource Guide: Children of Alcoholics, 1991).

A child loses his childhood when he lives with an alcoholic parent. To others, he looks like any other child, dresses like any other child does, walks like any other child, until they get close enough to notice the edge of sadness in his eyes, or the worried look on his brow. He lives life from the standpoint of a victim.

The Study

The study was conducted in the city of Chennai. The sample consisted of twenty-eight children of both sexes chosen using purposive sampling technique. The sample consisted of just twenty-five per cent males and seventy per cent females in the age group of 11-13 years (25 per cent) and 14-16 years, (68 per cent). Two schools from the North and South of Chennai were chosen for the study. The teachers in these two schools were interviewed initially and asked to identify the children who belong to families with alcoholic parents. An interview schedule formed the tool of the study, which was administered to the children independently. The collected data was analysed using appropriate statistical techniques. The results are presented along with the discussion.

Results and Discussion

The analysis of the data clearly indicates the various aspects of the victimization of children of alcoholic parents. The effect of these victimizations on the life of the child has been discussed and supported by the results.

Effect of Parental Alcoholism on the Parent-Child Relationship

Majority of the children have expressed their love to spend time with their families (80 per cent). Most of them have meals often along with other members of the family (71.4 per cent). The remaining children avoid having meals along with the family. This is probably due to the fact that they do not want to face the alcoholic parent. Nearly half (46.4 per cent) of the children make their own decisions normally and the remaining depend on their parents. Majority of the parents do not go to the movies (64.3 per cent), clubs (100 per cent), or to parties (42.9 per cent).

Research studies show that alcoholic fathers are sometimes very loving and warm. They are caring and interested and promise to get the children all that they want. But, once he is under the influence of alcohol, the same father comes home late, getting the child worried, picks up quarrels and forgets the promises he's made. The parent's behaviour teaches the child that anger means violence, promises can be made but not necessarily kept and creates a dilemma as to what love is all about. They have problems in building positive relationships. In order to cope with these problems, the child resorts to a behaviour different form other children. Majority of the fathers are working in private firms (39.3 per cent) or run their own business (21.4 per cent). More than half the mothers are housewives (56.7 per cent). A small percentage of mothers work in private firms.

Contrary to other research findings that such children usually deny the fact that their parents abuse alcohol, 92.9 per cent of the children agreed to alcohol abuse by their parents. Majority of the parents have been alcohol users for more than 5 years (75 per cent). The major reason for the abuse is bad company (28.6 per cent). and extra-marital affairs (21.4 per cent) of their parents. The children (60.7 per cent) agree that the abuse of alcohol by the parents making their home life unhappy. Compared with non-alcoholic families, research has shown that, alcoholic families demonstrate poorer problem-solving abilities within the family. This increases conflicts in alcoholic families. Further based on clinical observations and preliminary research, a relationship between parental alcoholism and child abuse is indicated in a large proportion of child abuse families.

Effect of Parental Alcoholism on the Children's Education

Majority of the children attend school regularly (82.1 per cent) and like going to school (93 per cent). The main reason for not attending school are ill-health (7 per cent) and not feeling good enough to attend school (7 per cent). Majority of the children are average (53.6 per cent) or below average (36.7 per cent) in their studies. The teachers while identifying the children for the study also stated that these children have a poor academic record. More than half of the sample revealed that even while at school they think and worry about their parents. This affects their concentration in class.

Majority of the children (75 per cent) stares blankly at the black board when the classes are in progress. Surprisingly, 68 per cent of the children get their uniforms ready for school and pack their school bags all by themselves (85.7 per cent). The aspect of learning to be independent is evident here. A small percentage (6.7 per cent) of the children get academic help from their fathers. The rest of them either get help from their mothers (28 per cent) or study by themselves (64.3 per cent). Teachers of these children reported that most of these children are hyperactive and indulge in behaviour that seeks attention and provokes anger. They also have difficulty in remembering and completing their schoolwork.

A child's personality and reaction to parental alcohol dependence is unique. One child may fail in class but another may, to escape strees, study hard for perfect grades. In this sample, all the children are probably affected in a negative way, in that they fair not too well in their studies. Informal discussions with the children revealed that they feel they will be failures even if they do well academically. They often do not view themselves successful.

Psychosomatic Effects of Parental Alcoholism on the Child

Children of alcoholic parents are known to experience greater physical and mental health problems than children of non-alcoholic parents. In this study, forty-two per cent of the children fall sick often. Further, children of alcoholics have physical problems like headaches (33.3 per cent), tiredness (35.7 per cent) and stomach ulcer (16.7 per cent), although no specific illnesses are detected. They do not have nausea or enuresis as some children do. They also do not have any problems to sleep or symptoms of asthma. A quarter of the sample have sensory problems related to noise, bright light, heat and cold more often than other children.

Effect of Parental Alcoholism on the Child's Behaviour

A good portion (28.6 per cent) of the children have taken up the household chores and duties that the alcoholic parents performed. Some young children from alcoholic families are known to become exceedingly responsible, taking on parental roles towards their siblings and others. Responsible children usually take over the responsibilities of their parents. These children provide stability in the family and make life easier for the parents by looking after their siblings. They are independent, self-reliant and capable of achievements. They gain an 'early maturity' out of a need for survival.

Nearly fifteen per cent of the children have tried alcohol at some stage in their lives. Nearly ninety per cent of them consume alcohol rarely. There is a strong evidence that alcoholism tends to run in families. Children of alcoholics are more at risk for alcoholism than children of non-alcoholics.

Unlike results obtained from other studies, the children maintain close friends outside the school (64.3 per cent). They do not withdraw from their friends because of embarrassment and shame over the parent's drinking habit. Less than half (42.9 per cent) of the children are engaged in frequent fights with the other children. These children probably get irritated easily or show their anger or resentment on the parent by engaging in fights.

The children of alcoholic families generally feel that they are responsible for their parent's alcoholism. They need to recognize that drinking causes their parent's strange and unpredictable behaviour. In this study, a majority of them (67.9 per cent) do not feel that they are in any way responsible for their parent's behaviour.

A lot of them (67.9 per cent) have not made any attempt to stop their parent from using alcohol. This is either because they are too young to make this move or that the parent's behaviour frightens them.

In spite of the parent being an alcoholic, the children wish to look upon him/her as a role model in their lives(57.1 per cent). Children are not born with standards of evaluating behaviour. They are unable to decide what is right and wrong. When a parent under the influence of alcohol behaves in a certain way, the child 'copies' the behaviour of his/her parent. Even while at play, these children act the way the parent behaves. There are also chances that they will grow up to be alcoholics and resort to the behaviour as that of the parent, for example, physical abuse of spouse and children, verbal abuse, lying and cheating, etc.

Psychological Effects of Parental Alcoholism on the Children

Studies reveal that the family members of alcoholics—including children—are high-risk candidates for chronic depression, psychosomatic illness, social aggression, emotional detachment, isolation and suicide.

The children of alcoholics are isolated. They learn at an early age never to talk about what goes on in their homes. They are hence likely to develop emotional and psychological problems. Majority of the children in this study, that is 83.3 per cent, have low self-esteem and 71.4 per cent have high-level of aggression. Self-esteem was measured using the Rosenberg Self-esteem Scale (1965). The scale aims at gathering information on self-opinion, worthiness, successfulness and self-respect. A scale to measure aggression was constructed by the reseacher. Items for aggression instincts to kill, cause injury, take revenge, to fight, blame others for things, etc. Children with low self-esteem have negative self-image and poor self-concept. They do not believe in themselves or others and feels that they have nobody to depend on. No matter what effort they put in they feel it is depreciated.

Conclusion and Recommendation

The disease called 'Alcoholism' can rob a child of his childhood and destroy the opportunities he might have to a bright future. Children can be protected from many problems associated with the growing up in an alcoholic family. If healthy family rituals or traditions such as vacations, meal times, holidays, are highly valued and maintained and the active alcoholic is confronted with his or her problems, the child can be protected from many consequences of parental alcoholism. Efforts should be taken to improve the self-esteem of identified child. It is sometimes possible to identify child of alcoholic parent and provide intervention services. If the parent is receiving treatment, preventive services such as monitoring can be provided for the child through family counselling. Prevention activities can include information on alcoholism and resources so that assistance can be given to children of alcoholic parents through schools or community agencies. Any programme which aims at prevention of alcoholism should include parents as their target group. Educating and creating awareness about effective parenting would help develop a healthy and positive parent-child relationship. This would pave the way for a child's trouble-free, addiction-free future.

References

1. Ministry of Welfare, Government of India, New Delhi, 1989, Alcoholism and Drug Dependency—The Professional's Master Guide.
2. Nastasi, Bonnie K. and DeZolt, Denise M, 1994, School interventions of children of Alcoholics Addictions, ISBN.
3. Prevention Resource Guide: Children of Alcoholics, 1991.

TEN

STRATEGIES AND INNOVATIONS

Our criminal justice system is tilled in favour of the accused and the real victims of crime have by and large remained out of focus of the welfare agencies, government and judicial system. An overview of the plight of crime victims reveals that while the criminal justice system in west is getting geared unto espousing the cause of crime victims, in India the victims of crime remain neglected at every stage i.e.—investigation, trial, prosecution and most importantly their own rehabilitation. The victim is perceived merely as an object, a piece of evidence in the conviction of the offender. Our system provides little succour to alleviate the trauma and pathetic living conditions of crime victims.

It is mostly seen that the child victims are the most ignored category. For every horrendous tale of abuse and violence against young children that gets reported in the news columns, there are thousands others who shed silent tears, their cries for help unheard and their pain unnoticed. The increasing incidence of assaults on children, whether physical, emotional or sexual, is symptomatic of the violence that is pervading our society across all sections and classes. Child victimisation may range from the milder cases of neglect deprivation, verbal or emotional abuse, to the extremes of physical battering, maiming or even appalling sexual crimes like rape and incest. Victimisation of child has often been thought as the sickness of an industrialised and/or developed society. However, recent literature in India, though sparse and frequently subjective, has indicated that we have little to congratulate ourselves. Child victimisation evokes societal responses that are sharp and emotional. We need to consider this phenomenon dispassionately and objectively.

This article attempts to discuss the phenomenon in the light of experience and information gathered by Pratidhi in the course of its intervention with victims of child abuse. We begin by discussing the concepts interrelated to child abuse and its various manifestations. Finally, we end by describing some of the issues associated in intervention. Based on the experiences of Pratidhi, we feel, some generalisations may be made about possible professional and informed interventions in such cases and the factors which may be borne in mind while doing so.

Clarification, Definition and Categories

Any attempt to define and clarify the concept of child abuse runs into several difficulties. Firstly, the concept has largely been clarified in western contexts where it has been extensively studied. Secondly, there is some lack of clarity and specificity in the use of the term. To some extent, this is because of the multidisciplinary nature of the issue. Consequently, medical writers refer to "child battering" which focuses on the physical aspects, social workers to "child neglect" which focuses on the need for intervention, psychiatrists/psychologists to "child abuse" which connotes emotional aspects of the situation. Quite often, the terms "child battering", "child neglect", "child abuse", "child maltreatment", "physical abuse", are used by different authors to refer to the same situation.

At the very outset, let us define "child matreatment" since this forms a starting point for our inquiry. Child maltreatment is a generic phrase that covers a whole range of behaviour. ".... It covers all behaviour patterns, whether or not sanctioned by law and custom, which are in some way injurious to the child's health or social, economic, emotional or moral well-being."

Child abuse and neglect comprises a wide range of behaviour distinguised conceptually as well as operationally. For analytical purposes, such behaviour has been categorised under broad categories. It is to be noted that these are not mutually exclusive categories. For example, child prostitution may be categorised as child exploitation as well as child sexual abuse. Some of the broad categories are as follows.

Child Neglect: This occurs when parents or guardians fail to perform their duties and obligations which fall under responsibility. This includes denial of food, shelter, clothing, medical care education and toilet facilities or total abandonment.

Child Exploitation: This is a form of child abuse which yields some economic benefits to the perpetrator or someone else. Specifically, this occurs when a child is made to engage in economic activities which are harmful to its physical, social, psychological and moral development. This may take the form of employing children as servants, as street beggars, as child prostitutes, as hawkers, as apprentices, etc.

Child Battering: This occurs when, due to any physical abuse or non-accidental injury, the child rquires medical attention and treatment or leaves bruises. However, it has to be noted that physical punishment, as a disciplinary measure for bad behaviour, is accepted and often encouraged in many cultures.

However, punishment, physical or non-physical, becomes maltreatment when: it is too harsh for the child's age, or physical and emotional state; it runs against the community's norms and value orientations; and it is any way detrimental to the child's well-being and proper development.

Child Abuse: This occurs when ".... a parent or guardian knowingly misuses a privileged position over the child to commit acts 'of non-economic nature' which are not in tune with the societal forms and which are detrimental to the child's health and well-being." At a National Seminar on Child Abuse in India (1998, NIPCCD), the following was offered as a definition: "Child Abuse and Neglect (CAN) is the intentional, non-accidental injury, maltreatment of children by parents, caretakers, employers or others including those individuals representing governmental/non-governmental bodies, which may lead to temporary or permanent impairment of their physical, mental and psycho-social development, disability or death."

Child abuse may consist of any of the forms: Physical Abuse, Social Abuse, Emotional Abuse, Drug Abuse and Sexual Abuse.

Sexual abuse refers to any sexual act being misuse of the child by any care-taking or family related adult. This includes acts of incest, oral-genital contact, sodomy, molestation, etc. Sexual abuse can be physical, verbal or emotional and includes: fondling, exposing children to adult sexual activity or pornography, having children pose, undress or perform in a sexual fashion, "peeping" into bathrooms or bedrooms to spy on children and attempting rape.

Thus, it is seen from the above discussion that child abuse and neglect incorporates a wide range of behaviour ranging from simple neglect to sexual abuse and even murder.

It is, thus, obvious that our discussion of child abuse would cover a very wide range of behaviour. In view of this wide range, and for operational clarity, we shall focus on sexual abuse of children. However, the importance of inter-agency co-operation and role of parents in protecting children has also been discussed. The foregoing has been largely to emphasize that we are aware of other dimensions of child abuse and also to place our specific focus in a framework.

Some Facts about Child Sexual Abuse

Mostly, child sexual abuse is committed by someone who knows the child. The offender is usually a family member, trusted friend, acquaintance, person who regularly comes into contact with the child or a relative.

Sexual abuse often starts with a long process where harmless touching gradually crosses over the line to fondling. The child may not realize that fondling has become inappropriate.

Physcal force is seldom used because the child usually trusts or depends upon the offender. Physical evidence or injuries occur in only a small percentage of child sexual abuse cases.

Children who have been sexually abused feel many different and often overwhelming emotions. These can be put under following expression of feelings: Fear, Anger, Isolation, Sadness, Guilt, Shame, Confusion.

Protecting Children

Role of Agencies Involved in Child Protection

This section deals with the role of the agencies and other associated groups in relation to child protection and how their duties and functions should be organised in order to contribute to inter- agency co-operation for the protection of children. The responsibility for protecting children should not fall entirely to one agency: awareness and appreciation of another agency's role will contribute greatly to collaborative practices.

Social Services

The child protection work of social services departments should be considered in the wider context of all the department's work and more precisely in the context of its child care services. Field workers engaged in child protection work are also involved in a wide range of other child care work and they often work with other client groups. They are aware of the wide child care facilities provided and known to the department and can draw on these in order to provide support and treatment services for children who have been abused. These include day care facilities, residential accommodation and foster homes.

Police

It is usual for the police to dissuade the victim from lodging a report on many grounds. For the reason, few cases get reported/ highlighted and the entire vicious circle of non-reporting results in increase of abuse cases. The importance of police action in child abuse cases is such that even if there is no clear scope for prosecution, the process of police action in itself is going to be of great value in deterring offenders.

The police involvement in cases of child abuse stems from their primary responsibility to protect the community and to bring offenders to justice. Their overriding consideration is the welfare of the child. In the spirit of working together, the police focus should determine whether a criminal offence has been committed, to identify the person or persons responsible and to secure the best possible evidence in order that appropriate consideration can be given as to whether criminal proceedings should be instituted. Failure to conduct child abuse investigations in the most effective manner may mean that the best possible protection cannot be provided for a child victim.

The decision whether or not criminal proceedings should be initiated should be based on three main factors: whether or not there is sufficient substantial evidence to prosecute; whether it is in the public interest that proceedings should be initiated against a particular offender; and whether or not it is in the interests of the child victim that proceedings should be instituted.

The evidential requirement of the criminal courts is proof beyond reasonable doubt that the defendant committed the offence of which he/she stands indicted. The burden of proof rests with the prosecution, i.e., the defendant does not have to prove his innocence. It is usual for the police to decide that criminal proceedings cannot be initiated against a person.

Police/Social Services Consultation

Although in cases of child victimsation, both the police and social services have as their foremost objective the welfare of the child, their primary functions, powers and methods of working are entirely different. Whilst the police should focus on the investigation of alleged offences, the social services are concerned with the welfare of the child and other members of the family.

Difficulties will be encountered in joint inter-agency investigations but these can be minimised by the selection of specialist staff who undergo appropriate inter-agency training. However, it is essential that methods of joint working are established between the two agencies over and above the joint interviewing of child victims. There should be agreed procedures for the joint inter-agency investigation process which ensures that there is adequate planning and full consultation at all stages of any investigation. It is important that those engaged in child victimisation investigation and their supervisors fully understand the responsibilities of both agencies, the powers available to them and the different standards of proof that exist in relation to criminal and civil proceedings. This will assist to remove some of the tensions that can otherwise exist.

Health

All those working in the field of health have a commitment to protect children, and their participation in inter-agency support to social services departments is essential if the interests of children are to be safeguarded. Health professionals are major contributors to the inter-agency care of children which extends beyond the initial referral and assessment, participation in planning and the on-going support of the child and family. There will always be a need for close co-operation with other agencies, including any other health professionals involved.

Probation Service

Probationary officers may become involved in cases of child victimisation as a result either of their responsibility for the supervision of offenders, including those convicted of offences against children, or of their responsibility to the court for the supervision of children. They may be able to identify potential cases and bring in other agencies when, through their work, they become concerned about the safety of a child.

The Education Service

The education service does not constitute an investigation or intervention agency, but has an important role to play at the recognition and referral stage. Because of their day-to-day contact with individual children during school terms, teachers and other school staff are particularly well-placed to observe outward signs of abuse, changes in behaviour or failure to develop. School social workers and counsellors also have important roles because of their concern for the welfare and development of children.

Other Voluntary Organisations

A wide range of voluntary organisation provide services, including telephone helplines, to help parents, guardians under stress and children at risk. Some of these are national, such as Childline, which provide counselling for children with problems and help children in distress. Authorities should be alert to the opportunities to promote voluntary efforts in their area, and ensure that there is good liaison with voluntary organisations. Staff in these and other voluntary services concerned with children and families can also help by bringing children who are thought to be in need of protection to the attention of the statutory agencies—such as, Juvenile Welfare Board, Department of Social Welfare, etc.

The Community

The community as a whole has a responsibility for the well-being of children. This means that all citizens should remain alert to circumstances in which children may be harmed. Individuals can assist the statutory authorities by bringing cases to their attention. Relatives, friends and neighbours of children are particularly well- placed to do so, but they must know what to do if they are concerned, in addition to providing support for the family and children, which may include help with caring for children. They must also be confident, because of the difficult and sensitive nature of the situation, that any information they provide will be treated in a confidential way and used only to protect the interests of children. They should know too that early action on their part is often the best way of helping a family stay together as well as protecting children.

Role of Parents

Quite obviously, parents have a major and significant role in the prevention of sexual abuse of children. Their role cannot be balanced by any amount of professional intervention. Quite often, shameful incidents of sexual abuse take place because of parents taking the safety of their children for granted. However, this is not to imply that all incidents of sexual abuse are caused by the carelessness of parents. Such an assumption would lead to harmful feelings of guilt and all that those feelings may entail. Nevertheless, we list out here some elementary measures/responses that parents can adopt to prevent sexual abuse and also to respond in a helpful manner once the child indicates that she has been thus abused.

Sexual abusers can make the child extremely fearful of telling, and only a special effort can help the child to feel safe and talk freely.

As concerned adults, we want to prevent children from sexual abuse, but we cannot always be there to do that. We can, however, teach children about sexual abuse in order to increase their awareness and coping skills without frightening children, we can provide them with appropriate safety information and support at every stage of their development. We can provide personal safety information to children in a matter-of-fact way, with other routine safety discussion about fire, water, health, hygiene, etc. Although even the best educated child cannot always avoid sexual abuse, children who are well-prepared will be more likely to tell you if abuse has occurred. This is a child's best defence.

In this article, we have attempted to provide some basic information and leads for intervention. However, our focus here has not stressed professional intervention but rather intervention/response by parents, state agencies and voluntary sectors.

Reference

1. Ackley, Dana C.: *"A brief overview of child abuse"*, Social casework; Jan. 1997, pp. 21-24.
2. NIPCCD: *Report of National Seminar on Child Abuse in India;* New Delhi, NIPCCD, 1998.
3. Deblinger, E and Heflin, AH: *Treating Sexually Abused Children and Their Non-offending Parents;* New Delhi, Saga, 1996.
4. Late Michigan S.E.: *Report on Sexual Abuse of Children;* Deptt. of Social Work, Delhi University.
5. Wolfe, David A.: *Child Abuse: Implications for Child Development and Psychopathology;* New Delhi, Saga, 1987.
6. Home Office, Deptt. of Health, Deptt. of Education and Science, Welsh Office: Working Together—*A Guide to Arrangements for Co-operation for the Protection of Children from Abuse.* London, HMSO, 1991.
7. Hallet, C. and Stevenson, O.: *Child Abuse: Aspects of Interpersonal Cooperation;* London, George Allen & Unwin, 1980.
8. Tayley, Brain (Ed): *Perspectives on Paedophilia;* (London, Batsford, 1981).
9. Bhan, Sushila: *Child Abuse: An Annotated Bibilography;* New Delhi, Northern, 1991.

ELEVEN

VARIOUS FORMS AND PATTERNS

Any study on victims of crime poses two major problems. Firstly, official criminal justice records hardly provide any data on the victims since they logically relate to the offenders as principal clients. Secondly, the non-official surveys on crime victims which have so far been carried out mostly in developed countries are prone to some forms of "response error". In such a scenario, one can easily assume how difficult it is to highlight the problems of crime victims including victimisation of child in a developing country like India. There is no denying the fact that children in the developing countries are much more vulnerable to crime as compared to their counterparts in the developed countries primarily because of their sufferings from poverty and illiteracy on the one hand and inadequate state and societal responses to victimisation of child on the other. Keeping in view these major constraints, a modest endeavour has been made in this article to examine and analyse various forms and patterns of the victimisation of child with particular reference to the Indian context.

There is no uniform legal definition of 'child'. Different laws define it differently. Under the 1860 Indian Penal Code, child usually refers to a person under 12 years of age. The Juvenile Justice Act, 1986 defines 'juvenile' as a boy below the age of 16 years and a girl below the age of 18 years. Under Child Marriage Restraint Act, 1992 a male child means a person who has not attained 21 years of age while a female child is a person who is below 18 years of age. The Factories Act, 1958 and Child Labour (Prohibition and Regulation) Act, 1986 define child as a person who has not completed 14 years of age. Such varying legal definitions notwithstanding the commonly perceived norms prescribed a person below the age of 16 years as a child, between 16 and 18 years as a minor and above 18 years as a major. According to UN Convention on the Rights of the Child (CRC), every human being under 18 years is a child unless majority is attained earlier under national law.

Female Foeticide

Undoubtedly, the worst form of child victimisation is female foeticide as it results in the killing of a female child before she is born. It is most unfortunate that even after entering the new millennium, preference for the male child remains such a predominant socio-economic factor that in a large section of our society, including the middle and upper class, the female child, to quote an official of Indian Medical Association (IMA), " is still considered an avoidable social burden". The increasing misuse of technical advancement in medical science such as sex determination tests with ultra-sound scan is evident from the fact that the ratio of women to men has gone down from 927:1000 in 1901 to 972:1000 in the 1991 census which is 63% less than the world average. In Punjab and Haryana the unethical practice of sex determination tests and abortion of female foetuses appears to be so widespread that a 1997 survey showed the sex ratio having dipped to 750. A recent newspaper report outlines the following facts/data which are indeed a matter of great concern: • IMA activists estimate that 5 million female foeticide operations are conducted every year. • India has about 20,000 ultra-sound clinics, mostly unregistered and staffed by doctors unqualified to conduct these tests. • I n Punjab, Haryana and Uttar Pradesh mobile vans have taken such sex detection tests to the villages.

Female Infanticide

Female infanticide is another worse form of child victimisation which has been practised in our patriarchal, male chauvinistic society for the past several centuries. In fact, female infanticide was one of the agenda of the social reform movements in India during the eighteenth and the nineteenth centuries led by Raja Rammohun Roy (1772-1833), Ishwar Chandra Vidyasagar (1820-91) and other great social reformers. It may be partly due to the impact of these movements that the female-male ratio was much higher in 1901 as compared to 1991. Another reason for such higher ratio in 1901 may be due to non-availability of sex determination tests in those days. The lower sex ratio in the 1991 census indicates that in all probability the cruel practice of female infanticide still exists in our society alongside female foeticide.

According to an estimate of the United Nation's Children's Emergency Fund (UNICEF), biologically 105 boys are born for every hundred girls. However, with higher death rates among the boys in the first year of life, these figures should be more or less equal. Since this is not the case in India, it implies that many of the girl children who are born normal may subsequently go missing as victims of female infanticide. Majority of those who survive in this process later become the victims of gender bias prevalent in their domestic and social life. They are generally subjected to indifferent and inferior treatment as compared to their male counterparts.

Child Abuse and Neglect.

Child abuse and neglect are universal phenomena. They have two-fold effect in the sense that these are not only offences against society's most vulnerable sections but may also sow the seeds of crime perpetrated later in life by the victims themselves. In fact, the violence committed by youths quite often is traced back to the abuse and neglect they suffered in their early years.[1] Survey results in some countries have established the link between child maltreatment and later criminal behaviour by its victims. Such linkage results in growing acceptance of the concept of a "cycle of violence" that starts with child abuse and neglect.

One recent national study in USA revealed that being the victim of abuse and neglect as a child increases the chances of later juvenile delinquency and adult criminality by forty per cent. Even among children who are neglected but not abused, one in eight would later be arrested for a violent offence.[2] Child abuse and maltreatment are not confined to family life alone. They occur more frequently far from the victim's own house or in its vicinities. Schools, formal and informal custodial institutions, working places (in case of child labour) and streets (in case of homeless children) are common places of victimisation. The worst form of child abuse is rape, sodomy or sexual assault. One recent research study in USA showed that more female than male adolescents had been sexually assaulted (13 per cent of females in contrast to 3.4 per cent of males).

It also revealed that youths from lower income groups experienced higher rates of sexual assaults than those from middle and higher rates of sexual assaults than those from middle and higher income groups.[3] Similar data relating to India are not readily available since "victimisation surveys have still not gained complete recognition by researchers of victimology in India".[4]Nevertheless, "scarcity or absence of statistics on the toll of abuse in developing countries", according to an observer, "does not mean that child abuse does not occur there". [5]

•exploitation of children in the forms of child labour and child slavery etc.

Another worst form of child abuse is genital and without anaesthetic: it is painful, terrifying and traumatic".

It needs to be emphasised that although all forms of child abuse and neglect do not come under the purview of law and justice, they must have deleterious effects of various kinds on the victims. A lot of research needs to be undertaken by scholars in Victimology to analyse why child abuse is rampant in developed as well as developing countries.

Child Labour and Child Slavery

The term 'child labour' has been aptly defined by Homer Folks as "any work by children that interferes with their full physical development, their opportunities for a desirable minimum education or their needs for recreation".[6]

The term, therefore, applies to "children engaged in all types of activities whether these be industrial or non-industrial but which are detrimental to their physical, mental, moral and social well-being and development".[7]

In developing countries, a large number of children from poor families are victims of the exploitation of child labour. According to International Labour Organisation's Bureau of Statistics, there are now 120 million children between 5-14 years of age who are fully at work, while there are about 250 million children for whom work is a secondary activity. Of these, sixty one per cent are found in Asia, thirty two per cent in Africa and seven per cent in Latin America. India has the highest number of child labour. As per 1991 census, the number of working children is estimated to be 17.36 million in the country. In real terms, the figures must be much more than the estimated figures. For, the National Sample Survey Organisation estimated the numbers at 17.58 million way back in 1985.

The worst form of child labour is child slavery in the form of bonded labour which still exists in some parts of rural India. It is the end product of an extreme form of economic indebtedness which compels the parents to engage their children in household and agricultural work under inhuman conditions of a debt bondage. Although the incidents of child slavery have declined considerably in recent years due to governmental and non-governmental efforts, this socio-economic evil has not been eliminated altogether. This is why, on November 11, 1997 the Supreme

Court had brought under the purview of National Human Rights Commission (NHRC) the task of supervising the implementation of all laws relating to abolition of bonded labour.

In response, the NHRC constituted a group to study various aspects of bonded labour and submit periodic reports to the Supreme Court. In the socio-economic context of a developing country as ours child labour is often considered as a necessary social evil resulting from economic necessity of a poor family. Although the conditions under which the children work vary widely across activities and between different sectors, the fact remains that child labour not only leads to denial of education and recreation for the working children but also they are often exposed to various types of occupational health hazards that reduce their average life span. Children engaged in mines, quarries, glass, bangle, fireworks, carpet, metal and match factories and other such hazardous occupations under unhygienic working and living conditions are the worst sufferers of child labour.

Sexual Harassment of Working Children

Apart from the kinds of harassment, mentiond above, the working children, both male and female, are also subjected to exploitation in the form of sexual harassment by the employees and their associates. There are various forms and patterns of sexual harassment. As per the Industrial Employment (Standing Orders) Rules, 1946 as amended recently, any behaviour or any other unwelcome physical, verbal or non-verbal conduct of sexual nature shall be construed as sexual harassment.

Child Trafficking and Prostitution

The United Nations General Assembly, in 1994, defined trafficking as " the illicit and clandestine movement of persons across national and international borders, largely from developing countries, with the end goal of foreseeing women and girl children into economically oppressive and exploitative situations for the profit of recruiters, traffickers and crime syndicates". The UN Convention on the Rights of the Child, defines child prostitution as "sexual exploitation of a child below the age of 18 for remuneration in cash or kind".

Child trafficking and prostitution are the commercial sexual abuse of children resulting in denial of human rights of the victims. According to Amnesty International's report on CRC, "On just two established routes, from Nepal to India and from Bangladesh to Pakistan an estimated 9,000 girls a year are trafficked." Girls in other developing countries are also not free from this menace.

Child prostitution is the worst form of child abuse and exploitation. Its nature and type vary from one country to another, one society to another and from one age to other age. They may even vary in a society due to different religious and cultural practices of different social groups. A recent study conducted by Delhi-based NGO, Joint Women's Programme, reveals that most of the children engaged in prostitution are not paid for the first 5-10 years. Mental and emotional trauma apart, they are tortured, burnt and beaten. Many of them are to live with unwanted pregnancies, riddled with diseases or die of maternal mortality. The stigma of illegitimacy stubbornly persists, often propagated by the parents who live off them.[8]

There is wide variation in regard to numerical data on child prostitute. One study estimated a total of 100 million sexually abused children in the world, but did not distinguish between the categories of child prostitutes and sexually abused children.[9] According to an estimate by End Child Prostitution in Asian Tourism (ECPAT) in 1993, there were 1.5 million prostitutes in India with 20 per cent of them under 16 years of age.[10]

Children as Victims of Drug Trafficking and Substance Abuse

India is placed between world's largest drug growing areas—the Golden Crescent on the border regions of Pakistan and Afghanistan and the Golden Triangle on the borders of Myanmar, Thailand and Laos. Indian has become a conduit country for drugs moving from the Crescent and the Triangle to the western world, especially during the past one decade. Drug trafficking is now closely linked to terrorism and supply of deadly weapons and arms for terrorist activities. Children in India and countries on the Crescent and the Triangle are increasingly engaged in drug trafficking, especially as carriers. Children in large number, particularly from the lower strata of the society, have also become the victims of the menace of drug abuse in India and other developing countries.

The menace, according to an empirical study conducted in Delhi a few years back, [1] afflicts the children and the young persons, especially in the age group of 15 to 25 years, under the peer group pressure, the sense of curiosity and spirit of experimentation. "The contribution of the modern technological age," observes this study very forthrightly, "is that the more potent derivation of narcotic drugs and other synthetic drugs and psychotropic substances are a trap and other synthetic drugs and psychotropic substances are a trap from which even the casual experimenter can seldom escape without professional help."[2] The menace of drug abuse was initially confined to urban areas. But of late, it has spread its tentacles over semi-urban and rural areas too.

Children of developed countries are no less prone to substance abuse, i.e., a combination of drug and alcohol abuse. A recent study reveals that about 3.4 million adolescents aged 12-17 in USA have been drug or alcohol abusers.[3]

Children as Victims of Wars and Civil Conflicts

Another worst form of child victimisation has its roots in today's armed conflicts in which children themselves have been compelled to become instruments of war. They are lured or kidnapped to serve as soldiers as is evident from armed conflicts in Angola, Chechnya, Eritrea, Ethiopia, East Timor, Guina Bissau, Kosovo and Kashmir, to name a few. In Colombia, observes the recent Amnesty International Report on CRC, "child soldiers are sometimes called 'little bees', because their size and agility enable them to move quickly and 'sting' their enemy."

Not only this children are even exposed to vicious hate campaign as in Rwanda, Burandi and Bosnia. For, almost all the major wars today are civil conflicts, and as observed by a commentator very poignantly, "they are fought among people who know each other well. Compatriots and neighbours are engaged in combat with each other."[4] Children's exposure to hate campaigns in these wars have left them with severe psychological trauma. As this commentator observes further, "in the innocent mind, categorisation of separation on religious, ethnic and racial lines are introduced. Even when fighting stops, children live with the psychological trauma of war. They need sustained assistance for rehabilitation, though today their needs are largely ignored."[5] Children are also being used as instruments of war by militant organisations like the LTTE in Sri Lanka and the Talibans in Afghanistan.

Impact of war on children is multiple and severe. It leads to deprivation of children of their security, food, education and access to health. During war, the girl children are especially vulnerable to sexual abuse, rape and forced prostitution. War also compels the children to live a miserable life as refugees. The majority of today's 11.5 million refugees are women and children.[6] Armed conflicts in countries like

Angola and Sierra Leone have even produced a large number of limbless children, the victims of land mines. As Olara A Otunnu, Special Representative of the UN Secretary-General for Children and Armed Conflicts observes:

Children are truly blameless victims of conflict... Yet, today we are witnessing unspeakable abominations directed against children in situations of conflict... Over the last decade, two million children were killed... over one million made orphans, over six million have been seriously injured or permanently disabled and over 10 million have been left with grave psychological trauma."[7]

Migrant Children

With rapid urbanisation in developing countries as India, there has been large-scale migration of rural families to urban towns and cities. The children of migrated families have not only become the victims of instability and insecurity but also exposed to various forms of abuses and exploitation. They are subjected to "abusive employment practices and, worse still, are forced to work under conditions which are dangerous to their health and physical and mental development.[18] They are to live either under inhuman conditions in slums or near their workplaces outside the orbit of the family. As a result, they become vulnerable of the vices of urban life—sexual and other abuses and also social and economic exploitation. Many of them are also lured by criminal gangs and ultimately become adolescent offenders.

Child Torture

The horrifying tale of innocent does not end here, as child torture is another worse form of child victimisation. Unfortunately, child torture though being one of the most insidious evils against humanity, has not been defined in the law, not even in the UN Convention Against Torture. In developed as well as developing countries, children are often subjected to insidious and informal types of torture as in children homes. The working children in developing countries are often the victims of this kind of torture by their employees. The Indian police has earned notoriety in inflicting torture or other cruel inhuman degrading treatment not only against accused children in its custody but also innocent children to extract information about their parents who are suspected to have committed offences.

Epilogue

It is most unfortunate that victimisation of child in various forms and patterns continue to occur in developed as well as developing countries even ten years after the United Nations drew up its Convention on the Rights of the Child which has been adopted by all but two countries (Somalia and the US) in the world. Consequently, there exists a wide chasm between universal acceptance and universal observance of this humanitarian international instrument concerning protection and promotion of human rights of the child. No wonder that the rights of tens of millions of children all over the world are being flouted on an enormous scale. Contemporary human civilisation and world community are yet to traverse a long, long way in their tryst with a new world order which will ensure human rights of the child victims.

REFERENCES

1. Earle, Ralph B., *Helping to Prevent Child Abuse and Future Criminal Consequences*, National Institute of Justice (NIJ): Programme Focus, Washington DC. US Deptt. of Justice, October 1995, p. 2.
2. Widom, Cathy Spatz, *The Cycle* of Violence, NIJ Research in Brief, Washington, DC: U.S. Deptt. of Justice, 1992, 3; Widom, *Victims of Childhood Sexual Abuse—Later Criminal Consequences*. NIJ Research in Brief, Washington, DC: U.S. Deptt. of Justice, 1995, 4. See also, Earle, Ibid., p. 3.
3. Kilpatrick, Dean and Saunders, Benjamin, *The Prevalence and Consequences of Child Victimization*, NIJ Research Preview, April 1997.
4. Singh, D.R., "The International Crime (Victim) Survey in Bombay". In Zvekick, Ugljesa and Frate, A.A.D. (eds.), *Criminal Victimisation in the Developing World*, Rome, UNICRI, Publication No. 55, 1995, p. 96.
5. Suman, Somen K., "Child Abuse in India" Social Welfare, Nov-Dec. 1985, p.22.
6. Quoted, Stein, Emanuel and Davis, Jerome (eds), *Labour Problem in India*, New York, Farrar & Rinchart Inc., 1940, pp. 12-13.
7. Kulshreshtha, Jinesh C., *Indian Child Labour, Delhi*, Uppal, 1994, p.4.

8. For further details, see Ramaswamy, Anindita, "The Ultimate Abuse", *The Hindustan Times,* November 12, 1999.

9. Gathia, Joseph, *Child Prostitution in India,* Delhi, Concept, 1999, p. 15

10. *Ibid.*

1. Prashant, Saroj, *Drug Abuse and Society, Delhi,* Ashish, 1993.

2. *Ibid.,* p. 159.

3. *Supra,* n. 5.

4. Panicker Lalita, Traumatised Children of Deadlier Wars, *The Times of India,* Delhi, September 17, 1999.

5. *Ibid.*

6. *Ibid.*

7. Quoted, *Ibid.*

8. ILO, Report of the Director General, International Labour Office, Geneva, 1983, p.10.

TWELVE

PREVENTING VICTIMISATION

The period from birth to late adolescence is extremely important in the life of an individual. It is the formative and developmental period and experiences during this period shapes one's personality and character. But, it is noticed that most incident of victimisation take place during this period, as the children are unable to assert and are too innocent to understand that the are being victimised .

The concept of victim appears among the most ancient ones in humanity. Inextricably connected with the idea and the practice of sacrifice, the notion of victims belongs to all creatures. Most religion, for example, are fundamentally sacrificial. Early ritual literature from all religions offers abundant clues to the study of sacrifice and of its victims–human, divine, animal or inanimate. The epics and mythological sources provide sufficient evidence of the different types of sacrifice and victim, and contain a wealth of symbolic element connected to those rituals and practices.

Although interest on victim's role in a criminal situation is not very old, various face of victim's situation have come under scrunity and have spurred people into action. Although victimisation as the form of human sacrifice is very rare these days, victimisation goes on nevertheless. Most common among them are child labour, child prostitution, child beggary, sexual abuse and child marriage. At attempt is made in this article to deal with a few forms of child victimisation and to suggest some strategies for its prevention. Emphasis is given on parental abuse and neglect, sexual child abuse and child labour. Some forms of victimisation such as parental abuse in the form of child battering and neglect has not been well-documented in India because of supports provided by the extended family. However, increasing media coverage, emergence of nuclear family have forced us to conclude that child abuse is varied and includes beating, emotional abuse, abandonment and sexual abuse. They are often connected with parental expectations, marital discord, divorce and career families, poor housing, poor parental mental health, alcoholism and superstition.

Parental abuse and neglect had, till recently gone unnoticed in India. It is however a major form of victimisation of children. The social change, structure of modern family and inter-generational relationship has brought it to the forefront. The concept of child abuse and neglect has undergone considerable change over the years. In the beginning, baby-battering was in the foreground to which phenomenon of maltreatment was added. Neglect and violence are latest additions.

If we try to analyse the causes of child abuse and neglect, we must first understand the characteristics of abused children and the type of individuals, who would harm their children. Secondly, we must understand the situational factors that lead to abuse. This will enable us to establish a link between the individual, societal and situational factors, which precipitate child abuse.

There are theories to suggest that child abuse is learned behaviour and transmitted from generation to generation. Parents treat their children the way they were treated by their parents. Although we cannot deny the concept of cycle of abuse, we find that many children have survived neglected and abusive childhood and become successful parents in spite of it all and well-cared-for children turn out to be parental monsters. So the situation, rather than the cycle of abuse, seems more acceptable.

Parental authority and conquest for obedience is a major issue concerning child abuse and neglect by parents. Parents are heard saying that they would rather have dead children than disobedient ones. They rarely understand that no child is born disobedient. It is the relationship between the parents and children that make a child obedient or disobedient. Disobedience apart, lack of proper parental care due to broken homes often lead to serious delinquency. Children cannot be considered as sole property of parents anymore. They need to be considered, as human beings with a mind of their own. They must feel wanted, loved and trusted. Studies reveal that non-abusers manage to raise their families with relatively more success. What children need to grow to their full potential is support and guidance, not indulgence. This imbibes confidence in children and they are able to face the rough world gracefully. Parenting is not a power game where asymmetry of power should lead to child abuse.

Stress is one factor, which is widely accepted as the cause of child abuse. The origins of stress in such cases are jobs, finances, loneliness, isolation where children are made the scapegoat. What parents need to develop are coping skills for managing stress and not make the children victim of their stress, may it be related to job and economic issue of family matters. To combat stress, emphasis should be on a closer tie between family life and work life.

Parental screening, abused child therapy and parenting classes will help prevent child abuse. Counselling is needed for both parents, and children which will help manage and solve many a problem arising out of parent-child conflict. Child protection strategies must aim at changing structural inequality of our families. Last strategy to protect child from neglect and abuse will be to have child protection services, which will be always available to protect the child. However, for the rural poor, only education and awareness programmes can help.

Sexual abuse during childhood is one of the worst forms of child victimisation. Children are innocent, timid and powerless in front of adults, who take advantage of this situation and victimse them sexually, i.e., use them for the sexual gratification. Child sexual victimisation may be termed as sexual abuse, sexual exploitation, sexual assault, sexual misuse, child molestation, sexual maltreatment and child rape.

Too often, parents and other professionals believe that sexual abuse of children is committed by strangers. This is true in only about ten to fifteen per cent of the cases. Warning children to avoid unknown persons may be an unclear message to children. A manipulative person can easily win over a child, and before too long the new person is not a stranger but a friend. According to developmental theory, only by age six, a child can be taught the difference between the two forms. Yet, even if the word 'stranger' has been clearly explained the child might not know why strangers should be sidestepped. The child might not understand what he or she should do if someone approaches him or her. This can create and generate feeling of anxiety for children. The irony of it is that in at least eighty five per cent of the cases the child sexual offender, is known to the child. In at least twenty-five per cent of the cases the offenders live in the child's home.

A variety of behaviour is encapsulated within child sexual abuse. The most common among them are non-contact sexual abuse such as sexual comments, exhibitionism, watching pornographic film and videos and contact sexual abuse such as kissing, handling or fondling, vaginal or anal intercourse frottage (an adult rubbing against a child in a sexual manner) pornography and cyber sex. The child is never at fault if sexual abuse occurs. Most sexual abuses begin at an age when the child has no knowledge about what sexuality means. Sexually abusive situation are characterised by lack of consent, exploitation, secrecy and force.

Although every child has a potential to become a victim of child sexual abuse, persons who molest children have a tendency to look for children who can be easily controlled. Most molesters seek out children who they think will keep a secret. They will also look for children who are very respectful and cannot say no to adults. The children who live with their stepfathers, live away from their mothers, not close with mothers, fathers very dominating have more chances of being victimised by sexual abuse. People close to the child must look for some indicators, which is different for different age group of children of sexual abuse.

Children most often will not talk directly about sexual abuse and thus determining of a child is sexually abused is a complicated procedure. They do not tell straightforward that they have been abused as they are threatened or made to feel as if the abuse was their fault. Not all adults 'however' can sexually abuse children. It is perversions some people have who are paedophiles. This kind of pervert sexual behaviour is thought to be a result of emotional, physical or sexual trauma. The individual may be emotionally underdeveloped. Due to retardation and indevelopment, the individual may age in years but not emotionally.

Some behavioural theorists maintain that paedophilia is a learned behaviour where abusers become conditioned to responding to young, sexually underdeveloped bodies. In a patriarchal society, male being dominant, controlling and powerful connect with partners who are younger, smaller and weaker than themselves. Some people who engage in child abuse cannot get their sexual and emotional needs met in adult relationships. They do not have any inhibition and are able to overcome the moral and legal sanction against performing sexual acts with children. Lowering inhibitions can be the result of alcohol usage, social isolation or senility.

Sexual child abuse may be extrafamilial as well as intrafamilial. Contrary to the common knowledge, the abusers need not be always males. However sexual abuses by females with either male or female children are less harmful than abuse by adult males. Although the existence of female offenders is now beginning to be recognised, it is still met with great skepticism. Accepting the harsh reality that females can and do abuse children and adolescents in both gender groups, perhaps attacks one of the last remaining vestiges of cultural myth: the myth that mothers of females are always protective towards children and could not be abusive, violent, or sadistic, sexual offenders.

Almost common among the intrafamilial abuses is father-daughter incest; the most common sexual abuse. This incest is viewed as a result of internal and external forces in the family in which the father is seen as pathological and alcoholic and the mother as unassertive. Mother-son intrafamilial abuse although was non-existent till recently is now being reported although literature reference regarding it is very scant. Brother-sister incest, too, is a common form of child abuse, which is grossly underreported. One cause of incest between siblings could be sexual experimentation. It could also be as a result of family dysfunction, ill-defined and poor boundaries within the family. It is surprising to note that a small portion of grandparent population too is identified as being sexually abusive.

It is disheartening to note that child sexual abuse is on the increase. The latest police statistics show that three out of four rape victims in Delhi are minor girls. Worse, there is still no legal recognition of serious kind to sexual abuse like non-penile penetration and incest. Crime statistics reveal a gory picture. In the past decade, the rape of minor below sixteen, accounts for more than twenty-five per cent of the total rape cases while cases of rape of children below the age of ten years increases by twenty-six per cent. The dismal rate of convictions is even more disheartening. Less than ten per cent of the reported rape cases in India results in convictions. Of the 284 reported rape cases in New Delhi in 1992 there were only three convictions by 1995. Of the 309 cases in 1994 there was not a single conviction.

Prevention of sexual child abuse must address three areas. First, all concerned with children such as parents, baby-sitters, pediatricians, psychologists must recognise the situations in which abuse has been occurring.They can come togehter and learn to be more protective towards children and learn what to do if abuse is suspected. Secondly, prevention must concentrate on societal elements that encourage child sexual abuse, such as advertisers exploiting children's sexuality to sell products and services. Thirdly, healthy parenting skills must be developed increasing child's self-esteem. Building self-esteem in children makes them less vulnerable of being abused. If a child feels positive about himself or herself and has his or her physical and emotional needs met, then he or she is less likely to be abused. Parents can teach their children some basic safety rules and make them tell a trusted adult (may be parents) about what happens outside home.

It is needless to say that parents are the best protectors of children. While protecting the child outside home, they should always hold the hands of the young child while shopping or walking on the road or parks. They should know the exact route the child takes to school and help the child identify restaurants, small business, and homes of friends where they know that the child could run if help was needed. They must make sure that child is not away from school during school time. Child should be protected at all the places such as religious meetings, public toilets, swimming pools, etc.

At home, children should never answer a knock on the door. They should be taught to deal with all types of phones early in their lives, the parents must make a list of emergency telephone numbers. If alone they should not tell a strange caller that their parents are absent there but tell that they are unable to come to the phone and ask them to give the number so that they can ring back. If the child gets gifts, parents must find out who is giving the gift, what is in the gift and determine how the child exactly got the gift. One should never allow a stranger to photograph his/her child.

Intrafamilial abusive situations are much more complex. Once the abuser is identified he must be sent out of home or the child must be kept away from the abuser. Help may be sought from some organisations, which have now developed to protect children. Family members talking to the abuser about stopping the abuse will not be effective. If the father or the mother is the abuser due to whatever reason it is the duty of the other parent to protect the child. Children must be taught that the adults are not always right. Above all, the children should be encouraged to build self-confidence from an early age.

Child labour is one of the worst forms of victimisation where they are sent to work instead of their rightful place in school. Child labour is usually defined as participation of children between the ages of five and fourteen years in gainful activity. According to the latest International Labour Organization (ILO) report global child labour figure is 250 million and statistics show that India has the dubious distinction of having the largest child labour force in the world. In spite of the constitutional directive (Article 45 of the Directive Principle of State Policy) to provide free and compulsory education for all children until they complete the age of fourteen years, this social problem has grown unabated.

Poverty coupled with population explosion and illiteracy are the basic causes of child labour. Income of the child becomes essential for the survival of the families, which are invariably large. Children's employment is preferred because they work for less remuneration than adult labourers, they can be pressurised easily into the exploitative tactics of the employers, children being amenable to discipline and control of child labourer is trouble-free and not unionised. The children working for long hours and sometimes even during the night in poor, polluted and hazardous conditions under constant mental and physical strain results in stunted growth. They suffer from lung and eye diseases, backaches and often become victims of fire accidents. Unable to participate in leisure and recreational activities, these children become drug-addicts, spend time in gambling and smuggling. It affects their physical and psychological growth, which finally degenerates the whole socio-economic structure.

While considering strategies to prevent child victimisation in the form of child labour, we can first cite various legislations enacted from time to time. The obvious fact that in spite of these laws, child labour still prevails in contemporary society indicates that these legal mesures are cleverly violated by the unscrupulous employers due to inadequate enforcing and monitoring machinery. Banning child labour altogether will be a long-term strategy. What can immediately be done is to combat exploitation. Children must be released from dangerous occupations and bondage. There is a need to build public opinion against child labour. Women and youth organisations must come forward and shoulder this responsibility. Many NGOs have the reputation of being able to get closer to the communities who resist any attempt to tackle the problem of child labour. Greater social awarencess, low cost job-oriented education and encouraging more women to the work force will go a long way in eradicating child labour.

References

1. Ahmed, Iftikhar "Getting Rid of Child Labour", *Economic and Political Weekly,* July 1999.
2. Emilio Viano, "Victimology: The Development of a New Perspective" Victimology, Vol. 8, 1983.
3. *The Hindustan Times,* November 19, 1999.
4. Julianu Whetsell—Mitchell, "Rape of the Innocent" Taylor Francis, USA 1995.
5. Segal, Uma A., "Child Abuse in India: A Theoritical Overview" *Indian Journal of Social Work,* July 1991.
6. Singh, S.P., "Child Labour Malady and the Remedy", *Yojana,* July 1997.

[illegible]

Notes

[illegible]

THIRTEEN

GENDER BIAS AND CRIME

Independence brought with it the Constitution, with equality and social justice as its basic fundamental tenets. Constitutional mandates for equality and justice have considerably been diluted by a parallel regime of personal laws which continue to prop discrimination against women in the fields of marriage, divorce, custody, inheritance and succession. The personal laws, based on traditional socio-religious customs, continue to uphold male dominance over female needs.

Women are socialised as 'breeders' and 'caretakers'. This constitutes the definition of a 'normal' woman, a woman who will protect that patriarchal social order. Any other role by definition would be deviant. In a patriarchal order, gender becomes a normative system through which female behaviour is controlled. Definitions of deviance tend to be imposed on the powerless by the powerful. Given modern complex and stratified societies, with acutely conflicting interests such as those existing between men and women—deviance and control apparatus are created to prevent the deviant, i.e., the powerless from pursuing their interests (McDonough and Saari, 1987). Social control mechanism becomes a tool for oppression, suppression, exploitation and discrimination of women—the powerless; by men—the powerful.

Socialisation for gender role begins from the moment of birth. Parents treat male and female children differently and have expectations based on cultural definition of sex differences. Parents characterise daughter as weak, less attentive and coordinated, softer and more fragile and son is characterised as more alert, stronger, more coordinated and firmer. This perception coloured by sex stereotyping influences parents' behaviours towards their children, which subsequently shapes the children's self-concept and gender role expectation. Sex differences in socialisation experiences make women weaker and men stronger resulting in exploitation.

Criminal victimisation of women, young girls have been prevalent throughout the history of mankind. The problem is common to a particular time, place and culture. It is rather a worldwide phenomenon and has aroused much public opinion and concern. Female child has been victim of abuse, discrimination and exploitation at all the stages of her life. She is discriminated at every stage which affects her adversely in physical, social and psychological development.

Victim of Gender Bias

In all patriarchal societies females whether kids, adolescents or adults are believed to be treated as being inferior to males. Even parents discriminate between their sons and daughters. Psychologists are of the opinion that the personality of an individual is governed by early childhood experiences. Behaviours like dependency, passiveness and submissiveness in female children comes out of discriminatory child rearing practices. These behaviours nurtured over the years, makes the female children victims of various crimes in different situations.

Gender discrimination, the age old system of inequality and stereotyping of the role of women, have resulted in the low valuation of a female child. The parents always favour a son. This perhaps is the attitude all over the country with a few honourable exceptions. Girls are expected to be docile, modest, less talkative and submissive thus closing the doors of creativity and innovation for girls. Gender bias does not stop at childhood but also continues during adolescence, at the time of marriage, in the household of in-laws, in the process of decision making, emotional rehabilitation as a member of group; employment opportunities and participation in the political affairs. Traditionally, most of the parents inadvertently instill orthodox, traditional and patriarchal ideas into the minds of children.

Female child has been the victim of various forms of abuse, discrimination and exploitation at all the stages. She is discriminated at every step, affecting adversely her physical, social and psychological development. She is treated as inferior to a male child. She is deprived of nutritious food, proper education and other needs required for her growth and development.

Victim of Domestic Crime

The Indian family structure is patriarchal, patrilocal and patrilineal. Traditionally men dominated the social structures. The dominant forms of family organisation have been the joint family headed by a male. Even where the matrilineal system prevailed, the real authority vested with men—wife's brothers, father and uncles. Indian women have been the victims of deep-rooted traditional oppression and socio-economic inequality in a male dominated society. Even today women are subjected to various forms of discrimination, oppression and exploitation in spite of widely prevalent legislations safeguarding the women's rights. The various forms of domestic victimisation of women range from wife-battering, dowry-killing, desertion, rape, incest and sexual abuse, female infanticide to other varied forms.

Women are innocent victims of discrimination, torture and harassment in their own families. Crimes like incest and child rape are located within the home, out of the purview of public; invisible and inaudible. Incest, never spoken about openly, exists in all strata of society and is often the cause of lasting trauma that can mar the family life for the victim.

A great proportion of incest and child rape cases that have come to light involve father-daughter relationships. Damodar Kunalienkar, a psychiatrist attached to the Institute of Psychiatry and Human Behaviour, Goa related the case of 17-year-old Tara. She was forced into an intimate relationship with her father since the age of 15. The girl's mother was mentally deranged and her two brothers were too young to know what was happening. Fearful of telling to anybody Tara found a way out of her private hell by attempting suicide. After three unsuccessful attempts of suicide, the girl was brought for psychiatric treatment (*Femina*, Aug. 1994).

Responses to incest are so radically varied, ranging from trauma to outrage to acceptance, denial to open admittance. Depression, guilt, shame... and most startling of all... indifference. While some people argue that in a permissive society, child molesting has increased, a recent study in the U.S. revealed that almost 12 to 15 million female children are subjected to incestuous abuse every year (*Femina,* 1992).

Shrouded in myth, secrecy and taboos, sexual abuse of children or paedophilia continues to rise alarmingly in India, where three out of every ten rape victims are children below the age of 16.

According to the National Crime Research Bureau's latest report, the year 1996 witnessed a 34.6 per cent increase in the cases of sexual abuse of children between 10-16 years and a 14.3 per cent increase in the victims below 10 years, when compared to the figures in 1992. According to Dr. Achal Bhagat, seventy per cent of child sexual abusers target girls who fall prey to the lust of perverse adults.

There is no special and separate law for child sexual abuse/incest in India, with the result that the victim gets a raw deal and being a child is all the more traumatic for him/her as he/she is unable to understand as to what has happened to him/her.

Victim of Child Prostitution

From the ancient temples of Delphi to the modern Hindu temples of India, the regular sexual abuse of young girls as temple prostitutes has been a way of obtaining religious merit. The term commonly used for these prostitutes is Jogini or Devadasi. Historically, the Devadasis served a God to which they were ritually 'married' by dancing and singing in that God's temple. Around 5,000 girls are dedicated every year into this system in Andhra Pradesh, Maharashtra and Karnataka. These dedication ceremonies given religious sanction to a family's decision to prostitute a daughter—who is initiated into flesh trade at puberty.

It cannot be denied that more than religious devotion, it is the economic considerations that are paramount in most families decision to push a daughter into prostitution via the Devadasi dedication ceremony. The initiation ceremony is celebrated with a feast which is paid for by an upper caste man who has purchased the right to her virginity. The economic benefits for the family are immediate.

There are some castes that have traditionally accepted prostitution as their profession. The Rajna tribe in Rajasthan is economically organised around a system of child prostitution. This tribe is only one of many such in Rajasthan. The system of prostitution practices by this tribe is inherently child prostitution, as the girls enter prostitution by puberty. The eldest daughter is raised, being fully aware that the tribe's survival depends on her labour as prostitute. The tribe's economic and social organisation ensure that these girls do not question their fate. Other communities—Dehrehar, Gandharva, Bedias and Kanjuars—have traditionally accepted prostitution as a source of livelihood.

Surveys have claimed that fifty per cent of all the prostitutes in Maharashtra began as Devadasis. Girls from this system have been estimated to account for twenty per cent of the total girls in this illegal profession. About eighty-five per cent of the prostitutes in Delhi and Calcutta were compelled into the flesh trade when very young, entertaining about seven to eight clients in a day. Often during heavy menstrual periods, ice is used and they are forced to receive clients. Physical and psychological torture may be specifically employed to ensure compliance in many cases. The girl in prostitution is a victim of sexual slavery in the name of deep-rooted tradition, social custom, religion and culture—which is highly discriminative, exploitative, oppressive and suppressive for females from their childhood (UNICEF Report—1995).

It is a sad commentary on the social values of modern society that we can permit more than one million children in prostitution in Asia alone to remain in a form of sexual slavery which is akin to a living death.

Traditional discrimination against women has not come to an end irrespective of statutory provisions to that effect. There is little awareness among them about the existing social legislations to protect their interests. Patriarchal conditions and discriminatory socialisation patterns isolate women from asserting themselves in changing and redefining the social order which prop up discrimination against them. Until equality for women is made a reality through social attitude and its change, until concrete solutions are found to various gender-related problems, until men cease to consider women as their subjugated/ suppressed property—women will continue to be the victim of gender bias, faulty socialisation process, domestic crime and sexual abuse of various forms.

So far as legal machinery is concerned, it can play only a limited role in the social and economic emancipation of women. Law is an instrument of social change and regulates the social relations between the state and society. Women need to be educated on various aspects of legislations concerning them in order to take the maximum benefits of such legislations by which social justice and freedom from gender bias for women can be achieved.

References

1. Bowker, L.H. (1983), *Women, Crime and Criminal Justice System,* Lexington, Mass.
2. Chatterjee, A. Shoma (1988), *The Indian Women's Search for Identity,* New Delhi : Vikas Publishing House.
3. Elias, R. (1986), *The Politics of Victimisation,* New York, Oxford University Press.
4. Femina (1992), " Crossing Bloodlines-Incest : The Unspoken Trauma" Cover Story (June)
5. Femina (1994), "Battered Dreams—Villent Reality" -Cover Story (Aug.)
6. Krishnamurthi, Latha, "Human Rights of a Girl Child" in Devasia & Devasia (ed.) *Girl child in India,* New Delhi, Ashish Publications.
7. McDonough, J.F. and Saari R.C. (Eds.) (1987), *The Trapped Women: Catch 22 in Deviance and Control,* N.Y., Sage.
8. UNICEF Report (1995), *Child Prostitution: The Ultimate Abuse.*

[illegible] social structures of modern society that we can account [illegible] [illegible] [illegible] [illegible] of social [illegible] [illegible]

[illegible] national [illegible] [illegible] [illegible] perspective of [illegible] [illegible] the [illegible] [illegible] [illegible] [illegible] [illegible] [illegible] conditions and [illegible] [illegible] [illegible] from [illegible] [illegible] social order which [illegible] [illegible] equality for women [illegible] change, [illegible] [illegible] gender [illegible] [illegible] [illegible] women [illegible] [illegible] [illegible] [illegible] [illegible] [illegible]

Social [illegible] legal mechanism [illegible] [illegible] [illegible] [illegible] [illegible] [illegible] social relations between [illegible] [illegible] [illegible] [illegible] legislations [illegible] [illegible] [illegible] gender [illegible] for women [illegible]

[illegible]

1 [illegible]

2 [illegible] New Delhi [illegible]

3 [illegible]

4 [illegible]

5 [illegible]

6 [illegible]

FOURTEEN

CURSE OF THE UNBORN CHILD

We have a fundamental right to life. But surprisingly we don't have a fundamental right to be born. In the womb, we don't enjoy even a status of human being and that is why the killing in the womb is not considered homicide. What to talk of culpable homicide! By implication, we don't have even rights in the womb.

One can ask a question, is it true? The answer to this question is provided by the Indian Penal Code itself. There are, of course, certain provisions to check foeticide, but the Section 299 clearly says that it shall not amount to homicide to kill inside womb. What is the net result? We are going on killing unborn children, legally and illegally, in the womb. Since the illegality of foeticide does not attract severe punishment as compared to homicide, we are going on even identifying the sex of the child in the womb and then at times we kill it if the doctor says it is female child. There are large number of such cases creating a serious threat to the sex ratio and leading towards creation of an unsafe society, especially for women, and ultimately it turns against all human beings.

A question which demands an urgent answer is—Does an unborn child enjoy any rights, whatsoever? The question should be addressed immediately not only for the reason mentioned above, but for other reasons concerning the basic rights. After introduction of artificial insemination and appearance of surrogate mothers, some children lose their basic rights, of even knowing their parents. It is important, more so because the child loses other rights regarding property, for which the child is otherwise entitled to, in case of natural parents.

The term 'crime' largely signifies offences which are serious in nature. But this meaning will not do, because, it excludes the acts of omissions and commissions which are not so serious in nature as to constitute a crime. Therefore, the word 'crime' here, has been handled in a way so as to encompass the word offence; so that the meaning of the word 'crime' should include the whole gamut of our discussion. It would naturally include all the abuses and inhuman treatment which may not constitute a crime but victimise a child.

Let's now take up the term 'Child Victim'. A child can be a 'victim of crime' in two different ways. First, when the offence is directed against the child and second, when the offence is indirected against the child, but affects the child. For example, if a girl child is raped, the incident comes in the first category and if the girl witnessed her mother being raped in front of her and consequently traumatised, the incident comes in the second category. Now, the word 'child' comes in our consideration.

Here, we are totally confused. More so because its very definition varies from one act to the other, from one scholar to the other, and from one branch of knowledge to the other. It is a matter of great concern that in most of the laws the word 'child' has a meaning which covers the age only after birth.

It is common knowledge and which is also endorsed by linguists, semantics and lexicographers that a 'child' is a person who is below the age of 14. However, this knowledge does not lead us to the appropriate place except while we understand it or express it in common parlance. For each and every specific purpose, and it will not be an exaggeration to say that for almost all the practical purposes we come across a different meaning of a 'child'. The different laws give the meaning of a 'child' ranging from the upper limit of 12 years (Section 376 IPC) to 21 years (for marriage of a male child), but child in the womb, is not considered a child.

However, in the Indian Penal Code the Section 312 gives us the expression 'woman with child' which means a pregnant woman. We derive from there that the existence of a child starts from the womb of the mother. With the existence of the child he or she may face the danger of victimisation which has also been perceived in the Indian Penal Code. But unfortunately they are improperly protected against the various crimes other than miscarriage and their killing. There are only five sections (312-316) under the Indian Penal Code, which deals with miscarriage and death of an unborn child.

Even injury which may severely hurt the child in the womb but not cause killing or miscarriage is not considered a crime against the child under Indian Penal Code. No police officer or prosecuting authorities are filing such type of cases in our country. At the most they consider it as an offence against the woman with the child. Thus, it is proposed that the separate identity of the child even in the womb must be considered and appropriate laws should be framed to fully protect them against all types of victimisation—criminal or otherwise.

Mainly because we know of many cases of civil and criminal nature which hurt the interests of the unborn child.

Now another question arises here that endangering the life of a child in the womb below the age of the fourth or the fifth months of pregnancy when the woman be 'quick with child not the peculiar sensation which for the first time the woman feels, is prevalent in our society, under the garb of Medical Termination of Pregnancy Act (MTP Act) which provides for the termination of pregnancy by a registered medical practitioner where its continuance would involve a risk to the life of a pregnant woman or grave injury to her physical or mental health or where there is a substantial risk that if the child were born, it would suffer from such physical or mental abnormalities as to be seriously handicapped. Where the pregnancy is alleged to have been caused by rape or as a result of failure of a contraceptive used by a married woman or her husband, it would be presumed to constitute a grave injury to the mental health of the pregnant woman.

The MTP Act heavily protects the woman but not the 'child'. If the pregnancy is unwanted and is the failure of contraceptive, the woman suffers a grave injury to her mental health but if the pregnancy is terminated the child loses his or her life. The mental health of a woman can be restored later on but can the child who lost its life be restored by any means?

While asking this question we are well aware of the problem of population we are facing. Yes, any civilised person would like to limit the population of the world but not by means of cruelty. Should killing be the means of population control? Enthusiasts of the population control policy are continuously making efforts to control the population by adopting such a cruel means against the helpless unborn child. They also insist on amending the Indian Penal Code in the light of MTP Act. But, it has not been amended till date.

However, the practice is going on and we are unable to protect even the innocent child in the womb, which has not been conceived by any other way but in the wedlock of husband and wife. The ground for termination is that their contraceptive failed. It is another matter that they may not have used contraceptive at all. In this connection we can see Section 91 of the Indian Penal Code which refers to causing miscarriage as an offence, unless caused in good faith for the purpose of saving the life of a woman, independently of any harm which it may cause or be intended to the human. Therefore, it is not an offence by reason of such harm; and the consent of the woman or of her guardian to the causing of such miscarriage does not justify the Act. Now under Section 3 of the MTP Act pregnancy can be terminated. What a cruel practice it is?

Let us take an example, X has been 'presumed' to be causing a grave injury to the 'mental health' of Y. Y wants to kill or terminate X on this ground. Can any justice system grant a permission to terminate X? And if the permission is granted, can we call it a justice?

To put the record straight we would like to mention here that X has done nothing wrong to Y. The answer to the question would obviously be in the negative. Mainly because X has a fundamental right to life. Therefore we cannot do anything which leads to victimisation of X.

But, if Y is a woman and X is in her womb below the age of four weeks and if X is legally conceived, MTP Act may grant permission to terminate X on the ground that contraceptive measures failed or X is conceived without their intention or X is unwanted. X has obviously done nothing wrong and if there is anything wrong, it is on the part of X's parents. However, on the submission of the woman or parents that X is causing mental suffering to them, the competent authority may presume under the MTP that X is causing mental suffering to them. In this way the child is even prevented from the right to be born. It's certainly against the natural justice of the child because human beings enjoy a right to take birth. However, in the Indian Penal Code proper amendments to this effect are awaited. Many jurists are of the opinion that it is the failure of justice for the child. Does the killing of the child in the womb not constitute the violation of human rights?

The unborn child is not protected fully from any type of victimization other than miscarriage. We can take example of an unborn child who is injured in the womb but is not miscarried. At best the authorities may file cases against the guilty for hurting the woman but the victim child is generally ignored because people do not think that the child in the womb has also a separate identity. In this way, if a pregnant woman is killed, the FIR against the culprit is invariably filed for killing of the woman but not for the killing of the child in the womb. It is generally treated as a single murder.

As far as other laws are concerned mainly regarding compensation and insurance, the loss of woman is generally compensated but the child in the womb is simply ignored. Does our Constitution not provide assurance of a right to life even in the womb?

Now, we can take another example of victimisation of an unborn

Now, we can take another example of victimisation of an unborn child when the crime is not especially committed against the child but against the woman who bears the child. The woman suffers and consequently the child suffers. But what we are doing for the child?

Let us see Section 299 of the Indian Penal Code which is for culpable homicide. The explanation No. 3 of the Section says that the causing of death of a child in the mother's womb is not homicide. This homicide is culpable only when any part of the child has been brought forth though the child may not have breathed or been completely born. A funny thing is that the killing of the child in the womb is not even homicide. That is why, we are compelled to file cases of this nature in Section 312 of the IPC for causing a woman to miscarry and the culprit in rewarded only a minor punishment of a term not beyond three years or a fine or both. And if act is done to prevent child from being born alive or cause it to die after birth, the guilty can be booked under Section 315 IPC but the punishment is comparatively less than killing of human being. Even when the act amounts to culpable homicide of a child unborn the Section 316 provides lesser punishment. Only when the woman is "quick with child" the offence rewards imprisonment, which may not extend to seven years and of course shall also be liable to fine.

Obviously while law makes provision for the woman, the child in the womb is ignored. Under the comment on the Section 299 some definitions are given. 'Causes death' is one of them. Here 'death' means the death of a human being as defined under Section 46 of the IPC. But this word does not include the death of an unborn child as we have seen in explanation No.3 above. There are other things like immoral, illegal and unethical practices prevalent in our society hampering the development of born and unborn child which have not been covered under the Cr. P.C. and need to be catered through social, educational, religious and other platforms.

Now we can take another example of victimization of an unborn child when the crime is not especially committed against the child but against the woman who bears the child. The woman suffers and consequently the child suffers. But what we are doing for the child?

Let us see Section 299 of the Indian Penal Code, which is for culpable homicide. The explanation No. 3 of the Section says that the causing of death of a child in the mother's womb is not homicide. This homicide is culpable only when any part of the child has been brought forth though the child may not have breathed or been completely born. A funny thing is that the killing of the child in the womb is not even homicide. That is why we are compelled to file cases of this nature in Section 312 of the IPC for causing a woman to miscarry and the culprit is rewarded only a minor punishment of a term not beyond three years or a fine or both. And if act is done to prevent child from being born alive or cause it to die after birth the guilty can be booked under Section 315 IPC but the punishment is comparatively less than killing of human being. Even when the act amounts to culpable homicide of a child unborn the Section 316 provides lesser punishment. Only when the woman is 'quick with child' the offence invites imprisonment which may not extend to seven years and of course shall also be liable to fine.

Obviously while law makes provision for the woman, the child in the womb, is ignored. Under the comment on the Section 299 some definitions are given. Causes death is one of them. Here death means the death of a human being as defined under Section 46 of the IPC. But this word does not include the death of an unborn child as we have seen in explanation No. 3 above. There are other things like immoral, illegal and unethical practices prevalent in our society hampering the development of born and unborn child which have not been covered under the Cr. P.C. and need to be catered through social, educational, religious and other platforms.

FIFTEEN

FOETICIDE AND GIRL CHILD

The issue of child victims especially the girl child needs a humane approach as it has become a curse to the country—crime graph of which is increasing in galloping way. Of different facets of crime against girl child, problem of female foeticide has been cropping up seriously in our country. Despite the law against sex determination enacted in 1994 (The Pre-natal Diagnostic Technique Regulation, Prevention, and Misuse Act), female foeticide is still a serious menace. This article deals with pros and cons of the problem of foeticide and girl child and tries to suggest some measures to control the problem.

India is one of the few countries where the sex ratio is adverse to females because of high female mortality rate. While 12 million girls are born in India every year, almost 50,000 female foetuses are aborted in a year after sex determination. If this is the situation when the pre-natal diagnostic technique act is expected to go a long way in tackling this menace, the gravity of the problem cannot be measured and for this millennium it may pose as one of the important crimes of the country. Despite the fact that such crimes are viewed as social evil and bad, the reported incidents of such crimes continue to rise in magnitude. This calls for greater involvement by the society with greater awareness and attitudes towards such crimes to fight and combat this menace.

No less telling is the fact that despite banning sex determination tests, the Governments of Madhya Pradesh, Maharashtra, Rajasthan, Delhi and Haryana have not been able to check this evil. The National Crime Records Bureau (NCRB) being the only source of getting authentic statistical data on such crime, this article mainly referred to the NCRB data in focussing the grievousness of the situation. We do not know how far the information is correct as only reported crimes are taken into account. NCRB, in its latest edition of 'Crime in India'-1997 figured that the incidence of foeticide crime in India in 1994 was 45; in 1995, it was 38; in 1996, although the figure rose up to 39, increase in 1997 was remarkable, i.e. 57. The percentage of variation from 1997 over 1996 was recorded as 46.2 per cent, which shows an exorbitantly increasing trend. So far as the state-wise contribution of this crime to the national figure is concerned, Madhya Pradesh was leading with 36.8 per cent; Maharashtra contributed 33.3 per cent and Bihar with 7.0 per cent. Haryana, Rajasthan and Delhi shared 5.3 per cent during 1997.

Even though the decade started with the celebration of International Year of Girl-child, female child continues to get a raw deal, even the birth of a girl in the Indian society is also not welcomed properly. This is mainly because of the structural set-up of the Indian society is also not welcomed properly. This is mainly because of the structural set-up of the Indian society and the social attitudes towards the birth of girl-child. Although things are constantly changing, the old thinking of higher the education of the boy, greater is his matrimonial value in the matrimonial market and the parents accordingly want to exchange the boy for a girl with sufficient amount of immovable property, jewellery, hard cash and other items still persist in the country. Disagreeing with the system leads to serious crimes like dowry death, wife beating, etc. Thus, the attitude towards girls in India has not changed over the decades which stands in the way of economic, social and cultural developments of our national life.

In several parts of rural India, a mid-wife's fee is lower when the newborn baby is a girl rather than a boy. This practice is symptomatic of a widespread preference for male child among Indian parents. While an imaginative scheme, announced on the golden jublee of Independence, entitles parents of a new-born girl to a grant of Rs. 500, it has delivered little, if anything, in terms of positive influence on parental behaviour. Although the scheme endorses anti-female stereotypes, it does give parents an incentive to keep their daughters alive at least temporarily. In any case, grants for female births are a clumsy way of addressing to the problem of plight of the girl-child.

In the front of social status also, female children are more victimised as compared to male children. In the imparting of social benefits like health care, education, nutrition etc., greater care is bestowed on boys rather than on girls. One of the important primitive ideologies among the poor parents which still exists, is that girls suffer from poor education. In most of the poor families, parents find little meaning in sending girls to schools. One of the important reasons of depriving the girls of enrolment in the schools are their dual role in the family—first as domestic helper and second as baby sitter and to help their parents in a wide range of family vocations and in unorganised sectors like agriculture, animal husbandry, weaving, sericulture, beedi-making and so on. The main reason lies in poverty and environmental factors. Due to this, in most cases girls become the victims of several crimes like forced prostitution, trafficking, child marriage, etc. Their future depends on the whim of their parents. Child marriage not only deprives girls of health and nutrition but also education.

The Child Marriage Restrain (Amendment) Act of 1978 prevents marriage of a girl below eighteen years and a boy below twenty-one years. The NCRB report focussed that the child marriage occurred highest in Gujarat (37.2 per cent), and simultaneously in Bihar (29.5 per cent), Rajasthan (12.8 per cent), Himachal Pradesh (7.7 per cent) and Kerala (5.1 per cent). The latest report (Crime in India-1997) also reveals that of the seventy-eight cases reported under this Act in 1997, twenty-nine cases were reported from Gujarat followed by Bihar twenty-three and Rajasthan ten. Even though the offence is non-cognizable, the police can take the offenders into custody. It is reported that the police disposed off seventy-two cases in 1997 out of one hundred seven cases including pending cases from investigation of previous year. In sixty cases, chargesheets were laid by the police. Of the two hundred seventy-four cases for trial, sixty-five cases were decided by the courts, in which thirty-seven cases ended in convictions.

A recent research by SAKSHI, a Delhi-based Non-Government Organization (NGO) reveals that eighty per cent of women from all classes experienced some form of sexual abuse in their childhood. More than fifty per cent of these women experienced abuse within their own families or from acquaintances. Over twenty per cent of them have undergone serious and continuing form of sexual abuse by close relatives. So, the female victims are mostly affected in the society. World Health Organisation (WHO) states that one in every ten children is sexually abused. A few case-studies of victimisation of girl child are cited here for exemplifying its gravity. (A)A case, reported in the *Tribune* (January 7, 1993) tells of Amandeep Singh, a student of class VII, who was made to crawl four times along the fifty metre corridor of the boarding house and then caned on his thighs and knees. The reason is that he had forgotten to take his T-shirt from the store room for a rehearsal. (B) The *Tribune* cited another incident occurred in November, 1997. Sonu, an eight-year-old girl-child who was living at home with her parents, was often beaten, sometimes for a mistake and many times even when she made no mistake. (C) Lovely was seven years old. Her uncle, who used to visit often, used to put his hand under her dress to touch her whenever they were alone and sometimes asked her to touch him too. He said that he loved her very much. That was their secret.... He would be very angry if she told anyone.

Like Amandeep, Sonu and Lovely, there are so many female children in our country who are victimised of neglect, physical, emotional and sexual abuse. SAMVADA, a Bangalore-based NGO, surveyed on the different emotional reactions of victims of different types of assault or depression, anxiety, fear, worry, etc., during childhood. These are:

Emotional Reaction	***Percentage***
Sadness	31
Fear	8
Anger	19
Guilt/Shame	5
Shock	2
Helplessness	14
Disgust	7
Humiliation	3
Frustration	7
Confusion	2
Worry	2
Long-term Effects	***Percentage***
Worry	2
Hurt	48
Depression	19
Suicide attempt	2
Problems in Physical	6
Intimacy	8
No long-term effect felt/learnt to handle situation	17

It is only very recently that a Delhi-based NGO, Centre of Concern for Child Labour (CCFCL) has made some inroads into the field. The CCFCL, in a study, has divided the girl child in the domestic sector into two categories—one, who did household tasks and the another, who was engaged in outdoors-economic work. The study revealed those middle or upper middle class families with small children who preferred to employ young girls as domestic help because the help in that case not only came 'cheap' but also was considered safe. The study further observed that like all other women workers in the informal sector, the child domestic workers were subjected to the sword of false allegations ever hanging over them. The Delhi Police, for example, arrested a domestic girl some time ago on a complaint lodged by her employer that she had stolen gold ornaments. It later came out that the girl wanted to quit and had asked for her rightful wages, the charges were just a plot to restrain her. Thus, it is very clear that even though a number of legislative measures have been passed in India for the welfare of children, they have failed to make any impact on life of the girl child because of lack of social and cultural support.

Prospects

Now-a-days just like 'Help-Line' services, there are many 'Child-Line' organisations coming up. But we need to go further and make sure that everyone consciously promotes 'childhood' for all children whatever family or community they belong to. But many, who profess to be friends of children, are the ones who violate her innocence and dignity. Hence, a VICTIM-ASSISTANCE SHOP may be created at state level initially and gradually at district level and in the rural areas of different states. Functions of such a shop will be to propagate the curse of childhood and to get rid of such curse. They will have direct link with judiciary system and police authority. Local residents will be selected to run such shops and local police chief will be responsible to communicate with local citizens-in-charge of such shops. Modalities are to be prepared by the local police, citizens and local Government as per local demands and problems.

2. The question of Children's rights is a very big one covering all aspects of their livelihood and, therefore, it has to be dealt with in a 'holistic' manner remembering that rights are indivisible and interdependent. We have to deal with many categories of 'problem' children or those with 'problems' such as children of nomads, of victims of terrorism, of sex workers, of women in jail, of immigrants or aliens and of consaguineous marriages. There are juvenile delinquents, children with disease or children with physical handicaps and children who belong to poor families. From the 'womb' to the 'tomb', children's rights have to be defined and safeguards provided. The gender differentiation increases the vulnerability of girls in any situation, the girl child is worse off than the boy, not only because she has to contend with her biological society views the role of females and males in society.

3. The government decision to establish a National Commision for Children is to be welcomed so that it can help to implement their rights. A mere advisory and re-commission is not only unnecessary but will also be positively harmful to the interest of children. Therefore, a

commission with power and accountability for implementation is needed for justice to children to become real and accessible.

4, The child-abuse is a national problem and so the responsibility for the welfare of children does not only lie on the government alone, it is the function of the parents, family and the community. In fact, it is their failure and inability, which invites government intervention. Hence, since the 'morning shows the day', the parents have important duty to shoulder the future of child, protection of child from any severe consequences. Some tips are mentioned here for parents which may help to prevent physical, emotional and sexual abuse of children.

* Do listen to the explanation of the child before taking the stick to the child. Children can have problems too.

*Do encourage the child to participate in decision-making matters that concern them. This may help you to become less authoritarian.

* Do listen seriously when your child complains of seniors or teachers in school or elder children in the playground bullying him. It may be necessary for you to intervene.

*If sexual abuse is suspected, support acknowledge and accept what the child is saying and feeling. Disbelief and rejection by adults increases the helplessness and the self-blaming tendency of the child.

* When the child conveys unexplained aversion to adults, try to get to the root of the problem. The child may not know exactly what is wrong but the feeling will exhibit itself in aversion.

*Do be careful while entertaining your child to adults even if he be a trusted servant. Question and educate about the possibility of abuse.

5. The illegal abortion mainly in the private nursing homes should be looked into seriously. Although number of abortions are neither reported nor registered, it is sure that a survey in this respect will increase the statistical data shown by the NCRB. Rather, this may reflect as one of the important problems of our country. In this regard, policy should be enacted which may help in eradicating such illegal abortion.

6. If government feels that merely by legislating a law to amend the conduct rules of civil servants prohibiting the employment of children below the age of 14 years as domestic servants by them is sufficient, it would be a major setback on the part of government to the concern and the plight of millions of child workers in the country. The government should look into its proper implementation. Senior politicians also

expressed that the presence of twenty million child labourers in the country is a great concern for our country. The darkest aspect of this is the prevailing child prostitution. According to one estimate, about 7000 new cases of child trafficking are reported in India every year. If it is multiplied, one cannot imagine its severe consequences. The government should be cautious of such possibility and accordingly, it should take preventive measures to tackle the situation.

7. Last but not the least, the task of making public aware of the dark side of the problem of foeticide and infanticide is to be taken seriously by the society and the government. NGOs, in this regard, should play a pivotal role in the society and they should enter into the remotest corner of villages and propagate against such crimes.

References

1. *From Crime Policing to Victim Policing* by Ezzaf a Fallah St. Martin's Press, New York.

2. Report of *The Times of India*, New Delhi on "Courts need to protect Victims of Crime" July 1999.

3. News published in *The Hindu* 'On the Child Domestic – a Life of Mute Sufferings'– 23rd Oct. 1997.

4. News published in *The Hindu* August 18, 1999 under the caption 'The right to Childhood'.

5. 'Crime in India - 1997' -by National Crime Records Bureau, Government of India.

6. Article published in *The Hindu* by N.R. Madhava Menon entitled 'The Rights of Children'.

7. News item published in the *Tribune* on No. 1, 1997- 'Is Your Child Readily Safe'.

8. 'Dismal Fate of the Girl Child' by Ms. Uma Joshi.

SIXTEEN

FROM WOMB TO TOMB

"There is one rape every 54 minutes, one molestation every 26 minutes, one kidnapping/abduction every 43 minutes, one dowry death every one hour and 42 minutes, one act of cruelty every 33 minutes and one eve teasing every 51 minutes" (Government of India—Data Sheet on violence against women 1991).

Violence against women in their different walks of life, i.e., at home, at workplace and in public sphere is persistently on the increase and has come to be accepted as a common phenomenon. Violence against women is the manifestation of a historically unequal power relationship between men and women. The forces of development have further weakened women's position making them all the more vulnerable to societal violence. In this article, an attempt is made to understand the concept, its different forms, its magnitude and what could be done to mitigate the same. A bird's eye-view is provided and the complexities are untouched. The idea is to create an awareness on the need for a movement against violence as such and against those acts of crimes which are perpetrated only on women because they are women.

The Concept

As per the definition found in the Social Science Encyclopaedia violence entails inflicting emotional, psychological, sexual, physical and/or material danger. It involves the exercise of force[1]. The Country Report submitted to the fourth International Women's Conference at Beijing observes. It is now widely accepted that violence against women is not an isolated phenomenon. Much of it is related to social changes accompanying the processes of development and modernisation.[2] This clearly indicates that the issue cannot be analysed in a vacuum but in the larger context of changing values and norms emanating from modernisation.

Incidence and Magnitude

It is very disheartening to note that till 1988 no data on crimes against women were collected. It was only from 1989 that data relating to crimes against women began to be collected which relate to (a) the incidence of crimes committed (b) number of persons arrested (c) social background of victims. The crimes committed against women are broadly classified under two categories. They are (a) crimes identified under the Indian Penal Code (IPC) and (b) crimes identified under the Special Laws (SL.) Rape (Section 376 IPC), kidnapping and abduction (Sections 363 and 373), dowry homicides (Sections 302 and 304B), torture—physical and mental (Section 498A), molestation (Section 354), eve teasing or sexual harassment (Section 509), Commission of Sati (1987 Act) and indecent representation of women (1986 Act) are the crimes covered under these two categories.

Of the total crimes committed in India under the IPC every year about six per cent are crimes against women. According to Government of India statistics, the total number of crimes against women (under the IPC and the SL excluding murders) increased from 68,000 in 1990 to 1,06,000 in 1995. Thus crimes against women have increased by forty-five per cent in five years [3]. The types of crimes list indicates that about twenty-nine per cent are torture cases, twenty-seven per cent molestation cases, eight per cent immoral traffic cases, five per cent dowry homicide cases and half per cent are other cases. The magnitude of the problem can be well appreciated if we take data relating to one particular crimes say rape. While 2487 cases of rape were reported in 1971 the number increased to 13,754 in 1995 which works out to thirty-eight rapes every day or about three rapes every two hours[4]. Here it should be remembered that the actual number of cases that occur is many times higher than the number registered as many cases remain unreported. In cases like rape, it may be even 15 to 20 times more.

There is found to be high inter-state variations in the crimes committed against women in India. The highest number of crimes are recorded in Maharashtra followed by Madhya Pradesh, Uttar Pradesh, Rajasthan, Andhra Pradesh, Tamil Nadu and West Bengal. In 1995, of the 1,06,471 cases recorded under IPC and SL 15.3 per cent were in Maharashtra, 14.4 per cent in Madhya Pradesh, 11.2 per cent in Uttar Pradesh, 8.8 per cent in Rajasthan, 8.9 per cent in Andhra Pradesh, 8.2 per cent in Tamil Nadu, 6 per cent in West Bengal and 27.6 per cent in other states.[5] In the nation's capital, Delhi, according to Delhi State Commission for Women the rate of crimes against women is far higher, i.e. 34. 1 per lakh of population against the national average of 9.5 which indicated that problem goes far beyond policing and law and order.

The Life Cycle of Women and the Categories of Violence

Let us see how and what kind of violence is perpetrated against women from womb to tomb under various following headings.

(a) Female Foeticide

The right to be born is denied to a female child. Sex determination tests are widely resorted to even in the remotest rural areas to find out the sex of the baby only to kill, if it happens to be a female. It is learnt that about 4000 female babies are aborted in Tamil Nadu alone every year. There is gross underestimation since all cases are unreported and there is no way of estimating such death in the absence of maintenance of records. A survey of fifty gynaecologists in Mumbai revealed that 84 per cent of these doctors were performing tests to determine the sex of the child. The use of these services is not restricted to women from middle class but also include women from working class backgrounds.

There is a clear nexus among physicians, sex determination clinics and abortion centres all operating as a network on the basis of commisions. The Registrar General of India has admitted that 3.6 lakh female foetuses were aborted in India in 1993-94, an estimate based on hospital births alone and a very large number of these are believed to have gone for sex determination test. Though data are hard to obtain, private estimates put the number annually around two lakh. But an additional threat which causes much concern is the development of new pre-selection techniques such as electrophoresis, Ericesson's method, etc., which involve not detection but prior manipulation of the sex of the child. What is the future of the female race in such a context is the moot question which remains unanswered.

(b) Female Infanticide

In many families in the lower rung of the society if female child is fortunate enough not to be aborted then a grim future awaits her soon after her birth in the form of deliberate forced killing by parents/kith and kin. Female infanticide is common in several parts of Tamil Nadu, Rajasthan, Orissa and in certain other parts of India. When a girl child is killed in Usilampatti a village in Tamil Nadu people talk about the ignorance and poverty of the people that lead to this crime but what does not come to limelight is that this is happening in a community that has traditionally valued women as repositories of knowledge related to agricultural practices and seed cultivation and therefore were seen as an asset and not a liability.

With the advent of green revolution and the dominance of cash crop economy this knowledge has become redundant and with it the women who possessed this knowledge. Sanskritisation process has added fuel to fire. Every year, twelve million girls are born in India and roughly three million or twenty-five per cent of them do not survive to see their fifteenth birthday. One million die in the first year itself. Little girls are allowed to die because of malnutrition and diseases and intentionally not treated. Acts of 'omission' and acts of 'commission' account for the lower survival rates of female.[6]

Research studies very clearly indicate that gender discrimination and preference for a son have a growing negative impact on the sex ratio and life expectancy in a number of communities and geographical areas. Female foeticide and infanticide are fundamental violation of the first and foremost right of the child—the right to survive and hence education of masses on this vital issue is a must. The materialism and consumerism projected throgh advertisements create a new value system wherein people are respected for what they possess than what they are. Children of economically weaker sections develop a poor self-esteem because of this.

The media has an important role to play in bringing about the desired changes. It should play conscious and responsible role in changing the status of the girl child through dissemination of information, balanced reporting, depiction of positive roles, avoidance of gender stereotypes, more development news and literature, films that portray girls equal to boys, etc.

Girl Child Labour and Violence Against Girl Child Workers

Poverty forces many families to sent the girl children for work. They are denied the right to education. At the workplace, they are subjected to physical and mental torture of varying degrees. The International Confederation of Free Trade Unions (ICFTU) in its report "Child Labour: World's Best Kept Secrets" points out that there are an estimated fifty-five million children who are workers.[7] Female working children out-number males in both rural and urban areas. For every 1000 male working children in India there are 1193 female working children. The very denial of childhood is an offence or violence against children. When girls of seven to ten years are forced to act as surrogate mothers, it is nothing but violence of a subtle nature.

The problems experienced by girl child workers in beedi (cigar) industry in North Arcot and Tirunelveli districts of Tamil Nadu are worth considering here. More than fifty per cent of the workers in the beedi industry are girls. Girls are pledged for a paltry sum of Rs. 1000 or Rs. 2000 borrowed from the employers by the parents. These children are forced to work 12-14 hours a day. The supervisor has a long whip and sits at the entrance and if any child gossips, it is found to be slack in work the whip is used to beat the child. The rooms are cramped and ill ventilated. Sexual assault of girls of 12-14 years is common.

At the age of 15-16, the girls are withdrawn for marrying them off and employers also do not want grown-up girls since they believe that by that age they become slack in their work. Most of the children suffer respiratory diseases and the incidence of tuberculosis is high among the beedi workers in general. In Tirunelveli, beedi rolling is the occupation of one particular caste and for a girl to get married knowledge of beedi rolling is a must. For beedi rolling, the dust is supplied by the employers for prescribed number of beedies (normally 100) and there is always a shortfall of dust supplied. To make up the shortage girls borrow beedies for an interest, i.e., for every ten beedies borrowed twelve beedies are to be returned, the other two being the interest (popularly known in vernacular as 'vatti beedi' system). In the case of three girls such vatti beedi accumulated to such a huge number that unable to repay they committed suicide according to this case study.[8]

Child Prostitution

Child prostitution is another worrying factor. About fifteen per cent of the nearly two million prostitutes are believed to be children. Minor girls are preferred in the sex trade since they pose a lesser AIDS (Acquired Immune Deficiency Syndrome) risk to their clients. Young girls are purchased or kidnapped and then tortured and sold in various red light areas.[9] A hospital based study in New Delhi has shown that out of the 362 patients who were suffering from STD (Sexually Transmitted Diseases), 58 were below 14 years of age. A majority of the children below seven years were girls. Since below seven is not a sexually active age, the only inference is that they were all victims of sexual abuse[10]. In 1990 out of 9863 reported rapes 394 were committed on children below the age of ten and 2090 on children between the age of 10-16 years. Almost one-third of rape crimes were against minors (Home Ministry, GOI).

It is also clear from the same records that 194 suspicious persons were arrested for rape in Delhi in 1988 in which only four were convicted. One hundred twenty-seven cases of dowry deaths were registered in 1990 in which only one was convicted. A study on the profile of prostitutes in India reveals that at the time of entry fifteen per cent of the women were children and twenty-five per cent of the women were minors between 16-18. The Scheduled Castes women constituted thirty-six per cent, the backward class women twenty-four per cent, illiterate women seventy-one per cent, unmarried women 84.4 per cent, married women 10.6 per cent and divorced, deserted or widowed women five per cent.

Among the causes for entry, economy distress (44 per cent), desertion by spouse (24.5 per cent), deception (11.9 per cent), social custom and family tradition (10.5 per cent) and abduction and kidnapping (2.25 per cent). On their earnings the profile reveals that sixty per cent of the women earn less than Rs. 3000 per month and the actual earnings retained by them works out to Rs. 500-600 after the brothel keepers and pimps have taken their cuts and maintenance of the women's families. The average indebtedness ranges from Rs. 10,000 to Rs. 15,000 thus keeping the women under perpetual bondage. (Child Prostitution in the Twilight? A Status and Action Report).

Trafficking in Children

At the adolescent age, women are subject to lots of cruelty. Their free movement and mobility in search of better avenues of employment are highly restricted in view of increasing social violence against them such as eve-teasing, sexual abuse, rape, kidnapping, molestation, etc. Trafficking in women is consistently on the increase. Utter poverty urges many women of the Third World to migrate thus making them an easy prey for traffickers. Since several Third World governments are promoting export of personnel among which women constitute a significant portion, it becomes imperative to monitor the practices of traffickers in women such as mail order brides, fake marriages via domestic work, entertainment etc. Tourism as a way of economic development has now increased the possibilities for further malpractices.

Abuses against Married Women

Then comes the next stage in women's lives—the married life stage—wherein they are subjected to maximum domestic violence like dowry harassment/dowry death, physical violence, maximum workload both at home and outside, the discarded harmful reproductive technologies being tried out on them in the name of birth control, etc. Hazardous contraceptives such as Depo Provera, Norplant, Net-en are freely available or administered without any thought to informed consent. They have very serious consequences to the health of women. Women are used as guinea pigs. The torture meted out to widows is mental rather than physical in nature. Because of the social stigma attached to re-marriage young widows are forced to remain single only to feel insecure, face humiliation and fight a tough battle for livelihood. The mental torture caused to them by denying them participation in functions and ceremonies cannot be described in words.

Certain other social practices which accord humiliating status to widows are to be condemned very severely. The social institution of absorption of widows by the natal families is dying very fast and they are left uncared to fend for themselves. No doubt, female-headed households are on the increase at an alarming rate. It is a pity that the very same society which denies higher education and employment in the name of culture to women, leaves them high and dry with no alternative livelihood strategy. It is never realised that it is one form of violence against women.

Communal Violence

The worst form of violence that anyone could think of is the communal violence. The lower caste women are invariably the victims of caste politics. Any mass agitation by agricultural labourers for higher wages or better working conditions is suppressed by mass rape of women of these labourers by the rich landlords. Again one of the war crimes is rape of women of the captives or refugees by the soldiers irrespective of which country they belong to. Sometimes the very protectors of law indulge in crimes and stories of custodial rapes are common news in the modern days. In the name of religion the violence perpetrated on women has come to be accepted as a socially approved normal behaviour.

Causes for Concern

The causes for concern are quite simple to understand. They are—(a) Increasing incidence and variety of violence against women, (b) Girl children of 5-15 becoming the victims in increasing numbers, (c) Growing proportion of children in flesh trade, and (d)Large scale trafficking of women at intra and international level.

The United Nations Conference held at Vienna in 1993 upheld for the first time the concept of women's rights as human rights and any form of violence against women is violation of human rights. The conference recognised that "The Human Rights of women are unalienable, integral and indivisible part of universal human rights which meant that the full and equal participation of women in political, civil, economic, social and cultural life at the national, international levels and the eradication of all forms of discrimination on grounds of sex" are the priority of the international community. Human rights cover a whole range of rights relating to life, liberty, equality and dignity of the individual as guaranteed by the constitution or embodied in International covenants. But unfortunately in India both private and public violence against women is on the increase. The mass media continues to depict women as sex objects thereby degrading and dehumanising their life and encourages acts of violence against women and also reinforces traditional stereotyped roles.

Though the causes for violence against women are cited as many ranging from inability to support the family to insanity, one main reason that stands out predominantly is the continuation of patriarchy and unjust social order. Women's subordinate status and dependency are the major causes. Empowerment of women—economic, social, legal, political and cultural, i.e., a multi-pronged strategy to emancipate and empower women will go a long way in reducing the incidence of violence against women both at home and in society. Egalitarian outlook and equal sharing of power, work load, resources and fruits of labour is a must. The responsibility lies not only with the government but with each and every segment of the society.

It is a pity that in our country the need for counselling to victims of violence is not appreciated at all. Temporary shelter homes and rehabilitation strategies are other important requirements. But unfortunately the victims of violence are looked down upon with social stigma, further accentuating their misery. The outlook should change and this requires awareness among public at large on issues relating to violence against women. On the one hand, efforts should be directed to reduce the incidence of violence against women and on the other hand public should be enlightened on the need for after-care of victims and their legitimate right to claim justice. This calls for sea-change in social values and norms relating to human lives.

References

1. Stando Elisabeth A. 'Violence' Adam Kuper & Jessoca Kuper (ed) 'The Social Science Encyclopaedia' Routledge, London, 1996, p.186

2. Government of India, Ministry of HRD, Dept. of WCD—Fourth World Conference on Women, Beijing, 1995, Country Report, p.49.
3. Crimes in India, 1995, p.223.
4. *Ibid.,* 1995, p. 222.
5. Ibid, 1995, pp. 224 and 231.
6. UNICEF's Gender Equity: Towards Women's Empowerment in 'The Progress of India States', Nov. 1995, pp. 57-59.
7. Economic Times, 16.694.
8. Karunanidhi, Child Labour in the Beedi Industry, Unpublished Manonmaniam, Sundaranar University, Tirunelveli.
9. CBCI, Women's Commission Newsletter, Vol, IV, No. 3, May-June, 1997, p. 7.
10. The Hindutan Times, 4.3.94.

SEVENTEEN

AGENDA FOR CRIME VICTIMS

When a crime took place, concern of the criminal justice system all over the world till the middle of the twentieth century was to prosecute the accused and punish the guilty. Victims of crime and the problems faced by them during the investigation, trial and after the trial have been completely neglected since the State took over the responsibility of the criminal justice system. The orientation of the criminal justice agencies all along has been to focus on the phenomenon of crime, its perpetrator and to prove the guilt of the perpetrator and to get him a conviction. Only in the early 1940s, realization about the role of victims in crime and the need to undertake scientific research about crime victims began after the introductory expositions made by the pioneers in Victimology such as Hans Lion Henting and Benjamin Mendelsohn. Since then, several milestones have been made in the development of the science of Victimology and on the advocacy for the recognition of victims of crime in the criminal proceedings.

The first among the major landmarks in the field of Victimology was the collectivity of victim advocates comprising various sections of the society such as researchers and academicians interested in Victimology and practitioners in the fields of criminal justice system in Jerusalem in 1973 for the first time in the First International Symposium on Victimology and their decision to meet once every three years to share and discuss the developments in the field (Chockalingam, K. 1995).

The plight of victims of crime and of illegal abuse of power has been arousing concern in recent years. Proliferating instances of victimization, both of individuals and of vulnerable groups, have provoked feelings of empathy, of shared vulnerability and the need for effective preventive and remedial action. Though the response still lags far behind the need, there seems to be a growing recognition that the common bond of humanity and self-interest as well as the climate of insecurity and fear in which so many people live, require strengthened ties of social solidarity and joint action to reduce the suffering and damage which criminal and other illicit acts inflict.

The second landmark is the founding of the World Society of Victimology in 1979 during the Third International Symposium on Victimology in Germany to promote empirical research on victimology, and to focus attention of the nations and criminal justice systems of the world on the need to render justice to victims. Since the founding of the World Society of Victimology, Triennial International Symposia on Victimology have been sponsored by the society and organized the participation of researchers and practitioners in the criminal justice system, with the unanimous view to uphold the human rights to victims of crime and abuse of power. Criminologists and Victimologists of the world have consistently felt that when the rights of offenders, suspects and accused have been protected through several international instruments such as the United Nations Standard Minimum Rules for the Treatment of Prisoners and provisions in the national constitutions, there was nothing at the international or at national level in most of the countries to protect the rights of the victims of crime and abuse of power.

Realizing the precarious conditions of victims of crime, the World Society of Victimology prepared a draft Victim Bill in consultation with experts from different countries of the world and after long deliberations at the Fifth International Symposium on Victimology at Zagreb in 1985 pressed for its adoption by the Seventh United Nations Congress on the Prevention of Crime and Treatment of Offenders held in Milan in September, 1985. For the first time in the history of the U.N. Congress on Crime Prevention, victims of crime and abuse of power became an item of the agenda for deliberations by all the countries leading to an intense debate resulting in a consensus among all the countries to have a declaration on victims with certain modifications. Finally, the Declaration on the Basic Principles of Justice for victims of crime and abuse of power was unanimously adopted by the General Assembly of the United Nations on 29th November, 1985. The adoption of the Declaration on victims by the United Nations is the third significant landmark and this instrument is a "Magna Carta" for the victims (United Nations, 1985).

The Declaration on victims envisages four important aspects of rights of victims of crime and abuse of power, viz., Access to justice and fair treatment, Restitution, Compensation and Assistance. A review of the position of victims of crime in the national criminal laws and the progress in the implementation of the U.N. Declaration on victims by the United Nations revealed that even after a decade of adoption of the Declaration by the General Assembly, not much attention was paid by majority of the nations to implement the provisions of this declaration, more particularly among developing countries.

Handbook on Justice for Victims and Guide for Policy Makers.

Concerned about the inaction and slow progress in the implementation of the U.N. Declaration on Victims, the U.N. Commission on Crime Prevention and Criminal Justice in May, 1996 adopted a resolution to develop two international documents, viz., (i) A Handbook on Justice for Victims (United Nations, 1998 A) and (ii) a Guide for Policy Makers United Nations, 1998 B) with the help of experts from different countries. Several groups of experts met four times during the last four years and the Fourth Expert Group meeting convened at Washington D.C. in April, 1998, in which the author was also a member, finalized the two documents. The Handbook on Justice for Victims is an elaborate document meant for the different practitioners including the frontline professionals in the criminal justice system, viz., police prosecutors, judiciary and correctional departments and other victim assistance professionals providing methods and techniques by which victims could be handled and assisted. On the other hand, the brief document, viz., the Guide for Policy Makers lists out the objectives of the U.N. Declaration on the Basic Principles of justice for victims of crime and abuse of power and the State's responsibility to implement the declaration by enacting new laws or incorporating new provisions in the existing laws to assist victims of crime and abuse of power.

Development in the Field of Victimology and Victim Assistance in India

Realizing the plight of victims of crime and abuse of power in India is all the more high, due to the vast differences in the socio-economic conditions and discrimination perpetrated in the name of caste, creed, sex and religion, illiteracy and many other factors by people among themselves and also by the agencies of the government in its various administrative functions, a national organization in the name of Indian Society of Victimology was established in Chennai in 1992. Its main objectives were to promote victimological research, victim assistance and dissemination of knowledge about the rights of victims of crime and abuse of power and to bring together people who are interested in victim empowerment.

During the last eight years, the Indian Society of Victimology has endeavoured to disseminate the victimological principles among the members of the general society and the agencies of the criminal justice system through its seminars, symposia and conferences. Two significant events in the annals of the Indian Society of Victimology deserve special mention here. Due to the consistent efforts of the Indian Society of Victimology, the Government of Tamil Nadu has established a "Victims Assistance Fond" (Government of Tamil Nadu, 1995) since 1995 through which three specific categories of victims of violent crimes, viz., murder, rape and grievous hurt are eligible to get a compensation of Rs. 10000, Rs. 5000 and Rs. 5000 respectively, recognizing the need of the victim, through this is only a token amount.

The Government of Tamil Nadu has allocated one crore rupees in the year 1995 (the same is renewed year after year) and effected some amendments in it in 1997 (Government of Tamil Nadu, 1997). In May, 1999, the Government of Tamil Nadu has extended the compensation to three more categories of victims, viz., women victims of kidnapping and abduction (Rs. 5000), victims of attempted murder in dowry harassment (Rs. 5000 if the victim dies), children of victims who commit suicide (Rs. 10000), women who are permanently disabled in a dowry harassment (Rs. 5000) Government of Tamil Nadu, 1999.

Not being content with this State scheme and also recognizing the need for a national level law for victim compensation, the Indian Society of Victimology prepared a Victims (Criminal Injuries) Right to Assistance Bill, 1996 drafted by an expert committee consisting of some retired judges of the Supreme Court, High Court, Criminal Lawyers, Professors of Criminal Law and Criminology under the chairmanship of Justice V.R. Krishna Iyer, which was sponsored by the National Human Rights Commission. This Bill was considered as an immediate measure to be taken at the national level to provide monetary compensation and other assistance to victims of crime and the same was forwarded to the-then Prime Minister, home and law ministers of the Government of India for adoption as a national law for victim assistance. Justice V.R. Krishna Iyer also addressed letters to the-then Prime Minister, the home and law ministers to consider the Bill for adoption as a national law.

The United Nations Commission on Crime Prevention and Criminal Justice also supported the initiative of the Indian Society of Victimology and wrote to the Government of India, in April 1998, for bringing out a national level legislation in tune with the U.N. Declaration on the Basic

Principles of Justice for Victims of Crime and Abuse of Power, to assist crime victims in India but so far it has not been done.

Third Biennial Conference of the Indian Society of Victimology

The National Conferences of the Indian Society of Victimology have always served as fora to project the cause of crime victims in India. The First Biennial Conference held in Madras in 1994 took up the subject of women as victims of crime as one of its main themes for deliberations, whereas the Second Biennial Conference held at the National Law School, Bangalore had deliberated on the only theme of 'A Comprehensive Victim Bill for India' and adopted the victim bill prepared by the expert Committee constituted by the ISV (Indian Society of Victimology, 1996; Chockalingam, K. 1998).

The main theme of the third Biennial Conference was "Child Victims of Crime Issues and Prospects" with the following two sub-themes:

1. Victimization of Child: Various Forms and Patterns.
2. Protection of Child from Victimization: Strategies and Innovations.

The preamble of the United Nations 'Convention on the Rights of the Child' (United Nations, 1989) states the significance of childhood and the need to protect it in the following words: The Universal Declaration of Human Rights, 1948, has proclaimed that the childhood is entitled to special care and assistance. The family, as the fundamental group of society and the natural environment for the growth and well-being of all its members, particularly children, should be afforded the necessary protection and assistance so that it can fully assume its respnsibilities within the community. For the full and harmonious development of his or her personality, the child should grow up in a family environment in an atmosphere of happiness, love and understanding. The child should be fully prepared to live an individual life in society, and brought up in the spirit of the ideals proclaimed in the Charter of the United Nations, and in particular in the spirit of peace, dignity, tolerance, freedom, equality and solidarity.

The need to extend particular care to the child has been stated in the Geneva Declaration of the Rights of the Child of 1924 and in the Declaration of the Rights of the Child adopted by the General Assembly on 20th November, 1959, and recognized in the Universal Declaration of Human Rights, in the International Covenant on Civil and Political Rights and in the Statutes and relevant instruments of specialized agencies and the international organizations concerned with the welfare of the child. The Declaration of the Rights of the Child states that the child, by reason of his physical and mental immaturity need special safeguards and care, including appropriate legal protection, before as well as after birth.

The Declaration on Social and Legal Principles relating to the protection and welfare of children, with special reference to foster placement and adoption, the U.N. Standard Minimum Rules for the Administration of Juvenile Justice (The Beijing Rules) and the Declaration of the Protection of Women and Children in emergency and armed conflicts, recognize that, in all countries there are children living in exceptionally difficult conditions and that such children need special consideration; take due account of the importance of the traditions and cultural values of people for the protection and harmonious development of the child; recognize the importance of the international cooperation for improving the living conditions of children in every country, particularly in developing countries.

Forms of Child Victimizations—International and National

The background paper for the workshop on the prevention of violent crime presented by the United Nations in its 9th U.N. Congress on Prevention of Crime and Treatment of Offenders held in Cairo in April, 1995 states that "in the U.S.A., homicide is one of the five major causes of death in young children". The same study quotes some alarming figures. In Brazil, four children are murdered each day, representing an increase of forty per cent over the year 1993; in the Philippines, Sri Lanka and Thailand, there are estimated to be more than five lakh cases of child prostitution. In the U.S. in 1992, 7000 children were killed using firearms. At least ninety per cent of domestic violence in Canada is targetted at women and children. In Asia, it is reckoned that one hundred million women are estimated to have 'disappeared'. According to the experts, this figure may be partly attributable to the selected destruction of foetuses, infanticide, and the abandonment of female children.

A recent study on the prevalence and consequences of child victimization sponsored by the National Institute of Justice in U.S. in 1997 and conducted by the National Crime Victims Research and Treatment Centre at the Medical University of South Carolina among 4023 adolescents and their parents indicate that a significant number of the youth of today have been victims of sexual and physical abuse and have personally witnessed incidents of violence against others. Extrapolating the findings of this study to the national adolescent population as a whole suggests that of the 22.3 million adolescents in the age of twelve to seventeen years in the U.S. today, approximately 1.8 million have been victims of serious sexual assault, 3.9 million have been victims of serious physical assault, and almost 9 million have witnessed serious violence. Nearly 2 million have suffered from Post Traumatic Disorder Syndrome (PTDS), and about 3.4 million have been drug or alcohol abusers as well.

Analysis of the survey information indicates a strong correlation between drug abuse and delinquency. Further findings indicate that more females than male adolescents had been sexually assaulted with 13 per cent of females in contrast to 3.4 per cent of males. Also young males had significantly higher rates of physical assault than females, with 21.3 per cent versus 13 per cent. The data also revealed that the youth from lower income groups experienced higher rates of sexual and physical assault than those from middle and higher income groups (Kilpatrick, 1997). The trend of these findings may be similar in many other countries too, including India.

In India, the child victimizations or child abuse have been found to take several forms—physical, sexual and emotional. The perpetrators of violence on children range from the friendly neighbour to the tough school teacher to the child's own parents. Some perverted streak in men and women impel them to hurt and injure children both physically and mentally. The abused children are hesitant to talk about their experiences because they are unable to comprehend or articulate what has happened to them and also because the people who abuse them have threatened them with dire consequences if they reveal it. While physical abuse takes the form of beating, inflicting burns, strangulation, battering and bites and is most prevalent among child workers and children in alcoholic families, emotional abuse is very common and happens in many homes everyday. Affluent families are unexception for the prevalence of child abuse. Parental favouritism, constant negative comparisons and castigation for being "under-achievers" can nag a child into depression. Often, it is the sheer neglect on the part of parents to identify the symptoms of abuse in their children that leads to extreme situations.

While children may not be able to explain what has happened to them in detail, they give off certain signals that must be watched out for. Physical indicators such as unexplained bruises, welts, bite marks, fractures, torn or bloody undergarments, difficulty in walking and sitting, venereal diseases and fatigue must be investigated. The more subtle behavioural disorders such as delinquency, violence, withdrawal symptoms, chronic depression, shying off physical touch, suicide attempts and hysteria over a prolonged period are also indicators that the child may be undergoing victimization or abuse.

Priorities of Action towards Justice for Victims

Creation of Awareness

Criminal Justice systems have a moral and legal responsibility to make all efforts to prevent crime victimization and also to provide relief and satisfaction to the victims. In India, creating awareness at all levels is the basic and immediate need to recognize that the sufferings of victims are unfortunate and the society condemns such sufferings and to motivate the society and people at large about the importance of preventing victimization and taking care of victims.

Even in developed countries where victim support and service systems have been sufficiently established, awareness campaign is an ongoing process. For example, in the United States, Congress designates one week each year usually in late April, as "National Crime Victims Rights Week" for the last two decades and it is declared by the President of the United States each year to highlight the needs of crime victims and the types of rights and services that could respond to those needs. Declarations are signed by many leading politicians such as State Governors and Mayors. During the week, national awards are presented to outstanding victim sevice providers from across the country. The week also provides opportunity for local communities to pay tribute to crime victims.

The U.S. Department of Justice sponsors the development of a Public Awareness Resource Guide for victim assistance programmes to use in planning "National Crime Victims Rights Week" activities. Hundreds of ideas to increase public awareness of victims issues have been presented in the guide. They include runs, rallies, memorial walls and sapling plantings; conducting forums, publishing editorials and broadcasting public service announcements; displaying posters and distributing brochures and other information in court buildings, school libraries and local retail establishments. Europe celebrates each year a "European Victims Day" with new initiatives being announced. In 1997, the European Forum for Victim Services issued a "Statement of Victims rights in the process of criminal justice" which focused on the rights for the victim to—

1. Respect and recognition at all stages of the criminal proceedings.
2. Receive information and explanation about the progress of the case.
3. Provide information to officials responsible for decisions relating to the offender.
4. Have legal advice available, regardless of their means.
5. Protection both for their privacy and for their physical safety.
6. Compensation both from the offender and from the State.

In the Netherlands, Victim Satisfaction Surveys (like customer satisfaction surveys) are regularly conducted by the office of the public prosecution.

A peer review system in the Police Department has also been establised in the Netherlands in which, after the victim has been questioned by a police detective, a second detective inquires of the victims regarding how he or she had been treated by the first detective. The responses are used to improve their training further. In Japan, a number of questionnaries regarding the treatment of citizens by the police are carried out both by the National Police Agency and some prefectural police forces. These are used as a means of improving the police treatment of victims and civilians.

The United States has created a separate section as Office for Victims of Crime (OVC) in the Federal Department of Justice and many other countries have also created a section for victims in their Home or Interior Ministries. On the similar lines in the Home Ministry of the Government and Union Territories, a separate section to deal with issues of victims of crime should be opened. This could be first step to recognise the problems of victims of crime and to chalk out programmes to alleviate their problems, to collect information and disseminate information about victim issues.

Victim Assistance is the Need of the Hour

What is most important in the case of victims of crime, particularly, child victims is the immediate assistance to be rendered to them to relieve them from victimization. Experiments have been initiated in Maharashtra, Tamil Nadu and a few other states to provide rescue to the children in difficult circumstances. For example, as early as in 1994, the Indian Council for Child Welfare, Chennai, set up a Crisis Intervention Centre to "intervene, prevent, rescue and rehabilitate children from all kinds of abuse". The Directorate of Social Defence, Government of Tamil Nadu has started a twenty-four hour phone outreach programme called "CHILDLINE" for helping children in distress in Chennai from April 30, 1999 onwards with a toll free telephone number of 1098. Any child in distress or an adult who sees a child in distress can call the number and provide details to the volunteers attending the call. Any child who is abandoned, runs away, requires help, lives alone on the streets, needs a place to stay, is abused or needs help to go back to the family can call the number for help.

While the Directorate of Social Defence is the nodal agency for the "Childline" services, two NGOs viz., Indian Council for Child Welfare and Don Bosco Anbu Illam function as the collaborating agencies receiving the calls and providing immediate assistance to the child. The response mechanism had been activated in such a way as to render assistance to children, depending on the needs of each case, within fifteen minutes of receiving the call. A log book records all calls received, details regarding the nature of intervention, action taken and subsequent follow-up activities would all be recorded in an effort to build up a data base of children's problem in Channai. "Childline" is funded by the Ministry of Social Justice and Empowerment.

When we are at the threshold of the third millennium, it is the duty of the State and Society to care for its crime victims and treat them with human dignity. Such duty is more paramount when it comes to child victims of crime who are defenceless in majority of the cases, I hope that the Indian Society of Victimology and other organisations, NGOs through deliberations will pave way for the statutory recognition of rights of victims of crime in general and child victims in particular.

References

Chockalingam, K. "A Review of Victimological Developments in India", *Japanese Journal of Victimology,* Vol. 3, No. 20, 1995, pp. 78-95.

Chockalingam, K. "March Towards Implementation of Victim Bill in India" in 'Society and Politics—Issues and Perspectives' (Ed) T.P. Sankaran Kutty Nair, Indian Institute of Police Studies, Thiruvananthapuram, 1998, pp. 550-68.

Government of Tamil Nadu "Creation of Victims Assistance Fund" Home (Police-XII) Department, G.O.M.S. No.----?89, dated 24.01.1997.

Government, of Tamil Nadu (1999) "Victims Assistance Fund—Provision of Relief to Certain Women Victims of Additional Crimes Against Women", Home (Police-XII) Department, G.O.M.S. No. 629, dated 10.05.1999.

Indian Society of Victimology, "The Victims (Criminal Injuries) Right to Assistance Bill" Draft Bill prepared and presented at the II Biennial Conference of the Indian Society of Victimology, at the National Law School of India University, Bangalore, October 5-7, 1996.

Kilpatrick, "The Prevalence and Consequences of Child Victimisation", NIJ Research Preview, April, 1997, 8 pages.

United Nations (1989) "Convention on the Rights of the Child" in Compendium of United Nations Standards and Norms in Crime Prevention and Criminal Justice, United Nations, New York, 1992, pp. 271-78.

United Nations Declarations on the Basic Principles of Justice for Victims of Crime and Abuse of Power, U.N. General Assembly Resolutions, 40/34, 1985.

United Nations Handbook on Justice for Victims—on the Use and Application of the United Nations Declaration on the Basic Principles of Justice for Victims of Crime and Abuse of Power, 161 Pages, 1998 A.

United Nations Guide for Policymakers—on the Implementation of the United Nations Declarations on the Basic Principles of Justice for Victims of Crime and Abuse of Power, 31.

Records for Young Children [illegible]

Government [illegible] Nepal [illegible] [illegible] Kathmandu, [illegible]. [illegible] of Child Rights [illegible] Addressing [illegible] [illegible] [illegible] (1989 [illegible]).

Indian Council of [illegible] Welfare, National [illegible] [illegible] Rights [illegible] [illegible] [illegible] and [illegible] Child [illegible] [illegible] [illegible] Conference of the [illegible] Society [illegible] [illegible] [illegible] [illegible] [illegible] [illegible] [illegible].

Kilpatrick, [illegible] [illegible] and [illegible] [illegible] American [illegible] [illegible] [illegible] pages.

[illegible] (1989). Convention on the Rights of the Child [illegible] [illegible] [illegible] United Nations [illegible] and [illegible] of [illegible] [illegible] [illegible] Criminal Justice [illegible] [illegible] [illegible] 1992 [illegible]

United Nations [illegible] [illegible] [illegible] [illegible] [illegible] Victims of Crime and Abuse of Power [illegible] [illegible] General [illegible] [illegible] [illegible] 1985.

United Nations Handbook on Justice for Victims on the Use and Application of the United Nations Declaration of Basic Principles of Justice for Victims of Crime and Abuse of Power [illegible] [illegible]

United Nations Congress [illegible] [illegible] on the Implementation of the United Nations Declaration on [illegible] Principles of Justice for Victims of Crime and Abuse of Power [illegible]

PART - III

PREY TO SEX

EIGHTEEN

SEXUAL ABUSE

In the last few years sexual abuse of children had increased considerably, and every tenth child in India was sexually abused. The preponderance of girl prostitutes from Nepal and Bangladesh can be attributed to prevailing abject poverty and ignorance in both these countries in comparison to India. The Government of India's Central Advisory Committee consisting of government officials and representatives from NGOs, first attempted to assess the magnitude of child prostitution, and found no reliable statistics either on the number of prostitutes in the country, or the number of child prostitutes.

The Convention on the Rights of the Child clearly lays down the role of the state in the protection of the child in Article 34, where it notes that the state will undertake to protect the child from all forms of sexual exploitation and abuse. Articles 35 and 36 state that all appropriate national, bilateral and multilateral measures will be taken by the state to prevent abduction, sale and traffick in children, coercion to engage in unlawful sexual activity, and all forms of excitation such as prostitution or pornographic performances. It also states that all children must receive the opportunity to discover their identity and realise their self-worth in a safe and supportive environment. But when a child is sexually exploited, what is denied is his or her childhood. The very basis of the child sex industry designating of a child as a commodity for sale and purchase demeans and dehumanises the child. It also serves the sexual drive of sexually immature men who seek emotional release by exploiting a completely powerless slave child.

The sexual exploitation of children does not occur in a vacuum but involves a more widespread exploitation, sexual or otherwise. Poverty and ignorance are the underlying causes of this worldwide phenomenon, as families rely on their youngest members to contribute to the household income. The child in prostitution is a victim of paedophiles who pose as tourists and of traffickers who force them into this trade.

All over the world, the child's vulnerability to commercial sexual exploitation lies in his or her family circumstances. The majority of sexually exploited children are either from marginalised families in the cities, and destitute families in the country, or children of women already in the sex industry.

The continued sexual abuse of children for commercial gain can no longer be hidden. The issue has now been brought out into the light of day where people can stare directly at it and see the potential for evil and horror and destruction which is always there in the heart of society.

In India, the demand for children comes mainly from the local population. However, India and other South Asian countries are slowly replacing South-East Asia as the venue of choice for foreigners, as there are fewer laws against child sexual abuse, and South Asian children can be bought more cheaply.

The Convention on Rights of the Child has been ratified by 178 countries including India. It gives the NGOs, lawyers, government officials, and police officers, no choice except to take all possible steps in ensuring protection of the rights of children. We do not need more legislations. We already have a number of laws which are not being implemented. The NGO 'role' has almost become a pattern of speech. The chosen rhetoric is that the NGOs are the closest to the target groups, that the NGO role is the critical one. It is a way of transferring responsibility from one sector to another. The government and we, however, cannot escape the responsibility. NGOs can be partners, not substitutes, in the government's efforts. There is a need to raise public sensitivity to these problems that confront us in our work.

The problem of child prostitution has to be addressed not merely through rehabilitation, but with greater emphasis on prevention. There are backward villages and districts that are the source areas for the traffickers. That is where the real problem is. The brothels in the cities are a symptom of the problem. NGOs working towards rural development should target such poor families that are forced to send their children to earn.

We do not have the skills to search the underworld mafia. It is dangerous. There are people who are making a lot of money in trafficking. We have seen the power of community action in Manila where the parents of the children went on a march and demanded justice; and in Goa where protests are going on; on the beach areas of Sri Lanka, where small community groups are committed to monitor the problem in order to protect their own children. The community has to rise up, and it is not something that is going to be easy.

In recent years, there has been growing awareness in the country of the menacing dimensions and implications of child prostitution. The difference between reality and application of the law indicates that the issue of child prostitution is more hidden than exposed. This sorry state of affairs rather create a number of serious problems in the country and the Human Rights Commission has decided to have this issue considered on regular basis by a core groups comprising, inter alia, the National Commission for Women, the Department of Women and Child Development, selected NGOs and UNICEF. This group is, inter alia considering adequacy of existing laws and the ways of improving their enforcement, necessity of making progress on such issues holding of public meetings, seminars in the specific areas and so on in order to remove or minimise the child prostitution.

There is a strong correlation between family abuse of children, especially girls, and the drive to enter the sex trade. The mother in particular, plays a central role in her daughter's life decisions. The evidences show that there is direct commercial sexual exploitation of children due to the family situations. Poverty despair and newly dislocating values promote such incidence of sexual exploitation among the children. Even though poverty is often said to be the cause of sale of children into labour, actually not of poor families sell their children. Some families sell the child due to poverty, unemployment, consumerism and other adverse situations. Sometimes, however, a child is sold into commercial sex by parents who have themselves sexually or otherwise abused the child. The child is found "ready" for sex and able to earn money for the family. Such parents get lumpsum money for their children and put their children into "bondage", a situation in which the child is forced to provide sex to earn money to repay the family's debt to the exploiter.

Commercial sexual exploitation of children is evident in an organised industrial sector from small business to large factories. There are people who use technology to sell the product to promote "good business". This "industry" is on abuse of children involved in deception, enslavement, bribery and corruption at different levels. The impact of commercial sexual exploitation on child has assumed staggering positions. The child loses its childhood, its dignity, often its future, These are unquestionable causes, but these are mal-effects of exploitation which are more miserable. The most obvious of these relates to the health of the child. HIV/AIDS is both a cause and consequence of commercial, sexual exploitation of children.

The evidence shows that children are being chosen as sex partners by the miscreant people who consider sex with a child as "safer". Having sex with a chid, it is thought, protects and abuse from a HIV/AIDS, because the child is more likely to be "clean". But the fact is otherwise because of their vulnerability and weaknesses. Children in prostitution who often forced to take more clients than adult might accept and are generally too weak to protest or avoid the situation. Moreover, children are physically more vulnerable to infection because of their socio-economic weakness. The 'virgin' child is sought by many customers as the "safest".

Nowadays another problem is reconstruction surgery which promotes commercial exploitation of sex with children making multiple operations. Thus, the child is more infected with HIV as is found through some studies. Thus, the innocent child is met with death sentence meaning thereby that his/her life may be left without any family or community life, dignity and options. There are, besides, various physical and psychological reactions among the children forcing them into sex.

Children trapped in the cycle of commercial sex are often physically abused, beaten, burnt, tortured and deprived of food, air, light and movement. They are also vulnerable to kidney infections, cervical cancer, early and repeated pregnancies and sexually transmitted diseases. Numerous studies have also shown high levels of abuse by children involved in prostitution. Drugs are often used to keep children taken into prostitution submissively. They may also be a self-medicating means to numb the pain of hunger or despair.

There are national and international laws and constitutional provisions for the safeguard of the children's rights. There are police and law enforcement agencies around the world to combat commercial sexual exploitation of children.

At the national level, many countries enacted laws making children's abuse a crime. In recent years there has been growing awareness of commercial sexual exploitation of children. Children are trafficked across borders. Exploiters travel to set up their network. Clients go to buy services on foreign shores for promotion of their "trade". Several countries have enacted extra-territorial legislation. As a result, the foreigners are arrested for child sex crimes, bribing their way to freedom and escaping to their home country. It is said that making laws is not the same as enforcing them. It is certainly difficult to make laws work well against such odds. It is more difficult when local laws make them scot-free and safeguard the culprits exploiting the children.

It is often neglected, for example, in the face of pressures to promote tourism in a country and authorities turn a blind eye.

The modern media and technology although develop consumerism leading to sexual trade, they can remove or reduce the menace to the minimum. The advent of the internet has opened up new channels of information for those seeking access to children for sex. The negative nature of internet technology means that information can be shared really time and again on "special requests" deal with by promoters and suppliers of children for sex. Pornographic images and video clips can be up-loaded and down-loaded anonymously. Besides technology the press and media also play a major role in the domain of commercial, sexual, exploitation of children, both positive and negative.

On the negative side the media contributed to the liberalisation of sexually explicit imagery and to shift any moral values. Satellite technology, international travel and support infrastructures means that such images are often receive in a non-supportive context. Many TV viewers are adolescent and their attitude to adolescence itself is worthless. On the negative side, many reporters investigating commercial, sexual exploitation leading to pornography and further sex exploitation. Journalists have unwittingly corrupted evidence by paying for stories, enabling criminals to escape conviction.

Press and media can play both positive and negative roles in exploitation of children for sex. The press and media can contribute immensely to advocacy, underlining positive moral values and human rights. They can support positive family values and inform parents when their children are at risk. They can hold children themselves to draw moral values on their own behaviour and to identify risk factors of their social situations.

According to the Convention of the Rights of the Child (CRC), child labour may be regarded as a denial of child right. Under this right come rehabilitation, protection of child workers and improvement of their working conditions. Hence regulation of these aspects of child labour is felt essential. Right to Education and access to recreation and to childhood itself are associated with the rights of the child. The concept of childhood is relatively of recent significance particularly in the context of children's rights. For the first time the French Revolution in 1789 led stress on equality, fraternity, and dignity of the human being from whom the rights of the man have emerged. In the 19th century, the children were not given any special importance rather their ignorance and weakness led to all kinds of torture, operations and misuse of their labour and comfort. It was taken for granted that child labour is due to poverty.

It is found that child labour has been due to the negative attitude of parents and of the society in general. Some argue that "work is experiential learning and good for the child". Children were suffering from various deficiencies and ailments and adequate care was not taken by the poof parents and the society. Hence, declaration of the rights of the child in 1959 is taken as a significant step in the "Best interest of the child". Nowadays ILO, UNESCO and other international agencies take interest in safeguarding the child rights particularly in relation to the exploitation of child labour. The CRC in fact devotes much greater attention to civil rights than to the economic, social and cultural rights.

The implementation of economic, social and cultural rights is made subject to the availability of the resources while civil and political rights have corresponding obligations and progressive implementation of economic, social and cultural rights. A country's richness is judged by the norms like "maximum extent of utilisation of valuable resources" in order to address child labour more effectively. With this background, child labour is now considered in a humanitarian as well as human rights approach.

Child labour is taken as a violation of civil and political rights or a violation of economic, social and cultural rights. However, all these rights are interacted and immediate steps need be taken for taking all these aspects or effectively breaking a point in the vicious circle. Of course, we cannot resolve the problem overnight, but no time can be delayed for taking adequate action in the matter. Under the CRC, there are various requests relating to child labour-discrimination, abuse, encroachment to privacy and recreation impeachment on the child's education and safety and security of the child.

Child labour is attributed mainly to exploitation, discrimination, powerlessness, caste and gender operation. There are various attitudinal factors which are responsible for taking children to hazardous jobs on dignified services and insecure and indecent life-callings. Even the World Bank is imposing restrictions on the misuse of child labour. It is estimated that the greater productivity of those children who remain in primary schools for reasonable time will enable them to earn over six times the cost of giving them the additional education. Primary education, says the Bank, is the largest single contributor to the economic growth rates of high performance.

Although a number of legislations have been enacted to regulate child labour, it has not yet been possible to bring child labour even to the minimum or to a reasonable standard. It is, therefore, insisted that there should be a Constitutional amendment to transfer the subject of education from a Directive Principle of State Policy to a Fundamental Right so that the government will be bound to provide minimum standard of education to every child.

Various NGOs are now active to control the quantum of child labour and reduce its harmful reactions and repercussions. Government has also set up a few committees to deal with child rights in its various sections of the society. It has also set up the National Human Commission to look into not only the human rights in general but also children's rights in particular. At present, a proposal is given to set up a separate commission for protection and safeguarding children's rights. India has tremendous armoury of legislations, regulations and statutes which call for the protection of the rights of children.

The Directive Principles of State Policy embedded in the Constitution of India seek compulsory primary education for all children. This is one of their basic rights and a goal still far from realisation. India is also a party to save International Conventions regarding protection of children's rights. India also ratified CRC in December 1992 which states in Article 32 "State parties recognised rights of the child to be protected from economic exploitation and from performing any work, i.e., likely to be hazardous or to, interfere with the child's education or to be harmful to the child's wealth or physical, mental, spiritual, moral or racial development". In ratifying this Convention, India has assumed yet another obligation to bring national laws and practices into conformity with international standards.

The UNICEF has identified the following causative factors relating to inequalities and abuse of child's right in the context of children's labour. These are:

— Bonded to pay up debts to landlords incurred by their parents;

— Working in situations in which their parents are unemployed; and

— Not paid the minimum wages and prone to physical, mental and sexual abuse by employers.

The Human Rights Commission has recently perceived that there is a growing recommendation in the seniormost policy-making circles of the country of the need for ending child labour, supporting with those employed in hazardous industries. This had led to the approval of series of constructive measures by the central government. Even the state governments have followed the suit and have implementing a number of restricting legislations.

In India, the government has taken steps to constitute a National Authority for the Elimination of Child Labour (NAECL) and also a National Child Labour Project (NCLP) which is being undertaken in twelve different areas of the country. The Commission is also most respectful of the fact that the Department of Education has deliberated on this matter carefully and that instead of All India Legislations on Child Labour, it has chosen to adopt a different strategy to achieve the goal of the Universalisation of elementary education.

NINETEEN

TRAUMAS OF RAPE

It is rightly being said that the reason why we have not been able to prevent child abuse is that we deal with the symptoms and rarely attack the root causes embedded in the society. Many of the propelling factors leading to child abuse are already known to us, e.g., poverty, illiteracy, broken homes, overwhelming mothers, social isolation, interaction between the social class and social stress. There are no concerted and co-ordinated efforts to tackle these roots of problems. Although great studies have been made in dealing with the problem of child abuse, it is still pandemic. It is clear that the problem is more widespread than previously though. The numbers of cases of child abuse are reported increasingly by the media.

The true incidents of child abuse culmination in sexual abuse often go unreported. It is a well-known phenomenon that unlike other crimes, sexual crime creates immense sensitivity in the society. People still do not like to discuss sex openly, and even today it is unthinkable in many sections that children can be sexually abused. Family plays a determinantal role either as a contributor and defender of the act by undermining it and not reporting to the police in due time. Preference is given to the protection of the family as a unit rather than to the individual child. In an illiterate, under-privileged poor family, a mother may be a constant witness to the sexual abuse of her child by her husband but she hesitates to disclose the affair to any person including her own family members for fear of winning the wrath of her husband and bringing shame to her family. She fails to realise that after-effects of this act are not only traumatic for her daughter, but also will continue to have permanent effect on her behaviour.

Myths about Child Rape

Before a diagnose is made of rape of small children it is necessary to discuss the myths and fantasies that enshrined the act so as to clear all misconceptions and handle the matter systematically. It is believed that children who are raped are primarily older teen aged children. It has been proved wrong by reports in the media of incidences of child rape of even below 3-year of age, well-supported by researches at microscopic level within the country and outside. It has been assessed universally that the mean age of sexually abused children tends to be around eleven years. Second false belief is that children who are raped are retarded. Though it is true that retarded children are more prone to a sexual abuse than a normal one but that does not deny the fact that any child can be a potential victim, given the right set of circumstances regardless of the child's age, race, intelligence, social class or neighbourhood.

It is also wrong to assume that child rape victims come mainly from the lower socio-economic family. Family income and social status both are unrelated to child abuse. The difference is that while a raped victim in a lower socio-economic home gets exposed to public scrutiny and comments, it is generally hushed and kept silent in an established esteemed family for fear of social shame.

The likelihood of children becoming victims of rape is not higher outside because the offender is often one's own kith or kin or some friend of the family. In fact, she is in more danger not only in her own home but also in the homes of her family friends. It is claimed with the support of various studies that three-fourths of child rapes occur indoors and only few are there which occur outside the child's home. There are many more myths, but they are gradually waning away with the people becoming more conscious towards this offence terming it not only barbaric and heinous but also demanding that the offender needs to be given life imprisonment.

To many people, the rape of a child is a terrible incident, yet somewhere there is a belief that since the child is small and is unconscious of the act she will overcome the shock quicker than her elder counterparts, and this is the biggest myth because the trauma left by the offence remains unexpressed at the same time causing severe mental damage and a blockage of healthy emotional stability which continues till old age.

***Symptoms of Rape*:** Sexual abuse such as rape is not often identified through physical indications alone. Physical signs such as difficulty in walking or sitting, torn stained or bloody under-clothes, complaints of pain or itching, bruises or bleeding, venereal diseases and pregnancy are there but there are also indications of behavioural change which may add to the traumas of Rape Syndrome. Several arguments can be made in support of a trauma specific approach. Studies have shown that sexually abused children, as a group, exhibit a greater prevalence of at least some problems than other clinical and non-clinical samples. Some logically related outcomes such as sexual behaviour problems constantly discriminate sexually-abused children according to Friedrich 1993.

Rape is an outcome, an internal crisis in the psyche of the offender, and results in the external crisis in the life of the victims. Rape Trauma Syndrome is a label given to a collection of syndromes identified as past rape indicators in the victim (Burgess & Holmstorm) (1974) and divide the rape trauma syndrome with two effects, one is the immediate disruption and disorganisation in the life-style of the victim in general and the second phase is the long-term effect in which some victims have nurtured suppressed feeling throughout the life while some attempt to reorganise their lives.

Studies have been done from to time to assess the traumas of rape and Peter (1976) is one of them who comprehensively described the child victims of his study. He found eleven per cent of child victims did not feel safe any longer at their place of stay while thirty-two percent showed more negative feelings for men they knew. Some of the children are less than usual and thirty-one per cent reported difficulty in sleeping. Nightmares were often seen and they cried out in sleep. Likewise Burgess and Holmstorm (1978) reported in their study that most of the children reported mild or moderate to severe symptoms. Very few children escaped with no symptoms.

It can be assessed from these studies that behavioural symptoms are many and they include general irritability, behavioural problems at school, acute withdrawal, depressive symptoms, running away from home and expressive of delinquent behaviour.

The long-term effect of minor rape is more harmful since it has detrimental effect on the self-concept and personality of the individual. A child who had shown little or no effect during the commission of crime stores up psychological dynamite that may explode during crucial point in her psycho-sexual development in later life. Among them can be courtship, marriage and child-birth. Sexual disorientation or psychoses were found by Peter (1976) to be related to childhood rape, who labelled this abuse as a *Psychological Time Bomb*. Moreover, it has been observed that victims of early rapes had an extremely low self-esteem. They felt worthless, rarely achieved anything satisfying to adults and could not succeed in their lives. Amy Katan, a psycho-analyst while studying a number of women who were raped in their childhood found her patients complaining of never feeling that they were complete women. They projected a displaced feeling of helplessness and pain of early childhood by turning aggressive against themselves or others.

Aggression turned towards self had been found to be continuously displayed in the form of exhibiting delinquent or criminal behaviour in engaging in sexuality or in other self-defeating behaviour. When the aggression was directed against others it resulted in an inability to get close to men because of suspiciousness, anger, rigidity, sexual unresponsiveness or need to be in control.

While justifying therapeutic treatment for rape victims, it must be acknowledged that rape raises certain critical issues for the victim especially when the victim is a child and for her family as well. The lives of the victim and her family members are disreputed by these issues. Parents find difficult to accept the fact that the child is no longer sexually innocent. Their attitude towards the child starts changing which becomes all the more shattering for the victim's mental equilibrium and unfortunately they bitterly fail to realise that their over-concern not only brings a guilty feeling in the child that she has done something wrong and she is a bad girl, but it also withdraws her into social isolation. Parents therefore need to know what happens after a sexual attack and attempt to understand the expressionless feelings of the child. They must encourage the child to discuss her problems with them, failing which, with a professional and seek counselling to regain a healthy and normal life. Unfortunately in many circumstances this does not happen. Parents besides being hysterical, urge the child to forget the unpleasant experience and refuse to talk about it with her. This attitude aggravates the problem and children continuously feel that they have done something terribly bad, for which the parents are extremely disappointed with them. Therefore, what is required is to make the incident less frightening so that the traumas are also less severe in nature.

According to Robert and Geiser (1979), such situation where child victims had experienceless traumas mentioned that if the attack was only once and the attacker was a stranger then the psychological injury is less. Also if the child received emotional support and understanding from elders and parents, and did not counter the ordeal of police questioning then the recovery from the emotional shock was quicker and easier than in other circumstances, facilitated further with counselling and psychiatric help. Feelings of fear, outrage, anger and guilt affect both victim and family and they are mitigated with proper intervention from a counsellor.

So far it is alright that therapeutic treatment is necessary for a rape victim, particularly a child, but what about the parents who are also thrown into a setback and undergo experiences which may be different in nature. They begin to feel guilty that they failed to protect their child. Some even lose confidence in their abilities to deal with future life crises. The feeling of powerlessness also engulfs them. Parents feel that they and their children are completely at the mercy of outside forces and are helpless to protect themselves. Besides any sexual offence, be it a rape or molestation of a child or an adult in the family, it becomes an issue of embarrassment for both victim and parents. Parents may not want neighbours, friends or other family members to know what happened to their child exactly in the same manner the child starts avoiding her peer-group in school, to the extent that she develops school phobia. There may be many other reactions emanating from rape, but it is conclusive that rape, especially of a child precipitates an emotional crisis in the victim and the family. The reaction to this stress can impair the mental health and functioning of both victim and the family. Timely crises intervention can help in preventing future emotional distress.

Incest: Many prefer not to think about incest. The public reacts with horror and disgust to any account of incest. Yet in spite of a strong taboo and legal sanction against it, incest occur every day, to a great degree than most of the people would imagine. Incest is also a sexual abuse leading to rape, the only difference is that while other rapes occurs outside the house, incest is committed within the house and the offender is none other than the victims's own kith and kin, be it her father, cousin, uncle or even father-in-law.

The other deplorable fact about incest is that while rape by a stranger is an incident happening once with the victim, incest continues over days and years like a scorpion gradually eating into the mental and physical condition of the victim. She silently bears the shameful act much to her tolerance. Only when her tolerance crumbles does she revolt and people come to know about her plight.

With the overwhelming impact of the traumas of rape, she has to remain in that environment maintaining the infamous relationship with the offender who can be her own father. This not only makes her terribly let down but also ruins her normal relationship with any other male-folk. Her life is coloured by violations. There is otherwise some opinion that the child victim sees the incest as a way of saving the family. She takes the guilt upon herself and endures the behaviour in an effort to keep the parents together. When the relationship is discovered, the child's guilt may centre more strongly on her failure to keep the family from breaking up.

The profile of the offender

While understanding the vulnerability of victimization and the traumas of a victim, the villain of the drama or the contribution of the tragedy should not be overlooked. Men who molest children are described as not only inept in their sexual lives but are also unsuccessful in other aspects also. Intermittent studies have revealed factors like social violation, unsatisfactory marital-sexual relationship, wife being mentally ill, passive, powerless or dependent, and marital discord, contribute making the individual rapist. Even then it cannot be generalized in all circumstances. In cases of incest some of the problems the offender faces are quite subtle, like power struggle with a child, boredom when not working or annoyance that a spouse has gone to work. The whole family involvement becomes an important precipitating factor to crime. These are however non-sexual problems and all child sexual abuse cannot be explained on the basis of the number or type of non-sexual problems. However, when designing a pragmatic treatment programme for offenders non-sexual problems have to be focussed to enable the offenders to get an insight and learn to solve the problems directly. In certain studies paedophiles have not only been discussed but also classified. Geiser (1979) had mentioned about fixated offender whose psychosexual development was disturbed in childhood and who was mainly paedophile. He is the paedophile, lover of children and he will repeatedly attack on this target group without remorse, but this is not so in the case of those rapists who turn to children for sex when their adult relationship gets disturbed. For any reason, whether it is marital discord or his passivity and dependency on his wife, this type of person regresses and develops intimacy with children and after winning their confidence rapes them. Child rapists are rarely mentally ill. They may be having emotional disorders but not to the extent that it impairs their judgement and rationality.

To support this hypothesis, Geiser quoted a study where adult rapists were compared with child-molesters and incidences of psychosis among paedophile was low. The study concluded that psychoses were not associated with sexual offenders. So to say that the child rapists do not show any particular psychiatric disorders other than sexual deviation. All do not agree with this finding assumption and Joseph Peter was one of them. In his sample of 224 probationer male adult sex offenders, he reported that all groups of sex offenders reported more symptoms of illness on a medical index than comparable groups of normal. The paedophiles in particular showed considerable immaturity, strong dependency needs, overall regression and a feeling of phallic inadequacy. Unable to attract adult women because of feeling of inferiority they turned to little girls for affection and sexual gratification. Unlike the other rapists, the paedophile, under stress, was found to be withdrawn and isolated. They were also more passive than rapists.

The vulnerability and the helplessness of the child make it all the more easier for the rapist to overpower her through treat, bribe or mild force since children rarely put up strong physical resistance. Therefore, extreme force is invisible in such incidents as with adult and adolescent rapes. Extreme is the mark of sadistic offender who intends to harm the child.

Judicial implication of child rape in India

There is no separate law for the act of sexual assaults on a child except that according to Clause Sixth of Sec. 375 IPC (1996). This particular section states that if rape is committed on a child who is not in a position to offer any substantial resistance, the mandatory sentence could be life transportation and if the act of sexual assault is followed with a murdering the mandatory sentence could be death sentence.

It is seriously being thought in the judicial section that to minimize the incidence of child rape there is a need for modification in procedural law for the trial and investigation of cases related to child rape.

The Committee of National Federation for Indian Women had focussed on lengthy procedure and questioning by the police which is prohibited in the existing laws of the minors. Rectification of the trials and amendments of laws to make the punishment rigid to the utmost are what every normal person in the society will desire.

Treatment of the Victim and the Offender

Group treatment for sexually abused children has frequently been recommended. Many researchers feel that child victim of rape will find it extremely difficult to disclose her experience to a therapist while she is alone than when she is in a group. It reduces isolation and facilitates peer-relationship in a manner impossible in individual therapy. This is however, sometimes possible because of the limitation of the number of cases coming for treatment, particularly in the younger age group.

Counsellor while talking to a sexually-abused child has to give extra concern to the dynamics of sexual abuse and the syndromes that children exhibit. In the foremost, exists the child's perception of safety, as to whether she feels safe. Secondly, she must be persuaded to give vent to her feelings thereby creating a congenial environment where she feels secured. Children of incestuous cases often put up a rigid resistance to any treatment. Fear of loss of family image and the relationship with the members of the family inhibit the child from stating her experiences. To get the cooperation of the victim, a therapist or a trained counsellor must use expressive therapy such as painting, drawing, writing or playing with dolls, particularly male dolls, enabling her to project her suppressed feelings mingled with shock and aggression on the external objects. This child through this process learns to communicate what has happened, thus reducing her isolation and provides an opportunity for sex education. Children have little knowledge of molestation and have trouble making sense of it. A child particularly needs to know that she is not the only one and that this has happened to other children also. This reduces her loneliness. Also, she can be explained that it is not she but the adult who is responsible for the act. That's way she does not feel guilty for the crime. In order to mentally as well as emotionally rehabilitate the sexually abused, child needs to know that while sexual abuse may make her feel different it does not make her look different from other children.

It is not enough to treat the victim alone. Incidences of sexual offences will remain unchecked as long as offenders remain unattended. While one victim gets treatment another may become vulnerable, as the rapist is always lurking somewhere. In circumstances where the crime has been committed intentionally and the child victim has died due to the injury of rape, there undoubtedly the offender should be given rigorous punishment including death, but where the criminal feels guilty and regrets for his act therapeutic treatment can be offered to him. Sometimes dissatisfaction of normal sexual life or rejection by the wife also leads to these types of deviant behaviour. Treating the offender alone in such cases will not help him to reform himself. It is necessary that family counselling be done and the individual is helped by reintegrating himself in the family fold. It is both difficult and critical when there is an incestuous relationship in the family and the therapist has to rebuild the normal relationship between the members of that house. This is possible only with the cooperation of the whole family and the offender is being made to realize the consequences of his act. We must not however mingle the treatment programme of this particular type with psychopathic criminals and with those who are mentally sick.

Paedophilic falls in this category. In order to prevent them from offending again it is necessary that they are exposed to long series of clinical treatment.

Measures to prevent sexual offences : (a) Uniform state laws are needed that define sexual abuse in detail, and penalties and treatment of offenders need to be standardized. (b) There is a need for national forums for the reporting of child sexual abuse. (c)There is a need for a broad public educational programme on child sexual abuse. Public awareness and discussion of the problem in seminars and media must be promoted, beginning with the education of the public with stress on the need to report cases of child sexual abuse. The largest single obstacle in doing something about child sexual abuse is the public's attitude of secrecy. It prevents victims and families from seeking and obtaining help. Child sexual abuse will not magically disappear if we do not talk about it. Rather, child sexual abuse thrives on secrecy. (d) A public educational programme should also include information abut the nature and incidence of child sexual abuse, and the community resources available to help children, parents, and offenders. As part of the programme, specific information about the needs of children and "how to parent" adequately should be made available. Courses in parenting and child care should be an essential part of the public school curriculum.

Few young children have had an adequate sex education. It is still commonplace for parents to postpone discussion and to avoid mentioning sexual activities until children are in late middle childhood or early adolescence, by which time the information is seldom needed. Younger children who have been sexually assaulted are thus left in a confusing situation. Quite often they do not understand exactly what happened to whom. (e)To guarantee psychiatric treatment of all identified child victims of sexual abuse communities need to institute treatment programmes specifically geared to treating the families and victims of sexual abuse. (f) any experts agree that the real trauma of child rape begins when it is discovered. This remark usually refers to the insensitive handling of the victim and family by the social and legal systems. Some people go so far as to claim that the child's contact with the police, courts and lawyers is often more traumatic than the original sexual assault, and advise against exposing the child to this process.(g) In order to help rape victim, all agencies and individuals dealing with child sexual abuse cases must coordinate their efforts. The people involved must come to understand the needs of the victims, family and offender. They must be helped so that their own feelings don't get in the way of rational, helpful action. (h) Professionals as well as the public need help with their feelings about child sexual abuse. The usual reaction in most people is an emotional and punitive one. In such a climate it is difficult to find much support for preventive, treatment and rehabilitation programmes. (i) Prevention of sexual abuse of children is part of a larger need for developing healthier attitudes toward sex. Some experts have suggested that the most important thing in preventing sexual abuse is teaching children that they have a right to say "no". (j) Part of preventing sexual abuse of children must necessarily involve general programmes to strengthen families. Obvious examples are day care centres, homemaker services, family counselling services, and parent education courses. (k) The handling of rape cases and the relevant laws should be re-thought. Instead of the legal response being based upon our emotional horror about the crime, the more serious crimes should be those, which involved force or violence, those that are repetitive in nature, or those which contain an exploitative profit element.

Suggestion

No raped victim should be treated in an undignified manner, particularly if the victim is a child. The consequences of the sexual offence traumatize the child throughout her childhood and even continue to create imbalances in her emotions when she enters the adulthood. It is often seen that a sexually abused individual either propels or commits sexual offence as a sadistic pleasure. If the whole incident is dealt at the right time and in an appropriate manner then a child-rape victim can easily be rehabilitated. She can enjoy life like any normal person.

References

1. Anna C. Salter, 1988, *Treating Child Sex Offenders and Victims,* p. 211, Sage Publications, The International Professional Publishers, Newbury Park, London, New Delhi.
2. Amy Katan, p. 28, *Sexual Misuse of Female Children in Hidden Victims*—The Sexual Abuse of Children by Robert and Geiser 1979.
3. Burgers Ann W, *Rape Victims of Crises* R.J. and Holmstrom-LL Brady Co. 1974.

4. Friedrich, W.N. Urquiza, (1986), *Behaviour Problems in Sexually abused Young Children,* Journal of Pediatric Psychology 11 (1) 47-57.
5. K. Kumar and Punam Rani, 1996, *Offences against children—Socio Legal Perspectives,* Chap. 7,pp. 72-73. Regency Publications, New Delhi.
6. Robert and Geiser, 1979, Hidden Victims. *The Sexual Abuse of Children,* Boston Press, Boston.

TWENTY

CHILD RAPE IN INDIA

A major chunk of the crime in the country's ascending crime graph is accounted by crime against children. Further, it has been observed that the proportion and number of crime against children is constantly on the rise specially in the past decade. Child rape below 16 years of age accounted for 28.79 per cent of the total rape cases reported in 1997. Further out of total crime against children, child rape alone accounted for 73.8 per cent (1997). Between 1993 and 1997 alone child rape registered 30 per cent increase.

Who can deny the fact that minors have always been vulnerable to lustful eyes. Rape itself is inhuman, but the rape of tiny tots is much brutal and heinous because of its detrimental effects on them. The rape of children is unforgivable as it causes physiological, mental and emotional injuries. Many a time such acts deprive the child of motherhood and even lead to death. In several instances, such children take to prostitution at a later stage because they are treated as outcasts even by their families. This alarming situation has awakened various social organisation who along with government support have been collectively addressing this menace.

Thus, efforts are on to prevent and save children from the vulnerabilities and exploitations to which they are subjected. Although such crimes are viewed as social evils, but the reported incidence of such crimes continues to rise in magnitude. It is to be noted in passing that in the Indian situation majority of such crimes are not even reported. According to one estimate for every sexual offence reported, at least three go unreported because of the fear of further trauma and embarrassment to the child as also to the family.

Child abuse is a gift of 'Uncle Culture'. It is very shocking, but true that most of the rapists are either family members of family friends. According to a study conducted in Bangalore and its adjacent villages reveals that about fifty-five per cent of men responsible for the abuse of girl children were family members—uncles, fathers, brothers, cousins, or relatives. Fifteen per cent of the 348 girls who put down their experience had, in fact, been seriously abused or raped before their tenth birthday.

In the present study, a spatio-temporal analysis of child rape in India is analysed. Firstly, the incidence of various crimes committed against children in India between 1993 and 1997 is observed. Secondly, the child rape pattern in various States, Union Territories and metropolitan cities between 1992 and 1997 is analysed. Lastly, an attempt has been made to understand the increasing rate of child rape as also to raise some pertinent questions related to the spatial aspect of child.

The data for this study is purely derived from a secondary source, namely, Crime in India—a Government of India publication.

Incidence of crimes committed against children in India-1993-97

The general penal code of this country and the various protective and preventive 'special and local laws, specifically mention the offences wherein are victimised and abused are categorised under two broad heads:

1. Crimes committed against children which are punishable under Indian Penal Code (IPC).
2. Crimes reported against children which are punishable under Special and Local Laws (SLL).

Among the various crimes against children in India, child rape (up to 16 years) accounted for the highest number in 1993—3393 cases. By 1997, there was a spurt in such cases—4414. It is clear that there is an alarming increase in child rape cases 30 per cent in just five years. Kidnapping and abduction accounted for 485 cases in 1993 and 620 cases in 1997, showing an overall increase of 27.8 per cent. Another crime which is on the increase and is a cause of much concern is foeticide which has increased from 45 cases in 1993 to 57 cases in 1997. This crime is committed in large numbers in various hospitals, clinics and dispensaries in all cities and towns of India. But the data is very much under-reported and is not at all a true picture of the actual situation. The incidence of abetment of suicide and selling of girls for prostitution went up by 18.2 per cent, 50 per cent respectively during 1996-97.

Child rape in India (1993-97)

Sadly and unfortunately, all the victims in rape cases during 1997, children alone accounted for 28.8 per cent share. The cases of rape of children below 10 years were on a rise every year in the country except in 1996 since 1993. From Table it is clear that child rape cases increased from 634 in 1993 to 770 in 1997, below 10 years of age. A similar increase is found in 10 to 16 years age group wherein the number increased from 2759 cases in 1993 to 3644 in 1997. When compared to the figures of 1993, the victims in the age group of 10 years increased by 21.4 per cent while those in the age group of 10.16 years increased significantly by 32.1 per cent.

Statewise incidence of child rape (1992-97)

A total of 2928 cases were reported from all the states in 1992 and 4107 cases in 1997. In 1992 and in 1997 Madhya Pradesh acconted for more than 20 per cent of all rape cases followed by Maharashtra and Uttar Pradesh accounting for more than ten per cent of total cases. More than five per cent cases were reported each from Bihar, West Bengal, Assam and Delhi in 1992 and West Bengal, Andhra Pradesh and Delhi in 1997. Bihar and Assam individually accounted for almost five per cent of child rape. Further, it is to be noted that the central part of India extending from Delhi and Uttar Pradesh in the north to Andhra Pradesh in the south, Bihar in the east and Maharashtra in the west, is much prone not only to child rape, but also to other crimes against children.

Incidence of child rape in Union Territories (1992-97)

On the one hand, Delhi reported 172 rape cases accounting for 93 per cent of total child rape cases among the Union Territories in 1992, and on the other hand, not a single case was reported from Dadar and Nagar Haveli, Daman and Diu and Lakshadweep. A similar picture emerged in 1997 with Delhi alone accounting for 97 per cent of cases. Lakshadweep, Daman and Diu continued to have no case reported and Chandigarh and Pondicherry accounted for only 3 and 2 cases respectively.

Incidence of child rape in the metro-cities of India

It is evident that Delhi, Bombay, Bhopal, Nagpur and Pune had consistently high incidence of child rape cases in 1992 as well as in 1997. On the other hand, not a single case was reported from Madras, Madurai and Visakhapatnam in 1992, whereas in 1997 only 3 cases were reported each from Madras, Ludhiana and Ahmedabad and no case was reported from Madurai and Patna. So it is unnecessarily true that urban areas are more prone to child rape as is evident from varying crime rate in the metropolitan cities which are meore prone to such crimes than others.

A framework for a geography of crimes with special emphasis on child rape.

Crime is basically an urban phenomenon not only as an outcome of combination of various factors, but also a chain reaction of circumstances arising one after another as a result of increasing urbanisation. Poverty and various forms of social disparities in some form or the other can be perceived as common in both urban as well as rural areas. However, in the rural context a relatively homogeneous set-up with strong social bond in a close-knit society where everybody knows everybody else, deter many people from committing various types of crimes. On the other hand, the heterogeneous set-up in urban areas leading to lack of social cohesion and increasing impersonality may tempt many people to commit various types of crimes. This explanation holds true as far as property crimes are concerned. In fact, most of the crimes (murder, attempt to murder, kidnapping and abduction, etc.) against persons are also one way or the other connected to property matters. But what about rape?

At this juncture the most pertinent question to be answered is why people commit such heinous crime like child rape? To answer this question, it is necessary to analyse the geography of this crime in a historical and socio-cultural context. From this study, it has been found that the central States of India are more prone to such crimes thus excluding the mountainous north, the coastal south, hilly and rainy east and the arid west. From time immemorial, various scholars such as Hippocrates, Aristotle, Herodotus, Strabo, Al-Masudi, Kant, Ritter, Ratzel, Huntington and others have emphasized the important role played by the environment on man's mental and economic well-being. As such, enormous and gigantic mountains enveloped with clouds, the mightly oceans and the unending desert landscape have as soothing influence on the mental state of its inhabitants. Thus, does nature play an important role in the reduction of various crimes including child rape in certain areas as against the other?

Historically, the Indo-Gangetic plain has been prone to plunder and rape by the foreign invaders from the West many of whom settled down in India and thier violent nature being perpetuated by the succeeding generations. In a recent article in the Sunday Review of The *Times of India* (21st Nov.,99) Mrs. Le bon, a socialite, accepted the fact that she has a wild spirit because of her being half Persian. Due to continuous upheaval in the political and socio-economic set-up in north and central India many people took to crimes as a way of life.

After independence, with better transportation network and peaceful political environment with adequate police protection, many of these professional criminals gave up crime and devoted themselves to sedentary occupations such as farming, but they have not been able to rid themselves of the inherent violent character in them. An outlet for it being child rape in appropriate opportunities in the environment. In fact people still continue to threat one another in terms of rape of the opponent's daughter, sisters and even mother, without even realising the magnitude of their loose talk. Even children who are abused are totally unaware of what they are saying. Does history play an important role in the occurrence of child rape in India?

The social set-up of India prior to Independence was based on the Zamindari system wherein the Zamindar who only owns the land in actuality, but considers himself to be the master of the peasants tilling his land and thus rape of young children and women was a common day-to-day phenomena. After partition of India and abolition of the Zamindari system, although the Zamindars gave up their land somewhat readily, but continue to consider themselves the masters of the peasants and thus rape of young women and children still continues. Is this pre-independence social set-up responsible for perpetuating child rape?

References

1. Tahir, M. (1996), *Crime in Delhi*, NBO, New Delhi.
2. Tahir, M. (1995), Rape scenario in India, *Police Research and Development,* Quarter 4.
3. Hussain, T. and Tahir, M. (1994), The ugly face of rape, *Link,* Aug. 28.
4. Hussain, T. and Tahir, M., (1992), Increasing rape incidents, *Link*, March 22.
5. Hussain, T. and Tahir, M.,1995, Impact of Policing on Crime, *Social Welfare,* Vol. 42, No. 1.
6. Ponnian, M. (1990), *Criminology,* Neelam, Delhi.

[illegible]

References

[illegible]

PART - IV

DAWN OF REASON

TWENTY ONE

THE AWARENESS

Child labour surveys based on recently developed methodologies have been carried out nationally or in selected areas of 19 countries or territories. These include Bangladesh, Cambodia, Costa Rica, Georgia, Ghana, Indonesia, India, Kenya, Namibia, Nepal, Pakistan, the Philippines, Senegal, South Africa, Sri Lanka, Thailand, Turkey, Ukraine and the West Bank and Gaza. New child labour surveys are either under way or in the process of starting or are being planned in the following countries: Angola, Belize, Benin, Brazil, Burkina Faso, Cambodia, Colombia, Costa Rica, Mali, Mongolia, Peru, Uganda, Vietnam and Zimbabwe.

Child labour surveys will be carried out as far as possible in all IPEC participating countries to optimise the complementary effects of IPEC and the Statistical Information and Monitoring Programme on Child Labour (SIMPOC). Given the effectiveness and popularity of the newly developed survey methodologies for quantifying child labour in all its different facets, an externally funded programme (SIMPOC) was formulated and launched at the beginning of 1998. SIMPOC, an interdepartmental programme between the ILO's International Programme on the Elimination of Child Labour (IPEC) and the ILO's Bureau of Statistics, is designed for a five-year period with the major aim of assisting individual countries in generating comprehensive quantitative and qualitative statistical data on child labour at the national level that is comparable among countries, sub-regions or regions.

SIMPOC is also aimed at capacity building of national statistical offices and ministries of labour for the production and use of such data on a regular basis in the future. For this purpose, under the SIMPOC programme, the staff of IPEC and SIMPOC are to be trained to design and carry out child labour surveys and analyse the data collected. The surveys are expected to become an integral part of the regular national statistical programmes; so that statistical information on child labour can be produced and disseminated at regular intervals.

A large majority of the countries listed above have undertaken the surveys under the auspices of SIMPOC. Through SIMPOC, comprehensive child labour information systems consisting of both quantitative and qualitative data will also be developed at national, international and regional levels with a computer programme that facilitates updating the database as new information becomes available. Such a database provide policy and decision makers with more detailed and better-quality information for the design, implementation, monitoring and evaluation of policies and programmes.

The dissemination of this data, through the publication of a regular trend report, is planned under SIMPOC—which will contribute considerably to raising public awareness and enhancing the understanding of the problem of child labour.

Since 1992, the ILO has taken the lead in developing methodological child labour sample surveys at national levels. The survey methodologies were developed to enable countries to obtain benchmark statistics on children's work in general or to produce statistics on specific core variables. These methods were first tested in four countries (Ghana, India, Indonesia and Senegal). Following their refinement and recommendations for quantifying child labour, several countries collaborated with the Bureau of Statistics in adopting the methodologies and conducting national surveys for collecting comprehensive data.

Based on detailed results of the experiments and national child labour surveys conducted in several countries using the newly developed methodologies, the ILO was able to:

—Produce regional and global estimates;

—Identify and quantify not only the different forms of hazard and risk working children face, but also the extent and nature of the injuries and diseases suffered while working; and

—Acquire much knowledge and experience, thereby enhancing considerably its competence for providing technical assistance to individual countries in designing and undertaking comprehensive child labour surveys and processing, analysing and using the statistical data obtained for formulating and implementing appropriate action programmes to combat the worst forms of child labour at the national and global levels.

To obtain a complete picture of the child labour situation, the information sought through surveys at the national level involved answers to the following questions, among others:

—Who are the working children and how many are there in the various countries?

—How old are the children when they start to work for the first time and how do they live?

—Why do they work and in which sectors are they engaged?

—What are their specific occupations and the conditions of their work?

—What types of exploitation and abuse do they face at work?

—How safe are they physically and mentally at their workplace or in their occupations?

—Do they also go to school? If so, what are the consequences of their work on their schooling? And if they do not go to school, why not?

—Who are their employers? Why do they employ them? And how do they treat them in comparison with their adult workers?

—How many children are engaged on a full-time basis in housekeeping activities of a domestic nature in their own parents' or guardians' households, thereby sacrificing their education?

—Do any children live away from their parents' or guardians' home, and if so, where do they live and what do they do?

—What are the perceptions of parents about their working children? What are the perceptions of the children themselves, and their employers?

The ILO Bureau of Statistics designed four survey approaches and tested them in a number of countries together with a supplementary inquiry. Three of the survey approaches were implemented, respectively, at the level of households, employers/establishments/enterprises, and street children. The fourth method tested was a "time use" approach. The supplementary inquiry was applied at the community level (cities, towns, villages). The main purpose was to determine which survey methodology would yield the best results. The surveys measured as many variables as possible, particularly in relation to the various non-schooling activities of children in the 5-14 age group, their characteristics and those of their parents or guardians, and so on. The principal variables considered for the investigation related to the following subjects as expressed in broad terms:

—The demographic and socio-economic characteristics of the children, including their schooling and training status, occupations, skill levels, hours of work, earnings and other working and living conditions and the reasons for working, as well as the hardships and risks, especially work-related or environmental injuries and diseases they face at their workplace which are detrimental to their health, education, and physical and mental development;

—The socio-economic situation of their parents or guardians, or other relatives with whom the children live, as well as the particulars of their employers;

—The migration status of the children and how they live (in particular those on the streets); where the children have been working, for how long and why they are working, their own immediate and future plans and those of employers using child workers; and

—The perceptions of the parents or guardians about their working youngsters and those of the children themselves and their employers.

The concepts, definitions, classifications and the like, used for the purposes of the experimental surveys in all the countries, were generally in line with internationally recommended standards concerning such elements as the economically active population, the labour force, classifications of industry, occupation, status in employment, age grouping, households, enterprises and establishments and so on, with some variations to reflect the unique circumstance of child work and the peculiarities of the individual countries.

Depending on the availability of basic information or demarcations regarding the general characteristics of the areas covered and the availability of appropriate sampling frames, the different elements considered for the stratifications included development levels of the selected, rural and urban areas—for example, poorly developed/well developed, slum/non-slum blocks, income classes (low, middle, high), overall rates of literacy/illiteracy of the general population, school attendance levels and so on. For the purposes of the experiments, a "child" was defined as a person between five and 14 years of age.

In the absence of a universally endorsed definition of "child labour", all activities of children were enumerated and quantified so that the data could be tabulated according to the different characteristics or categories of the variables included in the questionnaires. Depending on the level and nature of the quantified activities or variables, those which were judged or expected to have negative effects or consequences on the health, education and normal development of the working child were considered as falling within the boundaries of "child labour". The main focus of the surveys in all four countries was on the economic activity of the children, whether paid in cash or in kind, or in unpaid family work, thus respecting the international definition of "economic activity".

Some types of work or production for own household consumption, such as carrying water, fetching firewood, pounding and husking food products, were also considered as failing within the boundaries of economic activity. While the dividing line between economic and non-economic activities for cases such as the above is rather thin and not always obvious, these and many others (for example, preservation of fruit by drying or bottling weaving cloth, and dressmaking and tailoring), were considered to fall within the margin of economic activity or the "production boundary" as defined by the System of National Accounts. While schooling activities were measured in the majority of cases, in some instances non-schooling activities of a non-economic nature (especially household chores or housekeeping services provided in the child's own parents' or guardians' homes) were also estimated separately.

Both the "current" and the "usual" economic activity approaches were applied, the first in reference to activities during a short period such as the week (or seven days) prior to the date of the interview, and the second in reference to a long period such as the 12 months (or 365 days) preceding the inquiry date. The latter reference period takes seasonality into account, which is an important factor since a considerable proportion of children's activities is seasonal, including activities undertaken when schools are closed.

In all the selected areas the household-based surveys were carried out strictly on a relatively rigorous sample basis using a multi-stage (two-or three-stage) stratified sampling design. Using the household listing as a sampling frame as well as the basic information that was collected during the listing, all the listed households in each unit of the segment were then grouped into three strata as follows:

—Households with at least one paid child worker (in the specific age group);

—Households without a paid child worker but with at least one child working as an unpaid family worker (in the same specific age group); and

—Other households (in the same age group).

A specified number of households in each of the above three strata were selected by means of systematic sampling which formed the final stage sampling units. Through these sampling procedures or slight variations, between 4,000 and 5,000 households were selected to represent the sample size for the surveys in each of the four countries. Where suitable statistical software packages were not available in the statistical offices of the countries concerned, a self-weighing systematic sampling design with probability proportional to size (PPS) was adopted. This approach helped by providing a uniform weight for estimating totals. It also facilitated the computation of percentages, means and ratios of the population parameters directly from the sample data.

The questionnaire that was applied at the household level consisted of two parts. The first part was addressed to the head of the household to obtain information on the demographic and socio-economic composition of the household, including such aspects as housing facilities, household migration status and living standards and the education level and economic activity status of the household members.

The second part was used to collect the required information from the individual children themselves. As a supplement, a simple questionnaire was used to interview elected, and appointed leaders, administrators and the like, in the communities or towns and villages of the selected areas so as to identify the major local socio-economic characteristics, assess development levels and determine the differential in the incidence of child labour. During the household listing stage, basic information on a limited number of variables relating to each household and its members was also obtained to facilitate the stratification of the households in each segment and the sample selection of households.

The employer's questionnaire was addressed to the owner of the business or a designated respondent, seeking information on the particulars of the ownership, the goods produced and services rendered, the number of children and adults engaged, their working conditions, the reasons for using child workers, facilities and health care at the workplace and so on.

Probability sampling became prohibitive due to the absence of basic information which could serve as a master frame, such as an exhaustive list or directory of employers in respect of the areas selected for the surveys. In view of this problem, only those employers identified by the children themselves or their parents during the interview at the household level, or those enterprises known or suspected to be using child workers, were located and interviewed on a random basis. In this way, up to a total of 200 entities were identified and enumerated in urban and rural area selected in each country.

Special problems of collecting data on children working and living on the streets, an individual questionnaire was formulated and used to assemble information on variables relating to the schooling and non-schooling activities of such children, their living and working conditions, parents, migration status and so on. Therefore, for the children on the streets, a "purposive" or "convenience" approach was applied and as far as possible, enumerators who were selected and trained for the interviews were those who knew the core areas where such children were found. The children were visited in their localities in the evenings and in some cases at night if that proved to be more convenient.

Basic results

Variations exist in the results of the surveys conducted in the four countries owing to their differences in terms of social, cultural, political and economic development levels, average family size, household income and expenditure, literacy or illiteracy levels of the adult population and especially the school enrolment and attendance ratios of young children. The findings are also influenced by the differences in the reference period of the surveys, for example, whether it covers a schooling period, agricultural season and so on. For the same reasons, the findings also vary between any two areas covered by the survey within each country.

The statistical results from the surveys have proved the existence of a positive correlation—in some instances a strong one—between child labour and such factors as poverty, illiteracy, the level of rural community under-development, urban slum conditions, school truancy or dropouts, abandoned or runaway children, large family size, female-headed households, the parents'—especially the father's—occupations, and permanent absence or death of the father, among others. The household-based survey has been found to be the most effective means of investigating the child labour phenomenon in all its facets. As a result the data obtained through household surveys did not include information on such children who might have been working on the streets, although the number of such youngsters would be relatively very small in most countries. The best time to visit the sample households was found to be late afternoons or early evenings. While finding an adult respondent was relatively easy in the daytime, there was difficulty contacting the children themselves in the households during the daytime and proxy informants tended to be unreliable, especially concerning certain questions or variables.

In many cases the establishment-based investigation was not particularly successful, notably where it was difficult to identify employers and managers of workplaces. While it was hoped that the information obtained from the household heads and the children themselves would allow a list to be compiled of establishments where the children work, this proved difficult, mainly because many children were not available during the household inquiry and many adults were unable to provide the precise address of the children's place of work. Where a list or directory of establishments does not exist or cannot be compiled on the basis of the information obtained from the household-level survey, a micro-level approach can be taken in which the type of formal sector activities (industries, services) where children may be working are identified and the enterprises engaged in these activities are investigated.

In view of the fact that a large majority (90 per cent) of economically active children are unpaid family workers and some others are self-employed or casual labourers, this approach may often suffice. In a few of the countries where a proper sample survey of establishments proved difficult, small purposive or convenience inquiries were carried out which produced some interesting statistical results, though for the most part these were qualitative and not representative of enterprises as a whole. Another problem regarding the establishment-based inquiry was the lack of full, or even any, cooperation on the part of the employers, especially where the employment of youngsters under a specified age is illegal. For this reason, the use of the term "child activity" or "child work" instead of "child labour" in the survey instruments and by field personnel during interviews, may lead to a better response rate at all levels.

Conducting a well-formulated campaign, prior to the launching of the survey, in the various localities and at the national level to publicise the importance of the data to be collected for improving children's welfare could make respondents much more cooperative.

Homeless children are not represented in household samples since they have no usual place of residence or home. These children, however, face daily risks, hazards and exploitation that are detrimental to their mental and physical development. A purposive approach was applied using well-trained interviewers who were well acquainted with the inner city where such children usually work or congregate. In one country in particular, a micro-level inquiry was conducted successfully taking as a starting point the fact that most homeless children are usually found in large urban centres.

The interviewers were sent out in the early evening and often at night with a detailed questionnaire to interviewers at random the children they found. In many cases, the informal sector operators for whom the children work were also interviewed. The exercise resulted in useful statistical data, enabling the survey team to analyse the various characteristics of street children: age: sex: educational background: migration status and reasons for being on the streets; types of economic activity and occupation: earnings: living conditions (food, sleeping place, etc.); difficulties encountered; skills; future plans: activity patterns and background information of their parents, and so on. The survey experiment based on a "time use" module was not successful for the purposes of investigating children's activities and the intensity of their work. Even when presented with a long list of economic and non-economic activities, many children could not recall the activities in which they had been engaged during the 24 hours preceding the date of the survey.

Most children seem to remember only those activities which they most like, especially those in which they made "good" earnings. In many instances, it was difficult to consult the children themselves, and approaching proxies for this purpose was found to be futile since they could not account for the children's daily activities or their time allocation on each. Consequently, the results obtained from the "time use" exercise were found to be unsatisfactory. However, better-quality data may be obtained if the investigators or interviewers spend time in the area where the children can be found and interact with them and/or observe them throughout the day.

Unfortunately, this approach is neither practical nor feasible where the geographical coverage is wide and the sample size is large in order to make estimates at the national level. It is therefore recommended that, with the exception of a micro-level time allocation exercise, the application of a "time-use" approach to individual children to identify all their activities over a specific period of time (such as 24 hours) and to quantify the time devoted to each should be discouraged.

Recommendations on conducting surveys

The overall recommendation is to conduct a household-based sample survey which should be supplemented by surveys of employers (establishments and enterprises) and street children. Below are some details on each of these three survey approaches which could serve as technical guidelines.

Household-based surveys

The justification for these surveys and their suitability lies in the fact that by definition a household is a unit consisting of either an individual living alone or a group of two or more persons living together with a common provision for food and other essentials necessary for living. The only persons who are not represented through household-based sample inquiries are the homeless, nomads, and household members who are absent from the household permanently or for a long period at the time of enumeration. If such persons do not live in another household within the country, they will not be represented in a household-based national sample survey.

However, such groups normally only constitute a very small proportion of the total population within any specific age cohort. Even then, much in formation could be collected on those who are away from the households by addressing various relevant questions to the household head or a proxy. This information could, in turn, be used to design a more appropriate investigation of such persons to find out more details on all aspects of their activities, occupations, living conditions and so on. The use of households as units of enumeration could permit the gathering of a wealth of statistical information on all or any segment of a country's population, subject to the availability of resources.

The ILO methodological experiments carried out in 1992-93 and national surveys undertaken since then concerning child labour in several countries have proved the household approach to be the most effective means for it profound assessment of the level, nature and determinants of the practice at the national level. During such surveys, information could also be collected on the activity patterns of adults not only because the additional cost involved would be marginal, but because such data are important for studying the interrelation ship between the activities of children and the activities of other members of the same household and in particular, those of their parents or guardians. Besides providing a national picture, another advantage of a comprehensive household-based survey is that, if implemented through well-designed sampling and stratification procedures, it would permit segregation of the statistical information not only into rural/urban areas and informal/formal sectors, but also, and more importantly, into small geographical areas within any large geographical region or province.

The information on small localities would be crucial for formulating and implementing policies and action programmes appropriate for combating child labour in specific geographical areas or communities where the problem may be quite serious. The latter approach is much more efficient in many ways, particularly if the module is implemented as a supplement to an established programme of a labour force survey (LFS) conducted on a sample basis at the national level. This undertaking will not only result in substantial cost savings, but the operation could be achieved in less time. Operationally, it means that the module would be piggybacked into one of the rounds of the US and that the interviews for both the LFS and the module would be carried out at the same time.

Since the LFS questionnaire always seeks to enumerate the demographic and socio-economic composition of household members, there would be no need to repeat this part in the module for children. Through empirical studies it has been demonstrated that the incidence of child labour and the demographic and socio-economic characteristics of the "adult" household members are correlated positively or negatively depending on the different variables considered. Therefore, information on other household members has to be collected as well. The attractiveness of the modular option stems from the fact that there would be no need to list all the households selected in the initial stage of sampling, representing the primary-stage sampling units (PSUs), or to collect the basic information required for the stratification and selections of the second stage sampling units (SSUs).

Since there would be no repeat questions on the demographic and socio-economic characteristics of the children, the entire module would be considerably shorter. In addition, where the ILO and national statistics offices have collaborated closely in attaching a comprehensive child labour module to ongoing household-based surveys, significant savings have been realised. For example, in Turkey, where the module was attached to one of the two rounds of the national LFS, the cost of the operation amounted to only one-fifth (20 per cent) of the total resources that would have been needed if a stand-alone child labour survey had been conducted. A similar approach was carried out in Cambodia where the cost of the child labour survey component was about one-tenth (10 per cent) of the estimated total resources.

To avoid limiting the coverage of the incidence of various forms of child work, all types of activities (schooling and non-schooling, economic and non-economic activities) of children within a specified age group would be represented through sampling and enumerated and the volume or workload of their activities quantified, so that the assembled statistical information could be cross-tabulated by the different characteristics of the variables included in the questionnaire. Depending on the level and nature of the quantified activities or variables, those which are judged or expected to have negative effects or consequences on the health, education and normal development of the working children could be considered as falling within the boundary of "child labour".

The data should then be further dissected into various categories of affected children based on the degree of harm caused by the quantified activities. Since the comprehensive household survey would investigate all the activities of children in the particular age cohort, the data collected would make it possible to identify the specific occupations of the working children, their working conditions, accidents/ injuries/ illnesses suffered—including their frequency and gravity—problems related to the workplace environment, particulars of employers using children, the specific industries in which children work, the effect of their work on their normal life (including their schooling) and other related matters which would assist in assessing more fully the extent, nature and causes of child labour.

Declarations and resolutions seek to protect all children under 18 years of age from different types of harmful activities, it is strongly recommended that the survey of child labour should cover children from 5 to 17 years of age. One advantage of using this broad age cohort is that it would allow breakdown of the data obtained by different age groups, thereby satisfying the requirements of the various instruments, as well as national needs for respecting compulsory schooling regulations, labour codes and other legal requirements of individual countries. Examples of groupings are: 5-14, 15-17 and 5-17 years, the 5-14 age group broken down further by 5-9 and 10-14 years, all commonly used by most countries.

It may be useful to have the results also separately classified for children under 11, 12-13 and 14 years, in view of ILO Convention No. 138 and Recommendation No. 146 concerning Minimum Age for Admission to Employment (both adopted in 1973). Convention No. 138 generally prohibits economic activity of children under the age of 15, while making exceptions for those aged 14 years and for those between 12 and 13 years, depending on different circumstances in individual countries. It is also recommended that work of a domestic nature (household chores) performed by children in their own parents' or other relatives' homes where they actually reside should be included in the investigation of children's schooling and non-schooling activities.

The final data compiled on these children should then be tabulated separately from those relating to children who are economically active. Non-economic work of a domestic nature in the parents' or guardians' household would then be classified and tabulated into various ranges according to the number of hours during which such work was performed.

A threshold could then be established beyond which the activity could be deemed as constituting child labour. The above is based on the argument that many non-school-going children perform housekeeping activities in their parents' or guardians' households for various reasons, one being to make adult household members available for economic activity elsewhere. For many of these children this is a full-time occupation involving preparing and serving meals, washing clothes, cleaning floors, taking care of younger siblings, serving as messengers in and around the household and so on, all this at the sacrifice of the education and playtime to which each child is entitled under the United Nations Convention on the Rights of the Child.

Even those who attend school are found to be spending several hours a day performing such activities which are detrimental to their schooling, health and normal development to adulthood. Such children suffer fatigue which affects their school performance and many are exposed to hazardous situations, for example, cooking food over an open fire. Children who are put under the guardianship of relatives or other persons are especially susceptible to much abuse in these areas of work. The sampling approach to be adopted for surveys on children's activities should in principle be a multi-stage stratified sampling design to capture a good number of working children. Conversely, where there is a homogeneity of activities (in rural areas, for example), under-sampling (a smaller sample) could be considered.

Where statistical software packages are not readily available, a self-weighting systematic sampling design with probability proportional to size (PPS) of the population being considered should be adopted, since this will have a uniform weight for estimating totals and will also facilitate the computation of percentages, means and ratios of the population parameters directly from the sample data.

The sampling and stratification procedures to be adopted depend on the availability of basic information on various factors and at different levels. Uptodate information or demarcations regarding the general characteristics of the areas to be covered, the composition of the population and/ or the households within each area, and so on, would be required to serve as a master frame in designing several phases of sampling and stratification.

In the experimental surveys, the various elements or classifications considered for the stratification included: development levels of the selected rural and urban areas (e.g. poorly developed/well developed, slum/non-slum blocks); income classes (low, middle, high); overall rates of literacy/ illiteracy of the population; school attendance levels; family size, and so on. Again, depending on the sample size and the other factors, an over-sampling may be needed to capture adequately the incidence of child labour, which is more rare than finding an adult in the labour force.

According to ILO-IPEC experimental surveys carried out in Ghana, India, Indonesia and Senegal, the proportion of employed children among total child workers was found to be around 10 per cent. Thus, a survey of employers or establishments can give statistical information about only a small segment of child workers to supplement the results obtained through the household approach.

However, these child workers might form the most vulnerable section of all working children; some of them may be exposed to danger, maltreatment by employers, underpayment and environmentally bad working conditions. Such facts may not, however, be revealed through the survey of establishments as most employers will not divulge such information. Nevertheless, a survey of establishments employing child labour may be undertaken as a supplementary effort to find out more about the employers who have recourse to it.

The most important was the difficulty in identifying the establishments that employ child labour. Most developing countries do not have an updated or exhaustive national list or directory of employers. The task of preparing such a list and identifying those employing children in the ultimate areal unit is time consuming and requires considerable resources, both human and financial. Also, many establishment owners try to hide the fact that they actually engage children, and even if they admit to it, they may provide only partial information.

The alternative is to survey the establishments which employ the children belonging to the sample households. In spite of the problems that may arise, a survey of employers should be attempted.

The following alternative operational procedures, which can be modified according to national requirements and circumstances, may be considered:

—Constructing a list/directory of employers using *a* child workforce based on the responses provided by the children and their parents during a household-based child labour survey;

—Preparing, through local inquiries, a frame of enterprises employing child labour in the areas known to have a concentration of such units. For each unit, some broad information relating to the type of productive activity and the scale of operation may be ascertained;

—Selecting a sample of enterprises engaged in different activities in which children are known or suspected to be working; and

—Collecting the required information by interviewing all owners or operators of enterprises.

The main difficulty in applying the above operational procedures is the preparation of a proper framework. An alternative could be to list all the enterprises along with the listing of households in the selected areal units and elicit information as to whether or not they employ child labour. All the enterprises/establishments in each geographical unit in the sample for the household survey can be taken up. Such a scheme might also permit estimates of total child workers employed in enterprises. But it may call for a large number of ultimate areal units in the sample to obtain an adequate number of sample enterprises for the survey. Therefore, the strategy may be formulated according to the national circumstances of a country. The three possible strategies are:

1)As undertaken in the experimental surveys, a verification of the establishments in which the child workers identified during the household survey are reported to be employed;

2)A survey of all the establishments (employing child labour) located in the ultimate areal units in the sample for the household survey; and

3)A survey of establishments selected purposely from a list (prepared through local inquiries) of enterprises employing child workers.

Surveys of street children

Certain activities of children can prove difficult to quantify through sample surveys; for example, prostitution, trafficking and other illegal activities are not easy to investigate given that, for the most part, such activities are hidden. A purposive or convenience survey approach may have to be used to collect qualitative information. It may be possible to contact a few of the children involved in these activities who are willing to be interviewed.

However, much information can be gathered through the "key informants" system—contacting and interviewing knowledgeable persons in the community where the activities are known to exist. The investigators would have to be sociologists, psychologists, and social workers. Questions addressed to youths in the streets should relate to most of the variables directed at the children aged 15 years mentioned under the household-based survey. Additionally, street children should be asked to provide information on their migration status and reasons for being homeless or for coming to the present place, on living conditions (food, sleeping places and facilities, health and safety), on the background characteristics of their parents/guardians and siblings, on whether or not they are in regular contact with their parents/guardians and/or siblings, on their present difficulties or problems, and on their prospects or plans for the future.

The actual fieldwork for collecting data from street children may be operationally difficult within the general framework of a survey. There may even be some resistance from the group and in some cases it may even be dangerous to visit such spots for survey purposes. If so, help should be sought from local influential persons, social workers and the like and sometimes even from police personnel. The first operational step in the survey of street children is to identify the different places in the city where groups of street children usually gather to sleep. After identifying these spots, a sampling of them can be undertaken if they are numerous, but otherwise they should all be surveyed. If a city has a large number of such places where street children gather, an alternative procedure could be to survey those which fall in the areal units selected for the household survey in the city.

But since such places are not generally uniformly spread throughout the city, this scheme may not cover enough sample spots for the survey unless a special stratification is adopted. Therefore, an initial identification of such spots and a sampling of them may be more fruitful, particularly when such a survey cannot aim at statistical estimates for a larger geographical area. In the selected spots, a complete enumeration of all the children can be attempted if their number is small.

The children congregating at a particular place may often be homogeneous with respect to their activities and, therefore, if there is a large number of children in a given spot, a sample can be selected. To draw the sample, a list of all the children has first to be drawn up. Each child in the sample can then be interviewed to fill out the questionnaire. However, a survey of street children would have a number of limitations:

—The survey may not provide a reliable estimate of total street children by various categories, as the sample selected may not be representative;

—Children living individually on the streets may not be covered since many of them move from place to place continuously;

It may not be possible to get reliable information on some of the activities (illegal or disreputable) pursued by street children, which they may not want to report to the investigators; and

—If there is resistance in some places (or even threats of violence), the investigators may try to avoid collecting data in such places unless security is provided.

Interviewers of street children should be those who are reasonably acquainted with the areas and streets where the children are usually found, who may even know some of the children themselves and who are well trained in putting the children at ease, for example, by providing them with soft drinks.

Recommendations for interviewing children

The obvious way of collecting the information is by interview. A standard context for research interviews is the household-based surveys. But for reasons already explained, it is impossible to conduct indepth interviews with child workers inside an employer's workplace (or premises). The atmosphere is wrong, the timeframe is wrong, the employer may be obstructive; the child is most unlikely to be forthcoming and—fearing repercussions from the employer—may even give answers which please the employer, especially if the employer is present at the interview. This may also be true even at the household level, which makes it important to interview the child alone, particularly away from his/her parents or so-called "guardians".

Creating the right setting

Indepth interviews with children should therefore be conducted in a setting outside the place of work, preferably a place where the child feels safe and comfortable. Unless the interviewer has a great deal of experience in interviewing children, it will also be necessary to build up the child's confidence in the person concerned. Training in working with children will also be needed because creativity is needed to elicit correct information. Thus, interviewing children in depth, as opposed to asking broad questions, is best done over a period of time in a relatively unstructured and informal way.

The ideal setting is an existing project in which (ex)-working children are participating, for example, a drop-in centre or an education programme. If no such project currently exists, it is suggested that any attempt to collect in-depth information from the child workers at the employer's workplace or premises is postponed until it does. Here is a case where "action" should precede "research".

However, there is no need to feel that the task is impossible. Some NGOs have set up projects with the twin purposes of action and research in mind and have trained those who work with the children to collect information from them as part of their job. Alternatively, researchers might identify—with help from social welfare departments and others—an existing institution such as a children's home where some children are to be found, and conduct research among them.

In interviewing children about the effects of terms and conditions of work on their physical and mental well-being, it would be a good idea to seek advice from professional child care workers, as well as follow the suggestions below.

First, if you ask a child questions in a way which leads to a "yes" or "no", the child will probably answer accordingly. If you say: "Please tell me about . . . ." or "Please describe to me. . ." you are likely to get more information. Similarly, sometimes a "leading" question such as "What do you think of ... ?" or "What do you know (or "Do you know") about the difficulties (or other situation) at your school, or where you work, or with your employer, or at your home ...?" will result in more information.

Second, much information can only be gained indirectly. A child will not understand these words very well. So ask him or her to describe the whole day's activities, from the moment he/she gets up in the morning, right through until bedtime. Questions can be included about what the employer says and does; and about meals, sleeping space, rest breaks and so on. From the very specific, the child could then be asked more general questions about visits from family members, holidays, outings, pay, and the like.

Effects on well-being is more difficult. As far as health is concerned, you could include "before" and "after" questions such as: "How does ... compare to ... at home?" (food, bedtime, getting-up time, aches and pains). For psychological impact, you could ask about "my happiest times", and "my saddest times" and about contact with friends and relations. The most important thing is to create an atmosphere in which the child feels sufficiently comfortable to tell stories about his or her intimate experiences and reveal his or her feelings. This is why time, trust and the advice of child specialists are needed. Bearing in mind the delicacy with which interviewing should proceed, work out ahead of time what kind of subjects are relatively easy to open up and what kind should not be opened without caution. For example, you can start with questions about tasks, pay, and "gifts" such as shelter, clothing, home, and medical expenses.

Then proceed to working hours, where the child sleeps, food and care, how often he/she has a day off. From these responses you may spot natural openings to questions about the treatment the child receives and how he or she feels about it. If at any time the child becomes distressed, you can stop. In addition to noting the child's responses to specific questions, you may also want to write down some of your observations: "observation" is a useful research technique. Immediately after the interview is over, write a few paragraphs about the child. But in this case the colleague should be very unobtrusive and sit somewhere off to the side.

If the interview is conducted in a separate room with just the child present, there should only be one adult interviewer or the child is bound to feel overwhelmed. Have your observation headings ready ahead of time. For example: dress, cleanliness, facial expression, willingness to speak up, body language, signs of emotion, personality, ability to express him/herself. You may think you will remember all these things later when you read your interview notes, but very quickly one interviewee blurs into another.

Drawing, painting, acting, out and storytelling are revealing methods of eliciting information. They are especially useful in cultural settings where people are not used to being bombarded with questions.

Many NGOs use these kinds of techniques within non-formal education programmes. In Indonesia, *drama* and role-playing are used as a strategy for "breaking the silence" when working with children and young people who are socialised not to speak up in front of adults. Another technique is the focus group discussion. This is normally a semi-structured session with 6 to 12 participants picked for their special knowledge of the subject. Each group should have a facilitator trained in creating the kind of atmosphere which helps people speak up with confidence.

Factors and Causes

The incidence of child labour negatively correlates with per capita income, infrastructure development, school enrolment ratio, the position of women in society and female participation in non-agricultural work. It positively correlates with parental poverty, illiteracy, unemployment, underemployment, and the percentage of the labour force in agriculture.

Analysis of the incidence of child labour boils down to the composition of the household, the number of earning members, total earning vis-a-vis liabilities, and consumption pattern. In an extreme situation of a household below the poverty line with a meagre potential for earning, all members regardless of age and sex are required to work and have very little freedom to do otherwise. In a normal situation, however, a child's non-leisure time is available either for schooling or home-based work/income earning work in the market. There are undoubtedly competing claims on a member's time in a normal household. The way the household allocates the child's time depends *inter alia* on the household size and structure, the child's productive potential, and his/her parents (principally the mother) in home and market work, and the degree of substitution possible between the child and his/her parents (again largely the mother). The time allocation decision usually depends on the number of children which determines the income potential from child labour but this potential in turn also determines the desired size of the household. Children's income potential stems both from their work as children and the transfer of part of their income to the parents when the latter are old.

A recent review (Lloyd, 1994) of the evidence on this relationship from developing countries suggests that the larger the size of the household, the more limited will be the participation and progress of the child in school and the less the parents' investment in schooling. Lloyd's review reveals that the magnitude of the effect of household size is determined by at least four factors:

• The level of socio-economic development. The effect of household size is larger in urban or more developed areas;

• the level of social expenditure by the state (the effect of household size is less if state expenditure is high);

• family culture (the effect of household size is weaker where extended family systems exist; e.g. through child fostering);

• the phase of demographic transition (the effect of household size is larger in the later phases).

The extent to which boys and girls or all children are equally affected by household size is very much a cultural factor: families from urban slums in Tamil Nadu discriminate in order to provide a few children, principally boys, with quality private education. Where mothers enter the labour force, it is girls who must stay at home. In rural Maharashtra, if there are fewer younger siblings, boys benefit with more schooling and less work and girls must undertake tasks traditionally assigned to boys.

Research provides further evidence that poor households send children to work in order to augment household income and also as a safeguard against the uncertainties of income they face, such as the loss of a job, the occurrence of a natural calamity (flood, cyclone, drought, famine), failed harvest, prolonged ill health, etc. Such an interruption can be really threatening for poor households whose income is low, who have no savings, and are not in a position to borrow for want of collateral.

Most case studies of child labour do indeed identify the poverty of the household and low level of parental education as important factors in determining the incidence of child labour (ILO, 1992).

In rural areas the relationship between household size and child labour also depends on the extent of landholdings. There is evidence to show that children in landless and marginal farm households generally engage in wage labour while those in households with larger farms engage in agricultural work. The incidence of child labour increases with increase in size of the farm as the marginal contribution of children increases. This trend may be reversed in the case of large farm households where the landlord leases out land instead of operating it himself.

The supply of child labour is also determined by the characteristics of the community in which the household lives, especially the social infrastructure available, and no social infrastructure could be more relevant and powerful than education. If the system and form of education prevalent is dull, uninteresting and irrelevant many parents do not spontaneously send their children to school; instead viewing child labour as a preferred option. In an economic environment where there is shrinkage of jobs in the organized sector on account of rationalization, retrenchment or closure, and where survival depends on work, as in the unorganized or informal sector many parents would be inclined to conclude that taking children out of school and putting them to work will be the most sensible way of surviving.

The supply determinant of child labour relates to the labour market itself, and, therefore, any study of the former would be incomplete without a critical appraisal of the latter. In this study, an appraisal of the level of wages of both children and adults is relevant. It has been observed that flexibility in wages is a key factor influencing the employment of children. In competitive markets where wages are flexible, children can substitute for adults in the market place. In India, under the Minimum Wages Act, 1948, children are permitted to work for no more than four and half hours a day and entitled to receive fifty per cent of the wages of an adult. Since there are no ways of measuring the working hours in an informal work environment, in actual practice children are made to work the whole day while wages payable continue to be half those paid to adults. Besides, the same minimum wages law permits payment of wages in kind and also permits computation of these in cash. The prices of essential commodities (rice, wheat, cereals, pulses) vary greatly in different parts of the country and therefore, computation of the cash value of wages payable in kind is not easy. This gives rise to cases of under-weighment and cheating, and even though the arrangement may ensure easy availability of essential commodities or food grains, this is often less than what it should be. The usual assumption is that in a normal labour market situation where wages are at a floor level due to legislation or collective social action, adult workers will always be preferred to children as their productivity is much higher. If the Minimum Wages Act, 1948, provides, as in India, periodic review and revision of the minimum rates of wages for scheduled employments, and if this is rigorously enforced, it can deter the employment of child labour. Enforcement of the Minimum Wages Act, like the enforcement of child labour legislation, has, however, severe limitations. Establishments in the unorganized or informal sector, for whom minimum wages are notified, are scattered and bringing them within the purview of the labour law enforcement machinery has been found to be extremely difficult if not impossible. It is, therefore, a moot point whether mere fixation, review, and revision of minimum rates of wages would really be accompanied by a reduction in child labour as the process of enforcement of the law continues to be half-hearted and extremely frustrating. This is all the more difficult when, (a) wages are paid partly in cash and partly in kind, (b) payment is made against completion of specific tasks, (c) a group of people is engaged, as in agriculture, for performance of such tasks and the male adults invariably have a major say when it comes to apportioning wages for different components of a task and (d) the possibility exists of deductions on the ground that the end products do not conform to the specifications and for late delivery (as in *beedi* rolling, labelling, and packing which is a household industry but whose survival largely depends on the contractor).

All assumptions regarding the behaviour of labour markets tend to go awry in a situation, as in India, where there is no stability and durability of employment. Employment in the Indian labour market is susceptible to violent fluctuations and is characterized by rapid mobility of labour or migration. This has a considerable bearing on child labour in terms of employment status, wages, working conditions, and merits fairly detailed treatment.

Migration within the country could be of two types, i.e inter-district and inter-state. In yet another sense, the categorization could be determined by the mode of recruitment. One can migrate on one's own i.e out of one's own volition and freedom; one can also be recruited by a recruiting agent or intermediary or contractor or subcontractor of the principal employer for a specific purpose. Freedom of movement in any part of the territory of India and freedom to pursue any vocation of one's choice is a fundamental right guaranteed by Art. 19 of the Constitution of India. Migration being the movement of human beings in pursuit of certain desired objectives, such as better employment, better wages and better quality of life, is not in any way objectionable per se and is a normal social and economic phenomenon. It becomes objectionable only when it leads to exploitation leading to human misery and deprivation of the irreducible barest minimum to which every worker as a human being and as a citizen is entitled. It is objectionable when a person is recruited by an intermediary/contractor/subcontractor with promises and allurements that never fructify. It is objectionable, for instance, in the following instances:

- No agreement is signed between the recruiting agent and the person recruited.
- The person recruited is at a great disadvantage. S/he will often be from a rural background, landless, assetless, non-literate, and non-numerate with little awareness of the implications of leaving her/his home and going out in search of elusive employment and hence at the complete mercy of a third party.
- Cases where the person who is recruited is in debt to the local village landlord or moneylender and has found it difficult to repay due

to persisting landlessness and poverty. The intermediary/contractor/subcontractor pays some nominal advance to the person to be recruited to enable her/him to repay the debt incured, but then lures her/him to accept employment in another district or state in the expectation that this will yield rich dividends. This expectation is often belied, and in effect the migrant worker is lured from one debt trap to another. S/he will undoubtedly do her/his utmost along with other members of the family, including children, to repay the debt but the harsh logic of usury often makes this impossible.

□ Inter-state migration through recruiting agents without agreement is also fraught with many other undesirable consequences such as:

•The person who is recruited does not know the language of the state w here s/he is recruited.

•S/he is not familiar with court procedure.

•S/he is not a member of any trade union in the state to which s/he is recruited; there may not be any trade union at the place of work to safeguard her/his interests.

•In the event of accidents causing injury resulting in death or disablement there will be no one to champion her/his cause with regard to timely payment of compensation due under the Workmen's Compensation Act.

•The relatives of the migrant worker may be thousands of kilometres away and hence not in a position to come to her/his rescue. The children of a deceased migrant worker will be left to fend for themselves.

•Neither the principal employer, nor the contractor, nor the government of the state from where the migrant worker has been recruited will ordinarily come forward to safeguard the migrant worker's interests.

•Due to low wages and lack of unionization, the migrant worker would find it extremely difficult to plead her/his case in a court of law, and can ill afford the luxury of hiring a lawyer.

Tragically, people who migrate are not only poor but have large families to support either at the home if they remain there, or at the place of work if they are taken there. In a majority of cases members of the family too accompany the migrant worker. If it is a migration through a recruiting agent the law, i.e Inter-state Migrant Workmen (Regulation of Employment and Conditions of Service) Act, 1979, enjoins on the contractor/principal employer the responsibility providing suitable residential accommodation to the migrant workmen during their term of employment. However, the provisions of the law are in actual practice generally, only honoured in the breach. Residential accommodation is ordinarily not provided by the principal employer/contractor/ subcontractor, and whenever provided is far below the standard prescribed by law. Consequently, men, women and children are often huddled together in hovels that are at best suitable for rearing animals. There are ordinarily no arrangements for supply of potable drinking water to the tenements where the workers live. Men, women, and children are obliged to defecate in the open without any semblance of privacy. The hutments where they live are also vulnerable to pollution from dust, fumes and smoke emanating from heavy vehicular traffic as also from the chimneys of manufacturing plants. Exposure to such pollution at the place of work and stay makes the workers vulnerable to various occupational and respiratory diseases such as silicosis, pneumoconiosis, asthma, TB, anemia, and giddiness.

The social cost of migration is too heavy to be adequately described in words. The earnings are never adequate due to low wages and non-enforcement of provisions of the Minimum Wages Act, 1948. The entire workplace is full of middlemen like *thekedars* and *jamadars* who demand a cut for every transaction, those commissions being deducted from wages in violation of the provisions of the Payment of Wages Act, further lowering the level of the minimum wages. The meagre earnings of men are insufficient even for the very biological survival of the family, forcing their wives and children to work. This deprives women of their privacy and exposes them to the hazards of sexual harassment at the workplace, such harassment coming from the very people responsible for subjecting the migrant workers to ruthless exploitation at the workplace. It deprives children of their access to educational opportunity. Even if some minimal access to education through NFE centres is provided, rarely is there a literate environment in the home for children to reinforce what they have learnt in the classroom as their parents are non-literate and non-numerate. Besides, the children of migrant parents would find it far more profitable to be taught in their mother tongue while the medium of instruction at the place of work could be quite different. There is little scope for self learning or guided learning in totally alien surroundings that are not at all conducive to this.

Millions of innocent and guileless children of migrant parents are thus exposed to acute and heart-rending deprivation and exploitation for no fault of theirs. The joy and excitement of a normal childhood are totally lost to them.

This account has no intention of dramatization or sensationalization; it is intended only to portray what millions of children of migrant parents helplessly face. Their parents migrate from Santhal Parganas, Chotanagpur and the Singhbhum regions of Bihar, the Chattisgarh region of Madhya Pradesh (Raigarh, Durg, Bilaspur, Raipur, Rajnandgaon districts), eastern UP (Banda, Balia, Basti, Deoria, Ajamgarh, Gorakhpur, Jaunpur districts), the hill districts of UP (Dehradun, Nainital, Uttarkashi, Tehri Garhwal, Pithorgarh, Chamoli, Pauri, Kumaon districts), southern and western Orissa (Kalahandi, Nawapara, Bolangir, Koraput districts), the desert districts of Rajasthan (Barmer, Jaisalmer, Jalore, Sikar, Bikaner) to the plains of Punjab and Haryana, J&K, and hydroelectric projects and thermal stations of Himachal Pradesh, Delhi, and the north-east. They migrate on account of poverty, landlessness, and a total lack of assets. They do so being wholly unaware of the grim consequences of their action; of the perils of the debt traps ahead; of the perils facing their children.

A Magnified Problem

There are widely varying perceptions of the magnitude of the problem and this explains the widely varying statistics that are periodically trotted out. The ILO estimates that the number of working children in the 5—14 age group in the developing countries is 250 m., of whom at least 120 m. are working full time. Of these 61 per cent are in Asia, 32 per cent in Africa, and 7 per cent are in Latin America. The earlier ILO estimates had put the figure at 80 m. which evidently was a gross underestimation of the magnitude of the problem.

As anywhere else in the world, statistics on the extent of the problem in India vary greatly. According to all available indications, there has been a fall in the overall population of working children during 1981—91. The number of working children, according to the 1971 census was 10.75 m. which increased to 13.64 m. according to 1981 census, representing an increase of 26.88 per cent. The working children population according to 1991 census is 11.28 m. indicating that the number has fallen by 17.3 per cent during 1981-91.

The number of working children has fallen both in absolute and percentage terms. In 1981, out of a total population of 685 m., the number of working children was 13.6 m., which works out to about 2 per cent of the total population. In 1991, out of a total population of 838.6 m., the number of working children was 11.28 m., which works out to only 1.34 per cent.

The number of working children as a percentage of the child population has also fallen during 1981-91. According to the 1981 census, the child population (5-14 years) in India was 179.5 m., of which the number of working children was 13.64 m., indicating that 7.6 per cent of the child population were workers. According to the 1991 census the child population (5-14) was approximately 203.3 m., of which 11.28 m. were workers, indicating that 5.2 per cent of the child population were workers.

In 1981 the total workforce in the country was about 223 m. and the number of working children 13.6 m. or 6 per cent of the total workforce. In 1991, however, the total workforce in the country was 314 m., of which the number of working children was 11.28 m. or only 3.59 per cent.

The proportion of working children to the total labour force is also lower in India than in many other developing countries. Child labour accounts for 5.2 per cent of the total labour force in India as against percentages of 27.3 in Turkey, 20.7 in Thailand, 19.5 in Bangladesh, 18.8 in Brazil, 16.6 in Pakistan, 12.4 in Indonesia, 11.5 in Mexico, 8.2 in Egypt, 6.6 in Argentina. This is not, however, any consolation. The fact that the proportionate share of child labour as a subset of the total child population has been declining over time is also no consolation as the absolute number continues to be very large, and is in fact the highest in the world.

Professor D. P. Choudhury of the Department of Economics, University of Wollongong, Australia, has very precisely and scientifically classified the categories of working children in India. He has placed them in three categories. In the first, less than 6 per cent of about 13-14 m. full time child workers are employed for wages in activities that are prohibited under the Child Labour (Prohibition and Regulation) Act. In the second category are children employed for wages, but in activities that are not so prohibited under the Act. In the third category, over 80 per cent of India's full time and part time child workers are trapped in a situation where the parents of working children and their families work jointly within family economic enterprises (farms, household industries, petty trade). Small and marginal cultivators, sharecroppers, who are engaged in farming activities in the parched conditions of southern Orissa, central India (the Chattisgarh region), the desert tracts of Rajasthan are good examples of this. Professor Choudhury has graphically described this:

The average productivity in these enterprises is stagnant or declining. Output or income variability is very high and eking out an existence is a major challenge for survival. Due to population growth, demographic pressures and other urban industrial activities, environmental degradation in the hilly regions as well as plains has reduced the resource base of the working poor, the employers, self employed as well as family workers, forcing them to compete with each other and nature in an unfortunate race to the bottom.

A very large number of these children who are reported to be neither workers nor in schools (girls constituting a large majority) according to Professor D. P. Choudhury, are engaged in activities such as collection of firewood in rural areas, ragpicking in urban areas, and household work. These are not considered to be economic activities, and none of our laws provide any social or economic protection to this group. According to Professor D. P. Choudhury, these children, who he terms 'Nowhere children', numbered around 74-98 m. in 1991, the numbers varying across states. Neither at school nor at work, they represent a colossal waste of a sizeable percentage of potential manpower at its most formative stage on account of large scale educational deprivation. When they enter adulthood, the productive and reproductive stage of human life, without literacy they will be in no position to develop their innate capacities and skills and hence would constitute a major liability for the nation.

It is also abundantly clear from the above analysis that child labour in India is more a rural than an urban phenomenon. Approximately 90 per cent of the working children are in the rural areas, engaged in agricultural and allied activities. Cultivation, agricultural labour, forestry and fisheries account for 84.9 per cent of child labour. In urban areas, manufacturing, service and repairs account for 8.64 per cent of child labour. A major percentage of child labour in urban and semi-urban areas is in effect rural labour forced to migrate to urban areas due to poverty and other economic compulsions. Of these, only 0.8 per cent work in factories. The unorganized and informal sectors, both in urban and rural areas, account for almost the entire child labour force.

The distribution of child labour in different states appears to indicate certain co-relations. States with a larger population living below the poverty line have a higher incidence of child labour. A higher incidence of child labour is accompanied by a high drop-out rate in schools.

The incidence of child labour is partly linked to the level of socio-economic development of an area and partly to the attitude of the parents, employers, and socio-cultural compulsions.

The state-wise distribution of child labour in 11 major states in percentage terms, according to 1991 census, is broadly as follows:

State	*Percentage*
Andhra Pradesh	14.3
Madhya Pradesh	12.5
Maharashtra	11.4
Uttar Pradesh	10.5
Karnataka	8.3
Bihar	8.1
Tamil Nadu	7.1
Rajasthan	6.0
Orissa	5.1
Gujarat	4.5
West Bengal	4.4

TWENTY TWO

APPLICATION OF HUMAN RIGHTS

Childhood may be defined in terms of age but different societies have different age thresholds for demarcating childhood and adulthood. In some societies, age may not be a sufficient basis for defining 'childhood'. The fulfilment of certain social rites and traditional obligations may well be important requirements in defining 'adult' and 'child' status. In still others, the integration of children into socioeconomic life may begin so early and the transition from childhood to adulthood may be smooth and gradual, making it virtually impossible to identify clearly the different life phases.

The concept of 'child' may mean different things in different societies and at different times. In the context of child labour, a working definition of 'child' may be a person below the internationally agreed age limit of 15 years. However, different countries have different basic minimum age of employment.

The economic exploitation of children in India has always been an area of concern. In rural areas it is the fact that the child who does not attend a formal school is a working child. Collection of water, fuel, household chores and taking care of younger siblings all constitute important elements of a child's life. While many of these activities cannot be defined as hazardous work, inasmuch as they interfere with the normal development of the child and in the child's ability to reach his/her true potential they violate the Convention on the Rights of the Child. In the typical environment in which Indian children grow up the concept of a non-working, non-social going child simply does not exist.

The issue of compulsory education has always been something of anenigma. At the theoretical level very few disagree that all children should receive education, at least upto the primary stage, or with the fact that children should not work. In fact, the state has committed itself not only to the Universalisation of primary education but also to the abolition of child labour through various pronouncements, not the least of which are the Directive Principles of State Policy enshrined in the Constitution of India.

Democracy and its three pillars—liberty, equality and fraternity—enshrined in the Constitution of India are relatively meaningless in view of the fact that 120 to 140 million children are working in this country. Of these, 55 million children between the ages of six and 14 are languishing in servitude.

They are employed mostly in agriculture and industries such as carpet weaving, brassware manufacture, glass and banglemaking, leather, gem cutting and polishing, matches and fireworks, stone quarries, brick kilns and handloom. Socio-cultural factors, including the abominable caste system and ethnic and gender discrimination, are responsible for the perpetuation of the scourge of child labour. These factors exercise a significant negative influence, worse even than socio-economic factors such as grinding poverty, unemployment and illiteracy. Little wonder that 90 per cent of bonded child labourers belong to untouchable castes and tribes.

No government can scale down adult unemployment without curbing child labour. This is so because the maximum job opportunities created every year are preferentially given to children as their physical and mental vulnerability makes them easy to exploit. In addition, children represent the cheapest source of human labour. Our logical apprehension is that if we do not eradicate child servitude today, we will be responsible for perpetuating the poverty, abject misery and ill-health of 55 million adults in the country. It should be noted that the growth rate of the population is much higher among those communities in which unemployment is rampant. Obviously, if child labour is not controlled, impoverished parents will continue to succumb to the 'necessity' of enlarging the number of earning members in the family.

In India, an aggressive anti-carpet campaign was launched; the premises of manufactures were raided, children were liberated and their rehabilitation started. In addition, the issue has been publicised widely and political will has been generated for the total eradication of this menace.

The phenomenon of the sale of children is universal. The tragic circumstances leading to the abuse and exploitation of children cuts across the barriers between the developing and developed world.

As child labour entails the sale of a child, the following concepts of sale could also be considered: armed conflict; adult criminal activities; forced labour or abducted children; debt bondage; labour in the unorganised sector; labour in the organised sector; child prostitution; pornography and sexual exploitation; forced marriage; disabled children in the labour force; domestic labour; apprenticeship and family-supervised labour.

It is recognised that the exploitation of child labour is a form of sale of children. Generally speaking when one considers the notion "child labour" per se, it is not necessarily detrimental to children. However, when it gives rise to exploitation, usually be another party who has power over the child, it may result in negative consequences for children, both with regard to their rights and their development. It also constitutes sale because the child becomes the object of a transaction in cash or in kind. It appears that in many parts of the world, children are sold into several types of employment, either by their parents, guardians or other intermediaries.

Recently, the International Labour Organisation (ILO) estimated that there were some 88 million working children between 10 and 14 years of age. Instances of exploitation are to be found in all regions of the world but Asia and South America figure high in the number of children in difficult circumstances. It is noted that the worst forms of child labour exploitation often take place in the informal sector and small-scale industries.

At the international level, various instruments provide an umbrella of protection for child labourers. Under the auspices of the ILO, a series of conventions and recommendations on the exploitation of child labour has been developed. One key convention is Convention Number 138 which establishes 15 as the basic minimum age of employment, although reduction to 14 may be possible in developing countries. The ILO conventions and recommendations have been strengthened by the advent of the convention on the rights of the child. The CRC emphasises anew the issue of sale linked with child labour. Article 32 states that "children should be protected from economic exploitation and from performing any work that is likely to be hazardous or to interfere with the child's education, or to be harmful to the child's health or physical, mental, spiritual, moral or social development".

In East Asia, the sale and trafficking of children for labour exploitation is still rampant both locally and across borders. The issue is closely linked with the sex market. In Africa, the exploitation of child labour in the informal sector was reported in various countries in 1993. In particular, the girl-child is a victim of exploitative domestic service. At times, there is a link with the remnants of slavery, such as the sale of children for forced labour, particularly from certain ethnic groups.

In Central and South America, the number of children at work is large, especially as there is a vast population of street children. There were disturbing incidents of killings of street children during the past year. In this region, too, the problems of child domestic workers and the use of children in the informal sector are rampant. At the other extreme, children are at times employed to sell drugs. In Europe, the problem of child labour exploitation poses a challenge to many countries. This includes a specific linkage with children used as instruments of crime and as domestic workers.

In relation to child labour, the whole range of measures advocated by the UN Commission on Human Rights' Programme of Action for the Elimination of the Exploitation of Child Labour, 1993 should be implemented. There should be stricter law enforcement in the case of child labour, with more incentives for exemplary law enforcement personnel. All vestiges of bondage should be eradicated, and attention should be paid to the plight of the girl-child. The Programme of Action against Child Bondage, 1992, should also be placed as a priority for all parties concerned.

Child labour only happens in the poor world—while the vast majority of working children are found in developing countries, children routinely work in all countries. In every country, rich and poor, it is the nature of the work children do that determines whether or not they are harmed by it— not the plain fact of their working. Few people in the industrialised world, for example, would look upon the employment of a child to deliver newspapers for an hour or two before school as an exploitative form of child labour, despite the fact that the child will certainly be paid less than normal adult rates for the job. Often such a job will be encouraged in the interest of the child's gaining experience of the 'real world' of work and commerce.

Child labour will never be eliminated until poverty disappears—it is true that the poorest, most disadvantaged sectors of society supply the vast majority of child labourers. The conclusion often drawn from this is that child labour and poverty are inseparable and that calls for an immediate end to hazardous child labour are unrealistic.

The phrase 'child labour' conjures up a particular image: we see children chained to looms in dark mills and sweatshops, as if in a long and nightmarish line running from Lancashire in the 1830s right through to the South Asia of the 1990s.

Child labour has increased substantially in Central and Eastern European countries as a result of the abrupt switch from centrally planned to market economies. In industrialised countries, such as the UK and the US, meanwhile, the growth of the service sector and the quest for a more flexible workforce have contributed to an expansion of child labour.

Understanding all the various cultural factors that lead children into work is essential. But deference to tradition is often cited as a reason for not acting against intolerable forms of child labour. Children have an absolute, unnegotiable right to freedom from hazardous child labour— a right now established in international law and accepted by every country that has ratified the convention on the rights of the child. Respect for diverse cultures should not deflect us from using all the means at our disposal to make every society, every economy, every corporation, regard the exploitation of children as unthinkable.

Street child labour, virtually unheard of prior to the transition to a market economy, is now a growing problem in the Russian Federation. In Kyrgyzstan, in Central Asia, the numbers of children working on the streets, selling food and other products, have increased dramatically over the last three years. Many have dropped out of school or never attended classes. On the streets, they shine shoes, wash and guard cars, carry luggage, hawk flowers and trinkets, collect recyclables and find a myriad other ingenious ways to make money. The amount they earn may be small but is sometimes more than they would receive from formal-sector work.

In virtually every area of life and in every country as these annual state of the world's children reports have long noted, girls and women routinely bear burdens and endure treatment that reflect their unequal status. So it is with child labour. Working girls are often invisible, treated as if they did not exist.

All over the world, more girls than boys are denied their fundamental right to primary schooling. In some regions, including the Middle East and North Africa, sub-Saharan Africa and especially South Asia, the gender gap is still enormous. Educational equality between the sexes is being approached in East Asia and Latin America and the Caribbean, but elsewhere little progress has been recorded.

The exploitation of children is one of the consequences of complex situations of insufficient progress. ILO observed that 98 per cent of the economically active children are found in developing countries. The Special Rapporteur of the United Nations Sub-Commission on prevention of discrimination and protection of minorities also observed that poverty and exploitation of child labour go hand-in-hand. It is the poorest populations, at the lowest levels of human existence, who are forced to work the most prematurely. Children may be forced to work due to poverty but child labour in turn accentuates poverty. Children are engaged in jobs that can be done by adults too, thus depriving adults of jobs.

Employers prefer to hire children because they can extract the same work from children at lower wages, in the process bringing down the overall wages for such jobs. Thus child labour increases adult unemployment and reduces their income and thus forces adults to send their children to work to supplement the family income. The poor are thus caught in a vicious circle. Rather than improving the household income, child labour helps to reduce it. In a large number of developing countries, migration from rural areas has also intensified the problem of child labour. In most developing countries, developmental efforts have neglected the agrarian sectors, resulting in growing pauperisation of small farmers, increasing landlessness and rural differentiation. This has led to search for wage employment in commercial farms, as well as to rapid migration away from rural areas. Children from poor families are forced into the labour market to work either individually or as part of contracted family labour.

When a rural family migrates to the town, the adults are straightaway faced with a new and unknown environmental and labour situation. As a result of the instability and insecurity that this causes, the children are often sent to work so that the family may survive.

Countries having low literacy and school attendance rates generally have the most acute child labour problems. It has been often stated that education can bring the dramatic exploitation of child labour to an end. The example of the developed countries confirms this conclusively. The historical record reveals an astonishing correlation between the progress of education in Europe and decrease in the volume of child labour and the transformation of its very nature. A glance at the educational statistics shows that it is almost always the same countries that admit to being the most behind in school enrolment and teacher-student ratio, that have the greatest problems as regards the exploitation of child labour.

It is said that governments in developing countries lack financial resources for universal compulsory primary education and parents often find schools irrelevant to meet their needs. Many countries successfully made primary school education compulsory and universal when per capita incomes were low, poverty was widespread and parents would have employed their children had they been permitted to do so.

The relationship between child labour and illiteracy may not be one of cause and effect. Some countries have largely succeeded in eradicating illiteracy but remain confronted by the child labour problem, which is sometimes very acute. Sri Lanka is an example of a country that massively expanded its primary school enrolments in the 1950s. By 1981, 90 per cent of the primary school-age children were in school and 70 per cent of all children completed five years of schooling. Labour force statistics indicated a sharp decrease in the number of children in the age group of 10-14 in the labour force from 1946-63 as a result of school enrolment. Thus the importance of compulsory schooling in the struggle against child labour cannot be undermined. However, the educational system adopted by countries concerned must be meaningful and realistic and must adapt itself to the real needs of society.

The role of vested interests in perpetuating child labour also need to be highlighted. Employers often claim that there are types of work for which children are particularly suited. However, most work done by children can also be done by adults. The real reason behind employers preference in hiring children is the desire to maximise profits. Children can be made to work for long hours for low wages. Employers find it easier to deal with children because they do not organise themselves in trade unions, can be easily intimidated and are not capable of defending themselves and insisting on their rightful due. The notion of child labour is also rooted in the traditions and attitudes of the regions where it is practised, as a remnant of the past, a form of resistance to change.

In many societies, child labour is not considered a problem and is regarded as part of a child's normal socialisation even if exploitative work conditions are present. On the other hand, the attitudes and beliefs of policy makers in several developing countries regarding the respective roles of upper and lower classes have perpetuated the problem. It is often argued that the children of the poor should be prepared for their future roles from an early age. Child labour persists in some countries because of lack of political will to deal with the problem and because child labour laws cannot be adequately enforced because of shortage of qualified labour inspectors. Thus children work because of poverty, lack of compulsory education, rapid rural-urban migration and because of prevailing social, cultural and political attitudes.

Family farming makes the greatest use of child labour in the context of unpaid family assistants. In this type of labour it is not so much the child who is exploited by the general social system as the whole family.

The economic, social and cultural situation of the family obviously has repercussions on the child but he at least remains integrated in a social context that is in principle protective. Children are also engaged in family craftwork. The intricate rules governing the market for the crafts produced also makes possible exploitation and abuses.

As in the case of family farming, there is no question of wage and the situation remains one of joint production at the group level. This type of activity, in which the exploitation of child labour is no less real because it is indirect, to be found in most parts of the world. Craft piecework is a more highly evolved form than the previous type. It meets the same needs, is carried out in the some places, and employs the same manufacturing techniques. However, a middleman or a capitalist is involved who picks up the products from the families to market them, having first secured a more or less extensive and more or less excessive sales monopoly. The family no longer has direct access to the market. To be in a better position to exert pressure he gives a small advance on the wage.

The threat of exploitation is clearly greater and affects the child along with the family. Since payment is made on the basis of amount and quality of work, to earn more money the family calls upon its children and becomes the more or less willing and conscious accomplice of the middleman.

Children also carry out small tasks on their own account. However, two subtypes, differing radically, according to the level of development of the country, must be distinguished in this type of work. In developing countries, the child usually works in order to live and in order to survive. In developed countries children usually work in order to satisfy secondary or even superfluous needs. Small tasks called out by the child for third parties are different in that they produce a relationship of dependence which can very easily become one of exploitation. The seasonal labour of children in agriculture is more organised and also more prevalent. Seasonal labour is in general remunerative and is carried out under widely varying conditions. However, to the extent that it is work that is very difficult to control and in which middlemen are fairly numerous, the loopholes for abuse are quite large.

Learning how to work is a part of any sound and balanced education. Apprenticeship enables the child to try his hand at a task at a fairly early age and then to improve in skill until all operations have been mastered. But very frequently apprenticeship is simply subterfuge for evading legislation on minimum age. The exploitation of child labour is perpetuated through apprenticeship. More often than not, supposed apprentices are in fact working rather than learning and not being paid for it. Such a state of affairs may sometimes last for years. There is too much fake apprenticeship, which is merely a facade behind which there is nothing at all, since the activities performed require no qualification, provide no training and at best are carried out for paltry sums.

Maids-of-all-work in situation of virtual bondage are to be found everywhere. This type of child labour is very widespread. Bonded labour is the ultimate stage of exploitation of child labour. Debt bondage can arise in a number of ways. In agrarian societies land tenure patterns impose on tenants, sharecroppers and similar categories of workers obligations over and above household consumption requirements. In some cases, these obligations, may take the form of providing the landlord a share of the produce. But in others they may involve the provision of labour services, including those of children. The prevalence of such relations is known to lead to a severe and high incidence of debt bondage. Debt bondage is often also the result of the parents being given a loan to meet some urgent need. The debtor then has to repay by working. Parents may send children to work in the house of the moneylender.

In practice the debt does not decrease; it climbs ever upwards—a combination of usurious interest rates and outright fraud. These children may stay for many years, not knowing how long they must work or even the size of the debt they are paying off. While bonded labour is prohibited by law, it is still found for example, in parts of South and South-east Asia.

Children in most countries have always been used as prostitutes but the situation in some Asian countries, like Thailand, has been aggravated by the expansion of mass tourism. Both boys and girls are used in the flesh trade. In Sri Lanka, for example, the majority of child prostitutes are boys. The problem can also be analysed by examining the sectors in which children are employed. Sectors employing child labour vary from one country to another but child labour is most common in agriculture followed by service sector, largely in street trades and in third place industry.

Most child work is agricultural. Starting with light tasks, such as looking after animals, collecting firewood and fodder and drawing water, they later learn to sow and to reap. In commercial agriculture, on plantations for example, they often work as part of the family team: weeding, spreading fertilizer, tending plants, though they often share in the heavier tasks. The rapid urbanisation process of recent decades has led to a marked increase in child labour in the cities. Children work in a wide variety of street trades: as shoeshine boys, messengers, sellers of magazines, food, flowers, lottery tickets, etc. These children are often termed as street children because they may be literally living on the streets or at the place of their work. The boys very often work as waiters in roadside cafes and restaurants and as pageboys and the girls as hotel maids or domestic servants. Children who work in industries are generally employed in the informal sector. While in some industries children perform secondary tasks, they may also directly participate in the main tasks of production.

Where children work in a family undertaking, generally working conditions may not be too arbitrary. However, these traditional situations are declining in many areas, especially where plantation agriculture is becoming established or where there is massive out-migration. When children are employed outside the family, the way they are treated, as well as their conditions of work, are usually determined by the employer. The possibilities of ill-treatment are unlimited. Ill-treatment may include corporal punishment, abuses of all kinds, humiliation and frustration. Children are usually employed in the informal sector, where conditions of work are appalling and welfare facilities are conspicuous by their absence.

The tasks in which they are employed are generally monotonous and repetitive in nature and often they are ill-suited to the child's physical and mental capacities. The working conditions severely tax the child's physical and mental resistance as a result, for example, of suffocating heat in enclosed premises or exposure to rain or sun in open-air work. They may be forced to work in an awkward position in badly lit, badly ventilated, noisy or unhealthy premises, in damp and unhygienic surrounding, in an atmosphere contaminated with dust or gases, crammed together with other workers, in workshops without adequate safety devices, rest areas, medical and toilet facilities, having to carry excessively heavy loads, etc., all in violation of the principles set forth in international instruments to protect their rights.

Children who are more or less self-employed and child street traders generally feel they are freer than other working children. Despite their relative freedom, they too are an exploited lot because they too have to bear the demands of the market. Although many self-employed workers work in their own home, others have to travel varying distances to reach their workplace as many wage-earners do. When carrying out their activities they are hardly ever protected from the vagaries of the weather. They may be harassed by the police or by groups of youths or adults.

The length of time that children work each day and over the year varies considerably according to their schooling status, their parent's wish to keep them at work more or less continuously, how long the employer needs them and so on. Some children work only during the school holidays, at weekends, early in the morning or late at night. Seasonal work is also often undertaken by children, in agricultural work for tasks such as sowing and harvesting. In some countries, girls work longer hours than boys because boys spend more time at school. It is common knowledge that children in domestic service work long hours since they must be available at virtually any time to carry out their employer's bidding.

Some wage earning, children are permitted to take work breaks at fixed intervals during the working day. Others are not allowed to do so despite the fact that a child needs a break more often than an adult if he is to recharge his physical and mental batteries. The period of daily rest is often not sufficient, especially in agricultural work, industry, some service industries and domestic service. The weekly rest is sometimes granted and paid, sometimes granted but not paid and sometimes not allowed at all, i.e., the working week is a seven-day week.

When the child is a wage earner, he may be paid a salary, a daily wage or piece-rate wage. The wage that a child earns is much lower than those received by an adult for doing the same work. A still more flagrant example of exploitation of child workers is that of supposed apprentices who are in fact working than learning and are not being paid for it. Finally, in another types of exploitative relationship, payment is symbolic or non-existent or supplied in kind: food, lodging or 'presents' to the child or to the family.

Consequences of child labour

Sending children to work may seem a rational approach to poverty but employment of children has profound repercussions. ILO research shows that child labour is almost universally recognised as being undesirable, harmful for the children themselves and harmful for the future of their nations. When a child joins the workforce at a young age, he is deprived of the opportunity to educate himself and acquiring qualifications which will help him in getting a better job in future. It is, therefore, very likely that a child who has been at work from an early age will spend his whole life at the bottom of the social ladder. Thus child labour has become a mode of perpetuating an unjust social system and of ensuring the continued availability of subservient, unskilled, illiterate labourers who do not have the bargaining power to question the system that marginalises them and deprives them of their right to lead a decent life.

Many of the jobs that children do are harmful for their physical development. The physical susceptibility of working children also has a lot to do with the fact that they have very different capacities and needs from adults, and this fact is very rarely taken into account by employers. The manner of their employment, the nature of their work and the conditions under which they are often employed subject them to severe health and safety hazards. Work in agriculture is also characterised by certain hazards, particularly with the introduction of advanced farming practices, new techniques and chemicals. There is also prolonged exposure to heat, sunlight, dust, wind and insects and the high costs in terms of safety and health associated with work in commercial and plantation agriculture.

Children are particularly at risk from endemic and parasitic diseases, diseases of the respiratory tract, dermatosis and fatal accidents. However, these problems are multiplied several fold in industries. Work may be heavy and intense; it may be highly mechanised and extremely monotonous; it may involve the use of sharp and dangerous objects and toxic substances; it may be carried out in conditions of extreme heat, dust and noise.

Child workers in industries are faced with serious risks to their health and physical development. They may be required to undertake tasks for which they are entirely unprepared physically. In a number of industries children are exposed to lead poisoning which may have no noticeable effect on adults. There are claims that children's brains are detrimentally affected due to exposure to lead poisoning. There are documented cases of paralysis caused by the use of toxic glues.

There is documentation on the paralytic effects of a number of chemicals on children in Moroccan workshops where children were gluing suitcases and shoes. In these cases the toxic effects were accentuated by poor sanitation and ventilation and the younger the child, the more serious the paralysis. The risk of occupational diseases or accidents are higher among child workers because their growing bodies are not as strong as adult workers. Several studies show that child workers have greater health problems than adults even if both are placed in the same working environment.

There can be special risks associated with the working environment. Heavy loads and awkward body positions in particular can affect physical growth, especially the growth of bones, which are still soft in children. When a child is regularly bent under a heavy burden or is forced to stay in an unnatural position for long periods, deformation of the spinal column, pelvis or thorax may be the result.

A World Health Organisation report on child workers cites health hazards such as bony lesions and postural deformity attributable to such work as carpet weaving, embroidery and lifting heavyweights. Children generally work for long hours, which results in excessive fatigue and stunted growth. Poor children are generally malnourished but their work increases their energy requirement and calorie deficit. Moreover, if they suffer from anaemia, fatigue and inadequate sleep, they become more susceptible to accidents and infectious diseases. Excessively hot, damp or dusty conditions also create a milieu which favours the transmission of communicable diseases. Many of these diseases, for example, tuberculosis, may be very difficult to cure and involve lifelong illnesses.

Once again, malnutrition, anaemia, inadequate sleep, etc., lower resistance. Once infected at an early age, and through constant reinfection, it becomes difficult to break the vicious cycle of contact. In many cases workplaces do not meet hygienic standards. There is often no running water or toilet facilities. In these situations gastro-intestinal diseases nourish and it is difficult to break the oral-faecal cycle.

The self-employed child who has an accident or contracts a disease of occupational origin obviously benefits from no form of social protection. If the child is a wage-earner he is not usually protected either since in the vast majority of cases he is working illegally. If he is the victim of an occupational accident or disease he and his parents must be prepared for fearful and irreversible consequences. The official statistics reveal a very small proportion of the occupational accidents or diseases that affect children. Thus many jobs done by children are the cause of physical deformities and illnesses such as deformities of the spine, stunted growth, infections, burns, sores, etc., or else they may aggravate defects or maladies. Child labour involves both short-term and long-term health risks.

Child labour has mental repercussions also since the age at which he usually starts to work coincides more or less with a period of profound mental change in the child. The mental consequences of child labour are not just the result of the work situation but the violent change to which the child is exposed. In many cases children are separated from their families when they migrate to cities and other places in search of employment. An unfamiliar, often oppressive work situation, exacerbates the stresses and leads to socio-cultural disorganisation. There is a breakdown of effective communication, impaired human relations, insecurity problems of identification, a high prevalence of psycho-neurotic reactions and psychosomatic disorders.

With the spread of compulsory schooling in developed countries, the rapid and considerable improvement in levels of living and the enforcement of anti-child labour laws there was a significant decline in child labour. However, child labour is still prevalent in the developed nations, according to an ILO report. In the poverty pockets of the industrialised countries there may be as many as another 10 million or more working children, many of whom are not in school full-time and many may not be reached by health services. These children are found particularly amongst illegal migrant families; but also in certain occupations in the entertainment or publicity industries.

International action against child labour

The growing magnitude of the child labour has made it a cause for international concern. Efforts have been made at the global and national level by various international organisations along with their member nations to expose the problem and to cope with it. The beginning of the industrial revolution brought about the enactment of child labour laws. In the international arena, the first conventions indirectly protecting children began in the late 19th and early 20th century. Children's right emerged as a sub-category in the development of the rules of war and of the international labour conventions. The idea of grouping children into a distinct category was gradually promoted. Children have been a silent and unrepresented minority, they used to belong to one of those groups in history which Martin Luther King Jr described as "nobodies".

Non-governmental organisations played a very important role in giving shape to the rights of the child. The whole process started at the outset of 20th century, when some British women in Cambridge made a survey of the charitable societies at that time to determine what protection was provided to children. These pacifist women worked throughout the First World War to alert the general public to the plight of children in war-affected areas. After the war, they founded the "Save the Children" movement, whose lobbying led to the recognition of the rights of the child in the League of Nations. In January 1924, a committee was set up in the league whose scope included the protection of children in general. This was later divided into two sections, one of which was specifically devoted to child welfare.

The Geneva Declaration of the Rights of the Child was adopted in 1924. The Geneva Declaration recognises the principle that childhood is entitled to special care, assistance and safeguards. The Geneva Declaration contains a sentence that has become the motto of all supporters of the children's cause: "mankind owes to the child the best it has to give."

The General Assembly of the UN adopted on 10 December, 1948, a Universal Declaration of Human Rights. Portions of the Universal Declaration of Human Rights apply specifically to minors. It contains 30 articles, 21 of which spell out civil and political rights, and six articles deal with economic and cultural rights. The UN adopted a Convention on the Abolition of Slavery, the Slave Trade and Institutions and Practices similar to Slavery in 1956. This convention prohibits the exploitation of child labour in cases where children are delivered to another person for that purpose.

The International Covenant on Economic, Social and Cultural Rights imposes a general prohibition on the employment of children under a certain age and the employment of children in work constituting a threat to their health or morals. Though the Universal Declaration of Human Rights, 1948, implicitly included the freedom and rights of children, it was believed that this was not enough. It was felt that the special needs of children justified a separate document because children are particularly vulnerable to arbitrary deprivation of their human rights This led to the adoption of the Declaration of the Rights of the Child in 1959. The 1959 declaration enunciates general principles for the care and protection of children. It is mainly concerned with economic, social and cultural rights. It must be noted that it was in the preamble of 1959 declaration that the problem of implementation of children's rights was first mentioned. The preamble to the declaration states that the child because of his physical and mental immaturity needs special safeguards and care.

The Declaration of the Rights of the Child also prohibits the employment of children under a certain age and the employment of children in work which endanger their development. Principle 9 states: "The child shall be protected against all forms of neglect, cruelty, and exploitation. He shall not be the subject of traffic in any form. The child shall not be admitted to employment before an appropriate minimum age; he shall in no case be caused or permitted to engage in any occupation or employment which would prejudice his health or education or interfere with his physical, mental or moral development".

The Government of Poland submitted a draft Convention on the Rights of the Child to the General Assembly in 1978. In 1979, it submitted an amended version of the draft to the Commission on Human Rights. The General Assembly requested the Commission to give the highest priority to the question of completing the draft convention, "bearing in mind the children's rights are basic human rights and call for continuous improvement of the situation of children all over the world as well as their development and education in conditions of peace".

As a result, the General Assembly decided to set up a working group within the Human Rights Commission, which from 1979, the International Year of the Child, met regularly to complete the Convention. On November 20, 1989, the General Assembly at its 44th session adopted the Convention. It came into force on September 2, 1990, following ratification by the stipulated minimum of 20 member states. The Convention recognises the exceptional vulnerability of children and proclaims that childhood is entitled to special care and assistance. It is guided by the principle of "first call for children"—a principle that the essential needs of children should be given highest priority in the allocation of resources at all times. It obligates the state to respect and ensure that children get a fair and equitable deal in society. The Convention's provisions can be categorised under the headings of civil and political rights, social rights and cultural rights.

Article 3 states that "in all actions concerning children... the best interests of the child shall be a primary consideration". It implies that whenever a child's right is in the process of being affected, the focus must be on the child's welfare and not on the parents' or guardians' will. The extraordinary importance of Article 3 lies in the fact that for the first time it grants children the right to their best interests. Article 27 makes it obligatory for the state to recognise the right of every child to have a standard or living which may ensure requisite physical, mental, spiritual, moral and social development of each child. Article 28 of the convention imposes a liability on the state to recognise the right of the child to education and for that purpose it is expected on the part of each state to make primary education compulsory and it should be available to all children free of cost. The state is also expected to take measures to encourage regular attendance at school and the reduction of dropout rates.

Under Article 32 obligation has been imposed on each member state to recognise the right of each child for being protected from economic exploitation and from doing work of hazardous nature which may prove to be harmful to the health of the child or retard the physical, mental, spiritual, moral or social development of the child. Article 35 requires state parties to take all appropriate measures to prevent the abduction, the sale of or traffic in children for any purpose or in any form. As of 1995, 181 countries had ratified the convention.

The ILO has concerned itself with the question of child labour since its foundation in 1919. The abolition of child labour has been one of its basic aims since its establishment. At the same time, it has pursued a systematic policy of protection of working children from undesirable conditions of work. The ILO's traditional approach to child labour has been to lay down international labour standards through ILO conventions and recommendations. There are thus two main categories of ILO instruments concerning child labour: instruments prohibiting child labour, and protection of child labour The first instrument which set a minimum age for admission to employment was the Minimum Age (Industry) Convention (No. 5), adopted by the ILO General Conference at its first session in 1919. This convention fixed the minimum age for admission of children to industrial employment at 14 years.

At subsequent sessions the ILO adopted various other conventions and recommendations fixing minimum age standards for admission to employment in different sectors of economic activity. In 1973, the ILO decided that the time had come, as stated in the preamble to the convention, to establish a general institution on the subject, which would gradually replace the existing ones applicable to limited economic sectors, with a view to achieving the total abolition of child labour. Convention No. 138 provides that "each member should pursue a national policy to ensure the effective abolition of child labour and to raise progressively the minimum age for admission to employment or work to a level consistent with fullest physical and mental development of young persons". This age should not be less than 15 years. However, the above Convention provides the possibility of lowering these age limits in certain circumstances. Article 2 lays down that a country "whose economy and educational facilities are insufficiently developed may, after consultation with either the organisation of employers and workers concerned, where such exist, initially specify a minimum age of 14 years".

Moreover, a member state whose economy and administrative facilities are insufficiently developed may initially limit the scope of application of the Convention and may extend the scope at a later date. However, the provisions the Convention must be applicable as a minimum to the following: mining and quarrying; manufacturing; construction; electricity; gas and water; sanitary services; transport, storage and communications, and plantations and other agricultural undertakings mainly producing for commercial purposes, but excluding family and small-scale holdings producing for local consumption and not regularly employing hired workers.

Article 7 lays down that "states which have ratified the convention may permit the employment of children 13 to 15 years of age (12 to 14 for states which have adopted 14 years as a general minimum age) and of older children who have not completed their compulsory schooling, in 'light work' which is not likely to be harmful to their health or development" and not such as to prejudice their attendance at school or their participation in vocational orientation or training programmes". As regards work which is likely to jeopardise the health, safety or morals of young persons, the convention lays down that the minimum age for admission to any type of employment or work of this kind shall not be less than 18 years.

Article 3 provides that a country may authorise employment in dangerous work as from the age of 16 years on the condition that health, safety and morals of the young persons concerned are fully protected and that the young persons have received adequate instruction or vocational training in the relevant branch of activity. In addition, the International Labour Conference adopted the Minimum Age Recommendation, 1973 (No. 146) to supplement the Minimum Age Convention, 1973. This recommendation invites states to give high priority to planning for and meeting the needs of children and youth in national development policies and programmes and to extend interrelated measures necessary to provide the best possible conditions of physical and mental growth for children and young persons. It recommends that members take as their objective the progressive raising to 16 years of the minimum age for employment or work specified in pursuance of the Minimum Age Convention.

In countries where the minimum age for employment is still below 15 years, urgent steps should be taken to raise that level. In countries where the minimum age for admission to types of employment or work which are likely to jeopardise the health, safety or morals of young persons is still below 18 years, steps should be taken to raise it to that level. With a view to facilitating the goals set forth in the convention, the recommendation advocates the adoption of measures designed to achieve full employment of adults; the progressive extension of other economic and social measures to alleviate poverty so as to make recourse to child labour unnecessary; the adoption and extension of adequate facilities for educational and vocational guidance and training; the adoption of special measures for children who do not have families or do not live with them, as well as for migrant children; and the introduction of compulsory full-time attendance at school or participation in vocational training courses at least up to the age specified for employment in Convention No. 138.

While maintaining the long-term aim of achieving the prohibition of child labour, the ILO has also pursued a policy of fixing standards with the objective of protecting child labour against exploitation. This had led, since 1919, to the adoption of a number of conventions and recommendations prohibiting the employment of children and/or young persons in certain types of work and regulating their working conditions.

Legislation alone is not enough to deal with the problem of child labour. There is a wide gap between the legal instruments and the actual state of affairs as is borne out by ILO case studies. Child labour seems to be effectively abolished in the formal sector characterised by large enterprises using highly mechanised or capital-intensive techniques. Even here, it is not clear whether this is due to a strict enforcement of child labour legislation or to the fact that child workers are of little use and uneconomical in a production system which uses advanced technology and less labour input. In any case, child labour continues to be widespread in the unorganised sector of industry, agriculture and services in much of the developing world, despite national legislation prohibiting it.

There are many factors, responsible for the poor enforcement of existing legislation. The availability and quality of education along with the poverty of the families of school age children act as a brake on the effectiveness of legislation. The inadequacy and low standards of education results in a very high school dropout rate and undermines the parents expectations concerning the benefits of schooling. Moreover, governments lack effective enforcement machinery to monitor regulations and standards governing child labour. Such machinery is seriously deficient in most developing countries. The inspectorate system is generally understaffed and thus unable to cope with child labour. The introduction of social security contributions in respect of young workers has reduced employers' reliance on child labour.

Since child labour is closely linked with poverty, lack of development and inadequate schooling in the countries in which it is prevalent, child labour legislation must be accompanied by a wide range of measures concerning employment and income generation programmes, and by a reform and expansion of education facilities. Keeping these realities in mind, the ILO has not confined its activity to the establishment of standards and monitoring of the application of conventions.

In recent years, the ILO has supplemented its standard-setting work with research, information dissemination and technical assistance. ILO extends technical cooperation to member states to enable them to bring national laws and practice closer to the model set out in international labour standards.

The ILO technical cooperation activities focuses attention on eliminating forced labour or bonded labour and child labour in industries and occupations which are detrimental to the safety, health or morals of children. It recognised that employment of children in certain dangerous types of occupations, such as work which involves exposure to toxic substances, use of pesticides or insecticides in agriculture and recycling of household waste in dumping sites, may not be prohibited by national legislation, but should be eliminated.

The ILO recognises the fact that though it has been playing a leading role in the struggle against child labour, some of the action required to attack the underlying causes of child labour-poverty, insufficient economic growth and deficiencies in the education system—is within the competence of other international organisations like the International Monetary Fund (IMF), the World Bank, the General Agreement on Tariff and Trade (GATT) and the United Nations International Children Emergency Fund (UNICEF).

The ILO proclaims that diversity of mandates for action in the struggle against child labour should therefore be reflected in strengthened cooperation between the ILO and these other organisations and most importantly, by close collaboration with the UNICEF. Another way the ILO addresses the problem of child labour is through programmes and projects at the national and local community level. The ILO has committed itself to a major effort to halt child labour. The

International Programme on the Elimination of Child Labour (IPEC) came into being with a view to giving a new impetus to the ILO's operational activities in this field.

The operational structure of IPEC is based on ILO rules and procedures and on Memoranda of Understanding between the ILO and participating countries. The MoU finalises the agreement on the development and execution of national IPEC activities. It establishes the areas, principles and modalities of cooperation between the ILO and the government. IPEC seeks collaboration with other UN agencies, particularly the UNICEF, the United Nations Educational, Scientific and Cultural Organisation (UNESCO), and the World Health Organisation and also with international NGOs to avoid duplication of effort and to maximise the impact of all available resources against the problem. IPEC focuses on the worst abuses of child labour: hazardous work, forced labour, the employment of working children who are less than 12 or 13 years old girls and street children.

Organisations directly involved in initiating and implementing the action programmes include governmental institutions, policy makers and political leaders, in particular the ministries of labour, education, health and welfare and information and statistics. Partner organisations include NGOs, including voluntary agencies, workers and employers' groups, religious organisations and the media. The immediate objectives of the programme are: (i) to have enhanced the capability of ILO constituents and NGOs to design, implement and evaluate policies and programmes aimed at the elimination of child labour and the protection of working children; (ii) to have determined the comparative strengths and weaknesses of various types of intervention at the local and national levels for replication and adoption; and (iii) to have established mechanisms at both the national and international level capable of generating and supporting public awareness and social mobilisation campaigns to combat child labour.

In order to promote action against bonded child labour, the ILO, within the ambit of IPEC, organised the Asian Regional Seminar on Children in Bondage in Islamabad in November 1992. It was held in collaboration with the United Nations Centre for Human Rights and the government of Pakistan.

Elimination of child labour is also a key component of UNICEF's policy. UNICEF is the only UN agency devoted exclusively to the needs of children. Founded in 1946, initially to care for the children of war-torn Europe, its mandate was gradually expanded. UNICEF supports government efforts in providing services essential to the survival and development of children such as clean water, safe sanitation, immunisation and other health measures. It also seeks to provide to children skills essential for leading a healthy and productive life and thus education is a major priority of the UNICEF. UNICEF collaborates with governments, international agencies, NGOs, trade unions and legal experts to promote the elimination of child labour and integration of children released from labour into the educational system. It has been a major funding agency for improving the lot of children in general and child labour in particular. UNICEF has sanctioned $0.5 million for child labour programmes for the five-year period commencing from 1991.

The United Nations Educational, Scientific and Cultural Organisation (UNESCO) is another of the UN's specialised agencies. UNESCO has special responsibility for everything involving prevention of the various forms of discrimination and promotion of the educational and cultural rights. UNESCO has also been making efforts to combat with the problem of child labour.

Set up in 1946, UNESCO aims at promoting cooperation among nations through education, science and culture and thereby contribute to peace and security and enhance universal respect for justice, fundamental freedoms and human rights, including rights of the child. It has tried to attack the problem of child labour through the spread of education. Thus the efforts of these international organisations are in the right direction and indeed commendable.

The goal of complete abolition of child labour is still a distant one. In order to be effective, it is essential that international organisations arrive at programmes and campaigns suited to national conditions. Moreover, there is a need for greater coordination of efforts of international organisations in the struggle against child labour. International organisations also need to develop their campaigns within the framework of a partnership with concerned governments and NGOs if their efforts are to have a lasting impact on the status of the working children of the world.

The problem of child labour has assumed serious proportions. Their continued and widespread employment in the workforce is a denial of their basic rights. The repercussions of child labour are confined not only on the children individually but on the society as a whole because the contribution of these children to society in future will suffer on account of the sacrifices made in terms of their health and education.

Civil Rights

The Indian Constitution presents an impressive list of civil and political rights for children. (a) While the right of equality before the law and the equal protection of the laws is available to any person including children, Article 15(3) empowers the state to have special laws for children, only intended to enable them to enjoy the fruits of the equality guarantee. Examples of such laws include the Child Labour Prohibition laws and the Juvenile Justice Act. Class legislation is thus not only constitutionally permissible but also constitutionally mandated.(b) Taking note of the then prevailing exploitative practice of trafficking in human beings, particularly children, Article 23 of the Constitution has put a total ban on forced labour and made such practices punishable under law. (c) The Constitution in Article 24 has prohibited the employment of children below the age of 14 years in any factory, mine or in any other hazardous activity. (d) Besides, all the seven sets of fundamental rights in the Constitution are available to children with as much authority and accessibility as that with adult citizens.

There is a large body of case law which has not only developed the application of these rights to children but has also expanded their scope in order to make them meaningful. This was accomplished by the judiciary through harmonious construction of Part-III (Fundamental Rights) and Part IV (Directive Principles of State Policy) of the Constitution side by side with India's Treaty Obligations and obligations under the UN Convention on the Rights of the Child. Thereby the Indian judiciary has made a singular contribution for the universal development of human rights generally and of child rights in particular.

It may be concluded that in the matter of civil rights and freedom, the laws of the country stand very much in line with the global human rights movement and the UN Convention on the Rights of the Child (1989). India's ratification of the Convention in 1992 has generated renewed concern regarding the policies and priorities, obligations and commitments vis-a-vis children. In translating this concern into concrete actions, availability of trained personnel and greater accountability to legal obligations are being attempted. The courts have begun to take child rights and principles governing them seriously and have gone to the farthest limits to give every child, particularly the neglected and the delinquent, an opportunity to enjoy the minimum guarantees of law.

India is a union of states and under the scheme of governance envisaged by the Indian Constitution, all legislative powers are organised under three lists given in the Seventh Schedule. List 1 (Union List) contain matters in which the union parliament has exclusive power to make laws. Similarly, in respect of items in List II (State list), the state assemblies have exclusive power to make laws. List III, titled Concurrent List, contain matters in which both parliament and state assemblies have power to legislate. On matters not enumerated in List II or III, parliament has residuary powers of legislation (Articles 246 and 248).

While public order, police, prisons, reformatories, borstal institution, relief and the disabled, etc., are subjects of List II, a number of related matters like criminal law and procedure, family law, civil procedure, vagrancy, economic and social planning, social security, welfare of labour, education, etc., are items in List III. Many of these items relate to the rights of children. As such the status of legislative protection available to children and the extent of enforcement of available laws affecting their entitlements are dependent upon state governments.

There have been some positive developments in the period following the ratification of the UN Convention on the rights of the child. Following an international conference on the subject in March, 1994, an "Alliance for the Child" has been formed at the national level with the Chief Justice of India as its chairperson. This body has inspired an active interest in the problems of children viewed in the perspective of the child rights. Senior judicial officers, lawyers and police personnel have attempted to address the problems of children, particularly in the context of the implementation of the Juvenile Justice Act.

The National Human Rights Commission set up in 1993 has been taking an active interest in the implementation of children's right in the country. The Commission has been examining issues like child labour and related issues such as compulsory primary education, child marriages, child prostitution, female foeticide and infanticide in depth and is supportive of efforts by the non-governmental organisations and activists for furthering children's rights.

Name and Nationality

Prior to independence, nationality in India was governed by the British nationality and the Status of Aliens Act 1914. The concept of

Indian citizenship came into being only with the advent of independence. The Indian Citizenship Act 1955 provides for acquisition, termination and renunciation of Indian citizenship and other matters. A child born in India or abroad acquires Indian citizenship if either of his parents is an Indian citizen. A minor child ceases to be a citizen of India where his parents have renounced the Indian citizenship. But any such child may, within one year or his attaining 18 years of age, resume Indian citizenship by making a declaration to that effect.

Birth Registration

Article 7 of the CRC makes it the parents' responsibility to register the birth of the child. In India, there is a regular system of registration of birth, deaths and names. The Office of the Registrar General of India, under the Ministry of Home Affairs handles the subject of registering the birth and name of newborns as governed by the provisions of the registration of births and deaths act, 1969 (RED). Rules have been framed under this Act by various state governments between 1970 and 1982. Under the Act, registration of all births occurring in the country has been made compulsory and free of charge, if reported within the prescribed time-limit. At present, the period prescribed for the registration of birth varies from 14 to 21 days in various parts of the country. Section 13 of the Act also has provision for delayed registration for events which could not be registered within the normal reporting period. Under Section 12 of this Act, the first copy of the extracts of registration, which is also known as birth certificate is given free of charge. The necessary reporting form prescribed for the birth registration of a newborn contains an item on the name of the child. Concerted efforts are being made to create awareness for improving timely registration of newborns and thus ensuring that the correct age of the child, an essential prerequisite for children's rights, is known at all times.

In practice, it has been found that many parents do not register childbirth due to low levels of awareness, home-based deliveries and illiteracy. The Report on the Vital Statistics in India (1987) shows that coverage of births by the registration system is 100 per cent only in six states and three of the union territories. In order to increase the rate of birth registration, an element of compulsion for obtaining birth certificates has been introduced in certain urban areas. This includes compulsory production of birth certificate at the first school admission and for obtaining ration cards. This has improved the rate of registration of births. Media has been effectively used for promoting awareness of benefits arising out of universal birth registration.

The freedom of expression is a fundamental right which is available to all persons in India including children. The fact that this freedom, especially in case of children, may be circumscribed by the cultural ethos of any society needs to be acknowledged. The child's right to information is sometimes determined by parents or teachers which may sometimes be seen as limiting their rights. However such exercise is taken predominantly in the best interest of the child and should not be seen to prevent free access to Information or freedom of expression. The child's view is taken into account in a number of cases involving custody, fixing criminal liability, and giving evidence in court.

Every person in India is entitled to freedom of conscience and the right freely to profess, practise and propagate religion subject only to public order, morality, health and such other provisions as laid down in the Constitution itself. The Supreme Court of India has upheld the religious belief of a child belonging to Jehovah's Witnesses not to sing the national anthem in the morning assembly of the school. Similarly freedom of association and peaceful assembly is guaranteed under the Indian Constitution.

Bodily integrity and privacy are basic rights provided for in Articles 16 and 37 of the Convention. While personal liberty (right to life) is guaranteed by Article 21 of the Indian Constitution, freedom from self-incrimination, double jeopardy, unlawful arrest and detention are provided for by Articles 20 and 22. Traffic in human beings is prohibited under Article 23 and all forms of forced labour are outlawed. The court has developed Public Interest Litigation (PIL) as a strategy to provide wide access to aggrieved persons even through total strangers. Judicial remedies have come to be democratised through introduction of interim relief appropriate to the occasion. Thus medical justice, rehabilitative justice, compensatory justice, etc., have become part of human rights jurisprudence in India giving meaning and content to the right to life and liberty. One of the important set of beneficiaries of this judicial activism on the right to bodily integrity have been children.

—Children in bondage have been released and rehabilitated under court orders made at the instance of NGOs and journalists.

—Conditions of custodial institutions where delinquent and destitute children were kept have been improved to the advantage of inmates in a series of cases taken to the court.

—Humane approaches towards children in conflict with the law were adopted under strict directions of the court.

While such refinements in the rights of the child were taking place mainly through the judicial process, there have been reports of increasing victimisation of children through rape and related sexual offences and through forced prostitution. One explanation of this increase in reporting of such crimes could be greater awareness and openness due to effective advocacy for children's rights. Even then, all efforts are being taken to arrest this through effective and sensitised enforcement machinery, speedier trials and justice. A Central Advisory Committee on Child Prostitution has been set up to make suggestions for eradicating child prostitution. It has submitted its report. Suitable machinery shall soon be set up for implementing the recommendations. As a first step a Child Prostitution desk has been recently created in the Department of Women and Child Development to initiate the process.

An issue of great importance in this regard is the relevance of consent of the child or young adult in medical treatment. Usually, information on the child is gathered from the parent and decision on treatment is made with consent of the parents or guardians. However, there are situations in which conflict of interests may arise and the parents consent may not be in the best interest of the child.

The right to privacy implies that there should be in-camera trials for all cases involving juveniles. The present system provides this protection and reportage of cases involving juveniles or rape victims do not mention the name or address of the victim. However, this protection has not been extended to include law journals or publication of photographs of the victim.

The child's right to privacy implies that the child should be able to aspire for a decent living environment to meet his or her optimum needs. This right is especially important for girl children, adolescent girls and children living in urban slums who often have to share a one-room hutment with siblings and parents. Government's effective steps towards providing shelter for the homeless can go a long way in meeting this provision of the Convention. Although housing is a state subject, the union government formulates housing policies with regard to programmes and approaches for effective implementation of the social housing sherries particularly those pertaining to the weaker sections of society, to accomplish the goal of shelter for all. The Prime Minister's 20 Point Programme lays special emphasis on the housing needs of the disadvantaged sections of society. Currently, four social housing schemes, viz., scheme for the Economically Weaker Sections of the Society; Low Income Group, Middle Income Group, and Rental Housing Scheme, Rural House-site-cum-House Construction Scheme; and Indira Awaas Yojana are being implemented through the state governments and union territory administrations.

Any generalisation on the status of children's rights in the whole of India is risky, unfair and contrary to realities on the ground despite instances of relative neglect of children's welfare and uneven enforcement of laws in some parts of the country. Moreover, the performance of the higher judiciary has been particularly noteworthy in the context of enforcing legislation beneficial to children. It is through the High Courts and the Supreme Court that judicial remedies and procedural standards have been evolved and accountability established on issues of human rights. The Public Interest Litigation (PIL) which is a unique feature of the Indian judicial system has been successfully used in guarding the rights of children.

Priorities given for follow up action under civil rights and freedoms are:

—Review and revision of laws, particularly those relating to children to enable and facilitate affirmative actions by the state and address existing lacunae.

—Strengthening enforcement machinery to ensure translation of rights into reality.

—Making the existing Constitutional right to education a functional reality for all children.

—Comprehensive review of Juvenile Justice Act to make it more effective and child friendly.

—Sensitisation of the judiciary and the law enforcement machinery to the special needs of children.

—Promoting affirmative action by the state, communities and all concerned sections of society.

TWENTY THREE

THE REMEDIES

Education is one of the key solutions in the elimination of child labour. Children with no access to education have little alternative but to enter the labour market, often performing work that is dangerous and exploitative. Education and skills training help to prevent and reduce child labour, as:

— children with basic education and skills have better chance in the labour market; they are aware of their rights and are less likely to accept hazardous work and exploitative working conditions; and

— educational opportunities can wean working children from hazardous and exploitative work and help them find better alternatives.

The ILO and its International Programme on the Elimination of Child Labour (IPEC) has supported action research on many issues related to educational policies and programmes. It has also analysed the impact of action programmes with educational components on child labour, such as those providing non-formal education, (pre-) vocational training and other social support services for (former) working children and promoting their enrolment in formal schools.

There are many examples of effective educational programmes that are successful in preventing and eliminating child labour. The challenge is to mainstream such innovative initiatives into larger formal and/or non-formal education systems. Improvements in education systems are not enough, however. First, children who have been traumatised by work need rehabilitation. Secondly, the worst child labour abuses take place among the most vulnerable socio-economic groups in society. These groups can seldom afford education, even if it is available, relevant and less costly. Their children are sent to work, because the children's contribution and earnings are essential for family survival.

Measures to improve education need to be part and parcel of integrated programmes for disadvantaged population groups.

programmes which aim to empower the poor and abolish social discrimination by providing income-earning opportunities. These can be employment creation and poverty alleviation schemes, small enterprise development, minimum wage systems, credit systems and social safety nets for the most needy. The programmes should address both the need for income for adults and schooling for children at the design and implementation stages, so that they do not inadvertently encourage the employment of children along with or instead of the employment of adults. Finally, given that the supply of child labour is so large, actions to provide alternatives to children need to be combined with intensive awareness-raising in workplaces, among employers, managers and young and adult workers, and in communities. Workplace and community child-watch or monitoring systems need to be set up to ensure that new children do not enter the vacated jobs.

Strategies in Education

A whole range of interventions in education is necessary to attract children to school, and to keep them there and out of work. Investment in a country's human resources is crucial, not only for younger generations, but for socio-economic development as a whole. Therefore, renewed national commitment, policy reform and massive investment in basic education are vital to meet the challenge.

A holistic approach to education is required. Children should be provided with access to quality education from early childhood onwards up to at least 15 years of age. In the long term, this will be the most durable solution. However, given that many countries are still far from providing quality education for all, immediate remedial measures are needed. ILO-IPEC experience shows that even in countries where substantial progress has been made and average school enrolment ratios are high, there are still children from poor population groups who do not benefit from this progress. Transitional education has to be provided to prevent such children from taking up hazardous work or to wean them away from it.

They need to be equipped with basic education, practical knowledge and skills. Such education should consist of an integrated package of basic education, life skills and practical skills training and should ideally aim at main-streaming the children into formal education and vocational training systems. However, options also have to be provided to the children who are unable to continue formal education and training, so they do not re-enter the labour market as unskilled workers. The younger children may require skills that are useful in improving their quality of fife and can be developed further, while the older children generally require vocational counselling and practical training that can lead to income generation either through wage labour or self-employment in a broad array of employable skills.

A measure which can be undertaken relatively quickly and which does not require massive investment is the incorporation into children's and parents' education of explicit messages on the dangers of premature work and the rights of children to education, wherever there is a high risk of child labour.

Child Labour Issues

Education on children's rights can and should be integrated into the curriculum through social studies, health education, literacy and language learning. In this way children are also in a better position to protect themselves, express themselves, negotiate and assert their rights. Education on rights teaches them about their responsibilities to themselves and to others; it helps them become productive citizens of their own communities while receiving adequate care and protection.

Childhood Development Programmes

Integrated early childhood development programmes that address the physical, social, emotional and cognitive development of young children have in recent years received more attention and visibility because of their evident impact. Children who participate in various forms of these programmes are healthier, socially well adjusted and better prepared for learning experiences in later childhood. Thus, the programmes help prevent school failure, which contributes to children dropping out and being recruited for full-time hazardous work.

The more successful children are at school, the more persistent parents tend to be about keeping them there. At the same time, most early childhood development programmes involve a parent education component and are good entry points for educating both parents and children about the detrimental effects of full-time and dangerous work of children.

More schools are needed in communities with high concentrations of child labour, especially in rural areas, and these schools need to provide the complete basic education course and the necessary ingredients to meet the basic learning needs.

Both formal and non-formal education systems can be made more responsive to children who are at risk of premature work or who are already working. The structure of educational programmes, the content of the curriculum and the teaching approaches applied in schools should include relevant, useful knowledge and skills, which meet the developmental needs of children and prepare them to earn income later in life and become responsible adults in their communities. Innovative education methods which have been tried out successfully on a small scale in experimental non-formal education programmes should be incorporated and expanded in the formal education system.

Many initiatives have been undertaken in recent years to adapt educational programmes and make them more suited to the needs of former child workers. It has been found that quality non-formal education can act as a bridge between work and school and facilitate the entry of children into formal schools. However, the initiatives have been small scale to date and are often isolated from the mainstream educational programmes within the country.

Serious efforts still have to be made to further strengthen flexible non-formal remedial education programmes which provide adequate entry points into a country's educational and vocational training system. Non-formal education programmes have been established alongside the formal education system and accreditation and equivalency programmes have been developed to allow for an easier transition between formal and non-formal education.

In most countries, however, stronger linkages need to be created between the formal and non-formal education streams. For some older children, a few years of non-formal education will be the only option. These children need to be provided with an integrated package of general education, along with practical life and work skills so that they can re-enter the labour market at an appropriate age with more knowledge about their rights as workers and skills that will allow them access to better jobs.

Vocational education

Vocational training is often very popular among families which are prone to resort to child labour. Short-term vocational training is often combined with or delivered after functional literacy training and can provide immediate economic alternatives. However, there are issues to resolve in the definition and approaches to vocational education. A distinction must be made between more formal vocational training, which is usually longer term and systematically linked to apprenticeship programmes, and less formal training.

Most formal vocational programmes require close adult supervision and the available slots for students are limited. There are also non-formal vocational training programmes linked to both formal and non-formal education programmes which are often short term and deal with specific skills and topics that are not necessarily marketable or highly productive.

Non-formal education programmes can teach children skills that will provide immediate economic alternatives as well as psycho-social support. But these should not be viewed as a complete substitute for formal education, rather as transition programmes to facilitate the child's re-entry into the formal school system. In situations where there are no local institutions or schools offering such vocational education programmes, it may be necessary to provide scholarships. Practical skills training in the form of "learning by doing", experiments and arts and crafts are an integral part of basic education.

Vocational training should be geared to the provision of marketable skills that can be adapted to the changing needs in the job market. The gender bias in education is even more pronounced in the field of vocational training and specific attention needs to be given to facilitate girls' access. In most countries, better linkages need to be created between education and vocational training, and between non-formal and formal vocational training.

Rehabilitation programmes

Many of the most abusive types of child labour are hidden and few organisations have the capacity to identify and handle them. Child victims may also have developed various coping mechanisms and often there will be differences in the needs of boys and girls. Thus, special efforts are required to first identify the groups for priority action and then develop a range of appropriate interventions. It is essential to prevent children from becoming engaged in extreme forms of child labour. This involves intensive awareness-raising, and the provision of viable alternatives. In cases where organisations aim to withdraw children from the worst forms of child labour, the types of intervention need to include identification and rescue of children working under forced labour conditions, legal aid, intensive counselling and other rehabilitation measures for the children and their families.

Victims of human rights violations such as children in bondage and children forced into prostitution, domestic work or sweatshops in their own or other countries are often damaged and traumatised beyond recovery. It is therefore critical that these types of child labour abuse be prevented through effective law enforcement and large-scale awareness-raising in schools and communities where there is a high incidence or risk. Local community monitoring mechanism's should be activated to identify those at high risk and to monitor the situation of those who have been rescued.

Girls and women bear a major share of the burden of poverty. Giving girls access to quality education is a first essential step towards empowering them and enabling them to break through the vicious cycle of poverty. Successful strategies include intensive awareness-raising in communities where there are social and cultural constraints, provision of schools and childcare facilities near the girls' homes, recruitment of female teachers, promotion of gender fairness and equality at schools and investment in the education and skill training of mothers.

Prevention through family life education for boys and girls at school is still the most cost-effective measure. Special programmes to allow pregnant girls and young mothers to continue their education are also needed as these young women are otherwise forced to start working themselves and involve their children from an early age in meeting basic survival needs.

The lifestyle of street children has to be taken into account when designing education and rehabilitation programmes. In the first instance, peer or adult street workers reach out to street children to establish contact and gain their trust by involving them in street education activities, motivating them to participate in educational programmes and helping them acquire the basic skills that will enable them to learn in a structured environment. They need help to adjust to adult authority after being used to surviving on their own and developing a variety of defence mechanisms against adults who may have exploited them or who may have violated their rights.

Street education programmes which provide an atmosphere of freedom and democratic consultation and which build up rapport gradually and develop trust, have been more effective than enrolment in formal schools, especially at the initial re-entry stages. Non-formal education programmes are usually needed for a smoother transition between life and work on the streets and formal schooling. Special attention has to be paid to matching the learning methodology and process to the learning styles of street children. Hands-on-learning, experimentation and observation, and learning-by-doing are what they have been doing to survive.

Many street children may not be "school smart" but they are certainly "street smart". They are adept at problem-solving and assessing situations from the perspective of survival. They have worked and will assess the relevance of schooling to their immediate future in the world of work. It must be worthwhile for them to decrease their time on the streets and spend it in the classroom learning skills that help them improve their life. Many street children also need counselling services to cope with traumatic experiences of violence, sexual exploitation or other harassment at home or on the street. Rehabilitation for substance abuse may also be necessary.

Children who belong to ethnic groups need to be educated both in their own and in the national language and they should be taught about their own culture from the point of view of their community and not from an outsider's point of view. It is clear that children learn best in their mother tongue, in particular when they start school. At the same time, they should learn to express themselves in the dominant language of their country to be able to fully function in society.

The need to learn the dominant language—written and oral—has to be balanced with respect for the child's own language and culture. Adults in the community need to be actively involved as resources for the school in this respect. Several successful programmes have highlighted the importance of providing teachers who have the same socio-cultural and economic background as the children and of offering young people employment opportunities in their own communities. Indigenous communities usually belong to the most disadvantaged groups and seldom have access to basic services such as education, health, housing and employment.

Education programmes

Since they are usually the ones who decide whether children will work full time, stay in school and work, or study full time, it is critical to invest in parent education about child labour. There are various forms of parent education programmes offered by governmental and non-governmental agencies as part of early childhood development, literacy or health programmes.

The provision of information on child labour and on child rights and the organisation of workshops for extension workers from these programmes, can be ways of incorporating child labour concerns in these adult training programmes. Other forms of adult education through workers' organisations or trade unions and cooperatives which provide educational programmes for their members, and through other community-based structures or committees, should also be further utilised. Women's literacy programmes that emphasise child development, family life and children's and women's rights offer great potential for preventing and eliminating child labour and improving school enrolment. There is a tendency to look at women's and children's programmes separately or, at best, an incidental connection is made.

However, women and children's rights are intimately linked. Thus, women's programmes should include components to promote children's rights and address child labour exploitation and—vice versa—programmes geared towards children should pay attention to the situation of mothers as women with their own needs and rights. In addition, more and better jobs and social protection are needed for adults through the provision of income-earning opportunities for the poor, employment creation and poverty alleviation schemes, small enterprise development, minimum wage systems, credit systems and social safety nets for the most needy. Women's economic empowerment is an especially effective measure to strengthen vulnerable families. Programmes that enable them to learn skills (such as improved agricultural practices, entrepreneurship, specific crafts or food production) that provide them with resources to earn a stable income for the family and manage households by using labour-saving devices. or increase their access to credit schemes.

Workplace and community monitoring

Systematic efforts to ensure that workplaces and communities remain child labour free mean first of all that awareness raising activities should not be limited to the children and parents, but extended to all groups involved: employers, managers, and adult workers in workplaces, community leaders, service providers and enforcement agencies. In a second stage, monitoring mechanisms need to be set up to ensure that the children withdrawn from work remain and complete school and that new children do not enter work. This can be done in the schools or educational centres, in the workplaces and in the children's communities. In any workplace monitoring programme, the active participation of the concerned employers, manufacturers, contractors and subcontractors is critical, as the commitment to free all manufacturing and production processes from child labour may call for a change in established and traditional manufacturing and production practices.

The involvement of the concerned workers' representatives and local community groups as well as the concerned governmental agencies, is also critical. The involvement of children in the production and manufacture of goods for export has become a matter for international concern. Faced with outside pressure, some producers and manufacturers have turned to the ILO for advice on action to eliminate child labour from their particular industry. This has resulted in three instances in concrete prevention and monitoring programmes in the garment industry in Bangladesh, the football industry in Pakistan and its international counterparts and the carpet industry, also in Pakistan.

The result has been partnerships that span geographical and cultural boundaries, as well as positive changes in the attitudes and practices of the communities, in that the families have been willing to withdraw their children from work and send them to school.

The basic elements of the ILO-IPEC prevention and monitoring programmes are:

— Ensuring cooperation and collaboration of employers/ manufacturers, workers' organisations, district administration and other government departments;
— Assessing child labour involvement in the particular sector or industry;
— Assisting the participating employers/manufacturers in setting up their internal monitoring system;
— Operating an external monitoring team involving ILO project staff;
— Identifying and zoning monitoring area for visits;
— Establishing a monitoring database to collect, analyse and synthesise data, to indicate schedules, of surprise monitoring visits, and to prepare reports on progress; and
— Establishing linkages with the social protection component of the programme.

Social protection programmes provide viable and practical alternatives to the children and their families affected by the prevention and monitoring programme. These programmes support the withdrawal of the children from workplaces and prevent them from working by sensitising and mobilising the communities. They also provide services to rehabilitate the children withdrawn so that they can be integrated into mainstream educational systems and other developmental activities.

The basic elements of a social protection programme are:

- — Awareness-raising, mobilisation and counselling families through one-to-one contact and group meetings to prevent child labour and to encourage them so that their children participate in the activities of the village education and action clusters set up under the project; communicating with the families on an ongoing basis;
- — Group training of adults to form the family clubs/ committees for mothers and fathers to encourage them to play an active role in the programme;
- — Non-formal education to provide literacy, basic education and practical skills training to the children withdrawn and their younger siblings;
- — Recreational activities to foster social and physical development;
- — Health services through linkages with local health facilities;
- — Mainstreaming of younger children into formal schools;
- — Training in income-generation activities (adults): to follow up training in the credit/savings facility and training in various income-generation activities for the adults in the family;
- — Provision of a credit/savings facility to the adults in the family; and
- — Mainstreaming of children of employable age and adults into the labour market.

The establishment of local child welfare and vigilance committees is an effective tool which is increasingly being utilised in many countries. These committees can monitor, undertake action and even provide limited resources and services where necessary. Programmes which stress a participatory approach and actively involve the children, their, parents, community leaders and teachers are the most successful. Decentralisation of authority to local governments and community structures also has a positive impact and results in effective community participation.

Planning action programmes

Given the socio-economic situation of some countries and the lack of adequate resources and infrastructure, the complete elimination of child labour will be a lengthy process. But there can be no excuse for ignoring flagrant cases of child abuse that are an outright breach of human rights and an affront to the dignity of children. Clearly the children who fall into this category are those engaged in activities that pose a serious danger to their health, or physical or moral integrity; those who work in slave-like conditions or are subjected to forced tabour and those caught up in illicit networks such as prostitution, drug trafficking and pornography.

Some children are particularly vulnerable to this type of exploitation because of their age and sex, because they live and work on their own, or because they belong to socially excluded groups. Appropriate measures need to be adopted urgently to rescue children from these worst forms of child tabour. Prevention is crucial; but children must also be withdrawn from such activities and both they and their families provided with alternatives.

Sometimes, especially if a country is only starting to address child labour problems, there is resistance to begin to combat some of the worst forms, because of political and social sensitivity. The existence of these types of child labour is even denied and very few partners come forward who can effectively address the problems. None the less, at a minimum, the worst forms of child tabour need to be tackled immediately.

The most strategically positioned programme partners or initiators, governments have the main responsibility to make action a top priority. They need to take the lead in designing national policies and programmes and in allocating the necessary resources to enable implementation. When the policy framework is in place, care should be taken to translate it into feasible programmes and implementation guidelines and to inform and enable all stakeholders to take the required action. Without such a commitment, countries will have great difficulties in overcoming the problem. However, the task is too enormous to be handled by governments alone. A participatory approach and concerted action by all stakeholders is needed to eliminate child tabour. Successful examples of effective cooperation between different sections of local government, NGOs, employers' and workers' organisations, and local communities are emerging. Effective programme delivery has taken place through proper coordination between government structures at the national and local levels.

However, the implementation of multi-sectoral programmes by a range of different service providers is sometimes difficult. It has become clear that institutional mechanisms need to be set up to encourage joint planning and implementation for an effective convergence of services in countries where a start has been made in developing and implementing specific measures to combat child labour through education. Participation should ideally begin at the planning stages. Often, the lack of consultative mechanisms at the various stages of programme implementation or the exclusion of stakeholders from the processes of planning, problem solving and decision making engenders a sense of remoteness and powerlessness of the participating groups in relation to the programme managers and leaders. Active participation—not just token participation—is a critical element to developing a sense of ownership for programmes.

The main issues when starting a direct action programme is related to the partial or total withdrawal of children from work. But national goals must be defined in a clear, achievable and time-bound manner. If either the partial or the total withdrawal from work is defined as an objective and made a precondition for the children's participation, the programme design and content must reflect this.

In other cases, stipends are provided for the children to participate and withdraw from work. For programmes which opt for partial withdrawal, the design either provides for a schedule which allows children to study and work part time or, alternatively, less hazardous income-generating, opportunities are made available.

The ground rules are as follows:

— If children are involved in hazardous or exploitative forms of child labour, they need to be withdrawn completely. Child victims of human rights violations cannot be helped by the provision of support services while they continue to be in a slavery-like position. They must be rescued.

— If children are involved in work that harms them because of the working conditions or environment, a gradual phased approach may be used. The work hazards should be removed and children should gain access to education, but they can in a transitional phase continue to be involved in light work that is not dangerous.

Parents react positively to programmes where children work part time in light work and are involved in non-formal education. Even if this means a decrease in their income, it is more viable because of the continuing income. The parents also feel that the children are getting an education and learning practical skills which improve their employment opportunities for the future. Another approach that can be seen as a step towards the ultimate goal of children's withdrawal from hazardous working conditions involves campaigns for making the workplace safer. Adult workers as well as owners of workplaces can be recruited as volunteers to participate in training workshops so that they can monitor safety.

Nutrition, health and other incentives

Improvements in education are not sufficient to attract and keep children from very poor families at school. Many families of child labourers live on the brink of survival and many millions of children in the world do not go to school because they are malnourished or frequently ill. Many more go to school hungry and are unable to pay attention, concentrate and learn.

A nutritious meal makes a tremendous difference to a child's health and ability to learn. The school is also an important entry point for providing essential health services such as immunisation, detection of disabilities and childhood illnesses. Many organisations provide nutrition and health care to children through the education system and these have proved to be powerful incentives for parents to send their children to school. Besides school-based food and health programmes, organisations have experimented with providing other economic incentives, such as school uniforms, books or transport. Cash payments, such as regular stipends or scholarships, have also been provided. Schiefelbein has reviewed examples of such incentives in Latin American countries. These include cash payments for students, provision of school materials and allocating additional funds to schools or municipalities which provide services for child labourers or children considered at risk of child labour to enable them to provide more responsive and flexible programmes.

The various income-replacement strategies that have been tried in Latin America offer interesting examples of how effectively to provide for the needs of child labourers. Most require a combination of responsive local schools and the political will of national and/or local governments, which provide the necessary policy support and resources to implement income-replacement measures. An ILO survey on economic incentives for children and families to eliminate or reduce child labour also aimed to identify whether income replacement and substitution activities offered viable options in the battle against child labour.

Many of the incentives used by the NGOs which participated in the survey were directly related to schooling. Payments in kind were the most common form of benefits extended to children or their families. These included provisions for school uniforms or clothing, books, schoolbags and materials, school lunches or other food items, transport, or payment of school fees. Evidently, organisations which provide income-replacement services for child labourers, or for children who are at high risk of child labour, do so because the cost of schooling or the forgone income deters children from entering education. Thus, they raise the question of whether replacing the lost income of children who attend school full time would in fact be adequate to keep them in school. Another important finding was that the provision of cash incentives could lead to abuse and therefore many NGOs preferred to provide in-kind incentives rather than cash payments.

Support services are sometimes provided as incentives to attract parents and children to participate in action programmes. But it has been observed that some programmes offer too many incentives which make them more like welfare programmes. Among the disadvantages are: (i) high programme costs; (ii) the programme is not sustainable in the long term; (iii) child workers are perceived as privileged, because non-working while equally poor and disadvantaged children do not receive such benefits elsewhere; (iv) the practice may encourage more parents to remove children from school and send them to work in the hope of becoming eligible for similar benefits; and (v) parents of children who may not be part of the target group will insist on their children's participation, thus creating confusion and divisiveness in the community if they react negatively when their children are not admitted.

The major disadvantage is the difficulty of sustaining and replicating the programme since the participation of parents and children will be heavily reliant on the availability of incentives; thus the motivation for participation is mainly external. A careful balance must therefore be struck. One option is to encourage children's participation in running the programme. They can also work with younger children as peer teachers and participate in home visits, especially to other children who have been absent for a while. After they complete, their courses of study, they can also be asked to help with the programme activities and work as resource persons or volunteers with the other children.

In this way they can serve as positive role models and share their own experiences. Parents can be asked to work as volunteers for the programme and the activities can depend upon their individual talents and skills. Whatever time and energy they can contribute should be discussed with them from the outset and also clarified so that they will not view incentives as a hand-out but feel that they have something meaningful to contribute. Parents who actively participate in the action programmes are also more likely to better appreciate the impact or the benefits of these programmes for their children and ultimately their families. It is important to assess whether direct action programmes should focus only on the objective of generating income for the children and their families, or should also serve as income-saving or expense-reduction measures for the family. If the children can use what they make, or if the family, can eat what is produced through the programme, there may also be value added to encouraging such cost-saving measures towards self-reliance.

The approach of helping children and their families opt for participation in courses that also involve the production of goods that meet the basic day-to-day needs of the children and helping them to manage existing resources, may ultimately be more beneficial for the children. This approach will help them practice problem-solving and planning for very practical life needs and at the same time help them achieve a sense of fulfilment in being able to meet their immediate requirements. One of the more frequent reasons children drop out of programmes for their, education and protection is the difficulty they have in delaying the gratification of their needs.

Another important issue in setting expense-reduction measures alongside income-generation or replacement is the possibility that children and their parents can be helped to learn to be more realistic about earning possibilities and about basic needs versus additional or emerging needs. It is necessary to work closely with them and their parents, and clarify objectives with them at every step of the way.

It is important to determine whether the schools where the children are expected to enrol are actually receptive to the re-entry or the integration of working children. If they consider it as an imposition or a burden rather than as a responsibility, their attitude towards the children will be passive at best and negative at worst.

In relation to the mainstreaming of children into formal schools, some specific issues need to be considered:

— *The age of the children:* If children are older than the other children in the grade level for which they qualify, they usually feel uncomfortable, and often embarrassed, not only because they are older but because in most cases they also have difficulty in coping with the academic requirements. Former working children also find it difficult to adjust to the rigid structure and the regimen of formal schools.

— *Parents' expectations and attitudes.* Parents may react negatively or may be impatient with apparently slow progress through formal school, especially when they are used to their children being economically productive. With the loss of income, any activity that replaces their child's work will be viewed badly if they have not yet fully accepted the fact that it is a better situation for their children, a worthwhile investment even from their family's economic viewpoint, and a responsibility that they should fulfil. Another problem that affects the parents' attitude is the burden of school-related expenses (e.g., uniforms, food to be brought to school, school supplies and materials, books, and travel expenses).

— *Provision for follow-up and support programmes.* The need for follow-up support programmes, especially after the first year of re-entry into the formal schools is evident in the trends of programme experiences. Action programmes in different countries show that many children tend to drop out after the first year, especially when assistance for meeting expenses is discontinued.

In addition, there are some questions to consider in connection with the issue of mainstreaming working children into regular schools. In developing countries where job opportunities are still limited and where a large number of youths with college *or* university degrees are unemployed, it is not surprising that many disadvantaged parents doubt whether their children can compete in the job market with a primary or secondary education certificate. Few parents expect their children to be able to proceed to tertiary levels of education. That is why they may appreciate vocational training because they consider it more realistic for work opportunities. The experiences in education and child labour and the strategy for maximising education in the fight against child labour, clearly identify the expansion of early childhood development programmes as critical to meeting the needs of working children or those at high risk of recruitment in near future.

Research and case studies also show that disadvantaged children, who did not receive adequate health, nutrition and psychosocial cognitive and language stimulation in the early years of childhood are highly likely to experience developmental and learning problems and will have difficulty catching up. A number of mainstreamed children have to drop out because they cannot compete with other, often younger, peers and do not enjoy doing so. If there are younger siblings in the families of working children, they should be supported by facilitating their access to community-based early childhood development programmes and convincing parents that this is an important step to take for their children.

Mainstreaming of former working children or children who continue to work part time is only viable if there are support services for them. Parents need support and information so that they will be able to support their children. Teachers need help to understand the perspective of former working children and the pressures of adjusting to formal schools. It is critical if a country programme chooses to adopt this as the primary approach to the education and social protection of working children.

Most action programmes include various forms of awareness-raising activities directed at parents, community members, local school authorities, the business sector, and policy makers. These have been included based on the realisation that the understanding by these groups of child labour issues will be their basis for supporting the programme's objectives and activities. Ultimately, the programmes will also be the basis of their continued participation in concerted actions to prevent child labour, protect working children through community action, engage in needed policy reform and support effective law enforcement. When awareness-raising efforts are not considered investments of the programme, there can be problems. For example, teachers in formal schools may not develop a positive attitude towards non-formal education programmes provided by these action programmes if they are not informed in any way, especially in the planning processes.

Two Articles in the Convention on the Rights of the Child address the issue of nutrition. Article 24 says that "States Parties recognise the right of the child to the enjoyment of the highest attainable standard of health" and shall take appropriate measures "to combat disease and malnutrition" through the provision of adequate nutritious foods, clean drinking water, and health care. Article 27 says that States Parties "shall in case of need provide material assistance and support

Parties "shall in case of need provide material assistance and support programmes, particularly with regard to nutrition, clothing, and housing". India is making steady progress in limiting malnutrition, but the numbers are still too large and the rate of progress is too slow.

Nutrition Rights

In 1948 the Universal Declaration of Human Rights said in Article 25(1) that "everyone has the right to a standard of living adequate for the health and well-being of himself and his family, including food...."

The International Covenant on Economic, Social, and Cultural Rights, which came into force in 1976, says in Article 11: "The States Parties to the present Covenant recognise the right of everyone to an adequate standard of living for himself and his family, including adequate food, clothing, and housing..." and also recognise "the fundamental right of everyone to be free from hunger...."

While the idea of the right to food appears in many different contexts in international law, most are not binding. In some cases, as in the International Covenant on economic, social, and cultural rights, the obligations are technically binding on the states parties. However, because the obligations lack specificity and because there are no effective mechanisms for implementation and accountability, they are not binding in practice.

On reviewing the hunger data, Philip Alston and Katarina Tomasevski observed that "these statistics make hunger by far the most flagrant and widespread of all serious human rights abuses". The idea that people should have a right to adequate nutrition is an old one, one whose vision has not been fulfilled. However, its articulation in the Convention on the rights of the child suggests a new approach: Implementation of the idea of the right of adequate nutrition may be more politically feasible if it focuses on children.

Our principal obligation towards children is to promote their development, to be understood as empowerment or increasing self-reliance. The task is to increase children's capacity to define, analyse, and act on their own problems until they can become independent participants in society.

Who is responsible for children? The question is not whose fault is it that children suffer so much (who caused the problems?) but who should take action to remedy the problems? Many different social agencies may have some role in looking after children, but what should be the interrelationships among them? Most children have two vigorous advocates from the moment they are born and even before they are born. Their parents devote enormous resources to serving their interests. In many cases, however, that bond is broken or is never created. Fathers disappear, many mothers disappear as well. In some cities, hundreds of children are abandoned each month in the hospitals in which they are born. Bands of children live in the streets by their wits. Often children end up alone as a result of warfare or other political crises. Many children are abandoned because they are physically or mentally handicapped. Often parents become so disabled by drugs or alcohol that they cannot care for their children.

Children ought to get their nurturance from their parents. Failing that, they ought to get it from their local communities. Failing that, they ought to get it from the local governments. Failing that, it should come from their national governments. Failing that, they ought to get it from the international community.

Childhood malnutrition is one of those issues for which there should be a recognised obligation of government to provide some sort of services. As a matter of principle, there should be a recognised legal obligation of government to provide services to assure that every child is adequately nourished. The point is that there should be a clear duty of government, enshrined in law, to do what needs to be done if the family's and the community's response is inadequate. If the principle is accepted, there will still be a need for discussion of the exact nature of the services and the conditions under which they must be provided.

Community groups working on the local malnutrition problem should be able to rely on their local and state governments for help, whether for money, contacts, transportation, or moral support and encouragement. It is the responsibility of government to help such community groups. Moreover, the government should be grateful for the opportunity to help the community use its resources to deal with local malnutrition.

There have been efforts to gain recognition of a right to nutrition within individual countries and internationally. Unfortunately, this has often been equated with the general effort to alleviate malnutrition, and advocates of the right to nutrition have simply recommended ways of improving the production and distribution of food. Nutrition rights in international law are vague and soft. If the nutrition rights idea is to be implemented within nations, its meaning will need to be clarified in their national law. It is there, in national law making, that the specific, hard commitments can be made.

It is important to distinguish between the achievement of adequate nutrition and achievement of a right to adequate nutrition. Nutrition rights are based on the quality of protection one has against the occurrence of malnutrition. To assess the quality of the protection one has to look into the institutional arrangements that are in place, ready to act if and when disaster threatens. Past efforts to ameliorate malnutrition have all been valuable, but they have been matters of charity.

The motivating idea underlying the nutrition rights vision is that extreme malnutrition can be reduced by establishing clear rights to adequate nutrition in the law, and assuring the implementation of that law. The nutrition rights approach does not replace existing programmes for alleviating malnutrition, but rather it builds on and uses them. It can make feeding, health and education-based nutrition programmes more efficient and effective by making them more decisively goal-directed to end malnutrition.

According to UNICEF's 1993 report, *The Progress of Nations,* on average, developing countries have been devoting only about 10 per cent of their annual budgets to human priority issues: nutrition, water supply, primary health care, primary education, and family planning. Thus even poor countries could do more with their existing resources. The main argument of the rights approach, however, is not that nations should spend more but that they should spend better.

A clear distinction should be drawn between the broad notion of children's interests involving many different things such as shelter and a nurturing environment, and the more limited subset of those things that are—or should be— formally recognised as rights in law. Soft rights are not spelt out in the law, or if they are there is no strong and effective mechanism to assure their implementation. The CRC and other international human rights instruments in themselves establish only soft rights. They can be transformed into hard rights which are clearly articulated in the law and are accompanied by effective implementation and accountability mechanisms. Hard rights have a history of case law through which the meaning of the right is tested and refined. There is clear recourse in law for individuals whose rights are not fulfilled and clear public accountability.

Rights are important because without clear rights, those who are more powerful, more highly educated, or better connected have an advantage in obtaining services. Clearly established rights empower the weak, levelling the playing field a bit so that the weak are not so disadvantaged. Rights can be truly hard only where there is a strong and effective legal system in place. In many countries there is no such system. However, where it is absent it is nevertheless worth advocating the hardening of rights as part of the broader effort to pursue a civil society.

Many nations are divided into smaller jurisdictions, perhaps provinces or states; these smaller units might be able to establish their own nutrition rights systems. Provinces could then be assessed in terms of their nutritional status and the most needy provinces entitled to specific services. In some cases provinces, in turn, might manage their nutrition rights system by focusing on still another administrative layer—districts within the province.

Laws, rules, guidelines and principles can be introduced or adapted to conform to a nutrition rights system at the global, regional, national, state or district levels. Even the rules of access to individual service programmes can be modified to assure that clients are treated as if they had rights to the service.

Just as different levels have different responsibilities, they also can have different rights. For example, some services might be assured to individual children while others are assured for households, villages, or districts. Thus multi-layering means there are distinct nutrition rights and responsibilities, both within units and across units, in a hierarchical structure,

The nutrition rights idea, while based on the use of the law, is not based on punitive sanctions against wrongdoers. There may be some cases in which children go hungry because they have "bad" parents. In such cases, the law should be more concerned with ensuring that children do not have to pay for the sins of their parents than with ensuring that their parents do have to pay for them. In much the same way, it would be foolish for the international community to think about punishing bad governments.

To the extent possible, government's approach to its citizenry should be in positive forms. Similarly, the citizenry's "holding the government to account" should be positive. In a negative approach to accountability, a government agency assigned the duty of preventing abuse or ending malnutrition could be sued or fined in some way.

In a more positive approach, designated nongovernmental organisations could be given an award or "bounty" of a small sum of money for each needy child they find and present for services.

It is important to distinguish between monitoring and reporting on nutrition status and monitoring and reporting on nutrition rights. In my view, reporting on the status of nutrition rights should cover five distinct but interrelated components: (a) the nutrition problems; (b) government's service programmes in response to the nutrition problems; (c) the law relating to nutrition rights; (d) implementation, the extent to which the law is effectively carried out; and (e) accountability, the institutional arrangements for holding government to account in fulfilling nutrition rights.

It is important to know what categories of individuals suffer from what sorts of malnutrition problems. The most important form worldwide, protein-energy malnutrition, can be gauged by measuring the heights and weights of children and comparing them with the heights and weights of well-nourished children.

If nutrition rights exist, there must be government-sponsored services to assure that people are adequately nourished. Services should be preventive, to keep malnutrition from occurring, and remedial, to undo malnutrition after it occurs. Preventive services may include such things as health, education, water supply, or immunisation programmes, or programmes to keep people from being displaced from their land. Remedial services for those who are malnourished or at risk of malnutrition may include feeding programmes, clinics or land reform programmes.

There are several things one would want to know about government-supported service programmes related to nutrition. It would be useful to have information about their targeting and selection of beneficiaries; staff selection, supervision and training; community participation; management information systems; sustainability and replicability; and their impact and cost. In systematic reporting, nutrition service programmes should be listed and then characterised, following a simple outline to specify their main features.

Given the magnitude of the malnutrition problem and the level of resources available, judgements should be made as to whether the eligibility criteria are too high (excluding many who should be served), too low (including many who should not be served), or about right.

Many nutrition programmes concerned with protein-energy malnutrition as indicated by low weight or low height are misdirected in terms of their intended coverage. Growth failure is most active between six and 24 months of age, which is thus the main "window of opportunity" for prevention. Actions targeted to children beyond, say, three years of age are not likely to be very successful in reversing their growth retardation because their low weight or height is likely to have originated in their first two or three years of life.

Assessing the law

Nutrition rights must be enshrined in the law with as much clarity and detail as possible, specifying not only the rights of citizens but also the specific duties of government to fulfil those rights. Of course one must also look further to see if what is written in the law is effectively implemented.

Clear nutrition rights can be developed for different kinds of malnutrition. For example, in countries known to suffer from marked iodine deficiency, laws could be established to require government to assure that salt is iodised and other measures are taken for those who show signs of iodine deficiency. In some cases, where communities are likely to be responsive, the law may require nothing more than systematic growth monitoring to make sure that the community identifies children in need of special attention.

Reporting for the international human rights agreements should include descriptions of the ways in which national law has been or is in the process of being modified to take account of the commitments made by the nation upon becoming party to the international agreement.

Often laws that are on the books are simply ignored. Promises may be made but not implemented. Thus it is important to study the extent and effectiveness with which the law is carried out. This means going back to the government's service programmes and reviewing them not in terms of their own state goals but in terms of the goals set out in the law

In a complete system of rights, means must be established for holding government to account if its duties are not fulfilled. It is important to strengthen the law regarding nutrition rights in the books, and also to strengthen the use of that law by assuring that it is fully implemented. Hard rights require effective mechanisms of accountability.

In addition to asking whether there are government agencies which regularly assess the performance of the nutrition service programmes, we should also inquire whether there is clear legal recourse for individuals who do not get the services to which they are entitled.

Goals as Rights

People of different nations suffer from different types, intensities and distributions of malnutrition, with differing causes. Moreover, they have different resource bases and they all have many other concerns. Thus they will set their goals for dealing with malnutrition differently. However, there is now a broad global consensus on how these goals should be framed. At the World Summit for Children held at the United Nations in New York in September 1990, most heads of state signed the Plan of Action for Implementing the World Declaration on the Survival, Protection and Development of Children. Among the major goals specified in the plan was the following: "Between 1990 and the year 2000, reduction of severe and moderate malnutrition among under-five children by half."

Supporting goals specifically related to nutrition were:

i) Reduction in severe, as well as moderate malnutrition among under-five children by half of 1990 levels:
ii) Reduction of the rate of low birth weight (2.5 kg or less) to less than 10 per cent;
iii) Reduction of iron deficiency anaemia in women by one third of the 1990 levels;
iv) Virtual elimination of iodine deficiency disorders;
v) Virtual elimination of Vitamin A deficiency and its consequences, including blindness;
vi) Empowerment of all women to breastfeed their children exclusively for four to six months and to continue breastfeeding, with complementary food, well into the second year;
vii) Growth promotion and its regular monitoring to be institutionalised in all countries by the end of the 1990s;
viii) Dissemination of knowledge and supporting services to increase food production to ensure household food security.

These eight "supporting goals" have merit in themselves and also can be viewed as important means towards achievement of the major goal. These goals have been endorsed repeatedly, both before and after the World Summit for Children, by many international bodies including the World Health Organisation Assembly in 1990, the UNICEF Board Session of 1990, the United Nations Conference on Environment and Development in 1992, and the International Conference on Nutrition in 1992.

and moderate malnutrition to half the 1990 level by the year 2000. Nevertheless, the basic form of the language can be retained, with a fresh start and a new commitment.

Consider now a transformation in thinking. Imagine that the nation's commitment to the goal of the reduction of severe and moderate malnutrition among under-five children by half over the next 10 years is so serious that it is willing to assure its citizens that they have a right to its achievement. Imagine that the government is willing to take on the achievement of this goal as a real duty, one on which it could be called to account for its performance.

Of course it may be that the goal is too demanding, and the government is not willing to make such a firm commitment. For the purposes of this discussion, other formulations could be substituted. For example, the government might be willing to make such a strong commitment only if it was limited to children under two years of age, or only if was limited to severe malnutrition. The specifics are open to discussion. The point here is that, whatever the details of its formulation, one way to interpret nutrition rights is in terms of a firm commitment to a specific nutrition goal.

This perspective meshes nicely with the argument that poor countries are not to be excused from assuring nutritional and other economic, social, and cultural rights on the grounds that they can not afford it. Instead, there is a positive requirement for progressive realisation of the goals based on clear plans and the commitment of resources commensurate with the nation's capacity. Accountability is based on monitoring to see if good progress is being made towards achievement of the goal. If the programme is not "on track" there should be some legal mechanism for calling the government to account and pressing it to take the action that is required.

Nutrition Rights in India

Mr A.T. Dudani of the Society for Citizen Concerns has been exploring the prospects for strengthening children's nutrition rights in India. Through his efforts, a question regarding the current status of children's nutrition rights was raised by Mr V.K. Hariprasad in parliament in December 1993. The question was:

"Will the Minister of Human Resource Development be pleased to state: (a) whether Government is enforcing and promoting various programmes for the Convention on the Rights of the Child and if so, the steps taken in this direction and results obtained and achieved;

various programmes for the Convention on the Rights of the Child and if so, the steps taken in this direction and results obtained and achieved; and (b) whether the nutrition of children is receiving full attention and if so, the details of any action plan made state-wise?"

The answer, preparedly the Department of Women and Child Development and provided on December 7, 1993, in the Lok Sabha and December 10, 1993 in the Rajya Sabha, was as follows:

"The Government of India has ratified the UN Convention on the Rights of the Child. Appropriate legislative and administrative measures are being taken for implementing the Convention by the concerned Ministries/ Departments.

"A National Plan of Action for Children has been adopted under which goals have been fixed for the decade 1990-2000. The Plan seeks to cover the programmes in the areas of child and maternal health, nutrition, water and sanitation, education, children in difficult circumstances and adolescent girls. All sectors have reviewed their programmes for strengthening, keeping in view the goals set in the National Plan of Action for Children.

"A number of child care programmes for improving the nutritional status of children are being implemented. The Integrated Child Development Service (ICDS) programme is a major intervention for providing a package of services including supplementary nutrition to 16.3 million children under six years of age. Nutrition supplementation is also being provided to children under the scheme of creches (3,00,000 children) and Balwadi Nutrition (2,29,000 children). A new initiative to improve nutritional status of adolescent girls has been started, on a selected basis, in 507 ICDS projects. Again, through nutrition education programmes the mothers are also being educated and empowered to look after the nutritional needs of their children better.

"The Department has identified 180 focal districts in the country based on the criteria of poverty, concentration of Scheduled Castes and Scheduled Tribes and high crude birth rate. While expanding Child Care Programmes, preference is given to these focal districts."

The reply offered in parliament discussed the situation with regard to nutrition-related programmes, but more is needed to fully address the question of nutrition rights. It is also important to know something about the nutrition problems, the relevant law, the extent to which the law is implemented, and the mechanisms of accountability for ensuring that the law is implemented.

The government's statement confirms that the level of effort has been high, but it does not address the question of effectiveness. As in other countries, targeting is always difficult. It is expensive, and it can be politically unpopular. According to an overview of India's nutrition programmes prepared for the World Bank, "direct nutrition expenditures per child were pitifully low precisely in the very states that account for a larger share of the nation's severely malnourished children." The productivity of expenditures intended to alleviate malnutrition should be systematically assessed so that individual programmes can be adapted for greater effectiveness and reallocations can be made towards more productive programmes.

India has tried many different kinds of approaches to alleviate malnutrition, some successful, some not. One major lesson is that where programmes are not held to account and required to show their effectiveness, they lose sight of the original intended target. The argument here, however, is not that an entirely new programme of action should be launched, but that the programmes in place that are supposed to help alleviate malnutrition should have their effectiveness assessed more systematically and should be held accountable for their performance.

At the outset, existing programmes should be examined to determine where the rules of access could be adapted to conform more closely to a system of rights. To illustrate, one promising possibility is in Tamil Nadu, where the Tamil Nadu Integrated Nutrition Programme (TINP) was introduced in October 1980. It focuses on feeding children at nutritional risk as demonstrated by growth faltering based on weight-for-age. In July 1982, the government introduced the noon meal programme, covering all children between two and five years of age regardless of their nutritional status. In September 1984, coverage was expanded to include all poor children going to school, up to the age of 15. The new service protocol, based on careful targeting of services, has proven effective:

"Children ages six to 36 months were weighed each month .... Supplementary feeding was provided immediately to those who were severely malnourished, and feeding for children with faltering growth was provided after one month (for children ages six-12 months) or three months (for children ages 12 to 35 months). The children selected were fed for at least 90 days. If they failed to gain at least 500 grams in weight, they were referred to health care, and feeding was continued for up to 180 days. Intensive nutrition education was directed at mothers and to those who were nursing while pregnant.

"The project cut severe malnutrition in half and prevented many at-risk children from becoming malnourished".

Participants were fed only when required, with the result that food was only 13 per cent of the project's total cost.

In the view of Dr. Anuradha Khati Rajivan, Collector in the Pudukkottai District:

> In the state of Tamil Nadu, it is now possible to think of the feeding programmes for children as entitlement programmes. Here the term entitlement is being used in the sense of a right, something accepted by the society and political leadership and which is unlikely to be questioned for reasons of resource constraints ... Budgetary pressures have not led to cutbacks for the feeding programme... The noon meal programme now has a first call on the state budget along with food subsidies of the public distribution system and electricity subsidies.

It is still not a hard right because there are no explicit laws assuring children of this entitlement and providing some recourse in case the right is not fulfilled. However, it might not be difficult to make those adaptations. The number of beneficiaries has been increasing steadily, straining the budget. If it becomes necessary to limit the categories of those eligible, it may at the same time be feasible to provide legal assurances for those who are designated as eligible.

A sustained campaign could be launched to strengthen children's nutrition rights in India. Participants in the initial planning meeting should include officials from the relevant ministries and government agencies, representatives from non-governmental organisations concerned with law, human rights, children, and nutrition, and representatives of key governmental and non- governmental international organisations. All will have roles to play in the effort. The purpose of the campaign would be to put an end to extreme malnutrition among India's children through the establishment and effective implementation of clear laws regarding children's nutrition rights.

The planning process could have three major components: a review of the existing situation with regard to children's nutrition rights, goal-setting, and the formulation of a strategy for meeting the goal. Goal-setting should be informed by the nutrition goals set out in India's National Plan of Action for Children and other relevant national and

Goal-setting should be informed by the nutrition goals set out in India's National Plan of Action for Children and other relevant national and international documents. Alternative formulations should also be considered.

The implications of adopting a particular nutrition goal as a right should then he worked out in terms of the strategy, the programme of action that would lead to its achievement. The legislature should not be presented only with a vague goal, but should be asked to make a firm commitment to the complete package.

A radical approach to strategy formulation could be based on semi-privatisation of the effort. If the government decides it really wants to end extreme malnutrition among children it could have that effort managed by a semi-private organisation under contract. The operators of this "Nutrition Rights Corporation" would have a performance-based contract such that they would be fully compensated only if they were successful. The government could specify the goals and set out detailed ground rules, and then put out a formal request for proposals for providing the service, in effect putting the task out to bid. This method could be tested and refined in two or three states with strong support from the central government. In time, a full multi-layered system could be established, with separate management corporations for each state, all functioning under the guidance of a central headquarters office. While the goal-setting and operational guidelines would be established centrally, much of the planning and execution could be decentralised and highly participatory. The bidders would have room for creativity regarding these issues.

Even if it is politically infeasible, thinking in this way suggests the sort of business-like thinking that is needed. Close attention must be given to the bottom line of achieving reductions in malnutrition, just as any business venture must give close attention to the bottom line of profitability. Clear and strong incentives need to be established to assure that the goal is pursued efficiently and effectively.

India has excellent nutrition programmes "on the ground" and devotes substantial resources to the alleviation of malnutrition. However, the purposes of these programmes vary a great deal. As any military commander knows, assets on the ground become more effective if they are coordinated and goal-directed, all pointing in the same direction. India's resources for alleviating malnutrition could be used more efficiently and effectively if they were organised in a goal-directed programme based on clear nutrition rights.

[illegible] Arabic for Chinese [illegible]

[illegible]

PART - V

LEGAL ASPECTS

TWENTY FOUR

ROLE OF THE CONSTITUTION

The Constitution of India, enacted *inter alia* on 26 November 1949, the following Resolution:

We, the people of India, having solemnly resolved to constitute India into a

Sovereign democratic republic and to secure to all its citizens:

Justice, social, economic and political;

Liberty of thought, expression, belief, faith and worship;

Equality of status and opportunity;

And to promote among them all

Fraternity assuring the dignity of the individual and unity of the Nation;

This Resolution, which became the Preamble to the Constitution, was not a sudden or dramatic improvization but the culmination of series of pronouncements made before its adoption. To quote from the text of the Resolution moved by Pandit Jawaharlal Nehru on 13 December, 1946:

(5) (a) Wherein shall be guaranteed and secured to all the people of India— justice, social, economic and political; equality of status, of opportunity; and before the law, freedom of thought, expression, belief, faith, worship, vocation, association and action, subject to law and public morality; and (b) wherein adequate safeguards shall be provided for minorities, backward and tribal areas and depressed and other backward classes

The same ethos and spirit that characterized the Resolution moved by Jawaharlal Nehru was also reflected in a statement by Mahatma Gandhi outlining the goals he envisaged for independent India:

I shall strive for a constitution which will release India from all thraldom and patronage and give her, if need be, the right to sin. I shall work for an India in which the poorest shall feel that it is their country in whose making they have an effective voice; and an India in which there shall be no high class and low class of people, an India in which all communities shall live in perfect harmony

The provisions of the Constitution that set the goal for Indian democracy were broadly enunciated and adopted by the Indian National Congress at Karachi in 1931:

In order to end the exploitation of the masses, political freedom must include the real economic freedom of the starving millions. The state was to safeguard the interest of industrial workers ensuring that suitable legislation should secure them a high wage, healthy conditions, limited hours of labour and protection from the economic consequences of old age, sickness and unemployment. Women and children were also to be protected in various ways and accorded special benefits.

The spirit of this Resolution as also the spirit of the statement made by Mahatma Gandhi and Jawaharlal Nehru has been more concretely reflected in Part-III and Part-IV of the Constitution. Part-III deals with Fundamental Rights and Part-IV deals with the Directive Principles of State Policy. The Fundamental Rights are enforceable, and if any citizen feels that any of those has been contravened s/he can move either the High Court or the Supreme Court by an appropriate petition and seek redress. Although the Directive Principles are not enforceable or justiceable in this way, they were nevertheless viewed as being fundamental to the governance of the country. Their significance was lucidly and forcefully enunciated by Dr B. R. Ambedkar in a statement made in the Constituent Assembly:

In enacting this part of the Constitution the Constituent Assembly is giving certain directions to the future legislature and the future executive to show in what manner they are to exercise the legislative and the executive power they will have. Surely it is not the intention to introduce in this part these principles as mere pious declarations. It is the intention of the Assembly that in future both the legislature and the executive should not merely pay lip service to these principles as mere pious declarations. Instead they should be the basis of all legislative and executive action that they may be taking hereafter in the matter of governance of the country.

The same spirit was reflected in yet another statement by Pandit Jawaharlal Nehru:

The service of India means the service of the millions who suffer. It means the ending of poverty and ignorance and disease and inequality of opportunity. The ambition of the greatest man of our generation has been to wipe every tear from every eye. That may be beyond us but as long as there are tears and suffering so long our work will not be over.

It is in this broad perspective that the following provisions of the Constitution that have a direct bearing on child labour need to be analysed.

Art. 23:

Prohibition of traffic in human beings and forced labour.

Traffic in human beings and *begar* and other similar forms of forced labour are prohibited and any contravention of this provision shall be an offence punishable in accordance with law.

Art. 24:

Prohibition of employment of children in factories etc.

No child below the age of fourteen years shall be employed to work in any factory or mine or engaged in any other hazardous employment.

Art. 39(e) and (f):

Certain principles of policy to be followed by state:

The state shall, in particular, direct its policy securing (e) that the health and strength of workers, men and women and the tender age of children are not abused and that citizens are not forced by economic necessity to enter avocations unsuited to their age or strength, (f) that children are given opportunities and facilities to develop in a healthy manner and in conditions of freedom and dignity and that childhood and youth are protected against exploitation and against moral and material abandonment.

Art. 41:

The right to work, to education and to public assistance in particular circumstances:

the state shall within the limits of its economic capacity and development make effective provision for securing the right to work, to education and to public assistance in cases of unemployment, old age, sickness, and disablement and in other cases of undeserved want.

Art. 45:

Provision for free and compulsory education for children.

The state shall endeavour to provide within a period of 10 years from the commencement of this Constitution for free and compulsory education for all children until they complete the age of fourteen years.

Art. 47:

Responsibility of the state to raise the nutritional levels, and standards of living of its citizens and to improve public health.

The state shall regard the raising of the level of nutrition and the standard of living of its people and improvement of public health as among its primary duties and in particular the state shall endeavour to bring about prohibition of the consumption except for medical purposes of intoxicating drinks and of drugs which are injurious to health.

Art. 39(e) and (f) basically imply the right of every citizen to live with human dignity and honour free from exploitation. The principles enunciated in this Article are unexceptionable.

So far so good. The real dichotomy or contradiction lies in the provisions of Art. 24 and Art. 45. Art. 24 prohibits employment of children, but only in factories, mines, and hazardous employment. In other words, it is a qualified and not a total prohibition. Nowhere in the Constitution, is there any definition of the expression 'hazardous'. The simple dictionary meaning of 'hazardous' is 'dangerous', and this should be understood in relation to a particular form of work, undertaking, process or activity. There are processes or activities such as agriculture that may appear to be apparently harmless but undertaking them may be fraught with risks such as handling dangerous chemicals and toxic substances in the course of spraying pesticides. That is also the case with regard to horticulture, plantation, pisciculture, and sericulture. The collection of minor forest produce may, if performed skilfully, not be dangerous but there may be hidden dangers such as snake bite, insect bite, a fall from a tree, etc. that may prove fatal to both adults and children. In tribal and forest areas the entire family, comprising adult parents and children goes out to collect minor forest produce. They leave early in the morning, say at 4 a.m., and negotiate the entire forest track barefoot. In the process they may be injured but since they have no alternative livelihood they must perforce put up with such ordeal. Collection of minor forest produce, such as *sal* seed or plucking *tendu* leaves, or collection of resin or nuxvomica or *gumkaraya* entail a great deal of travel within the forest spread over long hours, while the forest product collected may not provide a decent livelihood partly because of its perishable nature, partly on account of the problem of the storage necessitating distress sale, under weighment and consequently unremunerative price paid by middlemen. The members of such tribal families are generally not able to return from the forest till the late hours of the afternoon and when they return they are weary and exhausted. School hours would by then be over and the children would be so fatigued that the question of their attending even a non-formal school in the afternoon would be a remote possibility.

This is precisely the dilemma posed by the provision of Art. 45. Its intention is unmistakable, i.e. the responsibility of the state to provide all children in the 5-14 age group with facilities and opportunities for free and compulsory schooling. Millions of children in India are, however, so disadvantaged in terms of birth, caste, sex, geography and topography that it is impossible for them to go to school even if they want to. It is purely external circumstances that dictate this rather than their parents' choice not to send them to school. Parents care for their children far more than any body else, and since education is one of the tools for promoting their well-being they are concerned about providing them with this.

The question that, therefore, arises is whether it is enough to speak in terms of the state providing free, compulsory, universal, primary and elementary education, as Art. 45 does, which sounds platitudinous? Would it not be better to speak in terms of creating conditions for this by minimizing or alleviating the distress of parents caused by their harsh work environment that will permit them not only to send their children to school but permit their retention and participation for sufficient length of time to achieve effective minimum levels of learning?

A few other questions that arise from this analysis and are relevant are:

1.If employment of children is prohibited in factories, mines, and other hazardous forms of employment, does it follow that children are permitted to be employed in non-hazardous or the least hazardous forms of employment?

2.If non-hazardous or the least hazardous forms of employment are permissible, where remains the scope for free and compulsory primary education?

3.Does it mean that children can continue to work and study at the same time?

4.If so, what will be the curriculum, course content, textual materials, the timing and duration of work and study, who will be responsible for coordinating these and evaluating their impact, what will be the mechanism for bringing these children into the formal system of education?

These and many other questions arise and must be answered. If 21 m. children are born, 8 m. of them die, and 13 m. survive annually it does not mean that they are all uniformly placed. There are children born to normal biological parents and reared in normal conditions; children born of parents at one place but adopted by foster parents and brought up elsewhere in an environment devoid of the natural love and affection of biological parents. There are children who are born to parents that are poor, landless, and assetless with nothing to fall back upon at their place of domicile and are, therefore, forced to accompany them from one place to another in search of better avenues of employment and higher wages. They, in the process, are deprived of stability and the innocent pleasures of a normal childhood. There are children with a normal IQ and normal faculties capable of absorbing and assimilating all that they are required to in the normal course; others are born with neurological disorders whose receptivity and retentivity are limited and who suffer severe learning disability. There are also other physically, orthopaedically, and visually handicapped, and mentally retarded children whose ability to learn is severely handicapped. There are areas that are prone to salinity where the inhabitants are victims of fluorosis and guinea-worm, iodine deficiency, and goitre. There are other areas where acute malnutrition is the norm and normal learning, retention, and application are inconceivable.

It is well-known that work, unless it is creative, interesting, and challenging, can be extremely harmful to young children. That is not to undermine the dignity of manual labour but merely to point out that there are strict limitations on the forms, content and extent of work that young children can safely undertake. How can children afflicted with malnutrition and other crippling disabilities be expected to cope with the stress and exhaustion of work and at the same time grapple with the rigours of non-formal education. It is necessary to ponder over this question and what it is likely to lead to before making a policy decision and implementing it. In the ultimate analysis, if children and their parents have no viable alternative to non-formal education or combining work with education, *we* will just have to accept an arrangement that is decidedly the second best.

TWENTY FIVE

PROVISIONS OF LAW

Law is a framework, an enabling mechanism. Labour laws like labour policy are society's response to certain basic needs of the individual, the society, and the nation. These needs being divergent and often conflicting, law acts as an instrument reconciling these conflicting needs.

The roots of laws on child labour, like laws on a host of other subjects relating to social protection, regulating the working and living conditions of workers are to be found in the Resolution that was drafted at the Karachi session of Indian National Congress in 1931. Its highlights were:

- The state shall safeguard the interests of the industrial worker.
- It will secure for the worker a living wage, healthy conditions, and limited hours of work.
- It will provide a suitable mechanism for the settlement of disputes between employer and workmen.
- It will ensure protection against economic insecurity arising out of old age, sickness, unemployment, and death.

In addition the Resolution highlighted the following:

- Labour will be freed from serfdom and conditions bordering on serfdom.
- Protection of women workers and special provisions for maternity leave.
- Children of school-going age should not be employed in factories and mines.
- Workers shall have the right to form unions to safeguard their interests.

These highlights of the Karachi Resolution were incorporated in the final report of the Labour Sub-Committee presented to the Indian National Congress in May 1940. The highlights of the report are:

- Working and living conditions of children including hours of work, would be regulated.

• The minimum age of employment of children should be progressively raised to fifteen in correlation with the education system.

• Working hours should be limited to forty-eight hours per week and nine hours per day.

• A mechanism for fixing wages should be established in order to secure for workers a living wage and a minimum wage.

Two years before the Karachi session of the INC where the historic Resolution referred to was adopted, the Whitley Commission *Report of the Royal Commission on Labour in India* (GOI, Calcutta, 1931) was shocked by the appalling conditions of children working in factories and observed:

In many cities large number of young boys are employed for long hours and discipline is strict. Indeed there is reason to believe that corporal punishment and other disciplinary measures of a reprehensible kind are sometimes resorted to in the case of smaller children. Workers as young as five years of age may be found in some of these places working without adequate meal, intervals or weekly rest days and 10 or 12 hours daily for sums as low as two annas in the case of those of tenderest years.

The Commission, therefore, appropriately recommended legislation to fix the minimum age for employment of children at a higher level than that obtaining in many industries. In the following years the minimum age for employment of children was fixed at 12 years under the Factories Act and 15 years under the Mines Act.

The recommendations of the Royal Commission on Labour that were finalized in 1931 came up for discussion in the Legislative Assembly and the Children (Pledging of Labour) Act, 1933 was passed. This may be said to be the first statutory enactment dealing with child labour. This law prohibits parents and guardians from pledging the services of a child. Basically what it implies is that as children are incapable of exercising the most appropriate option, parents and guardians are supposed to act in their best interests and not to pledge or mortgage their services.

The Children (Pledging of Labour) Act, 1933 was followed in quick succession by the Employment of Children Act, 1938. This law, that has now been replaced by the Child Labour (Prohibition and Regulation) Act, 1986, was quite narrow and restricted in scope and content. It sought to prohibit employment of children below 14 years in occupations relating to transport of passengers by rail and in work relating to the handling of goods within the limits of any port. The Act fixed the minimum age of employment at 14 years for those engaged in *beedi* making, carpet weaving, cement manufacture, cloth printing, dyeing and weaving, match manufacture, mica cutting, tanning etc.

The Employment of Children Act, 1938, suffered from the following infirmities:

- The Act did not attempt a formal definition of the child.
- It was unclear and ambiguous in its scope and content inasmuch as it classified children into two categories for the purpose of prohibition and regulation of their employment. The first category of children were those below the age of fourteen who were prohibited from working in five occupations listed in the Act. The second category were those who had completed 14 years but were below seventeen. They could be employed in the prohibited occupations provided they were allowed a period of rest.

This is a flawed arrangement inasmuch as in a society afflicted with endemic poverty and chronic malnutrition there is little distinction made between a child of 14 years and over that. Provision for a rest period or any other regulatory measure does not prevent a vulnerable human resource from being damaged.

The Child Labour (Prohibition and Regulation) Bill was introduced and passed in both houses of Parliament in August 1986 with a view to prohibiting the employment of children in certain types of jobs and regulating the conditions of employment of children in certain others.

The statement of objects and reason in the Bill reads:

There are a number of Acts which prohibit employment of children below 14 years and 15 years in certain specified employments. However, there is no procedure laid down in any law for deciding in which employments, occupations or processes the employment of children should be banned. There is also no law to regulate the working conditions of children in most of the employments where they are not prohibited from working and are working under exploitative conditions.

The Bill seeks to achieve the following objects:

- Ban the employment of children, i.e. those who have not completed their fourteenth year in specified occupations and processes.
- Lay down a procedure to decide modifications to the schedule of banned occupations or processes.
- Regulate the conditions of work of children engaged in forms of employment in which they are permitted to work.

• Prescribe enhanced penalties for employment of children in violation of the provisions of this Act and other Acts that forbid the employment of children.

• Establish uniformity in the definition of child in laws concerning them.

The introduction of the Bill generated a lively debate in the Indian Parliament in which members cutting across party affiliation debated and provided rare insights into this age-old social issue. In course of the debate the members in particular took exception to the following:

• The proviso in clause 3, part 2 of the Bill which says, 'provided that nothing in this section shall apply to any workshop wherein any process is carried on by the occupier with the aid of his family or to any school established by or receiving assistance or recognition from Government.'

The members had also expressed apprehensions and reservations regarding the following:

• Past experience shows that labour laws are never implemented. The Child Labour (Prohibition and Regulation) Act will become yet another exercise in futility.

• Hazardous work does not become safe merely because it is performed at home.

• Any scheme of exemption provided in a law is bound to be misinterpreted and misused.

• The intention of government should be not to regularize child labour merely because it exists.

• A one sided and half-hearted approach of banning child labour in few establishments and regulating it in few others without adopting a holistic or integrated approach, without solving the problem of poverty and economic deprivation, without enforcing the Minimum Wages Act, without resolving the problem of universal enrolment and retention of all children of school-going age in the formal school system will serve little purpose.

The apprehensions and reservations expressed by the members were genuine and continue to be valid to this day. The proviso to Sec. 3 of the Act has resulted in large-scale misinterpretation and misuse of the provisions of law, and is per se misconceived. The nature of a hazardous occupation does not change merely because it is performed at home or in any part of the residential premises with the help of family members. The *beedi* industry, with its rolling, labelling, and packing operations, is a hazardous occupation. The continuous bending causes backache; continuous inhalation of tobacco is harmful to the respiratory system, and none of these problems is minimized because the operations are carried out at home. It is another matter that widespread poverty and the dearth of other more worthwhile and lucrative occupations have driven millions of families to take to *beedi* rolling. The same applies to carpet weaving which entails sitting in a particular posture for long hours, in an unhealthy environment, subjecting the worker's fingers to continuous strain at a time when they should be used for writing and arithmetic. The logic and rationale of granting exemption under proviso to Sec. 3 is, therefore, not easily established.

Similar doubts also arise in regard to determination of age. Sec.10 of the Child Labour (Prohibition and Regulation) Act reads:

If any question arises between an inspector and an occupier as to the age of any child who is employed or is permitted to work by him in an establishment, the question shall, in the absence of a certificate as to the age of such child granted by the prescribed medical authority, be referred by the inspector for decision to the prescribed medical authority.

This is a provision of the law that is most difficult to implement. The inspector represents the prosecution and the Act puts the onus of proving age on the prosecution. In other words, the Inspector appointed as such under the law is not only required to inspect the establishment, observe and record acts of omission and commission on the part of the employer in regard to violation of the statutory provision on employment of children but also to record the age of the children employed and establish their ages before the trial court with the help of the prescribed medical authority. We know from experience how difficult it is for the prosecution to establish points of law relating to the age of a child. In India, registration of births is at best erratic and is conspicuous by its absence in most rural areas, and to compound matters births are seldom correctly recorded. There are scores of examples of educated and self-seeking parents reducing the age of their children at the time of their enrolment in the formal school system with ulterior motives (such as the added advantage in the matter of public employment). It is doubtful whether the ages of the 100 m. plus children in the 5—14 age group who are out of school, have been correctly recorded, and in the absence of correctly recorded birth certificates it is extremely difficult for an inspector to establish their age before a court of law. There is very little growth monitoring in India in the absence of an established mechanism or procedure for this. Besides, children between 12-16 years in rural areas may, due to malnutrition and stunted growth, physically look much the same.

The correct procedure should be to arrive at such conclusions through field enquiries by the inspector. Even if parents do not reveal the true facts about age, the truth will invariably surface if enquiries are made in the neighbourhood and the purpose of these is made known. Once the Inspector has arrived at a particular conclusion on the basis of field enquiries it should be treated as being final and conclusive unless the employer succeeds in successfully rebutting it. This is the existing provision in Sec. 30 of the Beedi and Cigar workers (Conditions of Employment) Act, 1966 and Sec. 104 of the Factories Act, 1948, and reflects the spirit of the judgement of 16 December 1983 in the Bandhua Mukti Morcha case (writ petition No. 2182 of February 1982).

The definition of both 'establishment' and 'occupier' in the existing law is also quite narrow and restricted. If our intention is to aim at the eventual abolition or prohibition of child labour in all industries, all occupations, and all processes we cannot restrict the definition of establishment to 'shop, commercial establishment, workshop, farm, residential hotel, restaurant, theatre or any other place of public entertainment' as in the present law. There must be an enabling provision empowering both the central and state governments to notify such other workplace as may meet the requirement of law.

Similarly, the present definition of 'occupier' in the existing law is fraught with limitations and difficulties. According to the present definition, occupier in relation to an establishment or workshop is one who has ultimate control over the affairs of the establishment or the workshop. According to this definition, the owner of the establishment or workshop is liable to prosecution for violation of the provisions of the Act in his capacity as 'Occupier'. However, there are various processes and occupations, especially those where employment of children is prohibited, that are earned out in the establishment or workshop on behalf of and under the supervision and control of a manufacturer who contracts out such manufacture to the owner of the workshop or establishment. The contractors also have under them a network of subcontractors. Appropriately, therefore, all such contractors and subcontractors should also share responsibility for acts of omission and commission and should come within the meaning and legal definition of 'Occupier'. This will help to fix responsibility and secure compliance with the provisions of the Act.

Part A of the schedule to the Act lists the occupations in which no child can be employed or permitted to work and Part B some of the processes.

The occupations and processes cited in Part A and B of the schedule are somewhat limited, but additional occupations and processes can be added on the recommendation of the Child Labour Technical Advisory Committee constituted by the central government. Thirteen occupations and fifty-one processes have been added to schedule A and schedule B respectively with effect from 23 October 1998 on the recommendation of the Committee.

The Act does not use the word 'hazardous' anywhere although employment of children in certain industries/occupations/processes has been prohibited ostensibly on the ground that they are hazardous or dangerous. It is very impractical and unrealistic to distinguish between hazardous and non-hazardous occupations/processes. Certain industries/occupations/processes, like un-mechanized agriculture may on the face of it appear to be harmless or non-hazardous but the introduction of mechanization, spraying of pesticides, etc. may make agriculture extremely hazardous for children. It may, therefore, be desirable to do away with this artificial distinction and prohibit employment of children in any form in industry as a whole.

There are a number of other gaps and omissions, conceptual, definitional, and operational in the existing law, and these continue to be exploited to the disadvantage of working children and the advantage of unscrupulous elements in industry and commerce. Examples are children employed in the carpet weaving units of Bhadoi, Varanasi, and Mirzapur and children rolling *beedies* along with their parents in Andhra Pradesh, Bihar, Gujarat, Haryana, Himachal Pradesh, Madhya Pradesh, Maharashtra, Karnataka, Kerala, Orissa, Rajasthan, Tamil Nadu, and West Bengal.

A proviso to Sec. 3 of the Child Labour (Prohibition and Regulation) Act, 1986 reads:

Provided that nothing in this section shall apply to any workshop wherein any process is carried on by the occupier with the aid of his family or to any school established by, or receiving assistance or recognition from, Government.

The workshop referred to in this proviso must be construed to mean that of the occupier as defined in Sec. 2(vi) and its members have to be of the occupier's family. This means that members of a family of a person other than the occupier to whom the occupier, for the purpose of manufacture, has handed over the raw material to complete the process elsewhere, including his own home to be returned to him, does not receive protection.

In the manufacture of *beedies* a *beedi* contractor or subcontractor hands over the raw materials *(tendu*leaf, tobacco) to the persons employed for the purpose of rolling *beedies* and permits them to take the raw material to their homes to roll instead of rolling them in the premises of the manufacturer (occupier). The same is true in carpet weaving. Children may weave carpets at home along with other members of the family but they do so using raw materials delivered to them by the contractor/subcontractor or any agent of the manufacturer. According to a correct interpretation of the law, the home of the person employed for this purpose is not a 'workshop' of the 'occupier' within the meaning of the proviso to Sec. 3 and members of the family who assist at the employee's home are not covered by the expression 'his family' in the proviso. If such an interpretation is accepted, the weakness attributed to the proviso to Sec. 3 is invalid. Unfortunately, however, most state governments/Union Territories, and district administrations tend to include jobs, operations, and processes that are carried out within a residential premise as falling within the purview of the proviso to Sec. 3 and tend to extend the protection to workers who are engaged in these jobs, operations, and processes that are logically not extendable.

Similar problems have been faced in regard to determination of the age of the child. Sec. 10 and 16(2) provide for determination of age in the case of any dispute regarding age. According to Sec. 10 in the event of any dispute regarding the age of a child between the Inspector and the occupier, the question should be decided on the basis of a certificate of age provided by the prescribed medical authority to whom such an issue has to be referred for decision. The question is of the extent of the authority of the Court in deciding this. According to an interpretation of the law provided by a competent legal authority, Sec. 10 should be read to mean that it is open to the Inspector to adduce such evidence as he deems fit to underscore his reasons for not accepting the age shown by the occupier, and in the absence of a certificate of age from the prescribed medical authority, the provision requires the matter to be referred to the prescribed medical authority for obtaining his certificate. The prescribed medical authority is required in turn to take into account the material made available by the Inspector on the basis of which the latter has formed his opinion, when certifying the age of the child. This merely means that when the Court is unable to reach a definite conclusion on the basis of evidence already produced by the Inspector and the occupier in accordance with the rules of evidence, then the opinion of the prescribed medical authority has to be obtained as an aid in deciding the question of age. There is no further requirement or restriction in Sec. 10 on the power of the Court to determine the disputed age of the child.

Sec. 10 has to be read with Sub-Section 2 of Sec. 16. This provision specifies that a certificate of age granted by the prescribed medical authority shall for the purpose of the Act be conclusive evidence of the child's age. This provision means that the Court's power to determine the child's age, is taken away by Sub.-Sec. (2) of Sec. 16 declaring a medical certificate to constitute conclusive evidence. The effect of this transfer of the authority of the Court to the prescribed medical authority is the question. What the Act means by 'conclusive evidence' is not specifically mentioned and, therefore, we have to construe it as required under the Indian Evidence Act, 1872. Sec. 4 of the Evidence Act states that the expression excludes any evidence being offered in rebuttal. In substance, the existing provision transfers the power of determining a disputed question of age from the Court to the prescribed medical authority which is wrong because the latter cannot be deemed to be a substitute for judicial authority, and moreover medical evidence is merely an opinion to aid the Court in deciding a disputed question of fact.

In India there is no satisfactory system of recording the registration of births, and in the absence of this, notably in rural areas, it is extremely difficult to correctly determine the age of a child. Callous and unscrupulous establishments employing children below 14 years of age often tend to take advantage of this lacuna. They in collusion with the prescribed medical authority, obtain a falsified certificate. This creates enormous problems for the Courts, for they are obliged to treat the medical certificate as conclusive evidence under Sub-Sec. 2 of Sec. 16 of the Act.

While Child Labour (Prohibition and Regulation) Act continues to be the principal enactment on the issue of prohibition and regulation of employment of children, there are a number of other labour laws that are not so much concerned with withdrawing children from work as with merely specifying the minimum age of entry to employment in certain factories, mines, plantations, etc. and it is worth examining and analysing these provisions, as done below.

Factories Act, 1948

(Sec. 67): Prohibits employment of young children. 'No child who has not completed his fourteenth year shall be required or allowed to work in any factory.'

Plantation Labour Act, 1951

(Sec. 24): Prohibition of employment of young children: 'No child who has not completed his twelfth year shall be required or allowed to work in any plantation.'

(Sec. 26): Non-adult workers who carry tokens:

No child who has completed his twelfth year and no adolescent shall be required or allowed to work in any plantation unless:

(a) a certificate of fitness granted with reference to him under section 27 is in the custody of the employer; and

(b) such child or adolescent carries with him while he is at work a token giving a reference to such certificate.

According to the provisions of the Act, children below 12 years are prohibited from working in any plantation. The Act, however, permits a child of over 12 years to work in any plantation provided a certificate of fitness is in the custody of the employer and the child carries to work a token signifying that such a certificate exists.

In 1986, Sec. 24 of the Plantation Labour Act, 1951 was replaced by Sec. 24(b) of the Child Labour (Prohibition and Regulation) Act, 1986. The definition of child was also amended as a person who has not completed 14 years. Sec. 26 of the Act was amended to read:

Non-adult workers who carry tokens:

No child [*deleted*] and no adolescent shall be required or allowed to work in any plantation unless:

(a) a certificate of fitness granted with reference to him under section 27 is in the custody of the employer; and

(b) such child or adolescent carries with him while at work a token giving a reference to such certificate.

The implication of the deletion of Sec. 24 and amendment to Sec. 26 of the Act is that a child (below 14 years) can work in any plantation provided he is granted a certificate of fitness by a doctor. This was an inadvertent error and needs to be corrected by bringing further necessary changes in the Plantation Labour Act, 1951 with a view to prohibiting employment of children.

Merchant Shipping Act, 1951

(Sec. 109): No person under fifteen years of age shall be engaged or carried to sea to work in any capacity in any ship, except:

(a) in a school ship or a training ship in accordance with the prescribed conditions; or

(b) in a ship in which all persons employed are members of one family; or

(c) in a home trade ship of less than two hundred tons gross; or

(d) where such person is to be employed on nominal wages and will be in charge of his father or other adult near male relative.

Mines Act, 1952

(Sec. 45): (1) No child shall be employed in any mine, nor shall any child be allowed to be present in any part of a mine which is below ground or in any (open cast working) in which any mining operation is being carried on.

(2) After such date as the Central Government, may by notification in the official Gazette, appoint in this behalf, no child shall be allowed to be present in any part of a mine above ground where any operation connected with or incidental to any mining operation is being carried on.

Motor Transport Workers Act, 1961

(Sec. 21): No child shall be required or allowed to work in any capacity in any motor transport undertaking

Apprentices Act, 1961

(Sec. 3); Qualifications for being engaged as an apprentice:

A person shall not be qualified for being engaged as an apprentice to undergo apprenticeship training in any designated trade, unless he:

(a) is not less than fourteen years of age.

(b) satisfies such standards of education and physical fitness as may be prescribed;

Provided that different standards may be prescribed in relation to apprenticeship training in different designated trades and for different categories of apprentices.

Beedi & Cigar Workers (Conditions of Employment) Act, 1966

Prohibition of employment of children—No child shall be required or allowed to work in any industrial premises.

All the above laws suffer from the same weaknesses or infirmities as the earlier or later laws in relation to prohibition of employment of children in certain employments, such as:

- There is no uniform age of entry to employment;
- Prohibition of employment of children is not unqualified, but hedged with various conditionalities, some of which do not make any sense.

Just as there are a number of factors that contribute to the existence and perpetuation of child labour such as poverty, low adult wages, unemployment, and underemployment, large families and migration from rural to urban areas, illiteracy and ignorance of parents, traditional attitudes and values denying the equality of human beings, there are definite reasons for the failure to enforce the plethora of legislative enactments. Some of these are:

- The existence of a large number of establishments in a particular area with a very small number of inspectors making their inspection virtually impossible.
- An inspector responsible for enforcing a large number of laws in a large number of establishments within his jurisdiction is further handicapped by lack of mobility.
- The total lack of cooperation from the employers of establishments. When an inspector visits an establishment children are whisked away from the worksite and hidden rendering the exercise futile. Given such negative attitudes, it is very unlikely that the inspector will be able to get any definite evidence from other employees of the establishment.
- In a system that is ridden with middlemen and where accountability is not easily established, it is extremely difficult for an inspector to make out a foolproof case against any defaulting employer.
- The trial courts, functioning under the Anglo-Saxon system of jurisprudence, take a very casual view of offences committed under various laws relating to the age of entry to employment. They do not ordinarily take cognizance of the fact that given the existing realities on the ground it is well-neigh impossible to produce a foolproof case

of an offence having been committed by an employer. The penalties awarded, mostly of paltry fines, are negligible and most employers prefer to pay these fines rather than comply with the statutory provisions.

• Most of the loopholes can be directly attributed to the legal framework itself, and are not easily rectified. Amendments to existing statutory provisions have to wait for years as it is often difficult to arrive at a consensus on the text of the amendments, quite apart from the cumbersome and long drawn out nature of the legislative process itself.

• Not enough has been done to disseminate the provisions of the law to a population that is largely illiterate and at best semi-literate without easy access to information. Ignorance of the provisions of laws in general and labour laws, including those relating to child labour, in particular, among parents, among employers of small establishments, among the general public is enormous and continues across generations. The content of the law does not thus easily cross the four walls of the legislature once it has been enacted.

The Minimum Wages Act

The Minimum Wages Act was enacted in 1948 with the objective of fixing, reviewing, revising and enforcing the minimum rates of wages relating to scheduled employments to be notified under the law by the appropriate government, i.e central/state. The intention of the Act is to fix minimum rates of wages in employments in which the labour force is vulnerable to exploitation, i.e. is not well organized and has no effective bargaining power. It provides for an institutional mechanism and procedure for fixation, review, revision, and enforcement of minimum rates of wages. 'Minimum wage' has not been defined in the Act. In essence, the minimum wage represents the basic subsistence wage below which no employer can go although nothing prevents him from paying above this statutorily notified wage. According to the judgement of the Supreme Court, an industry or industrial establishment does not have the right to exist if it cannot guarantee payment of the minimum wage. However, the following five norms recommended by the Indian Labour Conference in its 15th session held at Nainital in 1957 are kept in view by the appropriate government for fixation and revision of minimum wages:

• Three consumption units for one earner.

• Minimum food requirement of 2700 calories per average Indian adult.

• Clothing requirements of 72 yards per annum per family.

• Rent corresponding to the minimum area provided for under the government's Industrial Housing Scheme.

• Fuel, lighting and other 'miscellaneous' items of expenditure to constitute 20 per cent of the total minimum wage.

The Supreme Court of India in its judgement in the case *of Reftakos Brett and Co.* vs *Others,* Civil Appeal No. 4336 of 1991, held that the following should be added to the norms and criteria already recommended by the ILC:

- children's education,
- medical requirement,
- minimum recreation,
- provision for old age,
- marriage.

The Supreme Court of India also held that expenditure on the above components should constitute 25 per cent of the total minimum wages and that this should be brought to the notice of the state governments/Union Territories as a guideline for fixation of minimum wages.

Viewed in this perspective the objectives of the Act are laudable and contribute substantially in protecting and safeguarding the interests of workers engaged in the sweated sector through regulation of their wages, hours of work, overtime, etc.

There are, however, two provisions in the law that have a direct relevance to child labour and which, in the context of our thinking on the issue, are not conducive to the central objective of elimination of child labour. These are sub-section 3 of section 3(a) and Rule 24 which read as follows:

(3) In fixing or revising minimum rates of wages under this section:

(a) different minimum rates of wages may be fixed for:

(i) different scheduled employments;

(ii) different classes of work in the same scheduled employment;

(iii) adults, adolescents, children, and apprentices;

Rule 24

Number of working hours which shall constitute a working day

(1) The number of hours which shall constitute a normal working day shall be

(a) in the case of an adult, nine hours;

(b) in the case of a child, four and a half hours.

(2) The working day of an adult worker shall be so arranged that inclusive of the intervals of rest, if any, shall not spread over more than twelve hours on any day.

There are two anomalies arising out of the above provision. One is that in rural areas and in the unorganized and informal sectors of employments it is extremely difficult to fix the hours of work and also to enforce the hours so fixed. Even though children are barred from working for over four and a half hours a day, in actual practice they work for over eight hours and sometimes even more ten and twelve hours. A recent study conducted by UNICEF of children employed in brick kilns in Thane district of Maharashtra confirms this. Even when children actually work for more than the stipulated hours of work they are not paid overtime. The provision of 'spread over', as in rule 24(2) is invariably honoured in the breach. Such unduly long hours of work are not in the interest of children and are likely to cause irreparable damage to their health, psyche, and overall development.

The second anomaly arises from a bare reading of Sec. 11. Sec. 11 deals with payment of wages. Ordinarily under Sec. 11(1), such wages shall be paid in cash. Sec. 11 (2), however, permits payment of wages either wholly or partly in kind where it has been the custom to pay wages in kind, and the appropriate government can authorize such payment of wages in kind after satisfying itself that it is necessary in the circumstances of the case to do so.

Payment of wages fully in kind has several limitations and disadvantages for the persons receiving such wages, e.g.:

- Kind could mean either foodgrains or cereals or pulses or cooked food. It could also mean clothing, medicines, and other consumables.
- There is a possibility of cheating in all such cases by under-weighment, supply of unwholesome food that does not conform to the minimum standards of nutrition as also supply of sub-standard grain unfit for human consumption.
- In a majority of the rural areas where wages are paid in kind a

proper system of weights and measures may not be followed, far less enforced by the Inspectors of the Food and Civil Supplies Department.

• There have been cases where in certain parts of Madhya Pradesh like Satna, Rewa, and Sidhi wages were paid in the form of kesri dal in the 1960s and 70s. Kesri dal has toxic elements and its consumption resulted in lathyrism to a large number of agricultural labourers who received it in lieu of wages. Even though growing of kesri dal has been banned by law it continues to be grown illegally in several parts of the country including Madhya Pradesh.

• The support price of certain foodgrains are fixed by government as also the rates at which such foodgrains, covered under the Public Distribution System (PDS), are sold. The PDS is not however, exhaustive and does not include all the foodgrains that are grown and consumed in a particular area. To illustrate, while support prices for rice and wheat are fixed there is no support price for ragi which is also not an item covered by the PDS. In such cases, where wages are paid in kind it becomes extremely difficult to determine the cash value of wages paid in kind on the basis of the widely fluctuating value obtaining in the market. In addition, the system of payment of wages in kind suffers from the following deficiencies:

• when wages are paid in kind it is difficult for the parents of the child to arrange for payment of school fees, purchase of textbooks and uniforms for which ready cash is necessary.

• there are several other pressing household requirements for which cash is essential.

Conditions have vastly changed since 1947. In 1947, essential commodities were available in plenty and at affordable prices and there was some sense in conceptualizing payment of wages in kind. Fifty-two years later when there has been a transformation in terms of physical infrastructure, savings facilities (in the form of banks and post-offices), and change in consumption patterns, preferences, and needs of the family, a portion of the minimum wages should be paid in cash to enable the recipient of the wage to defray these. In the context of school children in particular a direct link can be established between educational deprivation (parents not being able to buy textbooks and uniforms) and child labour in a dispensation that authorizes payment of minimum wages wholly in kind. This clearly underlines the need and justification for an amendment to Sec. 11 (2) to make it possible to substantial percentage of the minimum wage (say 75 per cent) in cash.

TWENTY SIX

CRIMINAL JUSTICE SYSTEM

As we look forward to the beginning of a new millennium with new challenges and opportunities, let us look back at the neglected issues of protecting crime victims. Our Government wishes to recognize the importance of the rights of victims of crime. "Justice", henceforth, "marches to a different beat".

I have always wondered what victims of crime have to go through in the Criminal Justice System and about their feelings and experiences as a victim-imagine these issues when the victims are children—the most vulnerable section of any society. Perhaps, you have to be victim to know what it feels like.

Although we are not dealing with 'natural victimization' my heart goes out to the hundreds of people, especially children, who have been victimized by the cyclone-hit districts of Orissa. A deathly lull has crept over the entire state where over one and a half crore people have been rendered homeless and atleast ten thousand people are either killed/ injured or missing. We are yet to recover from the most horrendous train tragedy in North India, sometime ago,. that claimed hundreds of lives of innocent victims including women and children due to the negligence of a couple of human minds. The lesson that these tragedies teach us is that we need to have better appreciation in disaster management. How can we be more careful in the future and prevent such victimizations? What can we do to assist the living victims?

Though general victimology is a scientific study of all kinds of victims, the scope of victimology here is limited to crime victims. When a person is harmed by a criminal act, the agencies that make up our criminal justice system have a moral and legal obligation to respond. It is their responsibility not only to seek swift justice for the victims but also ease their sufferings in a time of great need. Victimologists are concerned with the interaction between victims and offenders, victims and the criminal justice system, victims and the society and victims and the environment. This field has been increasingly recognized as an international field of research and action, transcending many cultural and legal systems in the last few years.

It is fifty-three years since our nation has got its independence and after we are yet to listen and respond to victims of crime and their advocates. The victims of crime are virtually invisible in the laws and policies that govern our criminal justice system. Tremendous strides are being taken by various legal and social bodies and also the Indian Society of Victimology, to enact victims' rights laws in our country. Hopefully, the Bill on The Victims (Criminal Justice) Right to Assistance - 1996, drafted by the Indian Society of Victimology, will be given due importance and consideration by the present government to frame a national legislation to assist victims of crime in tune with the United Nations Declaration of basic principles of justice for victims of crime and abuse of power.

During the past two decades, the United Nations has undertaken a number of initiatives to address myriad needs of crime victims at the international level. The Declaration of the Basic Principle of Justice for Victims of Crime and Abuse of Power was adopted by consensus in the United Nations General Assembly in 1985, reflecting the collective will of the international community to address to the interests and concerns of victims of crime. Considered as a 'Magna Carta' for crime victims around the world, the Declaration is based on the philosophy that victims should be treated with compassion and respect for their dignity. And that they are entitled to access the mechanisms of justice and to receive prompt redress for the harm they have suffered. India is proud to be a signatory to this Declaration.

Each year, millions of children are directly experiencing or witnessing increased violence and abuse in their homes, neighbourhoods and schools. Children from broken homes, abandoned and destitutes are easy targets of unscrupulous elements. Their tender age, innocence, lack of experience and absence of any guidance add to their vulnerability. The general penal code of this country and the various protective and preventive 'Special and Local Laws' specifically mention the offences wherein children are known to be victims. The statistical analysis in the 'Crime in India', 1997, discloses that there has been a gradual increase in the incidence of child rape in the figures of five years from 1993-97, followed by kidnapping and abduction, exposure and abandonment and the procuration of minor girls. Other crimes against children are infanticide, foeticide, buying and selling of girls for prostitution, abetment of suicide, foeticide, buying and selling of girls for prostitution, abetment of suicide and child marriage. These are the only statistics that seem to be available on child victims. What we lack is a national repository of all child victimizations that is published every year. In spite of the lack of exact data, the available statistics suggests that child victimization is a crisis of national importance.

Though accurate figures are unavailable, each year there are thousands of children who enter the multi-million dollar illegal sex market. Children are coerced, kidnapped, sold and deceived or otherwise trafficked into enforced sexual encounters. The damage, commercial sexual exploitation causes to the children, is unquestionable. Children are robbed of their natural sexual development and their sense of dignity and self-esteem as well. Their physical and mental health are put at tremendous risk. Their rights are violated and their only support may come from those who exploit them. Where have we gone wrong in our sense of priorities and responsibility, when children of a prosperous society like ours, are selling their bodies to supplement their livelihood and find a ready market in the flesh trade?

Over the past decade, new manifestations of child victimization have emerged. Advances in technology brought serious threats and potential harm to children. Video cameras are increasingly used to produce child pornography. Computers equipped with scanners and access to the internet are used to disseminate child pornography worldwide and to solicit children for sexual encounters.

Research also reveals new information about intergenerational cycle of violence. A link betwen early victimization and the later involvement in violent crime has been identified. Witnessing violence at home and in the community also have adverse effects on the child's mental health and development, including an increased likelihood in some children to become directly involved in violence, whether as victims or perpetrators, as they mature.

Such tragedies are not just a day's happening. They happened yesterday; they are happening today; and they will happen again tomorrow—unless the nation decides to give priority to what can now be done to protect the victimization of these vast sections of its children.

In dealing with the victimization of children, the role of law enforcement agencies is most crucial as any effort taken even in the best interest of the children should not cause secondary victimization. This calls for a sensitization of the personnel of the criminal justice system, particularly, the police as they are the first agency to come in contact with the child victims. Sensitization programmes should cover the prosecutors, lawyers and even the judges at all stages of the criminal proceedings.

In fact, I would go one step further and advise that sensitization programmes should extend to the legislators and policymakers. In the given situation, time is ripe to address the unique needs of child victims and outline the legal rights that can protect children from physical and sexual abuse, child abduction, trafficking and other types of crimes against children.

Victimization is a serious threat for Indian children and youth. Many State laws now exist to protect children from physical abuse. Reforms on issues based on children have taken place at every step of the criminal justice process. But today, like all other victims, not even a fraction of the nation's child victims receive much needed services such as emergency financial assistance, crisis and mental health counselling, shelter, information and advocacy within the criminal justice system. There are many victims and their families who do not actively participate in the criminal or juvenile justice processes. They are denied meaningful participation in the judicial system and services to get justice done to them. Policies, therefore, have to be formulated to protect the rights of the child victims and improve their treatment. The Indian Society of Victimology has already ignited the kind of legislative response necessary. It is therefore a challenge to the nation to renew and refocus the treatment of child victims of crime. There should be a comprehensive plan regarding how the nation should respond to child victims. Today, we have, besides academicians and scholars, a broad cross-section of the criminal and juvenile justice and allied professionals and workers in the victim service field. Let your voices be the guiding force for the hundreds and thousands of crime victims who go unheard every year. Let us develop a strategy for providing justice and comprehensive services to child victims of the 21st century. I urge every Indian who interacts with victims, from police officers to prosecutors, from judges to correction officers, from politicians to bureaucrats and the like to join this force and implement programmes and reforms that make sense for their own communities. Over these years, the doors of justice have gradually opened to some victims of crime. It is my great hope that our nation will move closer to the day when the doors of justice open for all victims of crime.

The Indian Society of Victimology is dynamic in evolving innovative approaches to help child victims, find justice and victim assistance for child victims and their rights through this conference. It is this dynamism that ensures response to the evolving understanding of the needs of the child victims. This is not the final word, it is a sound compass that will help hold the course true in the years to come. Let us have faith that legislation will improve in favour of child victims of crime in near future.

PART - VI

FURTHER PROSPECTS

TWENTY SEVEN

PROGRAMME OF ACTION

The national policy on child labour was approved by the Cabinet on 14 August 1987 during the Seventh Plan period. Under the policy, a project based plan of action was envisaged. Accordingly, nine projects were started in areas of high concentration of child labour:

- Match, fireworks, and explosives industry in Sivakasi in Virud-dhanagar district in Tamil Nadu.
- Precious stone polishing industry in Jaipur in Rajasthan
- Glass and bangles industry in Ferozabad in UP
- Brassware industry in Moradabad in UP
- Handmade carpet industry in Mirzapur, Varanasi, and Bhadoi in UP
- Lock-making industry in Aligarh in UP
- Tile industry in Jagampet in Andhra Pradesh
- Slate industry in Markkapur in Andhra Pradesh
- Slate industry in Mandsaur in Madhya Pradesh.

Subsequently, in 1994, National Child Labour Projects (NCLP) were launched in Sambalpur, Thane, and Gharwa.

The NCLP rests on a gradual, sequential, progressive and selective approach to the elimination of child labour. Since the magnitude of the problem of child labour is vast, it was thought appropriate that initially we should concentrate attention and action in areas with a high concentration of child labour. The NCLPs had the following components:

- Imparting non-formal education to enable the children released from work to receive functional literacy and acquire a level of equivalence with the corresponding grade and level in the formal system.
- Supplementary nutrition through midday meals.
- Income and employment generation through impartation of skills.
- Stepping up enforcement of child labour laws.

In regard to the first special schools were opened under each project that were to enrol fifty to seventy-five children on average in different classes corresponding to the grade/level of the students. These special schools were designed to impart instructional lessons in a non-formal mode by teachers selected though a special selection procedure involving the community.

While these nine special projects for rehabilitation of children released from hazardous work were being implemented (1988-94) the former Prime Minister of India Shri P. V. Narasimha Rao, made an important statement in his Independence day address to the nation on 15 August 1994 on the direction being taken for the elimination of child labour:

You know that there are around 20 million children in our country who should be attending schools but are not doing so. They are working in factories to increase the income of their parents. Working in the factories means end of their education and the children's development forever .... There are about 20 lakh children engaged in such hazardous vocations that tell upon their health adversely. We want to withdraw them from such industries and put them in schools in the course of the next four to five years. The only way to achieve this aim is to provide the parents of such children full employment to increase their incomes because the parents are so poor that they cannot sustain themselves without additional income earned by the children. If such parents are provided full employment and their income is raised there is no reason why they should not be sending their children to school willingly. . . . The new programme aims at improving the prospects of the children whose life may be ruined because of their early employment in hazardous industries.

Consequent to this announcement, a National Authority on Elimination of Child Labour was set up on 26 September 1994 under the chairmanship of the Union Minister of Labour and with representatives of the ten government departments relevant to the area of child labour, namely Labour, Education, Welfare, Textile, Health, Family Welfare, Information and Broadcasting, Women and Child Development, Rural Development and Expenditure. The National Authority initially conducted a series of review meetings to strengthen policies and programmes relating to child labour and also to coordinate the activities of the central and state governments with the objective of eliminating child labour.

Pursuant to the announcement a seminar of sixty-two Collectors, District Magistrates and Deputy Commissioners was also held in September, 1995 to facilitate the formulation of additional NCLPs. The seminar was attended in addition by the then Minister of Labour, Shri P. A. Sangma, Prime Minister Shri P. V. Narasimha Rao, Minister of Industry, Shri K. Karunakaran, the then Minister of Textiles, Shri G. Venkataswamy, and the Deputy Chairman of the Planning Commission Shri Pranab Mukherjee. Various issues concerning elimination of child labour such as surveys to identify and enumerate working children, generating awareness amongst employers, parents, and working children of the laws and issues involved, additional projects and special schools for enrolling the large number of children released from work were discussed at length. Eventually sixty-four additional NCLPs were sanctioned. These projects were to be administered by District Child Labour Project Societies specially registered at the district level under the chairmanship of the Collector and with the involvement of representatives of the concerned departments at the district level. By 1995—6, seventy-six NCLPs had been sanctioned including the twelve projects that had been sanctioned earlier. These have opened 1800 special schools under them with about 2500 teachers, in which about 1.05 lakh children who had been released from hazardous industries/ occupations/processes have been enrolled. Each school is to run a three-year cycle. In the first two years functional literacy is to be imparted to bring the children to a level of equivalence with the appropriate level/ grade in the formal system of education while the third year is to be devoted to imparting vocational skill training to the children. The central objective of the experiment is to fully equip and empower the children so that as they cross the threshold of childhood, they will enter adulthood with strength and confidence as productive and responsible members of civil society.

The functioning of these projects has been evaluated by the institutes of social science research on a selective basis in the states of Andhra Pradesh, Orissa, UP, Rajasthan, and Tamil Nadu. The institutes who conducted the evaluation are:

- Administrative Staff College of India for Andhra Pradesh
- Centre for Media Studies for Tamil Nadu
- Nabakrishna Choudhary Institute of Development Studies for Orissa
- Tribal Development Institute, Udaipur for Rajasthan
- Giri Institute of Development Studies for UP.

A gist of the findings of the evaluation studies on the performance of some of the National Child Labour Project is set out in the Annexe 1.

As several deficiencies and infirmities in implementation of these projects were found by the evaluation agencies it was decided to have a second round of intensive evaluation by constituting inter-ministerial teams from the Ministry of Finance, Planning Commission, Ministry of Labour, Department of Women and Child Development, etc. This intensive evaluation was conducted between March and May 1998. A gist of the findings of the inter-ministerial team is to be found in the Annexe 2 to this chapter.

The magnitude of the problem of child labour in India with regard to all industries/occupations/processes is very large. Special attention is being devoted to industries/occupations/processes where employment of children is hazardous to their very safety. We have been able to cover about 1.05 lakh children under the umbrella of seventy-six projects and 1800 special schools, and need approximately 300 projects to cover 2 m. children who need to be urgently released from hazardous occupations/processes and rehabilitated through a multi-pronged and composite approach encompassing education for functional literacy, midday meal for supplementary nutrition, arrangements for regular health check-ups, and vocational skill training for economic empowerment. These projects in their entirety were to be implemented over six years and would have entailed a financial commitment of Rs 2197.05 cr., i.e. at Rs 3796 per child per annum x 20 lakh x 3. Since resources of this magnitude were unavailable the Expenditure Finance Committee in its meeting held on 25 June, 1998 has only approved the continuance of the seventy-six projects and 1800 schools during the Ninth Plan period. This means that we will not even be able to touch the fringe of this massive problem. It is, therefore, utterly imperative and urgent that the additional NCLPs are sanctioned and made operational in different parts of the country, and in particular in those areas where a high concentration of child labour is employed in hazardous industries/occupations/processes.

Simultaneously, the Ministry of Labour has been maintaining close and constant liaison with the Ministry of Rural Development, the departments of Women and Child Development, Urban Employment and Poverty Alleviation, Health, and the Ministry of Social Justice and Empowerment, to endeavour to pool resources from a variety of sources by appealing to the good sense of these ministries to view the problem of child labour as not the problem of a single ministry or department but the concern of the nation as a whole. The former Shri Prime Minister P. V. Narasimha Rao had indeed issued a comprehensive demi-official letter to the Chief Ministers of all states to adopt a multi-pronged and composite approach to the problem of elimination of child labour encompassing eradication of parental poverty, unemployment, underemployment, and illiteracy, and the promotion of the health and well-being of all members of the family including adults and children through observance of hygiene, sanitation, immunization, and nutrition. As the content of this letter and the directions it contained continue to be valid, a copy of it has been reproduced as Annexe 3 to this chapter.

National Child Labour Projects

In accordance with the decision taken in the meeting of the Expenditure Finance Committee held on 2 December 1996 evaluation studies were commissioned to assess the effectiveness of the various components of the National Child Labour Project scheme. The studies were entrusted to the following Institutions:

(i) Giri Institute of Social Service, Lucknow;

(ii) Centre for Media Studies, New Delhi;

(iii) Administrative Staff College of India, Hyderabad;

(iv) Nabakrishna Choudhury Centre for Development Studies, Bhubaneswar;

(v) M. L. V. Tribal Research Training Institute, Udaipur.

2. The major findings of the evaluation studies are set out below:

District Child Labour Society, Kalahandi

1. The District Child Labour Society, Kalahandi, has to a considerable degree been able to achieve the immediate objectives of the NCLP. Under the present administrative arrangement, all the 35 special schools run by the local NGOs have been found to be functioning satisfactorily. The financial aspect of the project has been well-addressed and, barring some minor problems at the Block level, there is a smooth transaction process and timely flow of resources in the form of grants to all the special schools to meet the salaries of teachers, the midday meal expenditure for children, their stipends, and other running expenses. The recruitment of teachers, clerks, and cooks-cum-peons of all the special schools organized by the managing NGO has been found to be satisfactory.

2. All the special schools managed by the local NGOs of the district are playing a commendable role. The problem of drop-outs or frequent absenteeism is negligible. The educational progress of the students has been found to be satisfactory and the performance of around 20 per cent of them in their respective classes may be rated as above average. On the whole, these schools have been found to be more disciplined and better organized than the other primary schools in the district. In some cases the schools have supplied uniforms, utensils, and study materials free of cost, and others have made necessary arrangement to supply such materials to all the child labour students out of their own stipends. This has not only helped in the growth of an esprit amongst the child workers but also amongst their parents.

3. The nutrition programme in all the thirty-five schools has been functioning well and almost all the children in these special schools express full satisfaction with regard to the both quantity and quality of the midday meal provided. It is because of the stipends and the good quality of the food that some of the students who were working children do not hesitate to commute a long distance either on foot of bicycle. Regular attendance of students in these schools has beer found to be much higher, probably because of the good nutritious food provided.

4. Awareness generation activities to sensitize the public on the issue of child labour, however, has been inadequate. The project society of the district appears to have neglected this aspect and in consequence very few people appear to be concerned about the problem of child labour and the importance of its elimination.

5. The project should place greater emphasis on awareness generation activities and sensitization of the issue at the community level to achieve the goal of progressive elimination of child labour. There should, therefore, be provision for an annual recurring grant under this head with effective monitoring measures rather than the provision for one time lump sum grant of Rs 5 lakh provided by the Ministry of Labour.

6. The project should examine the welfare measures for its workers and staff starting from the Project Director to teachers, clerks, and cook-cum-peons at the grass-roots level. It has been found that the present pay package made available to the project staff is grossly inadequate in relation to their skill, ability, educational qualifications and, above all, labour inputs. This should be fixed on the basis of the pay structure and gross salary of similar categories of workers at the minimum scales prevalent in the district.

7. It has been observed that because of the importance placed on opening special schools and providing stipends to working children in order to achieve full time enrolment, the NCLP schools are emerging as a parallel system of education. This needs to be checked by initiating greater awareness generation measures.

National Child Labour Project, Malkangiri

1. Attempts need be made to improve the quality of teaching to enable all the children to acquire minimum learning levels. For this, teacher-training programmes need be organized at the district or state levels.

2. The syllabus should encompass the childrens' rights besides lessons to develop sound personal character and traits, a positive attitude, an understanding of the requirements for good health, nutrition, and cleanliness, the employment opportunities available and the qualifications necessary to achieve higher income levels. That apart, steps should be taken to enhance children's skills and capabilities.

3. Adequate attempts need to be made to generate public awareness regarding issues relating to child labour.

4. There should not be any delay on the part of the Project Authority in entering the Rs 100 per month stipend in the pass books in order to avoid any controversy between the Project Staff and parents of child labour.

5. On the whole, the performance of the special schools under NCLP has earned admiration at all levels of the village community for its positive contribution.

6. An awareness campaign through audio-visual media is more effective than the printed form of posters and leaflets as most villagers are illiterate. Folk dance and folk drama seem to be most effective vehicles.

7. The evaluation team feels that apart from the course content the teachers are prone to academic inadequacies. They, therefore, need to be trained to improve their knowledge and skills and henceforth persons below matriculation level need be totally eliminated.

8. Though there is no trace of teacher absenteeism, poor teaching is likely to seriously affect the students' progress. Teacher-training programmes need, therefore, to be organized at the district or state levels.

9. It was observed that educational opportunities need be enhanced for a large number of working children of the district with the creation

of appropriate vocational curricula, and these together with the other educational courses need be linked to the socio-economic opportunities that exist within the district or outside it.

10. The evaluation team expressed general satisfaction that the special schools have been successful in providing access to the basic levels of learning that is likely to stand future generations in good stead.

11. It was observed that, given the existing conditions, total prohibition or elimination of child labour is not possible, but through necessary rehabilitation measures by the NCLP, the magnitude of the child labour problem in the Malkangiri district can be considerably reduced.

12. NCLP Malkangiri should continue its activities more vigorously and with new initiatives. The project has generated sufficient enthusiasm amongst working children, their parents, and the villagers. Despite some weaknesses, the project is clearly yielding effective and positive results. Its major achievement is that the local community has been directly involved in all its activities, contributing to its success. It may, therefore, be viewed as a successful means to the total elimination of child labour in the district.

National Child Labour Project, Rangareddy

1. During the assessment year, the M. V. Foundation, after providing proper coaching to the children, has got a large number of them admitted in various government schools in classes II to VII. The Foundation, has also managed to provide lodging and boarding facilities for the students in hostels meant for the Scheduled and backward castes managed by the Social Welfare Department of the district administration.

2. Many of the camp inmates were earlier engaged in various occupations such as mining, construction, cattle rearing, agricultural labour and the chalk industry, but a large number attended to household chores only. The female working children were largely engaged in attending to household chores and occupations such as mining and chalk industry, whereas the male children were largely engaged in construction activities, cattle rearing, and agriculture labour.

3. The creation of Bala Karmika Vimochana Vedika (BKVV) or Forum for the Elimination of Child Labour with a firm commitment from teachers in government schools and with the active support of the district administration has provided a great boost to the initiative for the withdrawal of child labour.

4. The Foundation has not established any special school for the children withdrawn from work but depends on the 'camp' method. The inmates come from many surrounding villages. The innovativeness of the 'camp' teaching methodology is its greatest strength and its success can be gauged from the high rate of retention of the children enrolled in the mainstream schools up to the age of fourteen.

5. At this stage it is possible to say that 'camps', as the key component of the NCLP, is making a small dent in the problem of child labour in the Rangareddy district, and there is a need to continue these in the known areas of concentration of child labour in the districts such as Tandur, Basheerabad, and the chalk and mining industrial areas.

National Child Labour Project, Udaipur

1. Hazardous jobs are by and large, nonexistent in the Udaipur project area. The Child Labour Rehabilitation Programme launched in the Udaipur area appears to have directed its efforts to provide schooling to all categories of children engaged in any occupation who have been obliged to stop pursuing their studies to support their families financially.

2. A majority of the identified child labour may be categorized as working children and not as statutorily defined child labourers. Relaxed identification of norms facilitated inclusion of children not pursuing formal schooling and withdrawing of few children from formal schools and enrolling them in child labour schools.

3. The new NGOs who were selected to run the special schools were ill-equipped to cater to the educational/rehabilitation needs of child labour. Lack of a sound financial base came in the way of their being able to sustain the new schooling activity. There should, therefore, be objectivity in selecting the NGOs for the project activity.

4. The schools were found lacking a congenial atmosphere and their general quality was very poor and ineffective. The lack of effective guidelines about school curricula has created confusion both amongst the teachers and parents of the children attending the schools.

5. Irregularity in the release of grants blocked effective implementation of the supplementary food scheme.

6. The role of project staff in coordinating various field functionaries, including the NGOs beneficiaries, families of the children, and the DRDA does not appear to have been adequate.

7. The parents of identified child labour should be educated through the awareness camps much earlier if the next phase of the project is launched. Parental education and behavioural change is an essential

part of the project. Consultancy services may be sought by the project authorities from the TRI/SIERT for organization of the camps.

8. It may not be possible for the project authorities to raise the level of stipend beyond Rs 100 per month. However, adequate arrangements need to be made to compensate the parents for the losses incurred by them through provision for

a. assured work/job opportunity to any one member of the family under any governmental scheme such as IRDP, JRY, NRY.

b. providing credit facilities to develop earning opportunities at the household level.

c. transferring the targeted child to any of the Ashram Hostels run by the Tribal Area Development Department/Social Welfare Department in the project area.

9. The special schools have completed only one academic session of their existence. The experiment was virtually new, and as such, the observed weaknesses are not unnatural. Indeed, an encouraging beginning has been made to protect child labourers from exploitation and provide the best possible alternative, i.e. schooling facilities, to the liberated children.

Child Labour Project, North Arcot Ambedkar and Kamrajar Districts of Tamil Nadu

1. A majority of NCLP students in Kamrajar districts (62 per cent) and a smaller proportion (8 per cent) of children in North Arcot Ambedkar district were not child labourers and were not engaged in any economic activity.

2. A majority of children (80 per cent in Kamrajar and 72 per cent in North Arcot Ambedkar districts) who were child labourers at the time of admission in special schools were engaged in non-agricultural occupations.

3. The study reveals that of the total children going to NCLP schools in North Arcot Ambedkar district, two-thirds of them combine study with work while in Kamrajar district, 14 per cent of total children going to NCLP schools are economically active. The reason for the high incidence of work among NCLP children in North Arcot Ambedkar district is the prevalence of home-based beedi making work. The children are thus not withdrawn from work to pursue their education.

4. A household survey reveals that a large majority of students in North Arcot Ambedkar (99 per cent) and nearly two-thirds of them in Kamarajar (64 per cent) receive free textbooks from their schools. Over

90 per cent of students enrolled in NCLP schools in Kamrajar district receive stipends while in North Arcot Ambedkar district no stipend is given. In the latter, however, the proportion of children receiving uniforms is higher (84 per cent). Other benefits given to students include a monetary payment of Rs 2.50 to 3.00 per day per child in lieu of a midday meal.

5. Almost all the schools surveyed in Kamrajar district are run in rented buildings, while most of those in North Arcot Ambedkar district have their own. Schools set up in earlier years in Kamrajar district have better buildings and classrooms. In both the districts, especially in North Arcot Ambedkar district, children of all the three years study together in the same classroom.

6. The schools function from 9.30 a.m. to 4.30 p.m. and offer courses such as Tamil, English, Mathematics, Social Science, and Environmental Science. In Kamrajar district, all the schools offer vocational courses, but in North Arcot Ambedkar district, out of the 30 schools surveyed, six did not offer vocational courses. The vocaticnal courses taught include carpentry, tailoring, basket-making, simple wiring, book binding, embroidery, and screen printing.

7. In North Arcot Ambedkar district, the project was initiated very recently, so no students have passed out yet. The Kamrajar Project, which has been in operation since 1988, has seen 3000 students pass out.

8. According to the information from the school survey, ninety-one and 105 students discontinued in North Arcot Ambedkar and Kamrajar districts respectively in the 1996-7, academic year.

9. The results of a written test conducted for the third-year students in NCLP schools and class-V students in non-NCLP schools show that the level of learning of children in NCLP schools are much lower than those in formal schools.

10. Government-run schools offer no incentives to children to continue their education in formal schools after they pass out from NCLP schools, but NGOs reported that they encourage children to join formal schools by providing free textbooks and uniforms from their own funds. Some parents complained that the NCLP schools do not issue transfer certificates that would enable the children get admission in formal schools; only progress reports are provided, making it difficult for them to seek admission to formal schools.

11. Focussed group discussions conducted with parents of children studying in NCLP schools in both North Arcot Ambedkar and

Kamarajar districts revealed that most of the parents have had their children admitted in NCLP schools because they were over-aged for formal schools. Besides, it is easier for the poor families to get their children, admitted in NCLP schools which provide free textbooks, uniforms, and midday meals.

12. The NCLP scheme has made a modest beginning in addressing the acute problem of educating working children and has achieved a modicum of success in its efforts. The sheer magnitude and complexity of the problem demands more intensive and cost-effective approaches to eliminate child labour. There is a need for a concerted and well-coordinated effort among different government departments, on the one hand, and the various sections of the civil society, on the other. The Department of Education has a vital role to play in working towards improved access to and quality primary education, and evolving suitable systems of alternate schooling. The Ministry of Labour has to take initiatives in enacting suitable legislation, strengthening enforcement, and sensitizing the society about the evils of child labour.

Ferozabad

1. In the schools run by the District Council for Child Labour(DCCL), out of total 500 students, 200 are receiving vocational training, but in the schools run by Child Labour Welfare Society (CLWS), there is no provision for vocational education. The very purpose of these schools is defeated if vocational training is not imparted to students along with formal education. The level of vocational training in special schools run by DCCL has also been found to be inadequate. The number of students receiving vocational training is very small and the quality of the training provided in these schools is very poor.

2. The caste composition of the students in the rehabilitation programme in Ferozabad district indicates that around 85 per cent students in the special schools are from the SC and BC groups.

3. The facility for nutritional food, books and stationery were available to all students in urban and rural areas, but medical check-up was confined to only 17.49 per cent of those sampled. None of the students in the special schools was satisfied with the amenities provided. In the light of these findings, the quantity and quality of facilities available in special schools must be standardized.

4. On an average 68 per cent students were working while receiving education in special schools in Ferozabad district, as the data by year revealed.

5. An overall analysis of data relating to the reason why children attending the special schools work suggested that the cause was the low level of household income; priorities should be fixed in NCLP to incorporate programmes for enhancement of the household incomes of working children.

6. Of 362 working children studying in special schools fifty-six (over 15 per cent) were handicapped, had developed chronic diseases, or some other ailment. The magnitude of the ailments and suffering among working students showed that the very purpose of starting special schools had not been fulfilled. The least that is expected from the NCLP is that students enrolled in special schools should not be permitted to work as child labour and consequently should not be exposed to such incapacities and diseases.

7. An analysis relating to the extent of dissatisfaction among working students in urban and rural areas shows that a significant number of students enrolled in special schools for rehabilitation are still working, and a significant proportion of these are dissatisfied with the kind of conditions in which they are working.

8. The parents' view of the performance of the rehabilitation programme for working children indicated that in urban areas 84 per cent of households were satisfied in comparison to 74.6 per cent households in rural areas. Of the dissatisfied households in the urban areas a large proportion of the households complained about unsuitable schools timings and delayed payment of the stipend. In rural areas the parents reported the problem of poor quality of teaching and the inadequate and poor quality of the meal provided.

9. Expressing views on the kind of education required for children under the rehabilitation programme, 34.76 per cent parents sought formal education for their male children, while 49.41 per cent of them felt the need for technical education for their male children, 9.32 per cent of the sample households expressed a preference for the inclusion of both formal and technical education in the curriculum of special schools for child rehabilitation.

10. Many parents of working children in the sample households were not prepared to send them to school, and indeed saw no advantage from a monetary point of view to send their children to school. The kind of education imparted in special schools, according to them, is too inadequate to provide employment to their children in the future.

11. Information provided by parents of child labourers revealed that over 90 per cent children are engaged in different categories of

hazardous work in the glass industry of Ferozabad. The impact of the NCLP in curbing this practice appears to have been quite ineffective.

Inter-Ministerial Inspection Teams

Background

The scheme relating to the National Child Labour Projects (NCLPs) is an earnest attempt to overcome the pernicious problem of child labour, especially in hazardous industries. Starting modestly with nine projects in 1988, it now covers seventy-six projects spread across ten States, selected on the basis of concentration of child labour in the country.

2. Major projects are located in the States of Andhra Pradesh (20), Orissa (16), Tamil Nadu (8), and Bihar (8) which have the largest number of working children. Continuation of the scheme during the Ninth Plan is under the active consideration of the government.

3. In an EFC meeting held on 10 March 1998 it was felt that the inspection of a few sample NCLPs should be conducted by inter-ministerial teams in order to make an objective assessment of the progress made so far and to ascertain their strengths and weakness so that corrective policy measures can be adopted and appropriate direction given regarding the future operation of the scheme.

4. The inter-ministerial teams comprised the representatives of the Department of Expenditure, Ministry of Finance, Planning Commission, Department of Women and Child Development, Ministry of Labour and Controller of Accounts of the Ministry of Labour.

5. The inter-ministerial teams undertook extensive visits to the NCLPs at Rangareddy (Andhra Pradesh), Kalahandi (Orissa), Varanasi (Mirzapur-Bhadohi) (Uttar Pradesh), Sivakasi (Tamil Nadu), and Jaipur (Rajasthan). The NCLPs were so selected that old and new projects, the endemic child labour affected industries, urban and rural centres, and progressive and backward areas encompassing four major regions of the country were covered.

Observations and Recommendations

6. The major observations and recommendations of the teams are:

(i) The National Child Labour Projects (NCLPs) have been able to achieve the immediate objective of withdrawal of children from hazardous employment and ensuring their rehabilitation through education in the special schools. Performance of some of the projects is particularly noteworthy and extremely encouraging. The 'Camp approach' of Rangareddy, Andhra Pradesh; 'Mobilization of grass-root organization' in Kalahandi, Orissa; 'Motivating parents of working children of a conservative Muslim community to send their children to special schools through volunteers of the same community' in Jaipur are unique experiments that need support and are worthy of replication.

(ii) The National Child Labour Projects (NCLPs) have largely covered the intended target group, namely, children working in hazardous industries. The groups feel that there were considerable operational difficulties in drawing a clear line between children working in hazardous industries and those in non-hazardous ones for the purpose of targeting. The group recommends that the target group for coverage under NCLP should be children working in hazardous occupations. This would include both children working in hazardous industries/units as well as those working children whose work is deleterious to their health and their well-being.

(iii) Delays in release of funds to the projects and uncertainty about continuance of the projects were major inhibiting factors. They led to a great deal of demoralization and demotivation. These procedural bottlenecks should be ironed out at the earliest. Long-term planning to eliminate child labour is obviously very essential.

(iv) One of the principal objectives of the National Child Labour Project (NCLP) is to withdraw children working in hazardous occupations and mainstream them into the formal school system. As working children are from different socio-economic backgrounds, have different skills and experience, the normal schools are not in a position to cater to their specific needs. The rehabilitation centres essentially act as a bridge to facilitate their entry into the formal schools. The child labour projects have been able to make a dent on the problem and have been able to facilitate both the withdrawal of children from hazardous work and their gradual entry into mainstream education. However, the problem persists. It is necessary to continue the project approach during the current Five Year Plan.

(v) The aim of the NCLP is to enable working children to become productive and participative members of society. Therefore, apart from academic inputs, there should be strong pre-vocational and craft components in the education of children in the rehabilitation centres. An appropriate module for the curriculum should be finalized at the state level. The V. V. Giri National Labour Institute, Noida, could also be associated in preparation of alternative modules.

(vi) The existing NCLP scheme provides for payment of a stipend of Rs 100 per child per month. While this amount does not fully compensate the income foregone by the working children, it acts as a great motivating factor for parents to send their children to school. Therefore, the system of paying the stipend should continue.

(vii) Peoples' participation and the involvement of grass-roots level organizations are essential components for the success of this programme. The NCLPs at Kalahandi and Rangareddy have demonstrated this. It is recommended that the volunteers should be essentially from the local community and grass-root level organizations like youth clubs, mothers' groups, cultural and social organizations should be fully associated, share the responsibility, and run the rehabilitation centres.

(viii) The existing scheme does not provide for any institutionalized monitoring mechanism; an inspection system is virtually nonexistent. Some of the state governments have been monitoring the pace and progress of the implementation of NCLPs in their respective states, but their role has been limited because of lack of financial support under the scheme. It is, therefore, necessary that the monitoring and inspection mechanism, especially at the state level, should be created, strengthened, and fully integrated. It is recommended that some finance should be earmarked for each of the NCLP states and a specific role should be assigned to them.

(ix) The present scheme does not allow any flexibility to adapt to the local conditions. This is very essential. It is, therefore, recommended that while the broad physical parameters in terms of coverage and provision of welfare inputs should be prescribed, adequate operational flexibility should be allowed to be exercised at the project society level subject to the overall cost ceiling.

(x) The involvement of development functionaries of allied departments like Education, Health, Social Welfare, Rural and Urban Development, Panchayati Raj, and interaction with them at the district level, is necessary to exploit the potential synergy for the benefit of children covered under the project. Experience of the NCLP Rangareddy, which has been able to mobilize such allied departments, is worth replication.

(xi) The convergence of various social schemes, such as those run by the Social Welfare, Welfare, Urban and Rural Development,

Education departments should be encouraged. For instance, the facilities available under various residential welfare schemes for backward communities, the midday meal scheme, etc. should be synchronized, and the provision under NCLP should be permitted to be utilized for the benefit of children withdrawn from work.

(xii) Each child labour project society should confine its activities to the concerned district only. The district covered under the Mirzapur—Bhadohi Child Labour Project Society, Varanasi, spreads over the districts of Varnasi, Mirzapur-Bhadohi, and Sonebhadra. Separate project societies should be sanctioned for each of the districts to overcome the problems of logistics and jurisdiction.

(xiii) The group was greatly impressed with some of the new experiments undertaken by the child labour projects. It is recommended that some finance (core budget) may be earmarked from the allocation under the NCLP to encourage new experiments for the rehabilitation of working children released from work for possible adoption in other areas.

(xiv) There is need for adequate awareness generation against the evils of child labour and stepping up enforcement of the relevant labour laws. The awareness among people about the evils of child labour, particularly after the judgement of Supreme Court and follow-up action thereafter, is noteworthy. The tempo should be maintained.

(xv) Apart from inspection and regular monitoring of the child labour projects, there should be concurrent evaluation of the NCLPs through agencies that may be selected by the District Collector in order to assess the effectiveness of various interventions for suitable and timely corrective action.

Conclusion

7. The problem of child labour is not only socio-economic but also has a very strong human dimension. Looking to the magnitude of the problem that exists in varying degrees in many states across the country, a holistic and integrated approach is essential to tackle and phase out the problem. For this, concerted and sustained efforts as well as appropriate interventions by states and voluntary organizations are necessary.

8. Against this background, the NCLP, which has played a catalytic role in mobilizing efforts towards the elimination of child labour, needs

to be strengthened, particularly as elimination of child labour finds place in the National Agenda for Governance of the present government.

Circular on Identification, Release and Rehabilitation of Child Labour

1. Introduction

Child Labour is a pernicious practice, a denial of the joy of childhood and access to social opportunities (like education) which eventually impairs the personality and creativity of children, the evolution and growth of a full being. Within the broad ambit of child labour, the plight and predicament of girl children (irrespective of whether they are working at home or outside) is worse. Such a practice which is abhorrent to our social conscience should, therefore, be eradicated from our social-economic milieu. It is in this perspective that elimination of child labour and integrated development of children have been important objectives of all our development plans and social sector schemes. Prohibition of employment of children under 14 years of age is the essence of various legislative provisions. This central objective has been reinforced further in the Child Labour (Prohibition and Regulation) Act, 1986 according to which children under 14 years of age are not permitted to work in certain hazardous occupations as also in occupations defined and notified as 'Hazardous Process' and 'dangerous operation' under the Factories Act, 1948. In spite of the recognition of the pernicious nature of this practice and the corrective steps initiated through these legislations, the problem has continued to persist in several districts and in remote areas of the country. Recognizing the imperative need to eliminate this problem the Prime Minister in his Independence-Day Speech on 15 August 1994 had stated:

You know that there are around 20 million children in our country who should be attending schools but not doing so. They are working in factories to increase the income of their parents. Working in the factories means end of their education and the children's development forever. . . .There are about 20 lakh children engaged in such hazardous vocations, that tell upon their health adversely. We want to withdraw them from such industries and put in schools in the course of the next four-five years. The only way to achieve this aim is to provide the parents of such children full employment to increase their incomes because the parents are so poor that they cannot sustain themselves without additional income earned by the children. If such parents are provided full employment and their income is raised there is no reason why they should not be sending their children to school willingly.... A new programme aims at improving the prospects of the children whose life may be ruined because of their early employment in hazardous industries. . .*

2. Identification of Child Labour and Stricter Enforcement of Relevant Legislation

At present, the task of identification, release and rehabilitation of child labour is being handled mainly by the Labour Department officials. In order to secure the desired objectives, the following steps are necessary:

(a) In the districts where child labour is prevalent, a survey should be conducted under the overall supervision of the District Magistrate in a time-bound manner, to identify child labour, the nature of vocations and occupations in which they are employed, and also the families to which they belong.

(b) In addition to the Survey, inspections, and investigations must be intensified in order to locate the children and file prosecutions against the employers under the existing laws. Statutory inspections, at present, are carried out only by officials of the Labour Departments. They are inhibited in achieving the desired results due to large area, less manpower, and limited mobility. The district, block, and village level officials belonging to the Revenue Department and other Executive Magistrates should also be authorized to conduct inspections and empowered to enforce the provisions under various laws. The employment of child labour should be made a cognizable offence under the relevant acts and Executive Magistrates should be specially empowered to dispose cases pertaining to employment of child labour in a summary manner under all these Acts (as is the practice u/s 21 of the Bonded Labour System (Abolition) Act). Launching of prosecutions on employers of child labour should be a precondition for taking up of rehabilitation of the concerned children and the economic rehabilitation of their families.

(c) A Standing Committee of officers comprising of the following, under the Chairmanship of the District Magistrate in districts having child labour problem, shall periodically (at least once in a quarter) review the problem of child labour in the district, organize the survey, and fix up responsibility for the supporting officers for effective supervision, inspection, and strict enforcement of the legislative provisions. The Officers are: (i) Head of the District Revenue Administration; (ii) all Sub-Divisional Magistrates in the district; (iii) District Labour Officer; Chief Executive of the Zilla Parishad; District Educational Officer in charge of Primary Education; District Women & Child Welfare Officer; District Social Welfare Officer; (iv) one or two representatives of voluntary agencies working in the area of child labour; (v) one or two eminent social workers involved in release and rehabilitation of child labour; (vi) Project Director, DRDA; and (vii) Chairman of Zilla Parishad Standing Committee dealing with labour welfare. This Committee would be in overall charge of identification, release, and rehabilitation of child labour and coordination of all programmes relevant to education, economic rehabilitation, and convergence of programmes to families of child labour. It can enlist the support of members of the Vigilance Committees constituted at the district and subdivisional levels under section 10 of the Bonded Labour System (Abolition) Act, and other institutions and agencies which are engaged in similar nature of activities.

3. Rehabilitation of Child Labour

After identification and release of a child from employment, suitable rehabilitation of the child and the economic rehabilitation of the family are the two distinct and important issues which should be simultaneously addressed.

Children have often been compelled to work on account of economic necessity or on the priorities of current consumption of families; it is, therefore, essential to ensure that the Child is not an economic burden to the family. For this purpose, there will be a need for schools, hostels, and other institutions wherein these children could be admitted and their requirement of food, clothing, books, medical care, etc. could be met. It is important to note that primary schools and vocational training centres which cannot take care of these requirements in a consolidated manner cannot be effectively used for the rehabilitation of child labour. Only such schools which can provide the children with boarding and lodging facilities, support for their education and skill development, and can provide a measure of care and solicitude should be selected for this purpose. It is important to make arrangements for boarding and lodging in schools where such facilities are not existing in the districts wherein the practice of child labour is prevalent. In addition to various

Central and State Sector Programmes like the National Child Labour Project, District Primary Education Project, Non-formal Education, social welfare hostels, Ashram schools, etc. should be geared to meet the requirements of the educational and psychological needs of the child labourers. Special support will be provided by the 'Labour Ministry' for this type of educational and psychological rehabilitation of the child labourer in the districts with concentration of child labour, by expanding their activities under the programme of the National Child Labour Project.

4. Economic Rehabilitation of the Family with Child Labour

It is obvious that families to whom child labourers belong are the poorer sections of the society. The best method of eliminating child labour is to ensure that these families are enabled to have access to adequate opportunities for livelihood and to improve the quality of their life. In order to provide sustained livelihood to such families, the Ministry of Rural Development have agreed to provide to these families on priority basis the following benefits:

(a) Assured employment for two adult members in the family for 100 days each in a year under the Jawahar Rozgar Yojana (JRY); Intensive Jawahar Rozgar Yojana (I-JRY) or the Employment Assurance Scheme (EAS). It will be incumbent on the Collector of the concerned district to ensure this employment under any of these Rural Employment Programmes. The shelf of projects will have to be planned in advance so as to ensure that members of these families seeking employment during any time in the year get assured employment. Accordingly, such priority to these families would be emphasized under the relevant manuals of these programmes;

(b) In the matter of allotment of house sites and allotment of Indira Awaas Yojana (LAY) houses, the child labour's family will be accorded a very high priority along with SCs/STs and families of freed bonded labourers. All such families whose details are available at the district level would be given the highest priority in the allocation of house sites and in the construction of IAY houses.

In addition to the above mentioned benefits, these families will be provided assistance under IRDP as per the provisions of the revised IRDP manual with adequate investment for self-employment ventures in land based or related traditional occupations. The investment under IRDP and selection of occupation should be such as to enable these families to earn a minimum incremental income of Rs 5000 to Rs 7000 per year. Necessary linkages like training for skill improvement, supply of raw material and marketing facilities for products shall be made available to all these beneficiaries under IRDP by DRDA.

5. Coordination and Implementation Arrangements

There are several Government Programmes in the social sector Ministries/Departments of Women and Child Development, Health & Family Welfare, Social Welfare and Education, all of which have relevance to the rehabilitation of child labour and prevention of recurrence of the child labour phenomena. The concerned departmental officials shall inform this Standing Committee of suitable projects and surveys relevant to the elimination of child labour. A Special Standing Committee of the Zilla Parishad should be entrusted with the responsibility to coordinate all these programmes with the primary objective of eliminating child labour. In order to ensure that various programmes relating to elimination of child labour are implemented without any delay at the district level, funds from the Government of India and the State Governments concerned with these programmes may be made available directly to the Zilla Parishads. The Standing Committee of the Zilla Parishad can coordinate and take up the formulation of coordinated plans and the schemes for the benefit of child labourers. The DRDAs on whom the responsibility of economic rehabilitation of the families rests shall make available the funds and programmes as decided by the Standing Committee from time to time. The Standing Committee of officials referred to under para 2(c) above shall also submit a periodical review of the child labour situation in the district to the Standing Committee of the Zilla Parishad.

Official Policy

Child labour is a subset of the total child population and policy on child labour is also a fragment of national labour policy. The national policy on child labour is, therefore, a combination of how the nation views children vis-a-vis other segments of the population and how it views working children vis-a-vis the rest of the working population.

Both the components have been clearly and forcefully addressed in the first two paragraphs of the judgement of the Supreme Court in Civil Writ Application no. 465 of 1986, M. C. Mehta vs. State of Tamil Nadu and Ors. dated 10 December, 1996. Opening with a beautiful poem by Mamie Gene Cole, the judgement proceeds with the importance of the statement 'Child is the Father of the Man'. It proceeds to emphasize how a child should be groomed, and receive education and nutrition, so as to enable the petals of childhood to blossom to the flowers of youth and manhood.

In the second paragraph the judgement has highlighted how the vision of the founding fathers of the Constitution was oriented to nurturing and educating the future generation to pave the foundation of a healthy, vibrant, strong and self-reliant Republic.

India has throughout followed a proactive policy in handling the problem of child labour. Its essence is that all working children are also children and must be given the opportunities to develop into healthy well-rounded personalities. Reference has already been made to the specific provision of the Constitution that prohibits employment of children in hazardous industries and according to the Directive Principles of State Policy the state shall so direct its policy as to secure the health and strength of workers, so that men and women and children of tender age are not abused and that citizens are not forced by economic necessity to enter vocations unsuited to their age or strength, and that children in particular are given opportunities and facilities to develop healthily in conditions of freedom and dignity.

It is against this background that the government set up a Committee headed by M.S. Gurupadaswamy in its Resolution dated 6/7 February 1979 to inquire into the causes leading to and problems arising out of employment of children and to suggest suitable measures for their protection and welfare. The Committee had the following terms of reference.

- Examine existing laws, their adequacy and implementation and suggest corrective action to be taken to improve implementation, and to remedy defects;
- examine the dimensions of child labour, the occupations in which children are employed, and suggest new areas where laws abolishing/regulating the employment of children can be introduced;
- suggest welfare measures, training, and other facilities that could be introduced to benefit children in employment.

The Committee drew up a plan of action for the conduct of in-depth and diagnostic studies on the nature and extent of the problem of adequacy of the existing legal framework and the supportive measures for working children. It circulated a questionnaire amongst politicians, trade unions, social workers, welfare and other institutions, employers, parents of children, government organizations, and the general public with a view to eliciting information on child labour. The information so received was tabulated and utilized in the report of the Committee that was submitted to government on 29 December 1979.

The Committee recognized that a distinction had to be drawn between child labour and its exploitation. It perceived both as problem areas, though of a different kind, underlining that in all future action dealing with child labour this basic aspect would have to be taken into consideration. In the perception of the Committee:

'labour becomes an absolute evil in the case of child when he is required to work beyond his physical capacity, when hours of employment interfere with his education, recreation and rest, when the wages are not commensurate with the quantum of work done and when the occupation he is engaged endangers his health and safety?.

The Ministry of Labour considered these aspects of the problem of child labour. It recognized the need to protect child labour from exploitation and from being subjected to work in hazardous conditions that endanger such children's physical and mental development, and the need to ensure the health and safety of children at the workplace. It recognized that they should be protected from excessively long working hours and from night work, that work even in non-hazardous occupations should be regulated, and all working children should be provided with sufficient weekly rest periods and holidays.

The government formulated the national policy on child labour bearing these important aspects in view and announced the policy in Parliament in August 1987. The programme of action or action plan under the national child labour policy comprises:

- a legislative action plan;
- focusing general development programmes to benefit children wherever possible; and
- project-based action plans in areas of high concentration of child labour engaged in wage/quasi-wage employment.

Legislative Action Plan

The legal action plan seeks to emphasize strict and effective enforcement of the provisions of the Child Labour (Prohibition and Regulation) Act, 1986, the Factories Act, 1948, the Mines Act, 1952, the Plantation Labour Act, 1951, and other Acts containing provisions relating to the employment of children.

Focussing General Development Programmes to Benefit Child Labour

Various national development programmes exist with wide coverage in the areas of education, health, nutrition, integrated child development, and income and employment generation for the poor. These programmes will be utilized to create socio-economic conditions in which the compulsions to send the children to work diminish and children are encouraged to attend school rather than take wage employment.

Project based Plan of Action

Under this, projects were proposed to be taken up in areas of high concentration of working children with a thrust on the following activities:

- Stepping up enforcement of the Child Labour (Prohibition and Regulation) Act, 1986, the Factories Act, 1948, the Mines Act, 1952, and such other Acts within the project areas.
- Coverage of families of working children under the employment and income-generating programmes under the overall aegis of anti-poverty programmes.
- Formal and non-formal education of child labour and stepping up programmes of adult education for the parents of working children.
- Setting up special schools for working children where provision for education, vocational training, supplementary nutrition, health care, etc. would be made. If necessary, stipends would be given to children taken out of banned forms of employment to compensate for their loss in earnings.
- Creation of awareness through social activist groups and by other means so as to educate people regarding the undesirable aspects of child labour.

TWENTY EIGHT

CONCLUSION

The constitutional provisions on child labour are clear and unambiguous. The Constitution gives a clear direction under Art. 24 prohibiting the employment of children in any factory or mines or in hazardous jobs. It also directs the central and state governments to endeavour to provide, within a period often years from the commencement of the Constitution, i.e. 26 January 1950, free, compulsory, and universal primary education to all children in the 5-14 age group (Art. 45). The Constitution does not speak of total prohibition of child labour in all industries/occupations/processes, and so there does not appear to be a clearly intelligible correlation between the provisions of Art. 24 and those of Art. 45. If all children in 5-14 age group are to be enrolled for free, compulsory, and universal primary education, they evidently cannot go to work and if they go to work, they cannot go to school; both cannot obviously be done concurrently. As a large number of households in India are below poverty line and the victims of economic deprivation, poverty, and malnutrition, they are not able to send their children to school. Even if they are able to do so, given the exhausting work the children are forced to undertake, whether within the household or outside, they are unlikely to have the physical strength or mental focus to concentrate on and benefit from the education they receive. A reduction in school hours, as is usually the case in the non-formal system, is unlikely to make a perceptible difference, and, therefore, a combination of work and education is not desirable.

Regretfully, however, this reality has not been adequately understood and appreciated, for otherwise we would not have had this legislative anomaly. The Child Labour (Regulation and Prohibition) Act, 1986, which replaced the Employment of Children Act, 1938, has not succeeded in ironing out the lacunae of the earlier legislation, and is at best a patchwork attempt at reconciling the viewpoints of those opposed to child labour in any form and those opposed to total prohibition. The Child Labour (Regulation and Prohibition) Act largely tolerates employment of children, prohibiting them only from working in certain industries/occupations/processes which are clearly recognized as hazardous and which are specifically listed in part A and part B of the schedule to the Constitution and providing for no effective measures to rehabilitate those who will be released from work. Indeed, the Act says nothing about the rehabilitation of children released from work in contrast to the Bonded Labour System (Abolition) Act that speaks of rehabilitation of freed bonded labourers.

The authority to prohibit employment of child labour in industries/occupations/processes rests with the union government and has not so far been delegated to the state/union territory governments. When exercising this power the union government acts on the advice of a Technical Advisory Committee constituted under Sec. 5 of the Child Labour (Prohibition and Regulation) Act, 1986 in 1989 under the chairmanship of the Director General of the Indian Council of Medical Research. It has so far held four meetings, and on the basis of its recommendations the government has issued notifications prohibiting employment of child labour in thirteen occupations and fifty-one processes, which is by no means an exhaustive list. There are still a large number of children who are employed in rag picking, collection of raw hides and skins, leather flaying and tanning, accompanying their parents for deep sea fishing, fish processing and storage, collection of minor forest produce, etc., that have not been brought within the ambit of the prohibited category. Even in agriculture, there are occupations like applying fertilizers, spraying pesticides, driving tractors, threshing, harvesting, etc. that entail grave occupational hazards that need to be prohibited. This has, however, not happened and the pace of inclusion of new industries/occupations/processes in the prohibited category has been painfully slow.

Regulation in the context of employment of children is conceptually complex and suffers from severe limitations because a majority of the operations in agriculture, building and construction, beedirolling, labelling, and packing, stone quarrying, brick kilns, etc. are outsourced to subcontractors, and often to a number of layers of them. These subcontractors or middlemen come from a low strata of society, are generally ignorant of the provisions of law, and in the quest of quick gains, do not attach any importance to investment in the health, safety, and welfare of the people at work including children, treating them virtually as commodities rather than human beings.

That children not only continue to be employed in hazardous employments in the prohibited category of employment without any provision for their health, safety, and welfare is testified by a number of reports conducted both at the behest of the government and several international agencies. These underline that the health, safety, and well-being of working children are almost invariably compromised.

In a historic judgement, Civil Writ Application No. 465, M.C. Mehta vs. State of Tamil Nadu & ORS, in 1986 the Hon'ble Supreme Court of India issued a couple of directions regarding the release of children from hazardous and prohibited categories of employment and their immediate enrolment in the formal school system. In regard to children who are employed in the non-hazardous category of work, it permitted them to work for 4—6 hours a day and to receive education for two hours a day with a clear direction that the cost of such education should be borne by the employer of the establishment concerned. In other words, the apex Court has simply underscored the combination of prohibition with regulation set out in the Child Labour (Prohibition and Regulation) Act, 1986.

The conditions under which children should work for 4-6 hours a day, the facilities and amenities that should be provided to them at the workplace, the agency responsible for providing such facilities, details of curriculum, course content and textual materials to be adopted for the non-formal education to be provided to these children, the place where they should receive their instructional lessons and the agency for imparting the lessons have, however, not been spelt out in the judgement. Evidently, these have to be worked out by the authorities of the education department of each state/union territory whose responsibility it is to implement the non-formal educational system for children released from work.

Successful implementation of a non-formal educational system depends on a number of factors such as opportunities and facilities available at the workplace, the attitude of the employer, including both the principal employer and the contractor towards providing such opportunities/facilities, the children's physical and mental capacity to take advantage of the non-formal education provided, the overall attitude of their parents, teachers (instructors), and their (i.e. the working children) own to non-formal education. While over 7 m. children are receiving such education according to the information available with Department of Education, Ministry of HRD, little data is available on the content and quality of such education and its overall impact on the children in terms of their acquisition of the minimum levels of learning and their subsequent mainstreaming into the formal system.

Thirty-eight years have passed since the adoption of the Constitution and since the directive for provision of free, compulsory, and universal primary education to all children in 5-14 age group was issued and we are nowhere near the laudable goal, inasmuch as over a 100 m. children in this age group continue to be outside the formal school system. The informal mode of imparting education both by the agencies of the state/union territory governments and by the NGOs, which was an integral part of the Educational Policy of 1986 reiterated in the policy adopted in 1992, has not had the desired impact. Regardless of the differences and variations in the number of children who are out of school, the fact remains that such children are either idle or caring for siblings at home, or working with their poor parents, or are employed in certain farm or allied occupations/processes. Neither the decennial census on enumeration of child labour nor the NSSO Survey (1987-8) nor the latest educational survey conducted in 1989 (Fifth Survey of Educational Research, 1988-92, NCERT, Delhi, 1997) have thrown any light on what such a large number of children who are out of school and have been deprived of access to educational opportunity are doing, and at what cost.

The issue of total prohibition of employment of child labour in all industries/occupations/processes was clearly highlighted in the Common Minimum Programme of the United Front government (1996-8)

The United Front Government will, in close cooperation with State Governments take steps to build a just and humane society. The right to free and compulsory elementary education shall be made a fundamental right and enforced through suitable statutory measures. Special programmes will also be launched to take care of children and the disabled and to eradicate child labour in all occupations and industries.

In respect of the directive contained in CMP, the Department of Education, Ministry of Human Resource Development, sent a note to the cabinet requesting it to declare education a fundamental right of all children in the 5-14 age group by amending the Constitution (83rd amendment) and also to issue a directive to all state/union territory governments to enact a law and provide for the infrastructure necessary for this. As the Eleventh Lok Sabha was dissolved on 4 December 1997 the proposed Amendment could not be carried through and, therefore, the directives issued proved infructuous.

The National Agenda for Governance adopted by the successor government in March 1998 speaks of drawing up a comprehensive charter of rights for children while reiterating the need for education for all children in the 5—14 age group:

We will present a National Charter for children. Our aim is to ensure that no child remains illiterate, hungry or lacks medical care. We will take measures to eliminate child labour.

It is evident that both the announcements speak volumes of the political will, commitment, and determination to provide free, compulsory, and universal primary education to all children as also to work towards the elimination of child labour. This notwithstanding, the declaration remains unimplemented on account of certain imponderables that need to be properly understood.

We are a federal polity and education and labour fall within the concurrent list of distribution of powers in the Constitution, with both the central and state governments empowered to enact labour laws, including those concerning child labour. It has, however, been generally observed that the central government enacts laws on all major issues, formulates both central and centrally-sponsored schemes, lays down the guidelines, provides for the necessary funds in the budget (plan), devises the procedure and provides the mechanism for implementation. In actual practice, however, implementation of most of the plan schemes and programmes rests with the state/union territory governments. Given the varying political complexions, there are widely varying perceptions and priorities. That is why despite clear demonstration of political will and commitment by successive central governments, the laudable objective of eliminating child labour has not so far been possible.

The issue of total prohibition of child labour was placed before the conference of state Labour Ministers held in July 1997. The states/union territories found it difficult to endorse the suggestion of the Ministry of Labour in the background paper circulated to the conference proposing total prohibition of child labour on the ground that this objective had to be realized progressively and could not be effected overnight. All the state/union territory governments, however, recognized the urgency of providing free, compulsory, and universal primary education although they did not spell out the modalities of effecting this in any detail.

Total prohibition of child labour and provision of free, compulsory, and universal primary education should invariably go together, one supplementing and complementing the other. Equally, free, compulsory, and universal primary education will not be meaningful so long as children continue to be at workplace, whatever its nature.

That is not to cast any aspersion on any government or on policy formulators and implementors; only to underscore that nearly four decades after the constitutional provision was made compulsory universal primary education is nowhere in sight. There may be valid reasons for this, either in the form of lack of political will, of a clear order of priorities, or lack of adequate resources (human, material or financial), or more than one of these.

There is no point in discussing which or which combination of factors in responsible. We need to honestly and candidly acknowledge that despite the constitutional and legal provisions, nearly 2 m. children continue to work in the match, firework, and explosives industries of Sivakasi in Tamil Nadu, the glass and bangle works of Ferozabad in UP, brassware works of Moradabad in UP, the pottery units of Khurja in UP, the lock-making units of Aligarh in UP, the carpet weaving units of Bhadoi, Varanasi and Mirzapur in UP and several parts of J&K, beedi rolling, labelling and packing operations in AP, Bihar, Gujarat, Karnataka, Kerala, Maharashtra, Madhya Pradesh, Orissa, Rajasthan, Tamil Nadu, Uttar Pradesh, and West Bengal, building and other construction operations and brick kiln operations throughout the country, the stone quarries and slate making units of Markkapur in AP and Mandsaur in MP, the gem cutting and polishing units of Jaipur and diamond cutting and polishing units of Surat and Bhavnagar in Gujarat, the textile printing units of Varanasi and several parts of Rajasthan, and the garment units of Tiruppur in Tamil Nadu.

They continue to work long hours in harrowing conditions without adequate rest, and without payment of overtime. They handle dangerous chemicals such as potassium cyanide, trisodium, sodium silicate, hydrochloric acid, sulphuric acid, sodium hydroxide, chromic acid, borium hydroxide, and the like and inhale the dust and noxious fume emanating from the workplace. They suffer from a number of respiratory and other communicable diseases, that play havoc with their health and limit the possibilities of production efficiency leave aside mental development.

It is evident that the state as an agent of society has failed to provide any protective cover to millions of vulnerable children at their most crucial stage of development. Even though a handful of NGOs have undertaken highly innovative, cost-effective and result-oriented initiatives in few pockets of the country and produced striking results, the fact remains that in terms of coverage or spread this is negligible and uneven.

It is, therefore, necessary to mobilize, organize and motivate the children to articulate their pressing needs and analyse how pressure for their fulfilment could be applied.

It was a refreshing experience in peoples' development that in 1984-5 the then prime minister, Rajiv Gandhi launched what is known as 'technology missions' for eradication of illiteracy, supply of clean and potable water, combating infant mortality through immunization, making the country self-reliant in oil seeds, and setting up an efficient rural telecommunications system. A mission is also a programme, but unlike other programmes, it is imbued with a sense of urgency, has a definite time frame, a result orientation, an area specific approach, and cost effectiveness. When launching these five missions Rajiv Gandhi realized that the magnitude of all the problems was so huge as also the number of people affected that only an unconventional and unorthodox approach could yield the desired results at optimal cost within a short time frame. The essence of the new strategy in relation to the technology mission for eradication of illiteracy could be summed up as follows:

- Literacy is a basic human need, almost as essential as open air and pure water.
- Literacy does not connote simple alphabetical knowledge but functional literacy that not only provides access to information, communication, and a variety of skills (survival, occupational, managerial and entrepreneurial), but also through access to information transforms an individual into a complete human being.
- Acquisition of literacy has to be demand driven and not merely supply driven, People must naturally and spontaneously perceive it as almost as essential for themselves and their children as is the need for food and water.
- Such a demand can be generated by harnessing resources that are readily available and affordable. Our country has a rich folk culture that can provide an excellent vehicle of communication. People will be convinced about the need for and relevance of literacy when they see with their own eyes how literacy can transform their lives from ' illiteracy, innumeracy, indebtedness, bondage, etc., to a new life in which human beings are treated with dignity, equality, and respect and not as goods and commodities or statistical units of production.
- The community plays an important role in this process of generating demand. It may be heterogeneous, yet within it there are

numerous creative thinkers, writers, artists, etc. with a social conscience and remarkable capacity to communicate simply and intelligibly and to mediate between the sender and the receiver.

The National Literacy Mission (NLM) drew inspiration and strength from the earlier National Adult Education Programme (NAEP), but sought to make a radical departure in terms of the following:

- Identification and enumeration of non-literate and non-numerate adults through surveys, with information coming from the ground rather than working with mythical targets being imposed from above.
- The survey itself was intended to be like a festival deeply rooted in the native ethos and culture and to act as a powerful nucleating agent or instrument for the creation of an environment conducive to literacy through recourse to the rich and varied regional folk forms.
- Powerful messages rooted in the native language and idiom were conveyed through nukkad nataks, street theatres, skits, role play, simulation exercises, and disseminated amongst the people through folk cultural troupes whose members were professionally trained in the art of communication through workshops in different parts of the country.
- The programme was implemented in a campaign mode and directed towards total eradication of illiteracy and innumeracy in a particular area, be it a village or gram panchayat Block or tehsil mandal or district. It rested on area specific, time bound, cost-effective and result-oriented programme.
- The Total Literacy Campaign (TLC) rested on the premise that each one owns, each one contributes, and each one participates.
- On the basis of the survey, there was matching and batching between potential learners and potential instructors on a ratio of 1:10. The site for teaching-learning came through voluntary contribution either at the premises of the teacher or of the learner, or any other central place, including places of public worship.
- Voluntarism being the bedrock of the TLC, it became one of the world's most inexpensive literacy programme inasmuch as the per learner cost ranged between Rs 50 and Rs 70 and went up to Rs 80-Rs 100 only in exceptional cases (where the area of operation was a hilly/mountainous/forest area or desert tract with difficulty in communication and transport). The components of cost included the cost of teaching-learning materials, teaching- learning aids such as

blackboard, roller board, slate, chalk, duster, charts, poster. A minimal amount was utilized for conducting area specific surveys, environment building, for training, monitoring, and evaluation. No honorarium was paid to the volunteers or supervisors, who were expected to provide their services free.

- The teaching-learning materials were designed on the principle of what is known as improved pace and content of learning (IPCL). This principle rested on the premise that all learners are not equally endowed, with slow and fast learners, and others afflicted with serious learning disabilities. The IPCL was a sequential approach aimed at inspiring a sense of achievement and confidence in the student as s/he proceeded from stage to stage, providing faster learners the opportunity to gradually learn to teach themselves. In terms of materials, the IPCL used three integrated primers, at the end of each of which drills and exercises were provided to enable the learner to practise them on her/his own and develop confidence in being able to solve problems.
- In addition to self-evaluation by the learners, they were required to undergo three tests at the end of each of the three primers.
- While six months were spent on planning and preparation, including survey and environment building, designing the need-based IPCL primer, training, etc., six months were devoted exclusively to the teaching-learning process. It was anticipated that during this period, using the IPCL technique, the learners would be able to achieve the minimal level of literacy and numeracy necessary to provide an important entry point into the world of communication.
- Training is an important tool of human resource development, and this was recognized in the TLC. Training essentially implied training instructors but also encompassed training of resource persons and master trainers. A cascading approach to training was adopted, in which the trainees of today become trainers of tomorrow in the various categories. The training was primer-specific, dialogue and discussion oriented, rather than didactic. The strategy for a specific duration, included designing a learner specific training curriculum and course content, close monitoring and evaluation to ensure that eventually the volunteers had acquired the desired level of proficiency and expertise and would be able to transact instructional lessons on their own with confidence.
- Monitoring and evaluation were important components of the TLC strategy and was multi-dimensional, i.e. at the learning centre

level (which is coterminus with the village), the gram panchayat, Block, and district levels. Monitoring served as a tool for collection, compilation, and analysis of data to impart credibility to the information system, and served as a basis for correction on the basis of the feed-back regarding deficiencies and infirmities noted. For this purpose, a set of coordinators were appointed at the village, panchayat, Block, and district levels who were required to report the pace and progress of learning as also various other attendant problems associated with learning to the next higher level. The report of the coordinator was then discussed in the Saksharatha Samiti or coordination committees set up at the panchayat, Block, and the district levels to lend openness and transparency to the entire operation.

- Like monitoring, evaluation was also intended as a tool of correction rather than as a witch-hunting exercise. Evaluation essentially implied self-evaluation by the learners, evaluation by the instructors, by the village community, by the master trainers and resource persons, as also external evaluation by institutes of social science research or NGOs from outside. The evaluation was both concurrent and summative, covering both the content, and process on the one hand, and the impact of the entire teaching— learning process, on the other.
- At the close of the campaign and on the basis of the results of the evaluation, a total literacy declaration ceremony was held. An area, be it a village or a panchayat or a Block or even a district was to be declared as fully literate if a particular age group in the area had been fully covered say, 9-35 or 9-45 or 15-35, and if on the basis of evaluation conducted 85 to 90 per cent of the learners were found to have acquired complete self-sufficiency in reading, writing, and arithmetic.

This was intended as yet another festival like the survey, fully participative and communicative in character, to accord public recognition to the scores of volunteers, supervisors, and resource persons for their selfless and dedicated service to the campaign. It was also meant to be an occasion for reflection over what had been achieved during the campaign, what has been left unfinished, and the tasks and challenges for the future.

Ernakulam district of Kerala became the launching pad for the TLC on 26 January 1989, and was the first district in the country to demonstrate that total literacy was not a Utopian idea but was a feasible and achievable goal. The Ernakulam campaign was essentially meant for a target group of about two lakh potential learners in the 6—45 age group with the help of about 20,000 volunteer instructors in a record period of one year. The experiment became an important trend and pace-setter for the whole country. Close on the heels of Ernakulam, the TLC model was replicated in quick succession, in the whole of Kerala state (for the remaining thirteen districts), the whole of Pondicherry and Goa, and now in over 400 districts (out of 535) in the entire country.

The TLC model for Ernakulam was largely based on an experiment undertaken earlier on a substantial scale first in Vietnam (1945-77) and later in Cuba (1959-61), Myanmar (1969-74), Ethiopia (1974-9),and Nicaragua (1985-90). In these countries there was first a revolution which brought in its wake sweeping social, political, economic and cultural changes along with a change in the system of governance. Literacy was an offshoot of that revolution, and was facilitated by it. Indeed, the campaign for total literacy became an important springboard for national reconstruction. Stories of the success of the TLC in these countries have been meticulously documented and indicate that the campaigns were successful largely in view of the political will and commitment of the leadership of the national and provincial governments, and the mass upsurge and mass euphoria in the wake of the revolution that facilitated the process of social mobilization and enabled the use of literacy as a tool for a total and radical social, cultural, and political transformation. As the story goes, the pace of the campaign was not slowed down by the poverty of the people or the fact that there was a hangover of colonialism, imperialism, and dictatorship, or the dry, barren, landscape, or the numerous divisive social, cultural, and linguistic factors. It was said in Vietnam that the back of the buffalo provided the slate, the brick kilns the blackboard, the juice of plants the ink, and sticks from the forests the pen. In a country where the economy had been ravaged by a long era of colonialism and war, the political vision of Dr Ho Chi Minh and the great grit, courage and determination with which he pursued the campaign for total literacy as a tool of social, economic and cultural emancipation of Vietnam for thirty-two long years (1945—77) has few parallels in world history.

It is true that India is not similar to Myanmar, Cuba, Nicaragua and Ethiopia either in terms of the total area or population. India is at least six times larger than these countries, and its burgeoning population and the problems associated with such a multilingual and multi-religious country are mind-boggling. Conditions vary widely from state to state, region to region, district to district, and even within the same district. These diversities and variations notwithstanding, it was thought that the essence of the campaign approach adopted by these countries would be worthwhile.

As I noted in the opening section of Chapter 19, 'The Role of the Media', Mahatma Gandhi was the supreme communicator who between the 1920s and 1940s, well before television entered India, was able to galvanize an entire nation, on the one hand by the strength of his personality and, on the other, by communicating with the people in an idiom they could understand and through images and slogans they could empathize with because they were rooted in their subconscious, their history, traditions, and folklore. As such, he was quick to recognize that education, and the access to knowledge that it brought, was the key to communication, to mobilization, and to liberation. It was in this context that he mourned: 'it is a matter of shame and sorrow that millions in India are illiterate; they have to be liberated from the curse of illiteracy if they are to be truely liberated.'

In 1989 the Department of Education, Ministry of HRD with Anil Bordia as its secretary believed that if a similar campaign for total literacy was to be launched in India it could not be effected by the government but by mobilizing creative thinkers, writers, artists, scientists and educational activists, and volunteers and with the urge and commitment to work for mass mobilization for literacy, and to use their skills for mass communication. This gave birth to Bharat Gyan Vigyan Samithi (BGVS) under the leadership of the late Malcom Adishesiah in August, 1989. Promoting and facilitating the formation of the BGVS at the national level was a very positive and constructive move initiated by Anil Bordia who is now president, Lok Jumbish Parishad and himself an outstanding adult educator. The BGVS was a confluence of creative forces and energies and brought under its umbrella thousands of creative thinkers, writers, artists, playwrights, actors and actresses on the stage and on the streets, and adopted the unique strategy of harnessing folk culture and folk medium of communication known as kalajatha for mass mobilization. Cultural troupes were organized and training camps for these, songs were composed, slogans, nukkad nataks, role plays, simulation exercises were devised and eventually, on 2 October 1990, what is known as Bharat Gyan Vigyan Jatha (BGVJ) was launched. The BGVJ toured the country for a period of forty-five days (2 October-14 November 1990) and covered one lakh out of six lakh villages spread over 300 districts (of about 466 districts then). Those were difficult times when class and caste wars had unleashed divisive forces that were playing havoc with the lives of innocent people over issues of little significance. Undeterred the thousands of BGVS volunteers not only spread the message of literacy, and messages on a host of other issues of national concern such as national integration, communal harmony, equality and empowerment of women, conservation of environment, the small family norm and the like) utilizing unconventional and yet very effective modes of communication. The impact on both the literate and non-literate was unprecedented. The former were persuaded to act as potential instructors, the latter to use literacy as the weapon against bondage, deprivation, and exploitation. Thousands of people from all over the country pledged their solidarity and support to the TLC. As one volunteer eloquently expressed it:

This is my village, my panchayat, my block and my district. I was born and brought up here. I have breathed its air and drank its water. I have come up in life with the blessings of my parents, elders, guardians and teachers. My advancement in life has also been facilitated by no small or insignificant measure by the toil and travail of numerous poor, deprived and disadvantaged sections of the society. I owe a deep debt of gratitude to them. Should I not, therefore, part with a portion of my knowledge, information and skills in favour of those unfortunate deprived sections of the society who do not know what they do not know and who are victims of ignorance, illiteracy and innumeracy for no fault of theirs. That is the only way I can redeem my pledge to the society and the nation. This would be a matter of pride and distinction for me.

Once the groundswell had been created, it was possible to structure the TLC as a planned and coordinated movement. At the national level was the National Literacy Campaign Authority with a governing council and an executive committee headed by the minister of Human Resource Development and Secretary, Education, respectively. Similar bodies were set up at the state level. The body at the district level was known as zilla saksharata samiti (district literacy society) and similar saksharata Samitis were organized at the Block, panchayat, and village levels. All these bodies comprised of men and women of integrity and character who had vision, imagination, and a profound commitment to literacy. The key feature in all these structures was that while people would voluntarily contribute their spare time free to the campaign, only a few components of cost such as those of travel and some minimal pocket expenses were reimbursed. The spirit of the campaign could be summed up as: 'If you genuinely feel for the cause of total literacy join us and devote yourself to it wholeheartedly without expectation of any reward beyond the self-fulfilment and sense of accomplishment it brings. If you are thinking of joining us only because you feel you must be seen to be doing so it is best that you stay away rather than reduce your participation to a mere facade and act as a dampner on the enthusiasm of fellow volunteers.'

The campaign for total literacy was also to be the model for launching similar campaigns against a number of social evils and to campaign for other socially and economically worthwhile programmes and, as we have noted, encompassed many of them.

Could such a campaign approach be extended to the elimination of child labour?

Eradication of adult illiteracy in a campaign mode involved:

- Creating an environment for a groundswell of public support and participation.
- Conducting a survey.
- Compiling data about adult illiterates and volunteers willing to teach.
- Matching and batching the two.
- Training of instructor volunteers through a cascading approach.
- Designing the curriculum, course content, and textual materials through a workshop.
- Pre-testing the instructional materials and having them printed.
- Commencement of the teaching-learning process.
- Monitoring, supervision, and coordination at multiple levels.
- Evaluation and certification.
- Post-literacy and continuing education.

Elimination of child labour would involve :

- Conducting a survey through volunteers to identify and enumerate working children.
- Collecting and compiling survey data.
- Steps for releasing working children from the clutches of employers.

- Rehabilitating the children released through education, nutrition, health-checks, and vocational skill training.

The TLC adopted a carefully planned, coordinated and selective approach. Initially districts were selected that had a high rate of literacy and where there were an adequate number of volunteer instructors and there was likely to be widespread support for the programme. The demonstration effects of the demand for similar initiatives came from the neighbouring districts. These were carefully scrutinized on the basis of the same norms and parameters on which the earlier decision to launch the TLC in a particular district had been taken to ensure that the campaign did not degenerate into a loose or unstructured exercise. In the campaign the National Literacy Mission Authority with a Council and Executive Committee played a positive and supportive role as promoter, facilitator, and catalytic agent working in close coordination with Bharat Gyan Vigyan Samiti, and sought to ensure on the one hand blanket coverage and on the other, through provision for post-literacy and continuing education programmes that there would be no relapse into illiteracy.

Conceptually child labour and educational deprivation are synonymous as states of deprivation for which the actors are not responsible and find themselves in circumstances over which they have no control. We, therefore, need a catalytic or nucleating body to play a role similar to that of the National Literacy Mission or the Bharat Gyan Vigyan Samiti which will create the environment, mobilize the resources, train the functionaries and design the instructural materials to carry the enterprise forward to its natural conclusion.

I believe the same strategy and methodology that was used in the TLC can be effectively applied to the elimination of child labour and their rehabilitation. Since the universe of child labour is large, working children are from multiple socio-economic and cultural backgrounds, have manifold skills, traits and characteristics, a careful and selective approach will have to be adopted to make a perceptible impact. To begin with, areas with high concentrations of child labour working in hazardous occupations could be identified. The most important among these have already been listed in chapter 17, 'Role of Central Employers' Organizations'.

The next step would be identification and enumeration of these workers through a survey. In chapter 15, 'The Role of NGOs',

I discussed in some detail the methodology that should be adopted, the inherent hazards in and precautions that need to be taken for the conduct of such a survey, as also those relating to identifying and releasing working children. Key among these are:

1. It should not be a mere routine head-counting exercise, but one conducted confidentially after winning over the support and cooperation of the local community, the local administration, Panchayati raj bodies, local political leaders, and the police. This will ensure that the personnel involved are not exposed to intimidatory tactics on the part of the employers of working children and their parents and that the children identified are not spirited away at the time of inspection.

2. The names of the establishments employing children will have to be collected in advance not merely from the office of the Chief Inspector of Factories/Shops and Commercial Establishments but through discrete local enquiries with the help of the local community.

3. It should be a thorough enquiry of all establishments, hazardous, or non-hazardous, employing children, their working hours, the names of the middlemen recruiting the children, their addresses, and the like.

There is an essential difference between a survey of working children and that undertaken in case of the TLC. In the latter case it was part of a process of community mobilization undertaken in a celebratory spirit, with adult non-literates and non-numerates fighting shy of being identified as such and hesitant to be participants in a process meant for their social transformation. In the case of a survey for identification and enumeration of working children, it is not they but their employers who are opposed to their identification and therefore disengage or spirit them away, with the helpless children being given no option. Left to themselves they would undoubtedly prefer to be liberated from the workplace and go to school. It is, therefore, a special responsibility of the survey team to mediate with the children, and this entails a great deal of motivation, skill and tact.

In the TLC anyone who had the inclination and commitment to work as a volunteer, be it in the survey, or environment building, or the teaching-learning process, or training or monitoring/evaluation was welcome to join the campaign. It is possible to recreate a similar spirit albeit employing a different methodology, for the launch of a campaign for the elimination of child labour and infuse it amongst millions of teachers, students, women, youth, and others who, as normal human beings, feel for the plight and predicament of working children and could put themselves in their shoes and rejoice in being able to do something to help.

Selectivity and simultaneity have to be the two guiding principles. The release of children from the workplace must follow the process of identification and enumeration through the survey in quick succession, as so also their restoration to their families backed by a process of immediate treatment of those who may have been battered and traumatized by exposure to a very harsh work environment.

It has been observed that thus far a rigid and legalistic approach has been followed in relation to the release of working children. What is necessary, as we have also discussed in Chapter 15 on the role of NGOs, is a summary trial immediately on receipt of a report from the concerned agencies to enable identification of child labour, their release from work, and restoration to the custody of their parents to be simultaneous.

The ultimate objective of the whole process is the children's total rehabilitation, physical, economic and psychological. Nothing could be a more potent tool of such rehabilitation than education in the broadest sense, far transcending mere alphabetical literacy; education that, in addition to imparting alphabetical and functional literacy, will impart a wide variety of skills and infuse the child with confidence in her/himself and the ability to cope independently and successfully with the future.

The success of rehabilitation through education will depend largely on the content, quality, and impact of education. While on the surface the reported gross enrolment rate may appear to be very high (over 120) the net attendance rate is very low on account of drop-outs (66). According to the findings of the fifth educational survey report, 50 per cent of the habitations do not have a primary school, 7500 schools have no building, 125,000 are accommodated in a single room, and 60 per cent of them do not have any basic facilities such as drinking water, toilets, etc. Besides, 4000 primary schools have no teacher, 112,000 schools are single-teacher schools, and 25,000 primary school teachers are para teachers. Basic education in India today is neither free nor compulsory nor universal.

The issue of UNICEF's State of the World's Children, 1998-99 on education published by UNICEF, presented a grim picture regarding literacy for the world in general and India in particular. It is deeply tragic, as the report shows, that in the fiftieth year of the Universal Declaration of Human Rights and tenth year of the Rights of the Child

Convention we have 130 m. out-of-school children in the developing world of whom 73 m. are girls and 855 m., or one-sixteenth of humanity are functionally illiterate. Within India, while there are 142 m. children in the 6-11 year age group eligible to enter the school and 98 m. have been enrolled, only 63 m. have been retained (meaning thereby that about 80 m. are out of school) Expenditure on elementary education as a percentage of total expenditure has fallen since the Fifth Plan period from 59 to 48 per cent. India spent 3.7 per cent of its GNP(1993) on education and has an immense distance to traverse before this figure exceeds 6 per cent. It is tragic that we have the highest number of out-of-school children in the world and that every third illiterate in the world is an Indian. By the year 2000 India will be the most illiterate country in the world, with two-thirds of them being women. Within this broad spectrum of the wide gap between enrolment and retention it is shocking that 50 per cent of those who complete schooling do not achieve the essential minimum levels of learning. There are more girls than boys who are out of school and most of these girls are the members of the Scheduled castes and tribes, a majority victims of multiple deprivation. The UNICEF is of the view that all out-of-school children are working children and has presented a detailed macro- and micro-level analysis of the educational scene across the different regions of the world with examples of several innovative cross-regional and country experiences, how productive investment in education can be, how learning achievements can be scientifically measured, how learning can be a continuum for life and correlated to the protection and observance of the rights of the child.

It may sound defensive to say all this and yet speak of the elimination of child labour. It is important nevertheless to recognize that basic education is basic public good, that its denial is associated with higher mortality, higher fertility, lower productivity of the labour force, and generally poor quality of life. The ILO's World Employment Report, 1998-99(1998) has clearly and unambiguously emphasized the need to enhance the education and skill levels of workers. It has concluded that rapid technological change demands richer cognitive content in education and skills training, and that it is vital that systems be developed for lifelong learning. It is essential, therefore, that we take cognizance of the yawning gaps and deficiencies in our management of basic education and to take timely corrective action.

The question that remains to be answered in the context of simultaneity is how we are to ensure that children who are released from work do not remain victims of educational deprivation but are made active participants of the educational process. This dilemma is particularly significant as the existing system is riddled with loopholes, is largely non-functional, and suffers from a a great deal of wastage and leakage. At the same time children who are released from work should receive an education that is not the same as that aimed at a six-months literacy programme or two-year NFE but high quality education of the kind that Sri Aurobindo, Mahatma Gandhi, and Gurudev Rabindranath Tagore dreamt of.

It should be noted that all children who are released from work are not wholly non-literate or non-numerate. Many of them are semi-literate and may have dropped out from the formal school system at a very early stage. What is, therefore, essential is to first identify the educational levels and special educational needs of such children before enrolling them into the formal school system.

Wherever there are functional formal schools, the children released from work should be admitted to those after determining their educational level and special needs. With mobilization of teachers, motivation of parents, and the wholehearted involvement of the community, a positive environment conducive to formal schooling can be created. In such an environment both parents and children are self-motivated and child enrolment and retention in schools becomes automatic.

In areas where there are no schools or these are beyond a 2 km radius new schools should be opened by properly mapping the area and properly planning the school complex. Clearly, the highest priority for opening schools should be in those areas where there is a high concentration of children working in hazardous industries from which they must be released.

More important than making good the infrastructural gap is the planning and preparation to make schools functional and vibrant, and this must begin even before a survey for release of children is conducted. This could be done by more or less adopting the same innovative approach adopted by M. V. Foundation, Hyderabad, and would include:

- Mobilization of teachers
- Motivation of teachers and bringing about an attitudinal change through orientation and training.
- Designing curriculum, course content, and textual materials

through participative workshops involving creative thinkers, writers, and artists, pre-testing these for suitability before they are adopted.

• Assimilating essential lessons from few other innovative experiments such as those of the Bhagavatulla Charitable Trust, Katha, Alarippu in terms of environment building to generate and sustain the interest of teachers and students in the functioning of the educational system.

The most essential component of the environment building strategy is that neither parents nor teachers but children of school-going age (5-14) themselves should articulate their demands for free, compulsory, and high quality education through nukkad nataks, street theatre, role play and simulation exercises all over the country on the basis of a planned, coordinated, and concerted programme. The strategy adopted by Bharat Gyan Vigyan Samiti in launching a countrywide jatha and caravan to motivate sections of the society to articulate and register their voice for good quality primary and elementary education could be adopted to translate the strategy into concrete reality.

As the entire TLC programme was planned, directed and coordinated by the National Literacy Mission Authority comprising a council and an executive committee, for the rehabilitation of working children through education, we could think of a similar authority. Indeed, there is already a National Authority for the Elimination of Child Labour with the Labour Minister as Chairman. This is, however, largely an official body with representatives from nine ministries/ departments, and no representation of non-official/voluntary agencies nor of state governments. There is another parallel Central Advisory Body on Child Labour. Rather than having a plethora of bodies it is desirable to have a single broadbased tripartite national authority with representatives from central employers, central trade union organizations, NGOs, state governments (representatives of major states that will be targeted for a campaign approach at the first instance), ministries/departments of the central government (Home, Finance, Law, Information and Broadcasting, Rural Areas and Employment, Health, Industry, Commerce, Textile, etc.). While this body may be headed by the Prime Minister to facilitate decisive action and direction and better coordination, an executive committee may function under the umbrella of the National Authority which will be smaller, more compact and manageable without diluting the principles of tripartism. The executive committee should be headed by the Labour Minister, should meet more frequently than the National Authority and should consider and sanction projects in specific areas from an existing list of targeted areas (say Bhadoi, Varanasi, and Mirzapur) for elimination of child labour and rehabilitation of released children. A District Child Labour Project Society should be set up under the Societies Registration Act, 1860 with the Collector and District Magistrate of the district as its Chairman. This body would be responsible for formulation of the project, presentation of its salient features to the executive committee of the National Authority, and then be responsible for implementation of the project once it is sanctioned.

It will be its responsibility to conduct the survey, build up the appropriate environment, design the curriculum, course content, and textual materials, select and train teachers to conduct the teaching-learning process in a campaign mode, monitor and evaluate the pace, progress, quality, and impact of the programme, and the like. The district society should have representatives from all cross-sections of society apart from representation from government departments.

To sensitize the insensitive and initiate the uninitiated in the district administration hierarchy, (starting with the Collector downwards) a series of orientation and training workshops will have to be organized as was the case in the TLC. The sole objective of such orientation and training workshops would be to eradicate misconceptions and pre-conceived notions regarding child labour and to disseminate the right messages in the appropriate manner. The impact of all such workshops would need to be evaluated to ensure that the workshop produced a team of functionaries with the right attitudes, and perceptions regarding issues relating to elimination of child labour and who have the necessary skills and confidence to tackle the problem.

0000 As the Bharat Gyan Vigyan Samiti provided a prop to the TLC and acted as a nucleating agent for it we need a similar centre of support and prop to launch a campaign for the elimination of child labour and the rehabilitation of working children. As we have seen earlier, the BGVS was a remarkable confluence of creative forces and energies comprising of scientists, technologists, social and educational activists and people drawn from all walks of life. They included a large number of people of great distinction who had won recognition in their various fields at the national/international level and yet had the commitment to take time off from their lucrative careers and comforts to serve the BGVS and NLM with wholehearted devotion; to write songs, skits, plays, and slogans; to mobilize people from all walks of life across the country to work for universal literacy; to tour the country as mobilizers and organizers of cultural troupes that performed for the Bharat Gyan Vigyan Jatha, as trainers (Resource Persons, Key Resource Persons and Master Trainers), monitors, evaluators, and the like. No account of the NLM would be complete without mention of this legion of missionaries of education.

A similar structure can be created for a national campaign for the elimination of child labour. We have several institutes of social science and research and NGOs/voluntary social action groups of repute and standing, and no dearth of creative thinkers, writers, artistes, playwrights, cartoonists, teachers, lawyers, medical doctors, engineers, scientists who can be easily identified, mobilized, consulted, and involved. This body can function as the think tank for the national authority for the elimination of child labour. It would organize the strategy for a countrywide campaign to spread the message in favour of abolition of child labour and the rehabilitation of child workers through education and to create the material for popular street entertainment and slogans to spread it.

It would depute activists to visit selected districts with a concentration of children in hazardous industries/occupations/processes as part of the pre-appraisal mission to assist the District Child Labour Project Society to create a positive and supportive environment that will be conducive to elimination of child labour, formulate campaign oriented concrete project proposals for the consideration of the National Authority on Elimination of Child labour, to identify and form groups of persons from all walks of life who qualifying as trainers, to organize training workshops as well as workshops for designing the appropriate curriculum, course content and instructional materials. The BGVS type structure for the elimination of child labour will not function on parallel lines as a rival or competitor but in close coordination with the National Authority on Elimination of Child Labour, one supporting and reinforcing the other. All expenses for running this body will have to be provided for in the budget of the Ministry of Labour and, while it may have considerable functional and financial autonomy and flexibility, it would be subject to the same financial mores as any other public institution.

The adoption of a campaign approach through alternative structures at the national, state, and district levels should not be construed as an attempt to belittle or minimize the importance of the state authority. Indeed, responsibility for dealing with socially sensitive issues such as the elimination of child labour and the introduction of free compulsory and universal primary and elementary education cannot be left to any agency other than the state, least of all to market forces. The programme must have clear goals, a definite time frame, a clear strategy and a methodology for achieving its objective. As we have noted earlier fundamental rationale for substituting the traditional way of implementing a programme by a campaign approach is to accelerate the pace of implementation, and this approach also enables wide social mobilization for the achievement of the objective at the least cost.

The enforcement of the law relating to the prohibition of children in hazardous employment would continue to be the primary responsibility of the state. The track record of state's performance in the area of child labour law enforcement has not been very encouraging. Few prosecutions are filed and fewer still end in conviction. The prosecutions are often poorly conducted and the penalties in the event of conviction are generally in the shape of paltry fines that do not act as a deterrent. Also, the labour law machinery is inadequately manned and there is often collusion between it and the accused. It is, therefore, essential that measures are taken to sensitize all government functionaries, including the child labour law enforcement machinery and judiciary with the help of individuals who are themselves fully committed to the cause of elimination of child labour and are skilled communicators and trainers.

To overcome rigid and pre-conceived notions and inculcate the right attitude and approach it is necessary to create a conducive environment with the involvement of all the ministries, departments, departmental undertakings, public sector undertakings and other agencies, including NGOs, both at the central and state levels, as part of a continuing process rather than a one-time exercise. The central theme should be child survival, child protection, and child development, taking into its ambit the elimination of child labour. It should be repeatedly reinforced through songs, slogans, paintings, elocution and essay competitions, and stage and street theatre that child labour is one of the worst forms of deprivation, and ensure through environment building exercises that all policy formulators, planners, and implementors responsible for the enforcement of the Child Rights Convention (CRC), 1989 are fully committed to the issue.

Over the centuries mankind has immeasurably developed its capacity to understand itself and the world around it; to widen the frontiers of knowledge, technology, and skills and to harness these to its betterment. This march towards progress has not been without challenges, impediments, and vicissitudes (indeed, there have been times when it has brought mankind within an ace of self-annihilation) but through it all the human spirit has triumphed and the quest for something yet unseen and unknown that can be harnessed to human betterment continues. Through all this there has been the hiatus between, on the one hand, individual progress and self-aggrandizement and, on the other, the greatest happiness of the greatest number.

It is in the latter that mankind's greatest hope for happiness and contentment lies in dismantling the artificial barriers between the privileged of society and those who Rabindranath Tagore, in Ebar Phirao More, termed the 'dumb, pale and meek, the fatigued, the withered and forlorn', and to provide the latter with the opportunities to live without fear in dignity and to accord them equality and respect. As another Nobel laureate said, 'Our lives no longer belong to us' but to those who are in desperate need of them. Who are 'we' and who are 'they'? 'We' are the so-called educated strata of society to whom all the privileges, amenities, and opportunities in life are available as if of right; 'they' are the disadvantaged who, for no fault of their own making, are at the bottom rung of our stratified, selfish, acquisitive society. If we choose to do so we can certainly make their lives easier and happier by parting with a fraction of our inexhaustible reservoir of material wealth, knowledge, and skills. The choice is in our hands: do we have the sensitivity to make the correct one?

This sensitivity to the needs of others and the sharing of social opportunity has been evocatively expressed by Rabindranath Tagore in 'Upahaar' (Manushi):

> In the innermost recesses of the human heart
> The waves of the universe strike off and on
> The heart alone is sensitive
> Which responds to these waves
> Which is wide awake throughout the day and night. -

In these times when crass consumerism, greed, and rapacity are beginning to overtake the gentler mores of a caring and value-based society, these words could not be more relevant, and could be extrapolated to take into its ambit the release of child labour and the creation of an environment in which they can develop into educated, self-confident, and productive individuals.

Bibliography

Books

Acharya, U. — *Trafficking in Children and their Exploitation in Prostitution and other Intolerable Forms of Child Labour in Nepal*, 1998.

Boudhiba Abdelwahab: *Exploitation of Child Labour*: Final Report of the Special Rapporteure of the United Nations

Burra, Neera : *Child Labour in the Lock Industry of Aligarh, Uttar Pradesh.* (UNICEF, New Delhi.) 1987

Choudhry, D.P. : *Child Labour in India in the Asian Perspec tive'.* Social Change, 1997

Delores, Jacques : *Learining, The Tresure Within*, International Commission on Education for the Twenty-first Century, UNESCO, 1996.

Dingwaney,M. : *Bonded labour in India* (New Delhi, Rural Labour Cell). 1987

Dobash, R Emerson and Russel P. Dobash — *Violence Against Women- A Case Against Patriarchy*, Free Press, New York.1979

Edvin-H-Sulherland & Donald R. Cressey — *Criminology*, J.B. Lippin Cott Company, and Phila-Dilphia, Tenth Edition, 1978,

Effah, J. : *Modernised Slavery Child Trade in Nigeria* (Lagos, Constitutional Right, project). 1996

Elias Mendelievich : *Children at Work* (Geneva: ILO, 1979).

Fluman Rights: *Contemporary Forms of Slavery in Pakistan* (New York.) 1995

Gandhi, Mohandas Karamchand: *The Story of My Experiments with Truth*, (trans). Mahadev Desai. (Navajivan Publications, Ahmedabad.) 1981

Hammarberg, Thomas: *A School for Children with Rights*

Haq, Mahbutul, & Khadija Haq — *Human Development in South Asia*, The Human Development Centre, Karachi, 1998.

Hawes, Hugh, : *Health Promotion in our Schools, the Child to Child,* In association with UNICEF, 1997.

Jam, M.: *Bonded Labour: Justice through Judiciary,* Raja D. V. P Research Study on Child Labour in Match Industries in Sivakasi. (Madurai Institute of Social Sciences, Madurai.)1993

Miske, Shirley J. : *Developing a Girl-friendly Learing Environment*, Consultancy Report for UNICEF, 1997.

Mohanty, J. : *A Report on All India Juvenile Literacy Conference and Sishumela*, 1997.

Raman, Vasanthi : *Profile of Child Labour in the Carpet Industry Uttar Pradesh: Lucknow*. (UNICEF, New Delhi.) 1996.

Robert Ricci: : *The Rights of the Child*, (Essays on International Relations) South Asian Publishers,New Delhi 1991.

Sattaur, O.: *Child Labour in Nepal* (London, Anti-Slavery International).1993

Satyarthi, K. : *Break the Chains, Save the Childhood*, South Asian Coalition New Delhi.

Sawyer, R. : *Children Enslaved* (London Routledge).

Teddy Arellano: *Child Labour in South Asia*, Asian Labour Update. 1994.

Torres Rosa Maria: Repetition: A Major Obstacle to Education for All, Education News.

Usha S. Naidu & Kamini Kapadia : *Child Labour and Health*

Vidyasagar, R.: Report on Survey of Child Labour in the Match Belt, Tamil Nadu'. (Mimeo., Department of Social Welfare, Government of Tamil Nadu.) 1994

Vidyasagar : & R.C. Nambi : A Preliminary Report on Study of Child Labour in Hosiery Industry in Tiruppur.

Vijaygopalan S. : Child Labour in Carpet Industry A Status Report. (National Council of Applied Economic Research, New Delhi.), 1993

Weiner Myron : *The Child and the State in India, Child Labour and Education Policy in Comparative Perspective.* (Princeton University Press, Princeton.)

Reports

Administrative Staff College of India (Child Labour Action and Support Project), 1996. Eliminating Child Labour through Community Mobilisation : A study on an NGO's efforts to eliminate child labour in the carpet industry in Mirzapur. India (New Delhi, ELO)

Ann-Slavery International. 1990. Children in Bondage Slaves of the Subcontinent (London).

Bonded Labour Liberation Front. Excerpt from Into that Heaven of Freedom (New Delhi, July).1989

Centre for the Protection of the Rights of the Child", Bangkok: A vivid portrayal of children in bondage featured in a video called Paper cup.

Child Labour in Africa", International Labour Review Vol. 132, No. 2, 1993.

Child Labour in Diamond Industry of Surat City . (Operation Research Group, Baroda.) 1993.

Child Labour in Gem Polishing Industry in Jaipur'. Indian Institute of Health Management Research, Jaipur, (1992). UNDP (1991):Human Developement Report 1991. (Oxford University Press, New Delhi.) UNICEF (1989):United Nations Convention on the Rights of the Child. (UNICEF, New York.) UNICEF (1997): The Progress of Nations (L'NICEF. New York.) UN (1966): International Covenant on Economic. Social and Cultural Rights. UNTS. UN (1966): International Covenant on Civil and Political Rights, UNTS. "Explosion of Child Exploitation in South Asia", SAARC Link, 1993. "Programme for the Advancement of Girls' Education (PAGE)", Yearly Technical Report on the AGEI Programme in Zambi, 1998.

Child Labour In West too: 1LO", National Herald, May 30, 1993.

Child Worker in Carpet Weaving Industry of Jammu & Kasmir (National Labour Institute.) 1993.

Child Workers" in Asia Bulletin (Bankok). 1995. Excerpt from Vol. II, No. 1. 1995

Children's Resources International, Inc. and the Step Programme", information supplied by CRY, 1998. Problems and Prospects (Bombay: Tata Institute of Social Sciences, 1985).

Children in Sudan: Slaves, Street Children and Child Soldiers (New York) 1995.

Crime in India, 1991, National Crime Records Bureau, 1994,

Department of Women and Child Development, Government of India. 1994. Child prostitution-In the twilight, Report of the Central Advisory, Committee on Child Prostitution, India.

Educating Girls in Bangladesh: Exploding the myth" in Reaching the Unreached: Non-formal approaches and universal primary education, UNICEF, 1993.

Govt. of India, Ministry of Human Resources Development (Deptt. of Women and Child Development), Development of Women in India- A status paper

Government of India (1931): Report of the Royal Commission on Labour in India. (Calcutta.)

Human Indian Social Institute. 1995. Freedom from Bondage: Citizens Commission Bonded and Child Labour. First National Convention (New Delhi)1985.

ILO (1992): World Development Report (1LO. Geneva)

ILO. Report of the Committee of Experts on the Application of Conventions and Recommendation to the International Labour Conference, Report III, Part I A (Geneva). 1995-96

Industry of Moradabad (U.P.) (Govind Ballabh Pant Social Sciences Institute, Allahabad.)

Informal Sector Service Centre (INSEC). Bonded labour in Nepal under the Kamaiya system (Kathmandu) 1992.

International Labour Organisation, Child Labour: A Briefing Manual (Geneva: ILO), 1986.

Ministry of Labour, Report of the Committee on Child Labour (Nasik: Government of India Press).1997

Ministry of Women and Social Welfare (MOWSW), Nepal; ILO-IPEC. 1998. National Plan of Action against Trafficking in Children and their Commercial Sexual Exploitation (Kathmandu)1998.

Minnesot Lawyers International Human Rights Committee. Testimony in Restavek: Child domestic labour in Haiti (Minnesot)1990.

National Institute of Occupational Health, Ahmedabad (1980s): Annual Report. (Various Issues.)

NCERT (1997): Fifth Survey of Educational Research, 1988-92. (NCERT, Delhi.)

Operations Research Group (1993): 'Child Labour in Slate Pencil Industry of Mandsaur District, Madhya Pradesh.'

Reaching the Unreached: Non-formal approaches and universal primary education, UNICEF, 1993. Reaching Ugandan Children Out of School, Government of Uganda/UNICEF, 1998.

Report of the Committee on Child Labour (Ministry of Labour, Government of India, New Delhi.) 1979

Status and Problems of Leather Workers and their Future Growth Persective: A Study Based on Survey on Leather Workers in Unorganized Sector in the Districts of Agra. Institute of Applied Manpower Research, New Delhi.) 1995

Sub-Commission on Prevention of Discrimination and Protection of Minorities (Geneva: UN, 1983)

Summers, Lawrence H.: Education for All the Children, Policy Research Working Papers Series, World Bank, Washington, 1992.

The Education of Girls and Women: Towards a global framework for action, UNESCO, Paris, 1995.

The Factories Act, 1948 (New Delhi: Government of India,).

UNICEF, "Child Abuse and Neglect in a Global Perspective", E/ICEF/1986/CRP-4.

United Nations Commission on Human Rights. Report of the Working Group on Contemporary Forms of Slavery (Geneva); Annual Reports, see especially 1985-97.

United States Department of Labour. Forced Labour: The Prostitution of Children (Washington)1996.

United States Department of Labour. By the Sweat and Toil of Children, The Use of Child Labour in US Agricultural Imports and Forced and Bonded Child Labour (Washington, DC)1995.

V.V. Giri National Labour Institute, Noida, Exploring Child Labour Issues: An Abstract Service. World Declartion on Education for All 1996.

Articles

The Hindustan.Times, Promilla Kalhan, Behind the Scene-Better Deal for Women, March 7, 1988

The Indian Express, Wife Forgives an Unworthy Husband-May 8. 1985.

The Journal of Peasant Studies, Chandrasekhar, C.P. :'The Economic Consequences of the Abolition of Child Labour : An Indian Study. April, 1997

The Times of India, Dina Mehta, Family & Home Column-IN Violation of the VOWS, New Delhi, June 24, 1994.

The Times of India, H.C. Baveja, Removing the Stigma of Child Labour. 20 July 1994.

The Times of India, Samora Jha Nambiar, It can't happen to my daughter. July 24, 1994.

INDEX